FinTech
Research and Applications
Challenges and Opportunities

Transformations in Banking, Finance and Regulation

Print ISSN: 2752-5821
Online ISSN: 2752-583X

Series Editors: Sabri Boubaker
(EM Normandie Business School, France & Swansea University, UK)
Duc Khuong Nguyen
(IPAG Business School, France)

Presently, the banking and finance sectors evolve within a globalized and highly uncertain environment. Each business and financial decision requires careful consideration of country-specific and international factors due to high levels of shock transmission and volatility spillovers. Furthermore, it would be remiss to omit the COVID-19 health crisis, which caused harmful effects to all areas of the real economy and made profound changes in the way our firms, economies, and markets used to function.

Many other already well-known aspects, including the repercussions of quantitative easing policies, disruptive technologies in finance (e.g., FinTech, Big Data, Data Analytics, Artificial Intelligence, and Blockchains), as well as innovative financing instruments for startups (e.g., ICOs and crowdfunding) are currently revolutionizing banking and finance and posing numerous challenges to regulatory bodies and policymakers. Climate change emergencies also put pressure on governments and firms worldwide to improve policy on governance, corporate social responsibility, and sustainability practices.

This book series "Transformations in Banking, Finance, and Regulation" attempts to address these issues by focusing on transformative perspectives in banking and finance. Accordingly, it provides evidence-based guidance, recommendations, and pathways to assist businesses and policy decision-makers through an interdisciplinary and in-depth understanding of ongoing changes in the behavior of economic agents.

Published

Vol. 5 *FinTech Research and Applications: Challenges and Opportunities*
edited by Daisy Chou, Conall O'Sullivan and Vassilios G Papavassiliou

Vol. 4 *Modern Finance and Risk Management: Festschrift in Honour of Hermann Locarek-Junge*
edited by Tony Klein, Sven Loßagk, Mario Straßberger and Thomas Walther

Vol. 3 *Finance with a Purpose: FinTech, Development and Financial Inclusion in the Global Economy*
by Frederic de Mariz

For the complete list of volumes in this series, please visit
www.worldscientific.com/series/tbfr

Transformations in Banking, Finance and Regulation
Volume 5

FinTech Research and Applications
Challenges and Opportunities

Editors
Daisy Chou
RMIT University, Australia

Conall O'Sullivan
University College Dublin, Ireland

Vassilios G. Papavassiliou
University College Dublin, Ireland

World Scientific

NEW JERSEY • LONDON • SINGAPORE • BEIJING • SHANGHAI • HONG KONG • TAIPEI • CHENNAI • TOKYO

Published by

World Scientific Publishing Europe Ltd.
57 Shelton Street, Covent Garden, London WC2H 9HE
Head office: 5 Toh Tuck Link, Singapore 596224
USA office: 27 Warren Street, Suite 401-402, Hackensack, NJ 07601

Library of Congress Cataloging-in-Publication Data
Names: Chou, Daisy, editor. | O'Sullivan, Conall, editor. | Papavassiliou, Vassilios G, editor.
Title: Fintech research and applications : challenges and opportunities / editors, Daisy Chou, RMIT University, Australia, Conall O'Sullivan, University College Dublin, Ireland, Vassilios G Papavassiliou, University College Dublin, Ireland.
Description: New Jersey : World Scientific, [2023] | Series: Transformations in banking, finance and regulation, 2752-5821 ; vol. 5 | Includes bibliographical references and index.
Identifiers: LCCN 2022024379 | ISBN 9781800612716 (hardcover) | ISBN 9781800612723 (ebook) | ISBN 9781800612730 (ebook other)
Subjects: LCSH: Finance--Technological innovations.
Classification: LCC HG173 .F539 2023 | DDC 332--dc23/eng/20220526
LC record available at https://lccn.loc.gov/2022024379

British Library Cataloguing-in-Publication Data
A catalogue record for this book is available from the British Library.

For any available supplementary material, please visit
https://www.worldscientific.com/worldscibooks/10.1142/Q0375#t=suppl

Desk Editors: Nimal Koliyat/Adam Binnie/Shi Ying Koe

Typeset by Stallion Press
Email: enquiries@stallionpress.com

https://doi.org/10.1142/9781800612723_fmatter

Foreword

What is FinTech? The typical use of this terminology is to describe new technology that helps deliver financial services in novel, usually automated, ways. However, the more we look into it, the clearer it is that FinTech is 'not a niche within financial services or is it a sub-sector', according to how Ron Kalifa OBE described in the preface of his now well-known, Kalifa Review. It is, as the Review concluded, 'a permanent, technological revolution'. From its core concept to the end product, FinTech can be deemed as the new 'economy'.

It is widely acknowledged that the fundamental core of the rapid growth of FinTech is technology advancement. The boom in data innovations, technologies, and infrastructure such as cloud computing, decentralized finance, machine learning, artificial intelligence techniques, and blockchain, among others, has accelerated innovation in financial services including digital lending and credit, smart contracts, automated credit rating and payment services, and cryptocurrencies. However, FinTech and the major problems that have evolved around FinTech go beyond technological debates.

First, it is a revolution that is beyond a single market and is booming globally. Furthermore, in a break from previous technological revolutions, the knowledge exchange from West to East is reversed. For instance, observing the inaugural Forbes Asia 30 Under 30 lists over the last few years, many of the honourees are FinTech innovators and their experiences are replicated in countries like the UK.[1]

[1]See Forbes Releases 2021 30 Under 30 Asia List: https://www.forbes.com/sites/forbespr/2021/04/19/forbes-releases-2021-30-under-30-asia-list/?sh=63e57f446699 and an example of Johnny Mayo, one of the Forbes honourees.

Second, though an innovation centered on the financial services sector, FinTech naturally engages wider and multiple industry segments. The core of FinTech both in data science and in applications is multi-disciplinary by nature. For instance, Mexico's Restaurant Toks' coffee grower-suppliers pilot program offers an interesting example of a blockchain-based FinTech application, that allows Mexican coffee farmers to benefit from a completely trackable, auditable, ethical, and sustainable supply chain.[2]

The above example is one of many FinTech innovations currently underway. Another major innovation is the widening participation of financial services to non-finance professionals. For example, according to Deloitte's market research on the UK FinTech landscape, the UK's approximately 2,500 FinTechs are made up of 23 different specialisms in 8 broad categories. Since 2011, new FinTechs have been appearing in this space with an exponential growth rate. The innovations in niche areas (e.g., banking, lending, and RegTech) also exhibit exponential growth. There are 10 high growth FinTech hubs including a London superhub, three established hubs, and six emerging clusters. The entire FinTech UK annualized growth rate sits around 16%, compared to a 1.3% growth rate of traditional SMEs; it potentially creates more than £2bn Gross Value Added uplift over three years and 50,000 jobs.[3]

As FinTech presents enormous opportunities for growth and prosperity, it also presents great challenges. These challenges are not merely with specific issues such as risk management or application optimization. They are society-impacting challenges that are complex in nature such as data privacy and discriminatory biases in algorithms. Meeting these challenges requires strategic positioning on policy and regulation, skills, investment, internationalization, and national connectivity, according to the Kalifa Review. To be able to address these big ideas, the key is to encourage FinTech research that accommodates multi-disciplinary approaches and aims for deployable applications. This book, *FinTech Research and Applications: Challenges and Opportunities*, proudly presented by World Scientific

---

[2]See https://simbachain.com/supply-chain/.

[3]https://www2.deloitte.com/uk/en/pages/financial-services/articles/uk-fintech-landscape.html.

Publishing, strives to meet this objective. It contributes significantly to the literature on FinTech research, and as such, is an invaluable reference for practitioners, policymakers, and academics alike.

Professor Jing (Maggie) Chen
Personal Chair
School of Mathematics
Cardiff University
United Kingdom

https://doi.org/10.1142/9781800612723_fmatter

About the Editors

Hsin-I (Daisy) Chou is Associate Professor of Finance at RMIT University, Australia. She earned her PhD from the Queen's University of Belfast and has held positions at the University of Otago, University of Bath, and La Trobe University. She specializes in corporate governance and corporate finance. Specifically, her research interests include board of director behavior, executive compensation, Asian economies, and M&A activities in the US market. She was part of the research team that examined corporate governance implementation practices in Asian economies following the Global Financial Crisis, which provided a comprehensive recommendation to APEC member countries. She has published in well-known journals, including in the *Journal of Financial and Quantitative Analysis*, the *Journal of Corporate Finance*, the *Journal of Banking and Finance*, and others.

Conall O'Sullivan is an Assistant Professor of Finance at the UCD Michael Smurfit Graduate Business School, University College Dublin. His research interests are in the general areas of derivatives and fixed income securities markets. His published works have appeared in journals such as the *Journal of Banking and Finance*, *Energy Economics*, *Quantitative Finance*, the *International Journal of Theoretical and Applied Finance*, and the *Journal of Computational Finance,* among others. He has presented at major international conferences including the *European Finance Association* and the *Bachelier World Congress*. He was a Visiting Professor at New York University's Finance and Risk Engineering department in 2019. He is the current Programme Director of the B.Sc. in Economics and Finance at the UCD Lochlann Quinn School of Business and a former Programme Director of the M.Sc. in Quantitative Finance at the UCD Michael Smurfit Graduate Business School. He was a recipient of a UCD College of Business Teaching and Learning Award for Teaching Excellence in 2017 and 2021. He previously worked as a quantitative analyst and has consulted to several international financial firms.

Vassilios G. Papavassiliou is an Assistant Professor of Finance at University College Dublin, UCD Michael Smurfit Graduate Business School, and a Fellow at the UCD Geary Institute for Public Policy. He earned his PhD in Finance from the Queen's University of Belfast, United Kingdom. His research interests span the areas of market microstructure, high-frequency finance, liquidity, bond markets, financial contagion, FinTech, and banking and risk management. His work has been published in international finance and economics refereed journals. He has been a funded Research Fellow at the Bank for International Settlements (BIS) and a Visiting Scholar at the Bank of Finland's Research Unit and at EM Normandie Business School in Paris, France. He also holds a Research Fellowship at the

Rimini Centre for Economic Analysis (RCEA). He has served as a principal investigator for a number of funded research projects, and has been an expert reviewer of research grant proposals at the French National Research Agency. He has served as a member of scientific committees and has presented papers at leading international conferences. He is an Associate Editor of the International Journal of Finance & Economics. Dr Papavassiliou is the Banking and Finance Subject Area Head of Teaching and Learning at the UCD College of Business and a member of the College Teaching and Learning Committee. He has taught a variety of finance modules to both undergraduate and postgraduate students in Dublin, Singapore, and Athens. He also holds multiyear hands-on practical experience with careers in financial markets in various roles.

https://doi.org/10.1142/9781800612723_fmatter

About the Contributors

Annisha Akosah is a Software Developer at Xero in Wellington, New Zealand. She carried out this research as part of her capstone project for her Bachelor of Engineering with Honors degree in the School of Engineering and Computer Science at Te Herenga Waka — Victoria University of Wellington, New Zealand.

Silvio Andrae is an economist. Most of his professional experience has been in the financial sector. Since 2000, he has worked as a senior consultant in various FinTech projects in Latin America, Africa, and Asia. He is currently a senior adviser with the German Savings Banks Association. He is a specialist for various regulatory initiatives at the Basel Committee on Banking Supervision. Silvio Andrae studied and received his PhD at the Free University of Berlin.

Xin Chen is an MPhil student in Economics at Lingnan University. Ms Chen's current research interests include corporate finance, international trade, and the Chinese economy. Ms Chen has published papers in academic journals, e.g., *Small Business Economics*, *Applied Economics*, and *Economics Letters*.

Thomas Conlon is Associate Professor of Finance at the Smurfit Graduate School of Business, University College Dublin. He has held visiting positions at the Saïd Business School, University of Oxford, and Simon Fraser University. His research interests span asset allocation, banking, risk management, and FinTech. Recent research has been published in international scholarly journals such as the *European Journal of Operational Research*, the *Journal of International Money and Finance*, and the *Journal of Financial Stability*.

Prior to commencing his academic career, Thomas held senior positions in asset management and consulted for financial services firms.

Martin Crane secured BA, BAI in Mechanical Engineering from the University of Dublin, Trinity College in 1989, and a PhD in Computer Science from TCD's Computer Science Department in 1993. His research includes Mathematical and Computational Modeling and Simulation for problems in the Financial and Bioinformatics domains. He has co-authored some 75 peer-reviewed academic articles, and book contributions, and has presented his work at international conferences. During his 20 years of research at Hitachi and DCU, he has been PI on 11 externally funded projects worth a total of €1.5M. He supervised 13 PhDs and two research masters to completion, with four primary supervised PhDs in progress.

Bahar Bahramian Dehkordi is a Master of science in Economics and Business Administration from LUT University, Finland, and works as a junior researcher with Kouvola unit of LUT. Her research area interests are innovation, sustainability, Industry 4.0, digitalization, business model innovation, FinTech, logistics, and green management. She is also project manager in some projects run by the LUT Kouvola team. Her master's thesis titled Application of blockchain technology in sustainable supply chain management explores the potential of blockchains from a sustainability perspective through a qualitative study. Bahar is now pursuing her doctoral studies at LUT University in innovation.

Jennifer Ferreira is a Senior Lecturer in the School of Engineering and Computer Science, Te Herenga Waka — Victoria University of Wellington, New Zealand. Her research focuses on participatory and user-centered design of financial technologies. She is involved with community currency projects in New Zealand, notably The Wellbeing Protocol, an initiative bringing blockchain technologies to local economies.

Gianna Figà-Talamanca is Associate Professor at the Department of Economics of the University of Perugia. She obtained a Master's Degree in Probability applications in finance at the University Pierre et Marie Curie in Paris (France), and a PhD in Statistical and Mathematical methods in Economics and Social Sciences at the University of Perugia. She has been a recurring visiting professor at the Finance and Risk Engineering Department of the Tandon School of Engineering (New York University). Her research interests include Derivative pricing, Financial econometrics, Volatility modeling, Risk measures, and, recently, Cryptocurrencies and Sentiment analysis. She is currently a member of the Faculty of the Crypto Asset Lab (University of Milano-Bicocca), of the Scientific Advisory Board of Cryptovalues https://cryptovalues.eu/, and of the CiNI Cybersecurity National Laboratory (node of the University of Perugia).

Sergio M. Focardi is Professor of Finance at the Pole Universitaire Léonard De Vinci, Paris-La Défense. Sergio has published many articles in peer-reviewed journals and is the author or co-author of many books including *Money: What It Is, How It's Created, Who Gets It, and Why It Matters* (London: Routledge). Sergio keeps a site https://www.sergiofocardi.net/ with his lectures, videos, and commentaries on economies as complex systems subject to qualitative changes.

Jenna Gavin completed a BSc in Mathematical Sciences in National University of Ireland, Galway, in 2017. She completed a M.Sc in Computing (Data Analytics) in Dublin City University in 2020. During the masters programme, she completed her research project 'Constructing Cryptocurrency Investment Portfolios Using PCA and Community Detection' under the guidance of her supervisor Martin Crane. She is currently working as a Data Analytics Consultant at PricewaterhouseCoopers (PwC).

Xize Guo is from the School of Economic, Finance, and Marketing, College of Business and Law, RMIT University, Australia. Xize entered the Finance PhD program at RMIT in 2020. She graduated from the University of Melbourne with a master's degree in management (major in Finance) in 2019. Before she came to Melbourne, she received a master's degree in Natural Science from Chinese Academy of Sciences in 2017. She also obtained double bachelor's degree major in Science and Economics in 2014 from Peking University. She has been awarded several merit scholarships throughout her academic career. Her research interests lie in machine learning in finance, empirical asset pricing, and fund management.

Wolfgang Karl Härdle attained his Dr rer nat in Mathematics at Universität Heidelberg in 1982 and in 1988 his habilitation at Universität Bonn. He is Ladislaus von Bortkiewicz Professor of

Statistics at Humboldt-Universität zu Berlin and the director of the Sino-German International Research Training Group IRTG1792 'High dimensional non-stationary time series analysis', a joint project with WISE, Xiamen University. His research focuses on data sciences, dimension reduction, and quantitative finance. He has published over 30 books and more than 300 papers in top statistical, econometrics, and finance journals. He is highly ranked and cited on Google Scholar, REPEC, and SSRN. He has professional experience in financial engineering, smart (specific, measurable, achievable, relevant, and timely) data analytics, machine-learning, and cryptocurrency markets.

Xiaolu Hu is a Lecturer in Finance in the School of Economics, Finance, and Marketing, College of Business and Law, RMIT University, Australia. Xiaolu joined RMIT in 2018 after receiving her PhD in finance at RMIT. Before she joined the academia, Xiaolu had extensive working experience in the finance industry. She is also a CFA charter holder and actively involved in the CFA Melbourne society. Xiaolu has published high-quality research papers on established finance journals, such as *Journal of Banking & Finance* and *Finance Research Letters*. Her areas of research are machine-learning in finance, empirical asset pricing, fixed income market, and the Chinese capital market.

Fearghal Kearney is a Senior Lecturer in Finance at Queen's Management School, Queen's University Belfast. His research is primarily focused in the area of financial market analysis, with his specific interests including commodity finance, option volatility, predictive analytics, and financial technology. His work has appeared in leading international outlets, including the *Journal of Banking and Finance*, *Journal of Financial Markets*, *Journal of Empirical Finance*, *International Journal of Forecasting*, and *European Financial Management.*

Tristan Lim is a Researcher and Faculty Member at the School of Business Management of Nanyang Polytechnic, Singapore. His domain areas include Machine Learning and FinTech, among others. Tristan has experience spanning the private and public sector, in the areas of technology advisory, venture capital, and finance. Tristan holds postgraduate degrees in the areas of IT, Engineering, and Finance from Singapore Management University, National University of Singapore, and the University of Sydney. He is a CFA (USA) and CAIA (USA) charter holder, and a member of the Chartered Institute of Securities and Investment (UK).

Davide Mazza is Professor of Finance at the Pole Universitaire Léonard De Vinci, Paris-La Défense. He obtained an MBA in Finance and PhD at MIP — Politecnico di Milano School of Management, Italy, where he has been teaching and working as Research Assistant in Innovation Management for more than 6 years. He has also been a consultant at Deloitte, and has served as Scientific Reference and Project Manager at Commissariat à l'Energie Atomique et aux Energies Alternatives (CEA), the French main technology and innovation research center, in the context of a EU-funded project on technology and product innovation.

Martina Metzger is Professor of Monetary Economics at the Berlin School of Economics and Law. Previously, she was Executive Director at the non-partisan Berlin Institute for Financial Market Research. She also worked at the Division on Globalization and Development Strategies of UNCTAD. She was a Lecturer, Research Fellow, and Assistant Professor for International Economics and Macroeconomics at the University of Applied Science (Berlin) and the Free University of Berlin from which she holds a doctoral degree in economics. She is a member of the Institute for International Political Economy at BSEL. Since 2015, she is also a Lay Judge at the Berlin Social Court. https://www.hwr-berlin.de/prof/martina-metzger/.

Maria Nemilentseva is a Junior Researcher and PhD student at LUT University, School of Engineering Science, Finland. Maria's past education is directly related to that of finance and economics, MSc in Economics, and MBA degrees completed in Russia and in Finland. Maria's past work experience was within the financial leasing sector, and she primarily focused on the collaboration of banks and leasing companies within the financial market. Nowadays, Maria focuses on collaborative innovation and sustainable service development within the financial industry, FinTech sector. Her other research interests are Innovation Management, Strategic Entrepreneurship, and Design Thinking.

Nadia Pantidi is a Lecturer at the Computational Media Innovation Centre (CMIC), Te Herenga Waka — Victoria University of Wellington, New Zealand. Her research is in the areas of Human

Computer Interaction (HCI) and User Experience (UX), with a focus on understanding, evaluating, and designing for people's real world experiences with using technologies.

Marco Patacca is a Research Fellow at the Department of Economics of the University of Verona. He obtained a Master's Degree in Finance and Quantitative Methods for Economics and a PhD in Quantitative Methods for Economics, at the University of Perugia. He has been a Visiting Scholar at the London School of Economics and Political Science (UK) and at the New York University (USA), and obtained a postdoctoral contract at the Pôle Universitaire Léonard de Vinci (FR). His research interests concern Cryptocurrencies, Blockchain Technology, FinTech, and Sentiment Analysis.

Jennifer Pédussel Wu joined the Berlin School of Economics and Law in 2008 as a Professor of International Trade and Production. Previously, she was a Professor of Economics at the EDC Paris and an Assistant Professor at the American University of Paris. She has also been a Senior Fellow at the Center for European Integration Studies (ZEI), Bonn (Germany). She holds a BA degree in Economics from Oberlin College, and a MA degree in Mathematical Behavior Science and a PhD degree in Economics from the University of California, Irvine.

Raphael C. G. Reule finished legal studies with a state exam after working for the German government and private entities as a contractor. He is a PhD candidate and programme manager with the Humboldt-Universität zu Berlin since 2018. In his PhD thesis, RCG Reule is examining digital and surrogate finance.

Tim Riedler is a Research Associate and PhD candidate at the Department of Economic and Social Geography at the University of Cologne since 2020. He gained relevant work experience at the Max Planck Institute for Human Development, the NGO Global Innovation Gathering, and as a freelancer in a project of the Global Labour University. He holds a MA in International and Development Economics from the University of Applied Sciences in Berlin and a BA in Economics from the Berlin School of Economics and Law.

Keira Nicole Soutar is a Junior Researcher and PhD student at LUT University, School of Engineering Science in Finland. Keira's prior education was conducted at leading universities within Canada,

Germany, Sweden, and Finland, specifically in Global Business, HCI, and ICT Innovation. Keira has previously worked within various EU incentives focusing on health/well-being from the user perspective and experience of smart devices for elderly care. She also has experience in the software automation industry, specifically artificial intelligent automation. Her recent transition back to academia focuses on research of user-centered innovations within FinTech companies. Her most recent projects include those focusing on sustainable financial services, and development of a multidisciplinary sustainable Finance course.

On Kit Tam was previously the Deputy Pro Vice-Chancellor at RMIT and Deputy Dean of the Faculty of Business and Economics, Monash University. He has also served in the Treasury of the Australian Government, UNSW, and Philips (Hong Kong). He has published influential academic books and articles in prominent journals on China's financial and economic reform, corporate governance, and mutual funds. His research has received significant grant funding from major domestic and international bodies and corporations, including the ARC, Australian Academy of Humanities and Social Sciences, University of Maryland (US), Australia China Council, Ford Foundation, and ANZ Banking Group. He has held visiting positions at the University of California Berkeley, ANU, the University of Hong Kong, SOAS, and Columbia University. Professor Tam has been a consultant and adviser for major multilateral organizations and corporations including the World Bank, UNDP, Asian Development Bank, Lend Lease, National Australia Bank, MLC Finance, Bankers Trust, and Rio Tinto. He has served as a board director in financial institutions, state government organization, and companies in Australia and overseas.

Patrick Thng is a Senior Practice Faculty at the School of Information Systems of Singapore Management University, Singapore, where he is presently the Director of the Master of IT in Business (Financial Technology and Analytics). His research interests include strategic sourcing and vendor management, digital banking, FinTech, and innovation management, among others. Patrick was formerly the Director and Chief Information Officer of the World Bank Treasury and Finance. He also held senior and regional roles in the banking industry, including DBS

Bank (MD of Strategic Sourcing), UBS, ANZ Bank, and BNP Paribas. Patrick graduated with PhD (Management) from Singapore Management University, Master of Commerce (Hons) in Information System Management from the University of New South Wales, and Bachelor of Commerce (Hons, First Class) in Systems, Accounting, and Finance from the University of New South Wales. He is also an FCA (Australia) and ISACA (USA) charterholder, and a board member of several FinTech (Digital Banking, AI, and Customer Experience).

Yang Wang is a Lecturer in the School of Business, University of Dundee. Yang's current research interests include corporate fraud, corporate governance, and corporate social responsibility. Yang has published papers in academic journals including *British Accounting Review*, *Emerging Markets Review*, and *International Review of Financial Analysis.*

Yifei Zhang is a Research Assistant Professor at the School of Accounting and Finance, Faculty of Business, The Hong Kong Polytechnic University. Dr Zhang's current research interests include corporate finance and corporate social responsibility. Dr Zhang has published papers in academic journals, e.g., *Small Business Economics, Economics Letters, China Economic Review*, and *International Review of Financial Analysis.*

Elizaveta Zinovyeva is a PhD student of the International Research Training Group IRTG1792 'High dimensional non-stationary time series analysis' at the Humboldt-Universität zu Berlin. Previously, she has completed her Master's studies in information systems and Bachelor's studies in business administration at the Humboldt-Universität zu Berlin. Her research focuses on application of deep neural networks on sequential data.

https://doi.org/10.1142/9781800612723_fmatter

Contents

https://doi.org/10.1142/9781800612723_fmatter

Introduction

The environment for international financial services has become extremely competitive, and the financial services sector is more technology intensive than it has ever been. The recent global financial crisis, along with the financial implications of the COVID-19 pandemic, have revealed that the business models and regulatory frameworks in place in different countries are incomplete and insufficient to prevent further build ups of vulnerabilities in the financial services sector that can generate systemic risk in the financial system. In that regard, Financial Technology (FinTech) can be used to detect systematic risk build ups, enabling investors and regulatory bodies to take anticipatory action. Moreover, competition from non-bank financial intermediation and technology firms has forced banks and financial services firms to concentrate further on new business opportunities, new business models, and modernized market practices that are based on digital transformation. FinTech, although not a new concept, is a rapidly growing industry that uses technology to improve financial services, serving both consumers and businesses alike, but alongside these opportunities, regulatory challenges lie ahead.

In the last few years, there has been a rise in the number of banking institutions partnering with FinTech companies as they seek to digitize and modernize their regulatory operations. This increased interest in Regulatory Technology (RegTech) solutions highlights the need for improved management of regulations within the financial industry through technology that has come as a result of the 2008 financial crisis, and the urgent need for more efficient risk management.

FinTech has broad applications in areas such as mobile banking, insurance, fraud detection, cryptocurrencies, and financial markets forecasting. FinTech's main themes, including big data, blockchain, artificial intelligence, and machine learning, have reshaped the financial services industry in recent years and have offered new innovative products and business solutions. FinTech presents both opportunities and challenges for countries across the globe and is widely regarded as a key contributor to the development of the international financial services industry. Governments around the globe have recognized the significant benefits FinTech can bring to economic growth, productivity, and the competitiveness of globalized digital economies. Scientific research on FinTech is expected to strengthen an innovative economy, create new employment opportunities in the financial sector, attract developing businesses, and develop partnerships between business and academia, thereby offering opportunities for multidisciplinary cutting-edge research that lies at the intersection of finance and technology.

This book aims to provide insights on recent developments in the area of FinTech. The intended readership of the book spans both academic audiences and industry professionals working in the financial services sector who use (or intend to use) FinTech applications to improve their business processes. In the chapters that follow, we will explore the following themes independently: smart contracts and regulation, cryptocurrencies, machine learning with financial applications, and FinTech in financial services.

Chapter 1 provides a data driven overview and categorization of smart contracts, Blockchain-verified decentralized contracts, and critically assesses the current and potential future applications of smart contracts. The regulation of FinTech is analyzed in Chapter 2 where several regulatory measures are proposed to result in a more adaptive, proactive, and comprehensive regulatory environment for the rapidly changing financial market ecosystem resulting from the growth in FinTech.

Chapter 3 outlines a theory of cryptocurrencies that parallels the standard theory of money but with a different process of creation and distribution. The future evolution of cryptocurrencies and central bank digital currencies are also considered. Continuing with the theme of cryptocurrencies, Chapter 4 performs correlation and cluster analysis on a large number of different cryptocurrencies to arrive at a small number of community groupings and leading coins with potential application in portfolio allocation models.

Chapter 5 applies machine-learning approaches to distill large volumes of information into a tractable evaluation of borrower credit quality using loan application data from a peer-to-peer lending platform. The individual features that drive both the price of credit and the likelihood of default are further analyzed with the tools of Explainable Artificial Intelligence. In Chapter 6, Machine-Learning methods are applied to detect financial fraud in firms using a novel financial fraud dataset consisting of a large number of cases, pertaining to publicly listed firms in China. Both firm-level financial and linguistic features derived from annual reports are used as predictors of financial fraud. The role of machine-learning methods in mutual fund performance measurement is evaluated in Chapter 7. The machine-learning algorithms used for this task are introduced and their contribution to mutual fund performance measurement above and beyond standard measures is elucidated.

Chapter 8 proposes a strategy-risk outsourcing life cycle model for financial institutions embarking on outsourcing in the increasingly complex FinTech and financial regulatory landscape. This provides a simple-to-use end-to-end framework which can be utilized by the financial services industry to guide outsourcing decisions. Chapter 9 presents a user-centered approach to developing and evaluating a digital prototype mobile application for personal financial management. Design decisions are explored, the usability implications of those decisions are evaluated, and ways in which future tools could be enhanced are examined. The success of Estonia's FinTech scene is analyzed in Chapter 10 with a focus on the historical perspective that created the environment for this success along with a discussion of the empirical insights garnered from interviews with several Estonian FinTech experts. Chapter 11 explores the role of digital financial services used by migrants to send remittances, for example, mobile money systems and cryptocurrency-based systems, and how these digital remittance channels are often superior to traditional formal and informal transfer channels.

These 11 chapters provide a diverse and interesting coverage of various important topics in FinTech. We hope that academics, policymakers, regulators, and investors will benefit from reading the book where novel interesting results on the impact of FinTech on financial markets, investment strategies, business processes, and the regulatory environment are presented.

Hsin-I (Daisy) Chou
Conall O'Sullivan
Vassilios G. Papavassiliou

Part I

FinTech: Smart Contracts and Regulation

https://doi.org/10.1142/9781800612723_0001

Chapter 1

Understanding Smart Contracts: Hype or Hope?

Elizaveta Zinovyeva[*,†,||], Raphael C. G. Reule[*,†,**]
and Wolfgang Karl Härdle[*,‡,§,¶,††]

[*] *Blockchain Research Center, Humboldt University of Berlin, Germany*
[†] *International Research Training Group 1792, Humboldt-Universität zu, Berlin, Germany*
[‡] *Wang Yanan Institute for Studies in Economics, Xiamen University, China*
[§] *Sim Kee Boon Institute for Financial Economics, Singapore Management University, Singapore*
[¶] *Faculty of Mathematics and Physics, Charles University, Czech Republic National Chiao Tung University, Taiwan*
[||] *elizaveta.zinovyeva@wiwi.hu-berlin.de*
[**] *irtg1792.wiwi@wiwi.hu-berlin.de*
[††] *haerdle@wiwi.hu-berlin.de*

Abstract

Smart Contracts are commonly considered to be an important component or even a key to many business solutions in an immense variety of sectors and promises to securely increase their individual efficiency in an ever more digitized environment. Introduced in the early 1990s, the technology has gained a lot of attention with its application to blockchain technology to an extent, that can be considered a veritable hype. Reflecting the growing institutional interest, this intertwined exploratory study between statistics, information technology, and law contrasts these idealistic stories with the data reality and provides a mandatory step of understanding the matter, before any further relevant applications are discussed as being 'factually' able to replace traditional constructions. Besides fundamental flaws and application difficulties of currently employed Smart Contracts, the technological drive and enthusiasm backing it may however serve as a jump-off board for future developments thrusting well in the presently unshakeable traditional structures.

Keywords: Cryptocurrency, smart contract, Ethereum, CRIX.

1. Introduction

> All great truths begin as blasphemies.
>
> Shaw (1917)

Smart Contracts (SC): A key buzzword of our modern, fully digitized, and increasingly globalized media and scientific world amongst 'crowdfunding', 'decentralization', 'resource management', 'prosumer', 'blockchain', 'cryptocurrency', 'internet-of-things', 'digital asset regulation', and many more. The SC hype has reached the non-tech-mainstream, driven by an ever-increasing number of FinTech, RegTech, SupTech, LegalTech, and OtherTech startups, as well as governmental initiatives — yet most often disappear into the ether after some hype.

The basal common 'understanding' is that *blockchain* (BC) *applications* of so-called SCs are *self-executing* pieces of software/algorithms/codes/processes with a predetermined set of rules to be followed in calculations and other problem-solving operations. SCs are supposed to decentralize the authority over agreements and their enforcement by being purposely *self-enforcing*, with people across the whole world starting binding relationships without ever trusting — leave alone knowing — each other. This ideal in a new appearance represents a fundamentally different approach on organically grown contractual systems. A technology from the 1970s, the so-called *Electronic Data Interchange* (EDI), was driven by a similar ideal and equally hyped but eventually failed to deliver on replacing traditional contracting. While it was able to reduce some costs, it effectively enshrined the human inefficiency in decision making in the process (Sklaroff, 2017). Translated to today's even more information-driven times, announcing to work on some BC application attracts a lot of attention and investments to companies — even though the rate of delivery of BC-driven outcomes is negligible with such announcements incorporating respective buzzwords are observable as an attempt to take advantage of artificial premia (Akyildirim *et al.*, 2021). Therefore, research on a possible gap between an actual status of SCs (given by data) and their target status is mandatory.

From crops insurance, over supply chain management, to development assistance, manifold imaginary fields of SC application turn out to be either philosophical 'How nice the world could be' — papers or 'This is what we used, use, and what we will use' — outlets of very specialized fields to forcefully foster the idea of SCs. They all have one thing in common: they do not access the broad view on (1) what the technology can really deliver and/or (2) where it can be applied to real-world situations. Evolutionary, humans used clay, wood, or paper to enshrine their agreements to trade grain, Schnapps, or other values within a system supervised by some hierarchical structures. BC SCs promise to overcome this homeostasis. Seeing that many forwarded SC-oaths are surreal to be accomplished even through traditional means, we critically assess and identify these areas to find out, if this is all just hype or if there is hope. Through the use of datasets depicting in depth the activity and information flow of SCs on the Ethereum (ETH) network, we are able to research the facts and what SCs are used for contrary to the common belief:

- SCs increase technological literacy, assure increased inclusion, and participation rights?
- It makes sense for every economic endeavor to adapt to such systems?
- SCs are more than just a financial vehicle and really able to, e.g., fight hunger in underdeveloped countries?
- SCs really increase efficiency and security whilst reducing associated costs and procedural risks?
- SCs that follow strict structures to function are really more flexible than traditional natural language agreements?

With many teething issues to be overcome by such applications beyond being simple transaction monitoring software, the result to date is a realm of uncertainty which the construction in itself tries to prevent ironically. Especially terms like *smart*, *contract*, *authority*, and self-enforcing are highly ambiguous and not as safely defined as in traditional schemes. The most obvious issue, and one of the common misconceptions, is the colported independent self-executability of SCs — which is wrong, as an external input is always needed to order an SC to execute its code. The code is then indeed self-enforcing, possibly acting as a vigilante, leading to a superfluity of problems. Our work is inspired by the work of Oliva *et al.* (2020) with the aim to extend it with a legal perspective and a proposal of approaches to gain opportunities for further exploration. In this sense, we will crystallize, that as a fact, SCs are just another — yet ambitious — 'pathetic dot' regulated by the forces of the market, technical infrastructure, law, and social conception (Lessig, 1999).

In this research, we first identify the sources of the hype on SCs; second, we present algorithms of SCs to understand what SCs are actually doing. This responds to many inherent questions by creating a taxonomy and critical understanding of SCs. By outlining their framework and providing an extensive mapping of SCs based on the ETH network. Visually, we de-frame the Storytelling by outing their real fields of application and the costs that come with this fractional delivery on the promised list of miracles. Based on the research insight we got from the analysis of existing SCs, we propose an algorithm to identify a proper answer and solution to the question, if it makes sense for a given endeavor to invest into creating BC/SC frameworks.

The chapter is structured by giving an introduction to the existing research literature and subject in Sections 2 and 3, followed by a dataset disclosure in Section 4, a taxonomy of SCs in Sections 5 (Clustering) and 6 (Classification), eventually culminating in a critical status analysis and improvement proposal in Section 7, and ending with closing remarks in Section 8. All presented graphical and numerical examples shown are reproducible and can be found via www.quantlet.com (Borke and Härdle, 2018) and are indicated as USC. Moreover, an Appendix with further details, such as description of technical methods used and full plots, which were shortened here due to spatial reasons. Research data is obtainable through the https://blockchain-research-center.com/.

2. Outlet Review

2.1. *Recent research review*

To outline the dissonance between the mass of whitepapers/prosaic outlets in contrast to the actual data available for SCs, we conduct a data-driven literature overview gathering a rather diffuse impression. Researchers, for example, focus on a variety of aspects, among others, ranging from applications of SCs in healthcare and quality monitoring (Celesti *et al.*, 2020; Khatoon, 2020; Yu *et al.*, 2020), technical implementations and vulnerabilities (Ajienka *et al.*, 2020; Li *et al.*, 2020; Pierro *et al.*, 2020) to games (Scholten *et al.*, 2019).

One of the first research works dedicated to the empirical analysis of SCs is the work by Bartoletti and Pompianu (2017). The authors gathered a dataset of 834 SC source codes, which were then manually classified into different categories using the proposed taxonomy. The identified categories contained types like Notary, Financial, Game, Wallet, Library. Moreover, the authors were able to identify the design patterns found in the source code. Wöhrer and Zdun (2018) also dedicate their work to design patterns that are aimed to improve and facilitate the work of software developers and engineers working on applications for the BC, as similar problems may require similar solutions. One of the later empirical studies created by Oliva *et al.* (2020) propose the approach of cross-linking the data from various sources in order to scrutinize better their behavior: their activity level, category of what these contracts are, and source code metrics, like complexity.

An important research direction in this context is automatic source code classification. Although the idea of using machine learning for code classification is not very new, it is not that present in the ETH realm, as we will see later. Norvill *et al.* (2017) use unsupervised techniques and run clustering on bytecodes to group contracts with a similar purpose. Chen *et al.* (2018) use the machine learning method XGBoost on the opcodes and account data to identify Ponzi schemes. Wang *et al.* (2020) use different machine learning methods to identify security vulnerabilities in SCs. Many codes on the ETH BC are very similar and are quite often copied. Kondo *et al.* (2020) investigate code cloning on ETH and identify clusters of the code clones and inspect their behavior.

2.2. *Preliminary data basis*

In order to scan a wide-angle of exhaustive SC outlets, we utilized the Scopus citation and abstract database that gathers peer-reviewed research from around 11.7K publishers from different directions in science. The query retrieves the scholarly work from conferences and journals in the English language containing *Ethereum* or *smart contracts* in the title. Furthermore, the query is limited to work conducted in the areas like Business, Computer and Decision Science, and Mathematics. The exact query can be found in the respective Quantlet on Github. In total, the data pool lists 839 research outlets. Research publishing on ETH SCs began in 2016 and achieved a peak in 2019. At the date of retrieving the query, the year 2020 was ongoing, hence, we could not fully measure whether the amount of research in 2020 is higher or lower than in 2019. Nonetheless, we can see that the SC area's interest is not fading and is staying on a relatively high level. The topics of the examined research outputs were distilled from their abstracts and keywords. The analysis on the keyword level has not shown any interesting patterns and due to spatial reasons can be found only in the Appendix.

The gathered research papers were categorized into their dedicated topics using dimensionality reduction, clustering, and natural language processing techniques (bidirectional encoder representations from transformers, BERT, Devlin *et al.*, 2018) to subsequently inspect the most important words used therewithin. This analysis was performed on the abstracts to achieve higher specification. This step's technical implementation is described in greater detail in Section 5. The optimal amount of groups/clusters of 14 for this step was determined by the elbow (curve) method (see Appendix for further details): a heuristic to identify the number of clusters in a dataset (Thorndike, 1953). Figure 1 presents the scatter plot depicting our clustering of the existing research into 14 various topics. The manual assessment of the top identified most *important* words pointed to the following possible topics: Healthcare/medicine, Implementation/Storage, Vulnerabilities/Ponzi/Scam/Bugs, Voting/Trust, Research/Categories of Research, Programming language/Solidity/Software Development, Crowdsourcing/Sharing, Applications Development/Protocols, IOT/Smart devices, Verification/Deployment/Execution of SC, Food/Agriculture, BTC/Finance/ICO, Energy/Electricity/Gas, and Payments/Audit. In the Appendix section, Literature Meta-Analysis on the Abstract Level, you can find the plots with the respective 10 most important words for each one of the 14 topics, in terms of c-TF-IDF, which will be described in Section 5. We observe in Figure 1 that the topics are very diverse, yet inter-related, and express different distances to each other. Whilst there are no dominating topics present, we observe that some of the clusters are relatively similar in the size: e.g., Payments/Audit, Vulnerabilities/Ponzi/Scam/Bugs, BTC/Finance/ICO, and Programming language/Solidity/Software Development. The Healthcare/Medicine cluster is very isolated, which points out that these papers are rather unsimilar to all the others. As well as Energy/Electricity/Gas cluster seems to have its very own distinct features, as there are space gaps, which are meaningful in UMAP dimensionality reduction (see Section 5 and UMAP versus *t*-SNE Section in Appendix), between this cluster and the others. Interestingly, there are no clusters containing distinctly related machine learning keywords. Moreover, there are no clusters that would obviously outnumber all the others.

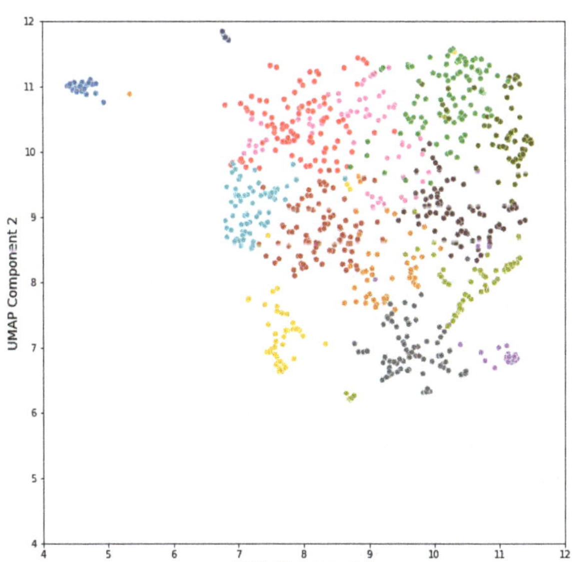

Figure 1. Grouping the existing research into 14 topics via UMAP.

This will be later of importance where we show that the existing applications are mostly dominated by the Finance/ICO.

Hence, after this first step into understanding SCs and structuring outlets on SCs, we see that there are no dominating topics and that they are diverse. This goes hand in hand with the common understanding that SCs can be readily applied to many diverse use cases. Further evidence to that can be readily collected to a basal Google search query or by respective Google Search Query Trends. Therefore, one of the aims of our work is to show whether the use-cases promised in the media or research can be realized within the SC concept or otherwise that the SC environment has significant technical and legal constraints and, in the end, is used primarily for one purpose — as a financial instrument. This fact would make BCs using the SC concept not significantly different enough from other CCs.

3. Science and Work

Governments, companies, clients, humans, in general, are making manifold kinds of transactions and agreements each day. Most are dependent on government-backed third-party entities to create *trust* in the given system. These highly centralized systems inject costs and risks into otherwise simple processes by being dependent on a stable workforce and intermediaries in order to keep this organically grown and comparably slow traditional *trust machine* running. This machinery is confronted by a rapidly increasing load of information and a plethora of interdependent data streams with increasing digitization. Smart phones and smart watches, for example, provide us with instant access to the whole of available knowledge of humankind, may it be location tracking or health data — yet, whilst the entry to knowledge may be easy, the real great leap forward is to understand and correctly employ this knowledge. Putting 'smart' into the name of any given product does not make it *smart* or even an *intelligent* idea to begin with. However, the idea of SCs as a tool to increase efficacy and objective decentralized controlling mechanisms is an essential approach on minimizing the possibilities of uncertainty and risks originating from human interference and 'allow a quarrelsome species ill-suited to organizations larger than small tribes to work together on vast projects like manufacturing jumbo jets and running hospitals' (Szabo, 1997a).

> A smart contract is a computerized transaction protocol that executes the terms of a contract. The general objectives of smart contract design are to satisfy common contractual conditions (such as payment terms, liens, confidentiality, and even enforcement), minimize exceptions both malicious and accidental, and minimize the need for trusted intermediaries. Related economic goals include lowering fraud loss, arbitration and enforcement costs, and other transaction costs. Szabo (1994)

Nick Szabo (1994) envisioned the now-famous concept of SCs to increase contractual efficiency and published it around fourteen years before the popularization of the BC technology through Bitcoin (BTC). Unfortunately, technical constraints forced this idea to become a more theoretical and abstract construction for even more complex use cases like the transfer of real estate ownership, shares in a company, or intellectual property. Szabo explained that a vending machine is the simplest form of an abstract SC: it is a technical device accessible to anybody who is eligible, designed to transfer ownership of a good when provided with a pre-defined input. Given the nature of a vending machine, it therefore also *controls* and *oversees* the actual value for the involved parties: the seller, by storing it, and the buyer, by granting access to it after corresponding valid input. It can hence also enforce the terms of the given agreement by either granting access to the requested value or asking for a fitting input — otherwise, the request gets rejected. Envisioned input for SCs is anything from payments, votes, or any other condition that can be expressed by code (Szabo, 1997b).

3.1. *Basic understanding*

The previously abstract ideas on SCs were ready to be transformed into a basic proof-of-concept status with BC technology's emergence. BCs are technically speaking a sequential and shared database managed and controlled by consensus algorithms for internal consistency. They can be designed as *permissionless/public* or *permissioned/private* system constructions, i.e., are defined by their read/write 'rights' to access the network (see further Härdle *et al.*, 2020; Lin *et al.*, 2021). ETH is a community-driven, open-source software platform that was the first of such BC systems to support SCs. Its Whitepaper was originally published in 2013 by Vitalik Buterin, before its public launch in 2015 (Buterin, 2020). The main elements of interest for ETH BCs, i.e., a chronological ledger of human-induced technological happenings, are peer-to-peer networks, consensus mechanisms, hash values, Merkle trees, and asymmetric key encryption. These are also some of the buzzwords employed by marketeers promoting endeavors based on ETH. They are repeated over and over again without explanation to confuse and subsequently impress possible investors — we will touch on these in Sections 3.2 and 3.3, as well as Appendix.

One of the key-points of ETH BC is to be not only just a *cryptocurrency* (CC) but also to allow a variety of opportunities through SC decentralized applications. But is it similar to other CCs? BTC is the de facto CC market driver and it can be seen as a speculative and very volatile financial vehicle, while ETH seems to be historically more of a technological driver which not submitting to this BTC regime as extremely — it is of course heavily influenced nevertheless (Keilbar and Zhang, 2020; Petukhina, 2021a,b) (see also the Cryptocurrency Dynamics section of the Appendix). We differentiate between two types of crypto assets: coins and tokens. One of the possible definitions is the following: a *coin* is a CC that runs on its own BC, whereas a *token* does not have their own BC and are run on another BC. BTC and *Ether* — the native coin of SCs and ETH BC are considered to be coins, as they run on their own BCs. Dai (MakerDao, 2021) and Golem (Factory, 2021) living on ETH are usually perceived as tokens. This difference may be important when different crypto assets are traded. While one can directly exchange tokens via internal applications, the coins, due to their non-standardized code protocols, can be exchanged only through external CC exchange platforms (Ledger, 2021). The difference is less visible in all other cases, and quite often, these terms are used interchangeably, or the tokens are called coins. In the following, we will differentiate between coins and tokens. One important type of crypto asset running on ETH BC is a *stablecoin* — a type of token, which price is designed to stay fix or, as the name says — stable with respect to another external asset, like gold or US dollar. It is designed this way to be robust against the volatility of the *Ether's* price. One example of the *stablecoin* is the USDC (Circle, 2021). The already mentioned Dai token (MakerDao, 2021) is also a *stablecoin.* Within the ETH realm, the tokens must follow certain standards to comply with its coding codex for their inception via an SC. These standards are proposed as *Ethereum Improvement Proposals* (EIPs) and *Ethereum Request for Comments* (ERCs) that need to be peer-reviewed and accepted by the community. ERCs are application-level standards for token standards, name registries, library/package formats, et cetera. Respectively for SCs, the ERC20 token standard is a set of functions that have to be followed as a mandatory 'styleguide'. The majority of ETH tokens are ERC20 tokens and have become famous through their *Initial Coin Offering* (ICO, remotely similar to Initial Public Offering (IPOs) in the traditional field). Besides ICOs, ETH's SCs also enable and define constructions like Distributed Applications (DApps), yet they most often just plainly represent transaction flows (see Sections 6 and 5). As said, Tokens are commonly emitted via ICOs, which can be seen as a crowd funding scheme — in other words: a lot of the created CCs are just tokens based on the ETH network rather than having their own BC network construction. Tokens can be *Usage Tokens* or *Work Tokens.* Usage tokens act like Ether — just within their respective DApp. Work tokens can be seen as shareholder identificators or membership cards, which means that one can interact within the DApp through this token, for example, to vote on who becomes the speaker of a given group.

For purposes of understanding the term 'Smart Contract' — as Hanna Halaburda (2018) with the Bank of Canada very critically outlines — we agree that the concept and actual modus operandi for the absolute majority of BC-based SCs is not new. Automated recurring payments between entities are an example of how SCs effectively define themselves nowadays. However, the elemental misunderstanding is with the idea of BCs. BCs are indeed not needed to gain the benefits from SCs when leaving the crucial aspect of immutability/non-modifiability and the utilization of BC technology out, i.e., by strictly following Szabo (1994)'s initial definition of *unbiased controlling.* In advance of Section 7.1, whereas Szabo (1994) defines SCs as a 'computerized transaction protocol that executes the terms of a contract' — hence every self-executing agreement like, for

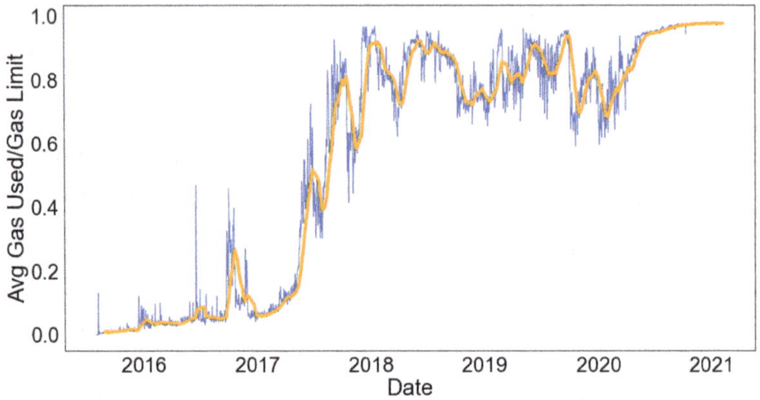

Figure 2. ETH network utilization (mean), 20150630-20210211.

example, related to a vending machine, an ATM, or an AppStore process — Buterin (2020) eventually defines them as any sort of script running on the ETH BC that follow certain defined standards for specified SC fields of employment (EIP, 2020). Of course, there are now plenty of other system constructions also supporting their individual kind of technological application for their individual purposes, yet we will only specifically look at ETH SCs as it has proven to be a stable system that has gained great market acceptance and steady network utilization (see further Section 4, as well as Figures 2, 6(a), and 14). ETH SCs are therefore realizing Szabo's idea of *control* by constructing BC-based, downtime-resistant, fraud-proof, and network audited systems. These operate without interference from a third party, by storing, verifying, and enforcing agreements automatically, therefore making human interaction redundant, hence aim to reduce process time and costs, while also improving transparency and trust.

3.2. *Understanding ETH*

ETH runs a so-called *account-based* BC, which means that these are the keypoints and central issue we need to look at after understanding the basic functional framework. An ETH BC block header contains, besides the hash of the previous block and other relevant information, three so-called *Modified Merkle Patricia tree*'s (tree also subsidized as *trie*) for its *state* system: state root (system state: account balances, contract storages, contract codes, and account nonces), *transactions* (TXs), and receipts (the outcome of individual TXs). These touch the overall state, i.e., information linked to blocks being added sequentially to the BC, as well as the individual state of certain entities, like some balance of value stored on an entity such as a given account.

In a Merkle tree parent/non-leaf nodes contain the hash of their children/leaf nodes, and the child nodes contain the hash of a block of data. Therefore, any change to the underlying data, i.e., the state, causes also the hash of the respective reference node to change. Since each parent node hash depends on the data of its children, any change to the data of a child node causes the parent hash to change. This would of course trigger a reaction up to the root node hash, but only the changed hashes will be propagated to a later block with respective parents of the later block — previous information contained in a already created block is unchanged. This means, that one does not need to compare all data across the network of leaf nodes for verification, as the root node hash provides a quick answer to that when looking up individual *addresses*. In return, confirming that some specific small amount of information belongs to the whole tree in question, is done easily via a so-called *Merkle Proof*. Only the minimum amount of nodes are modified to recalculate the root hash for a single operation as visualized in Figure 3. This creates systemic benefits as it is possible to store only a hash of the root node to represent the data at that point in time whilst keeping the data immutable on a previous block — see further (Appendix D in Wood, 2021), the Ethereum Wiki, and Buterin (2015). As this is

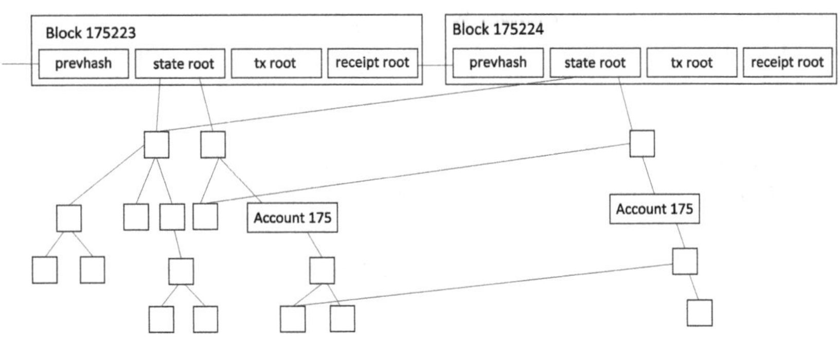

Figure 3. ETH BC visualization (adapted from Buterin, 2015).

mandatory understanding for the following sections: the state contains every account information present in the BC, however, the state itself is not stored in each block of the BC. It is, as outlined in Wood (2021), generated by processing each block since the genesis block, that is the initial/inception block of the chain of blocks, whereas each individual block will only modify parts of the state, but not the whole state. State trie information therefore exists independently of a referenced state root. Therefore Figure 3 presents that the state root in block 175223 (left) refers to two child nodes, and that the state root block 175224 (right) refers to one of the same child nodes as block 175223 with one new child node not referenced by the prior state root. Given that 175224 is the last block, the previous state trie information of block 175223 becomes 'irrelevant', when referenced in the state root of block 175224. This means, that only altered information is connected to the state root of a respective block containing this information and linking it to previous blocks. As each hash is unique, this means, that an imaginary block 175230 can also refer to information stored in the state root of block 175223, given that this old information is updated with new input, i.e., the overall size of data transferred can be kept low without loosing information.

Two aspects are important for understanding this system: First, adding subsequential blocks to the ETH BC that do not contain previous information, but only new or updated information, does not mean, that previous entries are forgotten/deleted/redundant. In contrary, each unique information has a corresponding unique hash, that forms a *hashmap*. The state root of block 175224 still references to previous entries present ad infinitum within the BC, hence allowing to reference values existent in the state trie of block 175223. Second, and this is important for the upcoming exegesis on accounts and TX, this *hashmap* creates a reference point for interaction on the BC. However, this referencing might be missing previous points contained in block 175223 or earlier, if one only loads data starting at block 175224, which might be referencing to information of block 175223. Hence that hashmap might miss information referenced in the state root of block 175223, for example, if an account has sufficient funds. Remember, that the whole state is not stored, but only the root hash. Conveniently, the ETH network protocol solves this by requesting missing information from peers — recall the structure and modus operandi of a BC. Even with only recent information at hand, i.e., missing the non-altered information of previous blocks, peers commit missing values needed.

With a basic understanding of the ETH BC at hand, we can now proceed to dissect which actors with which corresponding acts can be observed in this system. A TX can be described as simply sending some value, like say 1 Ether, from Alice to Bob, i.e., from one *address* to another, usually by using a *wallet*. That said value, however, is not in a 'wallet', but on the ETH BC linked to an *account*. TXs themselves do not need to be financial operations, but can also initiate systemic changes like creating an account. Therefore we first need to understand what accounts are, how they act and can be interacted with, and how these are uniquely identifiable. There a two distinct classes of accounts in ETH: *Externally Owned Accounts* (EOA) and *Contract Accounts* (CA, often just called *contracts*, hence unanimously used in relation to SCs).

An EOA is an entity that can be accessed and can validate TX through the individual secret *private key* (see Appendix for further details). It can consequently be identified by the extracted *public key* and the complementary *public address*. The public address can also be derived from respective in-/outgoing TXs connected to, for example, a given EOA. Moreover, it serves to store value like Ether and controls applications like wallets. One private key can generate multiple public keys and multiple other 'private keys' for certain applications (these are in fact not the real private key, but just private keys for an individual application, hence public keys that are kept secret within that system which then create further public keys in a mimikry fashion).

A wallet is a software client that allows to manage EOAs. One or multiple EOAs can be accessed via different wallets and the majority of wallet offerings can generate EOAs upon request. Wallets can be linked to further services like CC exchanges. Without going into further details, there are different kinds of wallets, like desktop, web, physical, and mobile app based ones, which allow features such as TX logging, multisignature, withdrawal limits, and many other functions. Wallets are therefore user interfaces, which are controlled via code and authenticated by an EOA's private key.

CAs, on the contrary to EOAs, do not possess a corresponding private key and are controlled by the inhibited information stored within: an SC with respectively coded functionalities. Individual

CAs are generated, when an SC is *deployed* with a TX — hence these two terms, CA & SC, are often used synonymously — and which is linked to the deploying EOA through means of *public key cryptography/asymmetric cryptography* and its *nonce* — and hold respective code and/or data (see above and Section 3.3). The state refers to information about individual accounts and consists of the accounts' balance (in Wei, see Appendix for further details), the nonce (the sequential number of TX sent from an EOA, which includes the number of deployed SCs/created CAs made by an EOA/CA, as they are TX as well), the storageroot (the root node hash of the account storage trie), and the codeHash (hash of the compiled SC, the *Ethereum Virtual Machine* (EVM) *bytecode*). Note: the nonce — differently to the *Proof-of-Work* nonce, which is a random number — is simply the sending accounts' sequential TX count and prevents *double spending*. CAs have a balance, a nonce, bytecode, and the root hash of a storage trees (the beforehand explained Merkle trees for TXs, receipts, and state). In contrast, EOAs do not host an SC, hence the bytecode and storage hash are empty. For CAs, the bytecode is the SCs code and the storage hash is the merkle root hash of all the key-value pairs in the CAs state. Only the codeHash represents an immutable field, as it contains the bytecode of the SC deployed to the BC — hence, an error in the code will exist persistently. The other fields are mutable, like the nonce, which increments when a TX created by this account.

There are two different kinds of interactions in ETH: TXs and *message call*s (MGSs). TXs are information packages, like debit or credit instructions of a given value, that are authorized by the interactor/sender through the *individual* TX *signature*. The authorizing signature is mathematically generated through hashing the respective information, like the above example of sending value from one address to another together with the private key by using the Keccak-256 algorithm — the result is the signed and hence authorized information. A MSG is equivalent to a TX, being only a local invocation of an SC function that does not broadcast or publish anything on the BC. They contain the source and target addresses, some data payload, some value like Ether, Gas and return data. A simple TX between two EOAs or an EOA to a CA is therefore straightforward with only three main parameters required: the interactor/sender account address, recipient account address, and the TX value. Parameters like the nonce, the *gasLimit*, and the *gasPrice* will be input automatically, for example, by using the Geth console (gasLimit and gasPrice will be touched on later in Section 3.3). Further parameters are related to ECDSA and accordingly used to sign a TX. The parameters *data* and *init* refer to SCs. Data is relevant for value transfer and sending a MSG to an SC, like altering a specified value. The init parameter is relevant for, as implied, CA creation, i.e., the bytecode utilized for initializing one.

MSGs are created, for example, when a CA executes certain SC *opcodes*, or when interacting through an EOA with an SC to check on a certain variable saved in the CA's state. CAs can communicate with other CAs through this functionality given respective coding (see further Section 3.3). MSGs are also called *internal transactions* — a very perplexing misnomer that may not be confused with TX, as they are not recorded on the BC, but can be derived from other ETH system functionalities and are actually reflected in the overall balance of the individual account over time, as they also consume *Gas* (which is a fraction of Ether — more on that later and see Appendix for further details). MSGs are, for example, the result of an SC initiating a value transfer to an EOA — like sending a Token after a valid and accepted TX has been received from an EOA for an ICO — or of calling another CA/SC to, for example, check their funds. Hence, CAs can only MSG an EOA to validate/execute a then *recorded* TX (that means publicly displayed on the BC). A MSG doesn't need to be signed, whereas the called account automatically has access to the identity of the calling account, which is most basically referred to initially in a variable called msg.sender. This variable information is stored in the constructor, which is a non-callable/MSGable function that is executed during the creation of a CA/deployment of an SC and permanently stores the address of the entity creating the CA/SC in the beginning. Note, that the actual ownership of a CA can be altered afterwards, given the ownership transfer function is coded in the SC. In other words: In the ICO example, one first needs to send some value, like Ether, to the CA that hosts the ICO SC in order to receive a defined value like a respective token in return through a MSG from the CA, or through the CA calling a EOA, which then transfers value to the initially interacting account through a BC-recorded TX or non-BC-recorded MSG after release.

Therefore the term 'self-execution' of SCs, as mentioned in the beginning, is wrong. Every chain of motion is triggered originally by an non-CA input. Whilst CAs are only able to send MSGs (which EOAs can as well) and transfer value through these MSG's respective to coded functions therewithin to other accounts. Importantly, TX can not be created by SCs (only 'internal TX', that are MSG). TX cause state changes by either a simple transfer of value between accounts (which changes their respective balance), similarly by sending a MSG to a CA (for example, to alter an SC value, which can be thought of like altering the balance of an account), or by deploying an SC and herewith creating a CA.

To summarizes, EOAs are controllable via private keys, while CAs are controlled via the individual SCs bytecode (see further Section 3.3). EOAs have private keys and are controlled by, for example, wetware through using software like wallets. Private keys can be used to create, through the trapdoor function ECDSA, multiple public keys that uniquely form derived addresses. Therefore, one EOA on the ETH BC can have multiple CAs linked through deploying SCs. Only EOAs can sign and hence send TXs, which are recorded on the BC, whereas a MSG are not recorded on the BC. TX/MSG's can be sent to a CA in which the respective SCs functions must run accordingly. Finally, only the most crucial information is stored on the BC like changes in account balance but not, for example, MSG's to check on a certain accounts' balance (these information can however be obtained through different channels).

3.3. *Understanding SCs*

Occasionally, SCs are seen as so-called *programmatically executed transactions* (PETs), i.e., technology for enforcing agreements. Simply put we can state that the execution of an SC just replaces third party trust with mathematical proof, that some conditions were fulfilled — nothing more, nothing less (given we are not dealing with nefarious external input). SCs can accordingly be seen as an enhanced *zero-knowledge protocol* or *proof* (see Appendix for further details). It only returns, that the predetermined conditions are fulfilled or non-fulfilled (*completeness*), that the conditions are clearly defined if conditions are not-fulfilled (*soundness*), and that nothing else was disclosed but the fact that the conditions are met by successfully terminating the process (*zero-knowledge*), and eventually it terminates the process with a given outcome like granting access to a motel room.

Creating agreements for a variety of codeable use cases as SCs, besides the above mentioned financial vehicles, has therefore several benefits:

- **Standardization:** Code, following systemic standards, modeled after traditional contractual counterparts, and proven by best practices, combined with a deterministic execution dependent on clearly pre-defined parameters, reduces risks and costs, while saving valuable time.
- **Automation:** Reduced procedural friction, by removing intermediaries, and increased transaction flow based on a BC or associated consensus system.
- **Certainty:** Code executes automatically as pre-defined, hence reduces risk (e.g., counterparty or settlement risk), and therefore creates trust in these deterministic digital processes.
- **Security:** Transactions are encrypted and uniquely identifiable by their hash and stored on a BC or associated construction.
- **Innovation:** Modular and adaptable code that automatizes the flow of digital assets and payments to incubate new business models. Coded regulatory compliance, for example data reporting, and specialized interdisciplinary regulatory BC-based nodes to comply with digital advancements.

To create a CA is therefore similar to how a self-extracting software installer works. During its execution, it configures the system environment and handles the information according to the given algorithm. In technical terms, SCs are account holding objects on the ETH BC that contain code with functions to store information or to trigger others. SC code is immutable once stored/deployed within the ETH BC and thus developing SCs is closer to hardware programming than say web development. CAs consist each of an individual SC code in a specific binary format called EVM bytecode representing opcodes and further respective data related to its state (see further Section 3.2). To deploy an SC, a CA needs to be created by sending a TX from an EOA to an empty address with the SC bytecode as data. CAs can also create other CAs, if the contained SC is respectively coded and the process in initiated by an authorized EOA — usually these CA/SCs are called *factory contracts*. The same process can be repeated ad infinitum resulting in CA 'clones', which just happen to have unique addresses as each EOA TX is created using a unique nonce (see Section 3.2). Modifying data in any of these does not have an impact on the other clones that have been created unless coded to do so).

Most SCs are typically written in *Solidity* before being compiled into bytecode, which expresses similarities found in object-oriented languages that include variables, arithmetic operations, functions, classes, string manipulations, and further programming elements. Access to this is therefore easy with some knowledge in Python, Perl, JavaScript, or C++. Other languages like Vyper or Bamboo can be used as well, but we will not touch further on these. The human-readable code in Solidity can not be executed directly but needs to be compiled to machine-readable opcodes/bytecode that is executable. These opcodes are allocated a byte each and create an efficient way of process control with, for example, 'stop' being plainly called with `0x00`. Accordingly, these define the management of contextual procedures, like how to handle certain functions, variables, and parameters. The SC runtime environment — that is embedded within ETH network nodes and responsible for executing contract bytecode — is called the EVM (see Section 3.2). The term 'virtual machine' (VM) has a strong overtone, and to clarify: the EVM is not a VM — it is an *interpreter* for the *assembly language* defined through Solidity (the beforehand mentioned bytecode), with every participating node running that interpreter. The actual hash of a given TX is not relevant for this operation until being recorded into the BCs block Merkle tree (see above Section 3.2), but only the data, the amount of Gas available and used and potentially also the SC code that is being called if it is such an operation. The EVM handles the state transition function which is composed of updates to accounts (balances & nonces), Gas (non-/used), bytecode execution, and mining (block creation rewards and block handling) — this is explained in extenso in the Yellow Paper (Wood, 2021). A buzzword often used to describe the EVM is *Turing completeness*, which simply refers to a system capable of solving any computational problem given enough resources — which in turn does practically not mean, that we can calculate the answer to everything (which is of course '42'). To make this more tangible: different from just the hosting of software — like the beforehand used example of an AppStore — ETH nodes not only process and manage but also execute these codes through their individual instance of the EVM, before they or their respective outcome are being propagated. As network participants predominantly care about gaining wealth, every node has to verify the results of individual computation thus benefiting fractionally from the respective fees for individual opcodes. Every function of SCs — in general every interaction, successful or not successfully, like transferring Ether — consumes computational power, which is monitored by the EVM and needs to be compensated through Gas to the participating nodes, i.e., the *miners* (see further Härdle *et al.*, 2020).

Contrary to the BTC realm — where compensation is paid per financial transaction executed, hence per newly created/*Proof-of-Work mined* block — the EVM system calculates the costs per function/opcode called (gasPrice), i.e., per computational power consumed at that given time compared to the network utilization (average gas used capped by the gas limit) under the expected time of blocks to be added (*block time*), and hence interaction can be cheaper given the amount of participating nodes and the amount of information sent to be validated at that time. This means, that the interactor can pay more Gas to have information validated more quickly, as each block in the ETH system has a maximum amount of Gas that may be spent within a block, i.e., a maximum of computational power and fee's that may be spend per block. Even if a block is created with no TX or no successful outcome at all, computational fees will be paid in Gas and there will be a block reward in Ether, which modifies the state trie and the state root — otherwise two consecutive blocks would have to have identical state roots. We will not touch at length on the so-called *block gas limit* (gasLimit), as it can change over time and is a question heavily related to especially the *scalability* of ETH's BC (for further details see the Understanding Smart Contracts' Network Section of the Appendix).

The parameters relevant to mining and SC execution explained in a nutshell are: *startGas* is the individual amount of Gas units assigned to individual opcodes and the maximum amount the creator assigns to be consumable. Partially synonymously, gasLimit sets the maximum price paid to execute an interaction in total and also denominates the total Gas that can be spent within a block. In the case of an interaction, gasLimit is paid upfront by an EOA. When an interaction is committed to the system, the value for the sum of individual startGas is reserved, leaving the value for *remainingGas*. Each further individual computation uses up Gas, therefore lowers the value for remainingGas until reaching an 'Out of Gas' exception if the interaction is not finished successfully beforehand, causing the CA's state to be reverted back to its previous state — there is no such thing like an SC running ad infinitum — hence, even if the interaction is not successful, the participating nodes gets paid. The incentive for the participating nodes to validate and execute information — i.e., to contribute computational power independent from its intentioned success — is therefore, that Gas is paid in advance and miners receive a guaranteed compensation for participating in the system. Any interaction, i.e., anything that requires computation, can not consume and run in excess of the *escrowed* amount of Gas, which prevents indefinite looping of executing commands. Reasons failed processing can be, for example, non-valid information and coding errors (i.e., non-compliance to standards, see further Section 3, or EVM exceptions with information processing), or just plainly missing sufficient funds on the interactors/senders end. Finally, the information processed by the miners is then stored in a new block on the BC and the miners receive their compensation, while unused Gas is refunded to the interactor to a maximum of half the Gas consumed. Therefore, if a code has a miniscule error that causes to EVM to run into an exception can waste a lot of resources, which is why ICO's (see further Section 3) may cost a lot of resources to begin with.

Figure 4 presents the most important factors of SCs, like the obvious dependence of Network Utilization to used Gas. We explicitly underline the difference between mere TX and ERC20-Token TX. Interestingly, we observe a higher correlation of ERC20-Tokens to VSCs than to TX. This indicates the increased usage of transparent coding for such endeavors, certainly fostered through the sum of ICO scams that have been ongoing. However, VSCs do not have a high correlation to the Network Utilization, indicating a subordinate role compared to, e.g., mere TX. Therefore we observe that whilst transparency issues have fostered the usage of VSCs, they are still not common ground for every application. With most applications being of a financial nature, the main point of interest is obviously Gas. Of course, the more complex an SC is, the more Gas it uses for its

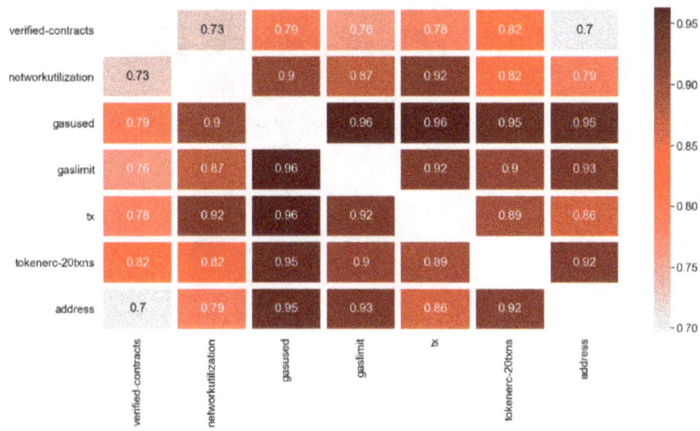

Figure 4. Network parameter correlation to VSCs, 20150630-20210211.

computational steps, yet Gas is more relevant to other proceedings on the ETH BC given the data analysis presented in Figure 4.

Importantly, the cost to run an SC can not be securely estimated upfront — contrary to simple TX. This incentivizes network participation, aside block rewards, and most importantly proper thought out coding. Clients like Geth inform interactors if not enough Gas is allocated for a given interaction to be executed. Entering a high Gas value can also end in spending more than what was originally intended, which once again incentivizes proper coding. *gasPrice* denotes the value of each computational step, i.e., each individual opcode. gasPrice is the amount in Ether to be paid for one unit of Gas utilized. As hinted to beforehand, miners can set a gasPrice threshold to prioritize or only accept respective interactions leading to others taking longer to be finished depending on the network utilization — remember, that the outcome is not important, as the miners are always paid out, hence *time is Ether*. SCs are employed to create tradeable digital tokens, e.g., through employing the ERC20 standard. These may represent a 'coin', an asset, a virtual share, a proof of membership, amongst other codeable entities (see further Section 3), and define how these tokens are meant to be distributed et cetera — in other words, they can act like a central bank (see further Section 7.2). As SCs themselves can not access data from outside their coded environment, so-called *oracles* are required — wording related to off-chain information streams that can change SC

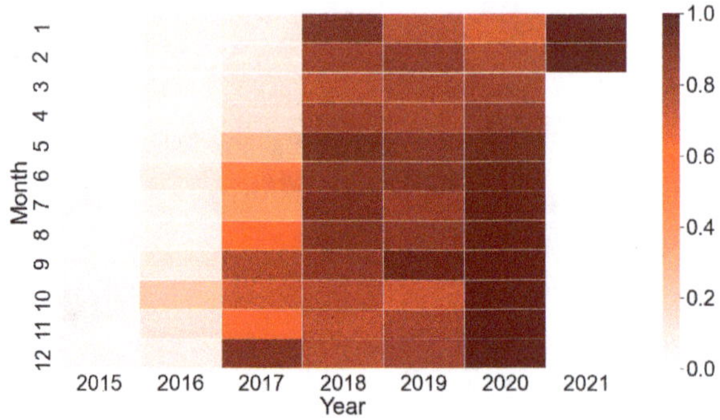

Figure 5. SC value, 20150630-20210301.

values and trigger events if their input is respectively coded to be accepted. There are different kinds of *Inbound Oracles* that provide off-chain data, like Software Oracles (essentially API's that relay, for example, price data), Hardware Oracles (for example, supply chain RFID sensors), or Consensus-based Oracles (like, for example, Gnosis). As this is off-chain data, the idea of a decentralized environment is put ad absurdum with these — potentially also nefarious — centralized data sources. Being dependent on only one source can be risky, unreliable, and potentially lead to market manipulations. On the other hand, there are Outbound Oracles, which enable SCs to send data off-chain (like unlocking a flats' smart lock). Figure 5 represents the normalized value in Ether being committed and locked to SCs — interestingly, this value has been on a high plateau since the COVID-19 crisis has started to really cripple real-world-based industries.

We observe that SCs are embedded in a very elaborate system with many functionalities. On the other hand, this means, that an entry into this realm and participation in it is bound to a quite demanding preliminary level of understanding how CCs work, or even how to access computer networks. The tale of 'banking the Unbanked' and creating financial inclusion, just to present the most obvious dissonance, is therefore debunked with either the possibility and/or infrastructure and/or knowledge of accessing this technology and its application are not given in most underdeveloped environment and/or does not present any visible benefits compared to traditional systems employed. Even with — already classic — Online-Banking, there still exist plenty of bank branches with employees to talk to customers, hence why should these — on an scale that really matters beyond a proof-of-concept — switch over to SC-banking? Furthermore, the strict structures imposed on SCs in order to function properly are in fact creating efficiencies, when only using them for simple tasks such as sending some value from A to B, but they therefore do not possess any kind of flexibility whatsoever, i.e., any application beyond numeric transactions are therewith hardly implementable.

4. Dataset

We cross-linked different sources. One of such sources is the State of the DApps (2021) (SDA) — a listing of decentralized Apps (DApps), where developers can list their DApps, additionally adding a category of the DApp (inspired by Oliva *et al.*, 2020). We only included DApps listed as open source types into our datapool. One DApp can consist of multiple SCs, similar to a normal App where an SC can be seen as one coding script. As one App consists of multiple coding scripts, one DApp consists of multiple interacting SCs. Using SDA's API in December 2020 we obtained a list of all ETH DApps and hash addresses of the SCs belonging to them. However, not all of them provide the information on the individual SCs belonging to them. Etherscan — a platform that allows to monitor transactions, blocks and SCs on the ETH BC — enables the verification of SC source codes for informative purposes through their API. SCs with available source codes are called *verified* SCs (VSCs). However, not all DApps provide us with VSCs or even list their hashes/addresses. Therefore, the amount of possible codes is reduced. Yet, Etherscan provides a list of last 10.000 VSCs having open source licenses. We hence got a labeled dataset with categories from SDA and a larger unlabeled dataset. A list of all SC addresses on the ETH BC up to December 2020 was obtained using BigQuery on Kaggle. For that, we created an SQL query analog to Durieux *et al.* (2019).

The first dataset that we are going to use for classification contains of 1428 observations belonging to 473 distinct DApps. 20% of observations were put aside as the test set. As we have a very small dataset, and some categories have very few observation, it was decided to summarize the categories except the first most-frequent

Table 1. Categories in the dataset 1.

Topic	Amount of SCs	Relative amount of SCs (%)
Exchanges	470	32.9
Finance	317	22.2
Games	272	19.0
Gambling	71	5.0
High-risk	60	4.2
Marketplaces	44	3.1
Social	41	2.9
Media	31	2.2
Property	29	2.0
Development	28	2.0
Governance	25	1.8
Security	13	0.9
Identity	12	0.8
Wallet	7	0.5
Storage	5	0.4
Health	3	0.2
All	1428	

5 to the 'other' category. The second dataset, which is unlabeled, consists of 16250 SCs (Table 1).

5. Clustering

In order to further understand the SC environment, it is hence not only necessary to understand the system they are deployed within, but moreover what kind of applications they are de facto be used for. Many media outlets, academic publications, and industry experts promise SCs that solve problems in digital notary, real-estate, managing transplantation organs, and many others, besides creating these processes to be more efficient and transparent. Can we actually find these categories in the existing applications on the ETH BC, or are these only hypothetical use-cases? The amount of TX that create individual SCs on the ETH BC count up to approximately 3.5B, see Figure 6(a). We can observe the total amount of SDA-listed DApps and the amount of the SCs that these DApps are consisting of. There are currently around 3.5K DApps on the ETH BC and 6.49K SCs. So what are all these 99% of the SCs saved on the BC used for?

To train a classifier that yields good performance for the data at hand can be very costly: researchers and industry experts would need to manually go through each observation and manually label it into pre-defined categories. In the case of source code, it is even more difficult, since only people having knowledge about this programming language may be able to properly categorize such data. Hence we first look into unsupervised approaches and other tools, like clustering. There exists academic work on the ETH data: grouping by the means of the bytecode (Norvill *et al.*, 2017), clustering the interfaces of SCs (Di Angelo and Salzer, 2020), or the nodes on the ETH BC (Sun *et al.*, 2019). To the best of our knowledge though, there is no research on clustering the whole source codes of ETH SC, so far. Every source code does usually contain comments of the developer who has written it. Some researchers even assess the quality of comments in the source code (Steidl *et al.*, 2013) or develop methods to automatically create the comments (Liang and Zhu, 2018). Therefore, one of our hypotheses is, that comments should describe what the code does and subsequently we can get a hint on what the whole program does. Comments are simply human-readable text, thus, based on the comments one may employ the same methodology used for natural language processing (NLP). One of the state-of-the-art techniques of NLP is the application of deep pre-trained transformers, such as BERT (Devlin *et al.*, 2018) or DistilBert (Sanh *et al.*, 2019), and their sentence embeddings (Reimers and Gurevych, 2019), which we are also going to use for our analysis.

As done in Section 2, we apply this strategy to our bigger unlabeled dataset to identify possible groups by using coder-comments present in SCs (inspired by the BERT-approach in Grootendorst, 2020). As we are dealing with a very high-dimensional dataset given by the comments in the source codes, our train dataset contains around 120K unique tokens and one SC can contain up to 14.6K of tokens (see Figure 6(b)) — the first step is therefore to reduce dimensionality. For this purpose we use the uniform manifold approximation and projection for dimension reduction (UMAP) technique, recently proposed by McInnes *et al.* (2018). This advanced method combines fast computational results with the ability to preserve the global structures. First, we encoded our data via BERT and only load the embeddings, i.e., the lower dimensional representation of words. Even though these embeddings are of lower dimension than the original data, it still has too many dimensions to perform clustering. Clustering methods are based on distances and the more dimensions the given data has, the more options arise to separate such data. We reduced our dataset to five dimensions through UMAP and used K-means clustering methods to identify 14 topics in the case of the above mentioned literature research example, see Section 2. UMAP was employed once again to obtain a reduction to two dimensions to be able to plot our data points. Grootendorst (2020) proposes a variant of TF-IDF — the class-based variant of TF-IDF (c-TF-IDF), which the author formulates as the following:

$$c\text{-TF-IDF}_i = \frac{t_i}{w_i} \times \log \frac{m}{\sum_j^n t_j},$$

where t is the frequency of each word, i (class), w (total number of words for ith class, m (number of documents), and $\sum_j^n t_j$ (total frequency of word t across all classes n). For each category, in our case topic, we identified the top of the most important words. Similar approach was used to group unlabeled SCs using their comments.

5.1. *Empirical results*

As described in Sections 4 and 5, our aim is not only to use labeled data but to try to gain knowledge from a by far larger unlabeled dataset. Here, unsupervised techniques become handy when no annotation is available.

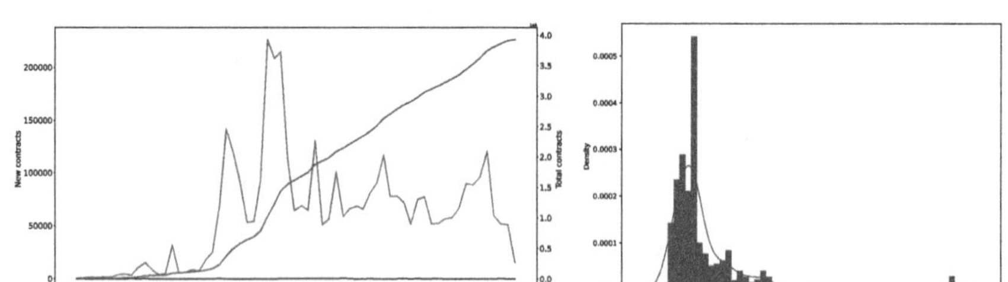

(a) (b)

Figure 6. (a) SCs created, 20150630-20201209. (b) Distribution of the amount of tokens per one SC source code.

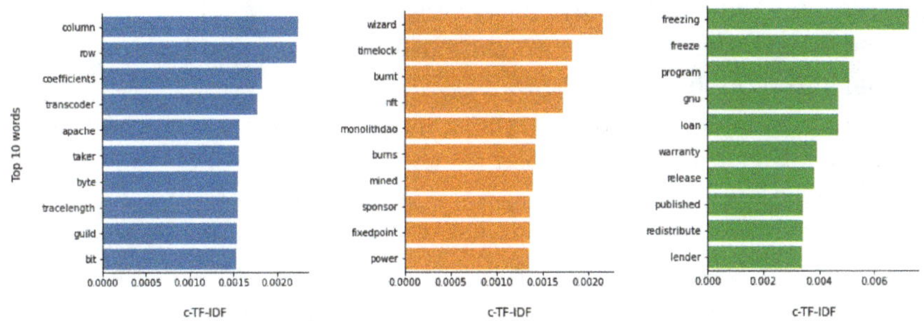

(a) Topic 1 (b) Topic 2 (c) Topic 3

Figure 7. Top 10 the most important words per cluster identified in the unlabeled SC dataset.

We apply the same technique of unsupervised clustering methods as in the beforehand Section 2 on the unlabeled dataset, specifically on the comments of approximately 13K open source SCs each having on average 1.2K words in the comment. We hence test, if this delivers us similar results as in the beforehand classification, and also if it will picture whether comments can help to better understand what individual SCs do and possibly even understand in what domain the respective DApp belongs to. The first insight is, that of 16,250 open source SCs around 17% do not contain any comments or their length is shorter than 10 characters or five words. These 17% were excluded from the analysis due to lack of semantic meaning necessary for the analysis. On the procedural side, we first applied UMAP on the remaining source codes to reduce the dimensions to 5 and ran clustering multiple times with different parameter of number of clusters to decide on this parameter using the elbow curve method with Davies–Bouldin score. Figure 7 presents the three out of 12 topics, where 12 is the optimal amount of clusters, according to Davies–Bouldin score (due to spatial reasons all 12 topics can be found in Appendix). Subsequently, the data was reduced further to two dimensions. Figure 8 presents the scatter plot of our unlabeled dataset, where each color identifies a different cluster and axes correspond to the first and second UMAP components. We can see that we have two main big clusters — the navy- and gray-colored clusters, followed by the smaller orange cluster, and all the other are rather spread everywhere and in two dimensions do not look like building proper interconnected clusters.

Yet, how can we interpret these clusters in Figure 8 and understand whether they are grouped by the category of their application (e.g., healthcare, notary, real-estate), their functionality, or rather just some other similarity measure? A closer look on the variables of the clusters reveals the most important words per cluster in Figure 7. On the first glance, we conclude that the majority of the keywords are very technical and reflect on the names of functions and/or variables commonly employed in SC codes. Apparently, the majority of comments do not really reveal any information apart technical implementations and describing what the respective function, interface or a library do. The only cluster having pretty much semantically-meaningful and understandable keywords from business application perspective is the third cluster, where some keywords are obviously related to loan business. Therefore, here we were able to show that

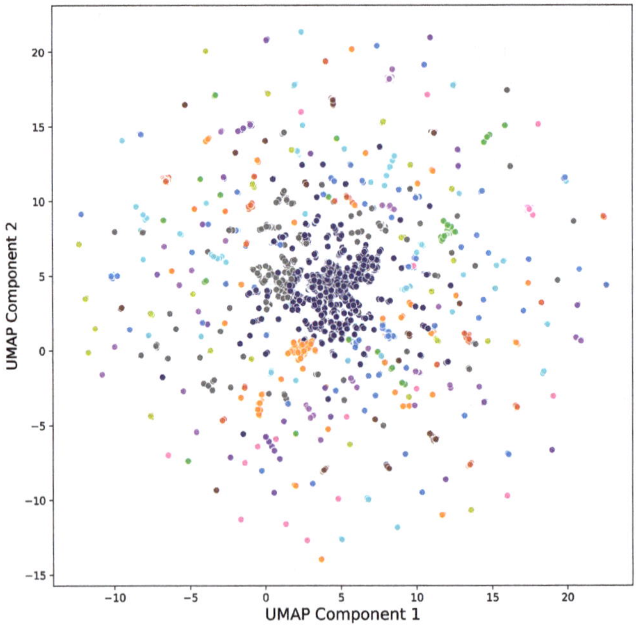

Figure 8. Grouping the unlabeled SC dataset into 12 categories.

the opportunities of directly trying to get the knowledge from the unstructured data without supervision are very limited and the supervised methods are needed.

6. Classification

Unlike traditional contracts, SCs are not written in natural language, which makes it hard to determine what each SC is about. We worked on a predictive model to classify SCs based solely on their coding. Previous approaches use to annotate SCs manually, as done by Bartoletti and Pompianu (2017). First, we decided to manually go through some SCs' source codes and summarize their application categories. Since, in this work we primarily aim to implement an automatic classifier that could improve such manual categorization, the description of the manual approach and challenges related to labeling such data can be found in Appendix. Nonetheless, the difficulties related to manual labeling of the data (e.g., the category of the SC is not always clear from the source code) speaks also for the difficulty to obtain a big dataset which is usually vital for automatic classification, therefore we need to rely on the very small dataset.

6.1. *Data pre-processing and feature extraction*

We created three columns for obtaining regular expressions to extract comments from the codes: source code (full code), source code without comments (only code) and only comments (comments). Moreover, as additional feature engineering step, we extracted names of functions, SCs, events, interfaces and libraries and joined to one string. There exist different approaches to extract features from the source codes. Possible approaches are to extract features like names, design patterns or even abstract syntax trees. For our work, we decided to treat our individual codes like text and used NLP techniques. In the case of traditional machine learning methods, since we do not need to preserve the sequential structure, we just use the TF-IDF weighting scheme. First, we separate our sequences into tokens — words in the code or specific punctuation marks that are specific for the programming language like parentheses, then each token is encoded into a numeric representation. For the encoding we use TF-IDF scheme. For the deep learning methods, we just encode the tokens with the ID, which is then embedded into a matrix to obtain dense vector representations of the words depending on the surrounding context in the sentence.

6.2. *Machine learning methods*

A classificator is trained on a variety of methods. Here, we employ a logistic regression, a Ridge regression (Ridge), and also an instance of Lasso regression (Lasso). As we just mentioned in Section 6.1, through encoding our source codes into TF-IDF vector representations, we obtain very sparse high-dimensional vectors. Since we have a such very high-dimensional data, we expect the Lasso regression to perform better due to inherent feature selection technique through L1 regularization. Moreover, we are going to use random forest (RF) and support vector machines (SVMs).

Deep learning methods are seen to be standard for natural language processing, yet, they usually require huge datasets. However, we apply three classical deep learning architectures for testing on the above mentioned data columns: gated recurrent unit (GRU), bidirectional GRU, and convolutional neural network (CNN).

Pre-training became a standard for many natural language processing tasks. Bidirectional Encoder Representations from Transformers (BERT) architecture invented by Devlin *et al.* (2018) allows the user to apply this deep learning architecture trained on a huge amount of data on a different task, e.g., text classification. These models achieve a state-of-the-art performance for many tasks. Moreover, they are able to work on relatively small datasets. Such architecture are usually pre-trained on huge text datasets. In our case, we have mostly the source codes, that differs from written and spoken human language, therefore it will not help us much. However, one of our tasks formulations includes machine learning on the comments. Therefore, we will be able to apply BERT on comments.

To summarize it, we are going to use traditional machine learning methods Ridge, Lasso, RF, SVM and classical deep learning methods GRU, BGRU, and CNN on full code, only code, and comments. Moreover, we apply BERT to the comments. Therefore, we will try to answer the question, whether it is possible at all to train a classifier on the solidity SC source code, whether traditional machine learning methods can better work on such small and high-dimensional dataset or they will loose to deep learning. Moreover, we will see whether it is better to train a classifier on the code, code with comments, or just comments, or even that, as opposed to spoken and written text, the sequential structure of the source code is not relevant at all to identify the category of the SC.

6.3. *Training and evaluation*

For training, we used cross-validation with three folds. Moreover, we performed a hybrid of manual and automatic grid hyper-parameter tuning. As we are dealing with a multiclass classification task with one class containing examples from the rest of categories, we draw upon the well established one-versus-all classification approach for the first five classes. For the evaluation, we used two metrics: Area under the ROC curve is equivalent to 'the probability that the classifier will rank a randomly chosen positive instance higher than a randomly chosen negative instance' (Fawcett, 2006) and the average precision — the metric which is seen as standard for unbalanced data sets.

6.4. *Empirical results*

Due to spatial reasons we present only the test performance, nonetheless, cross-validation performance can also be found in the linked GitHub repository. In Table 3, we see the results of classificator trained on the full code — without removal of comments. On the left part, we see the performance in terms of AUC ROC, which is relatively high for all categories. Methods of traditional machine learning methods outperform on average the methods of deep learning. One of the possible and very probable reasons is the small amount of data points, whereas the big size of a dataset is essential for application of deep learning methods. On the other side, as opposed to our expectation Lasso regression showed the worst performance across all traditional machine learning methods. RF shows the best performance in terms of AUC ROC in almost all categories, except high risk, where it is outperformed by the Ridge regression. Ridge shows the second best performance in all other categories. On the right part, we see the performance in terms of Av. Prec. Whereas the performance for classes with a higher amount of examples is still high, the classes that are outnumbered show much lower performance. Gambling and high-risk classes show the worst ability to be accurately classified.

Moreover, deep learning methods show a very poor performance for such unbalanced categories. In Table 4, we see the performance of the classificators trained on the code cleaned from the comments. It shows very similar tendency: a good performance of rather simple traditional machine learning methods like RF and Ridge and very poor performance of neural networks. Interestingly, there is no obvious tendency of outperforming between results on the source code with and without comments. In Table 5, we present results of predictors trained only on textual data — the comments extracted from the code. Again, traditional methods outperform deep neural networks. Some categories, such as Exchanges, show even better performance than classificators trained on code. A possible explanation could be the quality of the comments in the codes of this category. However, other groups show worse performance, except Gambling in terms of Av. Prec. Apparently, the comments allow the ridge regression to correctly pick the Gambling cases with higher precision and judging by lower AUC ROC, the False Positives rate increased. Interestingly, even BERT that is seen as a deep learning model that is able to deal with small datasets shows a very poor performance.

As we were able to show that deep learning networks, especially those based on recurrence and reflecting the sequential structure, show poor performance, it would be interesting to inspect, whether we are able to extract the most important features from the code. As explained in Section 6.1, we decided to extract the names of functions, events, libraries in the hope that they can be not only similar from the source code to source code, since as already mentioned many codes are cloned and copied, but also usually developers would name the variables and functions according to their behavior. In Table 6, we show the results of classification training of traditional machine learning methods, which have shown the best performance in the previous tasks. The aim was to show that not only can we extract meaningful information and the sequential structure is not important for our task but also that we are able to achieve sufficiently high performance using lower amount of features. And as we see in this table, we still have high performance, even though the amount of features was reduced by more than 3K.

Even though the differences between each mode: *Full Code* (FC), *Only Code* (OC), *Only Comments* (OCom), and *Extracted Features* (EF) might not always seem significantly different from each other, or on the opposite seem obviously different for some classes, we decided to test whether their performance results are significantly different from each other. For that purpose, using 14 different seeds to split the data, we ran our Ridge regression classifier multiple times for each cross-validation fold. Thus, for each mode we obtained 42 predictions for each class. Since we want to have the same classifier for each class, we averaged predictions between classes. The non-parametric Wilcoxon test (Wilcoxon, 1992) was chosen to see whether the differences in AUC ROC and Av. Prec. of different modes are significant. Double-sided, left-sided, and right-sided tests were conducted. Table 2 presents the pairs of modes and the null hypothesis H_0 which could not be rejected and the respective p-value. Using the test, we were able to show that even though when the classes are treated separately we do not see an obvious winning mode. If we want to use only one classifier, the best performance can be achieved while training it on the comments extracted from the source code (assuming the developers wrote accompanying comments).

Summarizing the results of these four tables: first, we can conclude that using supervised machine learning methods we are able to classify the source codes of SCs. Secondly, we highlighted the fact that no heavy computational architectures and algorithms such as neural networks are needed to classify the categories, and very simple Ridge logistic regression ran for each class independently will do the job sufficiently good not only for the over-represented classes like Exchanges and Finance, but will also show relatively good performance for rather smaller class of high-risk contracts. We were able to show that the common-sense telling us that the comments in the source code could give additional hint on the category of the SC is indeed correct. However, the presence of the comments in the code is required.

Table 2. Results of the Wilcoxon test.

	AUC ROC				Av.Prec			
Modes	**FC**	**OC**	**OCom**	**EF**	**FC**	**OC**	**OCom**	**EF**
FC	—	$FC < OC$ $p = 0.99$	$FC < OCom$ $p = 0.99$	$FC < EF$ $p = 0.99$	—	$FC < OC$ $p = 0.99$	$FC < OCom$ $p = 0.99$	$FC < EF$ $p = 0.99$
OC	—	—	$OC < OCom$ $p = 0.99$	$OC < EF$ $p = 0.99$	—	—	$OC < OCom$ $p = 0.99$	$OC < EF$ $p = 0.99$
OCom	—	—	—	$OCom > EF$ $p = 0.99$	—	—	—	$OCom > EF$ $p = 0.99$
EF	—	—	—	—	—	—	—	—

Therefore, we were able to show that it is possible to classify SCs by using their source codes quite accurately for the dominant categories: Exchanges, Finance, Games, High-risk. Such information can be useful not only for researcher who want to explore the remaining 99% of SC on the ETH BC, but also for the developers and investors. Especially the high-risk category is interesting in identification of possible risks.

After the algorithms were trained with satisfactory results regarding the achieved performance, we apply them onto new data. Here, we can apply our classifier on the unlabeled dataset to see what potential categories of open source SCs can be found on the ETH BC. We present the identifiable categories discovered by the trained algorithms, without the implication that these datapoints were correctly identified. Since the most important category to categorize is high-risk, and moreover we cannot assume that all source codes contain comments, we decided to take the algorithm that predicts this category best to out final prediction on the unlabeled dataset, which is the Ridge logistic regression running on the source code cleaned from the comments. However, one could argue that we want to identify all classes correctly, then the mode of the interest would be to train the classifier solely on the comments. Therefore, Figure 9 shows the categorization of our unlabeled dataset obtained by applying our trained Ridge logistic regression.

We note, that the **Finance** class outnumbers everything else, followed by the **Other — class** having all observations that have too low probability to fit one of the specified classes. The other classes, such as Exchanges, Games, High-risk, and Gambling represent only a very small fraction of the unlabeled dataset. This reveals, assuming our classification was similarly accurate as within cross validation and with test data, that the majority of VSC of this opportunity sample of SCs is dominated by the codes dedicated to financial services — 68% (**Finance** + **Exchanges** + **High-risk**) and around 10% to other 'entertainment' purposes. Only around 30% of them are dedicated to **Other** DApps — potentially including the use-cases promised by media like smart rental services, voting through SCs, or even transplants management — all the use-cases which made the SC technology such a hyped phenomenon.

Table 3. Classification results — Full code.

Method	AUC ROC					Av.Prec				
	Exchanges	Finance	Gambling	Games	High-risk	Exchanges	Finance	Gambling	Games	High-risk
Ridge	0.988	0.967	0.914	0.972	0.983	0.985	0.925	0.482	0.914	0.720
Lasso	0.961	0.927	0.714	0.917	0.847	0.962	0.844	0.238	0.804	0.554
RF	0.988	0.973	0.944	0.971	0.974	0.984	0.942	0.572	0.912	0.700
SVM	0.987	0.972	0.892	0.977	0.976	0.983	0.944	0.482	0.934	0.668
BGRU	0.970	0.848	0.767	0.795	0.860	0.963	0.699	0.149	0.422	0.256
GRU	0.966	0.712	0.749	0.818	0.897	0.956	0.443	0.102	0.442	0.486
CNN	0.972	0.950	0.804	0.908	0.840	0.972	0.880	0.155	0.672	0.482

Table 4. Classification results — Only code.

Method	AUC ROC					Av.Prec				
	Exchanges	Finance	Gambling	Games	High-risk	Exchanges	Finance	Gambling	Games	High-risk
Ridge	0.983	0.965	0.916	0.957	0.988	0.981	0.914	0.483	0.868	0.795
Lasso	0.960	0.915	0.832	0.922	0.934	0.959	0.813	0.363	0.769	0.656
RF	0.986	0.974	0.938	0.966	0.986	0.983	0.940	0.491	0.907	0.771
SVM	0.980	0.973	0.905	0.970	0.976	0.979	0.943	0.574	0.919	0.717
BGRU	0.946	0.282	0.461	0.744	0.763	0.952	0.157	0.049	0.448	0.508
GRU	0.949	0.802	0.779	0.692	0.888	0.952	0.615	0.121	0.299	0.350
CNN	0.952	0.895	0.707	0.868	0.781	0.953	0.794	0.100	0.663	0.168

Table 5. Classification results — Only comments.

Method	AUC ROC					Av.Prec				
	Exchanges	Finance	Gambling	Games	High-risk	Exchanges	Finance	Gambling	Games	High-risk
Ridge	0.991	0.959	0.880	0.972	0.976	0.986	0.910	0.508	0.912	0.701
Lasso	0.982	0.930	0.734	0.942	0.880	0.977	0.852	0.217	0.844	0.409
RF	0.984	0.972	0.890	0.974	0.977	0.981	0.937	0.452	0.924	0.675
SVM	0.988	0.963	0.879	0.978	0.976	0.983	0.921	0.511	0.933	0.626
BGRU	0.971	0.639	0.656	0.853	0.839	0.968	0.276	0.086	0.520	0.361
GRU	0.960	0.804	0.638	0.840	0.855	0.963	0.648	0.107	0.511	0.313
CNN	0.937	0.907	0.829	0.865	0.703	0.937	0.799	0.155	0.600	0.070
BERT	0.968	0.777	0.353	0.789	0.602	0.965	0.637	0.038	0.628	0.056

Table 6. Classification results — Extracted features.

Method	AUC ROC					Av.Prec				
	Exchanges	Finance	Gambling	Games	High-risk	Exchanges	Finance	Gambling	Games	High-risk
Ridge	0.988	0.963	0.883	0.957	0.971	0.984	0.906	0.462	0.870	0.735
Lasso	0.981	0.919	0.803	0.913	0.874	0.973	0.791	0.395	0.730	0.573
RF	0.989	0.971	0.864	0.961	0.973	0.985	0.928	0.474	0.899	0.719
SVM	0.980	0.963	0.877	0.971	0.970	0.978	0.932	0.489	0.915	0.754

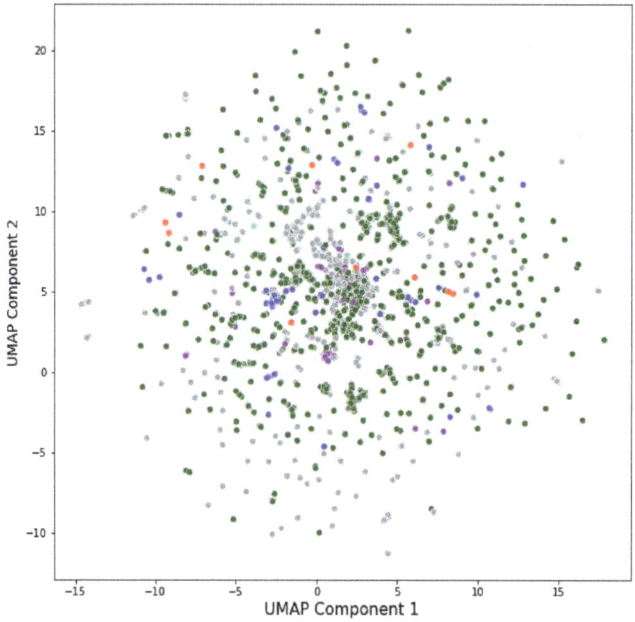

Figure 9. Classification of the unlabeled dataset — UMAP reduction to two dimensions: Finance (10009 SCs — 62%), High-risk (162 SCs — 1%), Gambling (60 — >1%), Games (506 — 3%), Exchanges (756 — 5%), Other (4757 — 29%).

7. Possibilities and Realities

7.1. *Defining smart contracts*

New ideas are generally only accepted, if they seem to improve on a given state. This, of course, with respect to the technological and legal frameworks, as well as administrative possibilities. The abstract question to be kept in mind is: Does it make sense for a given enterprise to invest into creating BC/SC frameworks? Whereas *traditional contracts* (TCs) are defined as a promise or a set of promises for the breach of which the law gives a remedy, or the performance of which the law in some way recognizes as a duty (Bellia, 2002), SCs consequently are software that, for example, facilitates the generation and transfer of BC-based crypto-assets (see further, e.g., Mik, 2019), and runs without human intervention once commanded to execute (see above PETs, Section 3.3).

Again, we must stress here: SCs do not execute without input, which can of course be a timed-coded threshold. SCs are *not* self-executing and respective information might not be stored on the BC directly, but has to be accessed via different sources. SCs do not possess a *will* to execute themselves, they just do what is being input. Legal laymen commonly define these as *contracts*, however, these terms are creating confusion: the terms of *account* and *transaction* can have very different meanings and so does obviously the term *contract*. Both fathers of this invention, Szabo (1997b) ('a computerized transaction protocol that executes the terms of a contract') and Buterin (2020) ('systems which automatically move digital assets according to arbitrary pre-specified rules') define and underline, that SCs are *not* contracts in the traditional terminus but means of contract execution — a definition, which is conform with Halaburda (2018).

The isolated full legal status of SCs, as pursued partially in the United States, does not change this and has no influence on completely different legal systems. However, for example, legislation in the state of Tennessee is of interest: 'Smart contracts may exist in commerce. No contract relating to a transaction shall be denied legal effect, validity, or enforceability solely because that contract is executed through a smart contract' (Justia, 2019). Yet, any further inclined discussion on this issue will open Pandora's box, as it misunderstands the technology way beyond its existence of being PETs, especially when mere supply chain reporting SCs are accepted as legal means of being 'contracts' instead of 'tools'. Of concern would be the SC application when being used to spawn then forcibly legally accepted loophole-'currencies' — just think about ISO 4217 with its three different US$ 840/USD (*cash*), 998/US$ (*sameday*), and 997/USN (*nextday*) being simple compared to the chaos created by the number of existing and already abandoned CCs (see further, e.g., deadcoins.com). The resulting issues of classification and handling these entities legally will result in an increase in insecurities. Hence, the discussion is a priori not even remotely leading to a result, as SCs were not even intended to *replace* the traditional instruments.

We propose the following definition to create the necessary — yet missing — connection between the factually more and more intertwined fields of information technology, statistics, and law:

> *Smart Contract*:
> Software algorithm that is a blockchain application, digitally signed, computable and potentially dynamic in state, given the input potentially immutable, non-physical agreement between two or more parties, that relies on a consensus system and conditional constructions which can dependent on potentially off-chain third party information input, that is creating or based on mutual relations and/or obligations which it seeks to technically execute in the event of undisturbed predetermined code procedures.

With the creation and emission of tokens being included in the above definition and whilst the legality of crypto-*currencies* is not undisputed in many legal systems, SCs can be independent from these and are therefore not necessarily prima facie a negotium non grata for any given legal framework (see further Ni *et al.*, 2020). A discussion, if one does or does not accept *cryptocurrency* as a *currency* and consequently a *statutory means of payment per se*, and thus of which type the agreement at hand is in a legal sense (exchange or purchase contract in that meaning) is redundant as it is at least an intangible asset.

Yet, as with any given advancement, CCs and SCs first need to stand proof to the legal system before they may be accepted as valid modus of exchange. Improving efficiencies and facilitate dependable results, the promised key advantages of using SCs, are conclusive repetitions of the industrial automation. Technological advances have fostered the human thrive of rather trusting a machine, than human information, to a level that non-physical processes can now reliably be mirrored by machines. Nonetheless, even with *deep reinforced machine learning* and other consorts of technical marketing language, the basic question of *smartness* is fundamental. Are SCs *smart* enough for taking the *responsibility* for decision making, thus can we speak of *contracts* that can even replace legal entities? An argument against that would be of course, that the *smart* human input is needed to kick-off SC processes — but where is then the *smart machine*? A code or document can only be as smart as the human initially writing it implying a plethora of possible sources for errors (see Section 3.3 and Appendix for further details). We will not touch on the controversial ideas of *code is law* (*Note*: a replacement of law by code was literally not what was envisioned by Lessig, 1999) as complex natural language can not be completely replaced by code at this given level of technological advance. There exists a wide variety of fields where SCs could nevertheless already be applied in a trade-off consideration. With many advances already accomplished towards the direction of mirroring traditional ways of interaction to digitized counterparts (recall IPO and ICO), a general comparison between SCs and TCs lead to a framework for understanding their potential:

- **TC**s are created by legal professionals using their *lingua franca*, handed out to each party as *physical* copies, and enforced by institutions such as courts using an agreed upon *legal codex*. These agreements are considered to be effective, if they stand the test of the law and according ruling. Their main problems can hence be broken down to their creation and enforcement being *time consuming* and *costly* due to the controlling intermediaries involved, as well as their outcome being potentially *ambiguous* given changing rulings or unclear wording.
- **SC**s, in contrast, promise to cut on these shortcomings by being *quickly* creatable through the help of *easy* coding and *seamlessly* understandable user interfaces. They purportedly define iura et obligationes the *same way* as TCs, hence are completely *deterministic*, while being *entirely digital* and therefore easy to mathematically proof and enforce, through algorithms and a given *consensus codex*, adding to *efficiency* and *verifiability*. These agreements are considered to be effective, if the agreed upon action, for example a TX, was performed without technological error.

If an SC can really be seen as a universal replacement to traditional agreements in a legal sense may be clearly answered at this given state: *No*. It's a technical possibility to automatize given relationships according to pre-defined rules that depend on predefined coded events, not necessarily replicating legal standards or legal relationships. In other words: they facilitate traditional agreements technically without being classifiable as such themselves. However, their functions and proven fields of application can already replicate certain traditional functions of agreements/ contracts.

We may mark the most basic understanding of what a traditional agreements should fulfill as we are pointing to the question of *replaceability* and the likely *replaceable* parts of our contractual system: (1) legality of the agreement itself, (2) definition of the parties, (3) definition of the subject et cetra, (4) offer and acceptance, (5) ability and/or intention of the parties to be legally bound, (6) capacity to satisfy contractual elements, and (7) signatures.

Taking this into account, the question of the *replaceability* of TCs with SCs is more tangible. We can see that certain contracts can, for a fact, be reproduced as coded Doppelgänger's. From the standpoint of automation, SCs present an analogous form of agreement/contract, where only details such as the contractual parties, date, subject, etc. have to be added — the easiest to understand example would be an ICO. Potential can also be seen regarding *adhesion contracts*, *shrink wrap contracts*, or *boilerplate contracts*, which refer to pre-defined standard form contract clauses and are commonly used for matters involving leases, purchases, insurance, mortgages, amongst many other use cases (with special regards to certain national limits these need to be differentiated from general terms and conditions). Such application fields could increase efficiency in contract law decrease processing time and hence also costs. Adhesion contracts are usually engaged as digitally signed *clickwrap* agreements that offer individuals the opportunity to accept or decline digitally-mediated contents. These electronic agreements are requested to appear as identical to physical contracts as possible. Although not accepted in all legal frameworks, documents which are signed electronically possess equivalent legal validity to physically signed agreements/contracts (see Appendix for further details).

7.2. *Implementation*

An ever increasing number of potential use cases are envisioned that try to mimic TCs in their function: insurance, mortgage, financial derivatives, human resources, supply chain management, to name a few. Typically each individual field is bounded by specific procedural legal standards and SCs are best applied where maximizing efficiency and optimizing cost-minimization, or the removal of traditional processes that require vast amounts of manpower to keep the checks-and-balances-system running, is a possibility. SCs presumably fit in these automation-gaps naturally, as many of the intermediaries become redundant with monitoring and information propagation being established via trustworthy standardized coding. Especially financial applications have regulatory requirements, like *know-your-customer* (KYC) to check if a participant is eligible for a given service according to regulatory watch-lists such as the Office of Foreign Assets Control (OFAC) Specially Designated Nationals (SDN) list. Keep in mind that, while one does not need a BC construction for these tasks of course, one does need it for fostering the idea of transparency and immutability (see further Sections 3.1 and 7.1). SC applications are predestined for systems where currency is not a necessary medium of exchange and centralized allocations are not feasible or preferred. SCs do not necessarily depend on CCs to work (in ETH they do, see Section 3.3), which imposes their adaptation also within governmental systems where CCs are deemed to be illegal. For example, organ donation and procurement could be improved through coded most favorable matching structures, where the inherent BC-based recording of input would be beneficiary especially regarding the legal patient's provisions that could be respectively stored data for and in an SC. We therefore note, that a crucial point to introduce an SC-based system is *risk control*. Risk pooling can be achieved in both SCs and TCs as a risk-sharing structure, yet modern technologies are obviously superior in these fields than paper-based auditing systems could ever be. Another critical point is thus *monitoring*, as a measure to continuously audit the contractual terms and to detect potential problems or breaches.

To make the legal handling of *particular* SCs replacing *particular* TCs more tangible, consider a motel doing a series of standardized and proven rental SCs with digital access codes to the apartments. Instead of relying on an intermediary, for example, a receptionist, to administratively keep watch on the payments, the landlord creates an SC factory to spawn individual SCs (see further Section 3.3) with all respective compulsory parameters. Additional actions like for example accommodation reporting to governmental institutions, may also be encoded through an beforehand outlined oracle to provide legit and trustworthy information on the individuals identity. If the conditions of this SC are met by the parties, i.e., that the exact rent was transferred to a given account and client information was forwarded successfully et cetera, then access to the rental object is granted. Yet, if the conditions required to be fulfilled are not met, then access is denied. This is arguably not a legal contract itself, but just a mean to process the corresponding TC itself. However, one could argue that this example could serve as proof for the replaceability of at least basic and often repeated TC cases. Adding to this is, that more than three quarters of the SCs we analyzed are serving the purpose of defining a value token. A selected few of them implement interesting distribution schemes like a Dutch auction or a collectible cards game mechanism, but most of them are made of repeating code patterns for a distinct variety of use cases. As a consequence, since not that many SCs consist of more than 600 lines of code, these SCs are much easier to read and understand once one is familiar with a small subset of code examples. Although this shows that the developers want to employ best practices in their code this does not necessarily mean that the reused code is secure and bug-free (see further (Cohney and Hoffman, 2020; Pinna *et al.*, 2019). Furthermore, nefarious SCs are harder to discern from regular SCs since their codes and the codes of legitimate SCs are so similar. This is underlining the fact, that previously isolated fields of IT and LAW are required to, and will be, increasingly intertwined.

An endless field of further imaginary applications in Sharing Economy, LegalTech, InsurTech, Dispute Resolvement, Royalty Management, voting, insurance contracts, electricity prosumer management, trade finance, escrow services, monitoring of regulatory compliance, copyright services and rights of use, traceability of products through supply chains and markets, or the famous field of Internet-of-Things (IoT) applications, and many more buzzword-flooded fields can be envisioned.

7.3. *Decentralized App versus 'traditional' App*

One of the key reasons for many startups to fail is the limited understanding of the hyped technology and most importantly its differences to already existing technologies. Some companies are even trying to follow the hype and force to implement such buzz-concepts as BC- and SC-based without properly understanding whether it is feasible and profitable on the stack they are using — bigger ones silently abandon such endeavors eventually.

SC — is one of such technologies, where the word 'smart' promises futuristic digital tools, whereas what SC really are — just a coding script running on the BC, a part of a decentralized App, similar to how interconnected multiple coding scripts written in Python, Java or other languages make up an App. Basically, DApps can do almost the same things (or even less, as it will be described further) as a respectively oriented normal Apps, while having the computational processing ran on the BC. Therefore, in this section, we are describing the key differences between Apps and DApps. Moreover, inspired by the flowchart proposed by Wüst and Gervais (2018) 'Where does Blockchain make sense', we are going to propose a flowchart for deciding whether one should choose DApp over a traditional App or vice versa. As one DApp consists of one or multiple SCs, our flowchart also aims to answer the question whether one should use SCs or not or in other words whether you should execute your code on the BC or not.

According to Laplante (2017), an application or App is a program or a bundle of programs that are designed to solve a specific problem. Usually, one refers to apps or to application software — to programs that run outside of the operating system. Usually apps are ran on the desktop, on mobile devices or in the webbrowser. Subsequently, we can identify webapps, mobile Apps or desktop Apps. However, in this work, we will refer to all of these three types as to Apps. The majority of Apps, at least of webapps, follow a centralized server-client model. Moreover, some are distributed and the new type uses the decentralization (Raval, 2016). In Figure 10, these three types of architecture are depicted. As we can see, in the centralized system, the most frequently found type of Apps, a central node controls the operation, flow of the information and interconnection between child

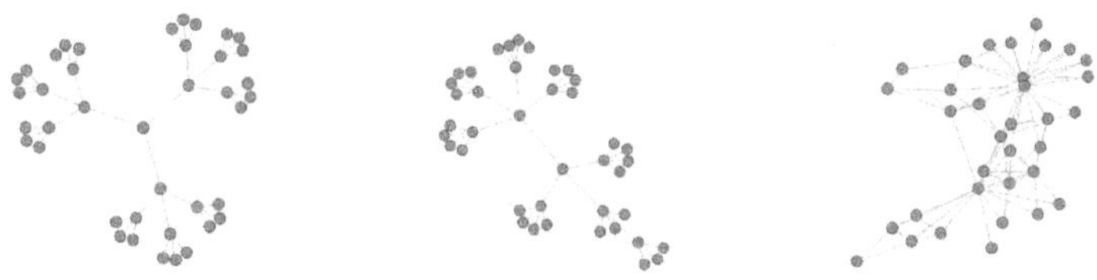

(a) Centralized (b) Decentralized (c) Distributed

Figure 10. Types of software applications Apps.

nodes. All client-nodes are dependent of the central node. Distributed systems allocate computation to different nodes, many big companies make use of distributed computations. Therefore, a system can be centralized and distributed at the same time: e.g., a company provides computation services, the computations are distributed among many servers (Raval, 2016), however, the company is itself the central node holding the responsibility of the services. So, if one server fails, nothing will happen to your data because of the distributed nature, however, if the whole company fails — all your data could get lost. Decentralized systems, on the other hand, implies that no node in the hierarchy is higher than the other and can give instructions as to what to do. And all nodes hold similar amount of responsibility for the functionality of the system.

Therefore, looking at the definitions of the DApps and 'traditional' Apps, we cannot say that these are dichotomous concepts, but rather DApp is a subset of the Apps. Subsequently, we will still speak of DApps versus Apps where Apps here can be web, desktop, and mobile Apps relying on a centralized or centralized distributed systems (having one main responsible authority if something will fail). According to Firica (2019), for an App to be classified as DApp, it must comply to the following criteria: (1) the App should not have a controlling entity, (2) be completely open-source, (3) operate autonomously, (4) work on BC, (5) use cryptography (for tokens that act as proof of the value of the node and are distributed through a rewarding system).

Even though we mostly agree with this list, the criteria that everything should be open-source might be correct, however, while going through multiple DApps and SCs on State of the DApps (2021) and Etherscan (2019b), we found many SCs and DApps that do not have an open-source license. In Table 7, we present the advantages and disadvantages of using DApps compared to traditional Apps.

While the majority of the criteria are quite clear without additional explanations or have been already mentioned in the previous sections, we would like to go in the details of complexity limitations. In this work, we address the complexity from two perspectives: first, the straightforward limitations of the code complexity, which is also related to the TX costs: to compile the code on the BC, payment of a fee is required. Code of different complexity requires a different fee. This fee is bounded to a certain value in order not to exceed it and

Table 7. Advantages and disadvantages of using DApps.

DApps	Apps
Advantages	
• Decentralization if one node fails, the data won't be lost • p2p validation • Mostly open-source • BC, proof-of-work make the systems trustworthy so it almost impossible to hack • Support CC • Transparency	• User-friendly, no technical knowledge required • Nothing needs to be installed (in case of webapps) • Can be designed to user's needs • Can be adjusted if designed wrong • New functionalities can be added
Disadvantages	
• TXs are very slow • The amount of TXs is bounded due to technical limitations of the system • TX costs: Creation of a contract or sending a TX requires a fee to pay • Cannot be taken down from the network • Cannot be adjusted or changed • Redundant storage of the data and redundant computations thus very high energy costs (Digiconomist, 2021) • Therefore — not sustainable • Complexity limitations of the code	• Can be hacked • If data is stored centrally, one electricity outage can lead to the data loss • TX costs: Information exchange in a presence of a third party is costly • Data is not always encrypted

not to consume all the balance for the code, which could mistakenly run too long. The second perspective of the complexity, which we are working with is the ability to make complex math computations. Even though, the DApp consists of 'Smart' contracts, their ability to do mathematical computation is very limited: only basic operations like Addition, Subtraction, Multiplication, Division, Modulus and Exponential (GeeksforGeeks, 2020) can be done on the ETH BC.

We propose a decision flow in Figure 11, which can help to decide whether it is useful to develop a DApp or if one should stick to a traditional Apps. Further, we refer to trust from three perspectives: first, as to resilience of the system in case of failure or outage — whether the data will not get lost, the system saves the last state and the usage of the App can be immediately continued, second — that the node provides sufficient security that no third-party can alternate the data or retrieve personal data they do not have access to, and third — probably the most important perspective — whether we trust the central authority that they will not manipulate data or the state of the system themselves. Therefore, we see that if we are not aiming to implement a CC or a cryptoasset and trust our central node, there are almost no incentives to use BC for developing Apps — DApps. Thus, speaking of DApps, we have one main question which needs to be answered — *do we trust our central node*?

7.4. *Shortcomings and legal handling*

Immutability is an obvious benefit with BC system constructions being coined as *trust machines*, yet, absolute immutability can also be insurmountable hurdle. To provide a brief framework one may keep the following points on BCs & SCs in mind:

- **Interactability:** Software and operational errors hardly removable or reversible, if at all.
- **Scalability:** Data storage and availability with permanent fixation of information to BCs and adjacent structures like the EVM, require increasingly sophisticated cloud- and physical-based management structures.
- **Sensitive content:** Illegal, nefarious, or confidential information hardly removable.
- **Regulatory issues:** Conflicting national frameworks on consumer rights and data privacy, or personal legal register information like the EU General Data Protection Regulation or Rome I Regulation, the US Gramm-Leach-Bliley Act and Fair Credit Reporting Act, or the SEC Regulation S-P.

Despite SCs offering interesting new opportunities in various use cases (see further Section 7.2), not many new solutions for existing problems are actually employing them, particularly in the legal industry, although they were intended as a replacement for TCs.

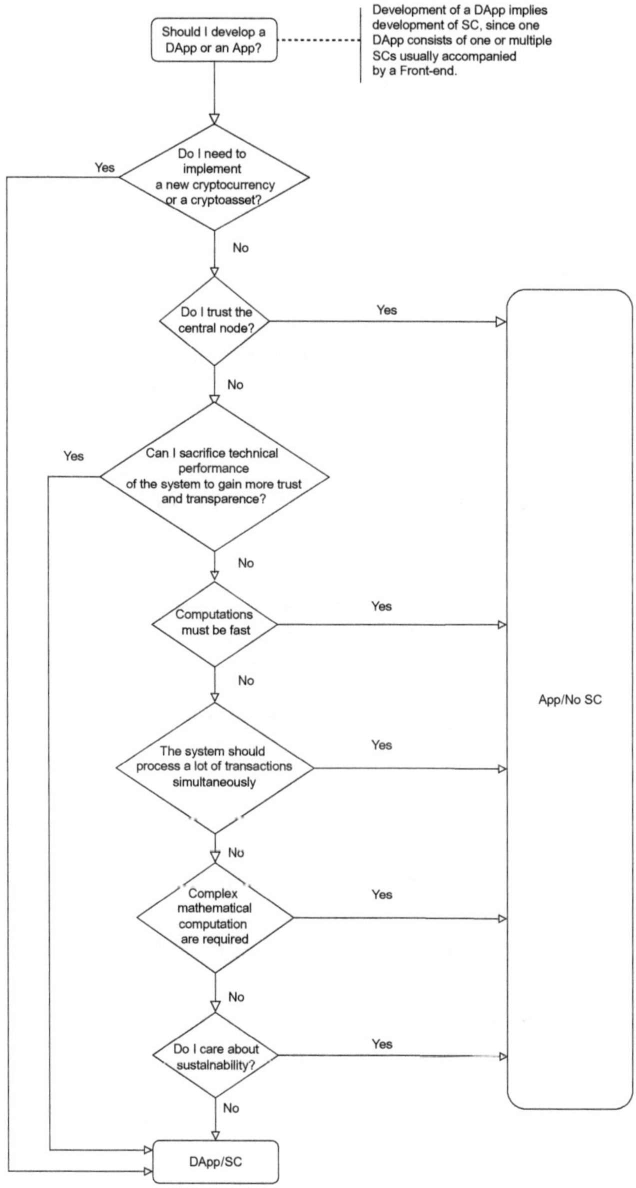

Figure 11. A flowchart to identify whether a DApp or an App is a proper solution.

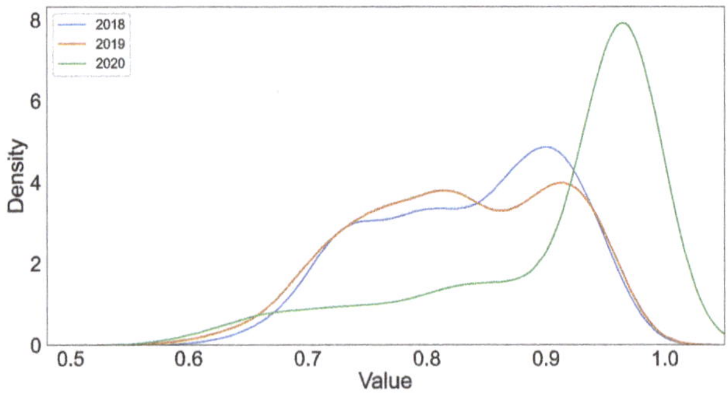

Figure 12. Network usage comparison, 2018, 2019, 2020.

Of course, there exist decent examples of companies putting the technology to use, such as the likes of Tracr (2019) and Inmusik (2019), yet the scale of the technology adoption is to this day rather small. While novelty and unfamiliarity surely are factors, another reason for that may be the beforehand mentioned scalability issues. An outstanding example is the very well-known CryptoKitties game SC (Dapper Labs, 2021). At its peak accounted for roughly 12% of all TX on the ETH BC (Quartz, 2017) leading to the amount of pending TX increasing by a sixfold (*BBC*, 2017) with execution time and costs of TX considerably high as the system got clogged with 'cats' (see further Section 3.3). Vitalik Buterin expressed more than once that scalability remains a bottleneck and hinders widespread adoption of BC platforms (Star, 2019). The ETH network utilization remains quite consistently over the 80% mark moving towards a constantly higher than the 90% region, as visualized in Figure 12. While some big players like UBS (2016) experimented with SCs, not much was heard about it afterward with disintermediation and decentralization through SCs, and BCs are rarely able to replace common structures effectively (Greenspan, 2016).

As outlined in Section 3.3 and Appendix, it is important to note that first and foremost, the code of SCs must be absolutely bug-free and secure from nefarious inputs as much as possible. Otherwise, exploitation of bugs or security flaws can be an insurance business and puts the saying of 'BC-based systems mean security' ad absurdum. An important factor affecting the quality of SC source codes and their legal handling is that only 1% of all SCs have a publicly available source code (amongst other sources, so-called *verified* SCs on Etherscan) (see further Nikolic *et al.*, 2018). The remaining 99% can only be read via the compiled source code. This does not necessarily mean that those other 99% of SCs have qualitatively better or worse code, but it would reinforce good practices and enrich the knowledge base of SC developers to have access to all source codes, preventing possible further DAO-esque incidents.

The DAO (Coindesk, 2016) — a construction typus, which can be seen legally as a cooperative, partnership, or unincorporated association with participants having usufructuary or usage rights — lead to a split/*forking* of the initial ETH BC into an altered BC, now known as ETH, and a BC that kept the exploited status quo, now known as Ethereum Classic (ETC). In fact, the ETH community regulated itself in the absence of jurisdiction, as the value lost during this happening due to bugged coding and nefarious exploitation of that error could legally not be seen as value back then — hence 'nothing' was stolen. This has since changed and respective assets are commonly seen as non-tangible assets, which can also be subject to taxation. Similarly, the software hosting project Edgeware — which accumulated investments of US$ 300,000,000 in July 2019, a month after going live — held an exploitable coding, which would make it unable to unlock and emit funds from their SC construction (Cohney and Hoffman, 2020) — an issue, which is also present nowadays, if the ETH SC coder simply forgot to include the function or to set the contract correctly as *payable* (see Appendix for further details). Finding bugs and imperfections inside the code just by looking at it is not easy, therefore it is hard to assess how good or bad the code of more complex contracts is and throughout testing is essential. This induces costs as repeated auditing and testing is required to be performed by specialists. Additionally, as it could be expected from Solidity being an object-oriented programming language (see Section 3.3), the *open-closed principle* of the object-oriented software design (i.e., open for extension, but closed for modification, see further Meyer, 1988) is especially important in the case of SCs, since it cannot be altered once an SC is deployed with a CA on the ETH BC unless the BC is forked at a point prior to the deployment. We did not encounter extension properties and outstanding modular development in the subset of the SCs we analyzed, yet, one could imagine that with time more and more examples of such missing elements could become available.

If SCs are really cheaper than their traditional counterparts is also often up to the field of employment. First off is the question, if it makes sense for a small or medium enterprise to actually invest in such an endeavor. This consumes a lot of development time and human resources, as well as a considerable amount of funds to make sure the codes are (possibly) free of bugs and exploits. On a second look the question is, if such an SC-based system makes sense in the long run for a plethora of cases. Here it is interesting to look at the price of Gas related to certain opcodes (introduced in Section 3.3 and denoted in Appendix). Table 8 presents the Gas cost for certain opcodes (see further Appendix G: Fee Schedule; Wood, 2021) and how much that would cost if done a million times with an arbitrary stable Ether exchange price of US$ 250. Executing the ADD opcode once will therefore cost 3×10^9 Gwei which gives a cost of 0.00000009 Ether and US$ 0.0000225 — respectively, done a million times, this gives US$ 22.5 (see further Ryan, 2017). When comparing this data storage and propagation technique — without taking the energy intensive mining process into consideration — to the pricing of cloud storage services, the benevolent reader may turn pale looking at the *SSTORE* opcode and ideas like: 'Just store a natural language version with the SC code' given volatile price structures like the previous maximum of US$ 1,427.05 for 1 Ether on 13 January 2018 (see further Figure 14 — not mentioning the costs to set up and understand such a system). Data received through the Ethereum Energy Consumption Index (Digiconomist, 2021) is providing a self explanatory overview regarding the cost in energy compared to traditional proceedings in Figure 13. Digiconomist (2021) and De Vries (2018) propose the Bitcoin Energy Consumption Index, where they estimate energy costs of TXs lying on the BC, the same approach they propose using to estimate the energy costs of ETH. Digiconomist (2021) show that the footprints of a single ETH transaction is equivalent to the power consumption of an average US household over 2.05 days and the annual footprint could be compared to the power consumption even of a whole country (e.g., compared to Lybia as of 15 March 2021, Digiconomist, 2021). For a deeper look into the statistics of the EVM we recommend, for example, Swende (2019).

As we have already touched on the issue of mining in Section 3.3, we just briefly want to add on the issues related to the costs of

Table 8. Opcode costs examples in Ether and in USD when done one million times (1 Ether = US$250, mining fees and energy costs not taken into consideration) Network energy consumption comparison with ETH, 20170527-20201210.

Opcode	Description	Gas	Ether	USD * 1M
ADD	Addition operation	3	0.00000009	22.5
MUL	Multiplication operation	5	0.00000015	37.5
SLOAD	Load word from storage	200	0.000006	1.5
BALANCE	Get balance of the given account	400	0.000012	3
SSTORE	Save word to storage	20000	0.0006	150

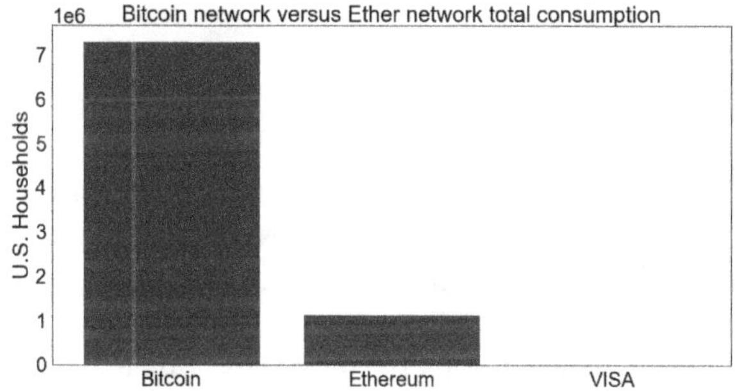

Figure 13. Energy consumption of BTC and ETH compared to VISA, 20170527-20201210 based on Digiconomist (2021).

mounting and running SCs contrasted to the grand scale of things happening in ETH. We saw, that the price of gas, the fuel needed for every action of SCs, is directly bound to the price of Ether. Therefore, not only the setup of some SC may be very expensive to ensure bug-free runtime, but on the other hand bug-free yet laboriously written SCs may consume more gas than actually needed for the individual application at hand. One can compare this to the energy consumption of badly coded simple action applications on a handheld device: having, for example, a badly written step counter on your mobile phone is a nuisance and needlessly consumes energy through requiring more computing power. Figure 14 visualizes, that hence the price of running the same SC can be very expensive to begin with,

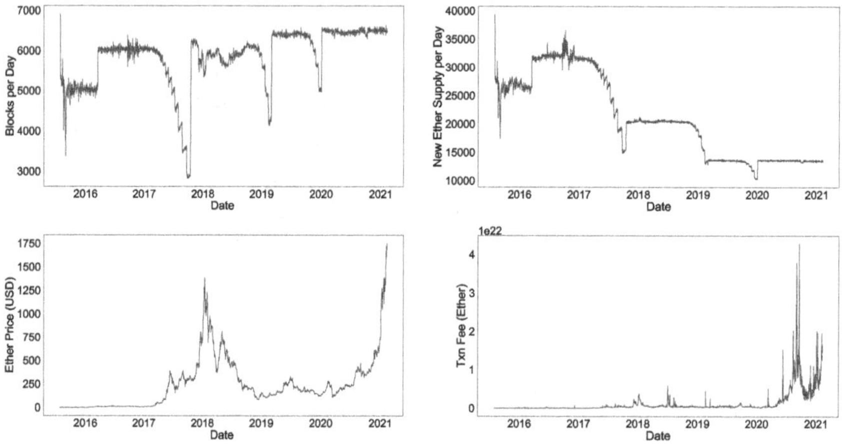

Figure 14. Network parameter time series, 20150630-20210211.

but depending on the market price of Ether, it can be even more expensive.

A discussion of the term *smart* is hence needed for a basic understanding of the potential decoupling between technological advances (code) and legal frameworks (natural language) which require insight into the source codes analog to raw natural language. At the moment, SCs can not adapt to situations dynamically, but instead only return based on the fulfillment or non-fulfillment of the pre-defined conditions. Indefinite legal terms commonly used, like 'to strive for' or similar, are not yet codeable and hence the technological aspects lack considerably behind flexibility offered by TCs. Is this state, however, a consequentially bad outcome? By recalling the quote by Nick Szabo from the introduction, this is not necessarily a bad result given the human nature (Szabo, 1997a). Without the intention to create an Osborne effect, extended usage of SCs is momentarily quite limited due to the lack of *smartness*. For example: any given SC, on a more advanced level than just financial TXs, cannot identify any violation as these can come in infinite forms and SCs are only coded to react according to respectively written triggers. As most issues for SCs are of a time-varying, stochastic, and humanoid nature — especially identifying problems *ante factum* — they require an agile technological and legal framework that is hard to implement at the given technological state (see Appendix for further details).

The question of *natural* or *legal* persons is also interesting to be looked at with advancing digitization. Can *Artificial Intelligence* (AI) can be considered as contractual partner in the sense of a legal person? Basically, if a given SC is coded to send or receive specific MSGs, it can be considered to be a smart post box or receptionist for inbound interaction and a messenger for outbound messages. Yet, if AI can hypothetically be considered a persona itself, or if the derelictio of software is possible and forces such entities to exist, can also be up to discussion. Any action of an AI should not pose a problem as long as the expressed will of the AI can be attributed to a natural or legal person. Considering the AI to be a legal person itself would only overly complicate the matter at hand (unless one would want to introduce an *intelligent* person, besides a natural and legal one), as there will always be a wetware point-of-origin. The person who initially wanted to express a will via a code, may it be an SC or an AI, needs to reassure that unwanted results are prevented, otherwise has to accept the unwanted consequences by implication or estoppel (attributable to a natural or human person in the sense of *falsus procurator* or similar to a blanquette signature). Eventually this becomes relevant, when looking at BC-based IoT applications of say autonomous vehicles, which are designed to transmit sensor data for insurance reasons in case of an accident, or also might address repair/supply stations to keep it operational.

Another grave aspect of SCs versus the legal reality is their incompatibility of eventual execution according to the coding and potential legal expectations or pleads of, say, a consumer as the counterparty. Whereas it has been often discussed how to employ SCs, these applications can be plainly nonsense with serious consequences for the applicator in certain legal frameworks. Whereas the example of locking a rentee out of a flat has been often used to outline this issue, it is important to also think of possible scenarios of the landlord selling a lien. This could be an autonomous driving car with an SC-coupled electronic lock which the rentee needs to go to earn a living. The SC would act like a vigilante given that this scenario can be coded and executed after being triggered. 'Fiat iustitia, et pereat mundus' does not work in the state that SC-applying civilizations have reached.

Whereas the idea of using digital signatures is already widely accepted in legal frameworks, advances such as the EIP712 (Ethereum typed structured data hashing and signing) should be observed critically. A major point for friction between legal systems and BC-based systems is present in the European Union (EU), most notably regarding the GDPR. Given this regulation, SCs as a replacement for TCs de facto *not* possible in the EU (at least in B2C realms). Notably, the SC standard ERC1812 (Ethereum Verifiable Claims) records Identity Claims containing Personal Identifying Information (PII) on the ETH BC (remember: immutable public database) is conflicting with the GDPR. However, the *legal legibility* of SCs should be seen as a *time decaying problem*. Knowledge and incorporation of codes as part of traditional constructions, just like the eventual acknowledgment of electronically saved parts of legal documents, will happen as the level of safety and standardization of SCs takes place. If SCs will become *smart*, in that if a piece of code is able to become a real competition to paper, is yet to be seen. Therefore, we are still waiting for the realm envisioned by Susskind (2013). While it is certainly true that members of the tech or law guild enjoy to create dense and impenetrable œuvres, one always has to take the elementary self-defining aspect of many BC enthusiasts of being *anti-establishment* into account — or as Sklaroff (2017) put it: 'How to Lease a Car from an Anarchist'. Most of what we commonly encounter as 'Smart Contract' is running against the self-definition of what the SC inventors themselves envisioned for their creation. Therefore, many overused terms such as *self-enforcing* and *unbreakable* need to be understood with a pinch of realism — from both a legal, as well as a technical point of view. As it stands today: Any smart contract will not protect from a smart lawyer in court or an enthusiastic hacker — not even a smart SC will. In the section Legal Example of the Appendix, you can find a theoretical hands-on example of legal handling, law enforcement and difficulties related to them within the SC-framework.

8. Closing Remarks

> There is no reason anyone would want a computer in their home.
>
> Olsen (1977)

Wetware, Hardware, and Software have an inherent need for evolvability in response to changing requirements, and SCs are no different. Though interest in SCs has taken off in the past few years, they have created — at the time of writing this — a bulk of 'hyped hopes' with only a fraction of the said miracles having been delivered. Yet, is there really no reason anyone would want to buy their home via an SC?

We have shown how the first system that enabled SCs works, and what SCs can and can not accomplish in contrast to the common narratives. Moreover, we proposed a methodological solution for the decision support on the appropriateness of using DApp and SCs for solving specific problems. While we critically assessed the narrative of SCs, we see the chance and hope that SCs provide the incentive to move onwards to more efficient and stable proceedings. Work towards this on the intersection with Ricardian Contrachts is already underway (Grigg, 2015, 2020). However, the fields involved in the matter at hand — explicitly Statistics, Information Technology, and Law — must cooperate and not claim the sole right to exist coupled with *papal-esque infallabilitas*.

We have proven, that the application of SCs is very restricted to this point, but every technology requires some patching before being able to cater the promised deeds to the target group. Hence, SCs have the potential to be Door Kickers to evolve the idea dramatically with most legal frameworks being abstract or adaptive enough to get it accustomed to it. Otherwise, at the given state, the question what SCs can and can not deliver will stay to be a question of Realism and Idealism.

Acknowledgments

Financial support of the European Union's Horizon 2020 research and innovation program 'FIN-TECH: A Financial supervision and Technology compliance training programme' under the grant agreement no. 825215 (Topic: ICT-35-2018, Type of action: CSA), the European Cooperation in Science & Technology COST Action grant CA19130 — Fintech and Artificial Intelligence in Finance — Towards a transparent financial industry, the Deutsche Forschungsgemeinschaft's IRTG 1792 grant, the Yushan Scholar Program of Taiwan, the Czech Science Foundation's grant no. 19-28231X / CAS: XDA 23020303, as well as support by Ansar Aynetdinov (ansar.aynetdinov@hu-berlin.de) are greatly acknowledged.

Appendix

A.1. List of Cryptocurrencies Used in This Research

Abbrev.	CC	Website
BTC (XBT)	Bitcoin	bitcoin.com, bitcoin.org
ETC	Ethereum Classic	ethereumclassic.github.io
ETH	Ethereum	ethereum.org
LEO	UNUS SED LEO	bitfinex.com (iFinex ecosystem)
USDC	USD Coin	centre.io/usdc

A.2. List of Abbreviations

Terminus	Abbrev.
Blockchain	BC
Cryptocurrency	CC
Smart Contract (general terminus)	SC
Verified Smart Contract (Source Code public)	VSC
Decentralized Apps	DApps
State of the DApps	SDA
Externally Owned Account	EOA
Contract Account	CA
Transaction (BC recorded)	TX
Call/Message ('internal TX')	MSG

A.3. Literature Research

A.3.1. *Literature meta analysis on the keyword level*

We present the most frequent keywords as a wordcloud in Figure A1. The keywords *blockchain*, *smart contract*, and *Ethereum* were filtered out since they were used to limit the query and therefore do not deliver any additional semantic information to differentiate between

Figure A1. Wordcloud of existing research keywords.

the outlets. Technical keywords such as *security*, *data*, *iot*, *solidity*, *distributed ledger*, and *decentralized* are the most frequently used. Unfortunately, these do not provide us with sufficient additional information to identify clear tendencies in the research. Each of these keywords could belong to any given paper in the field of SC research. Hence, bibliometric research on SC outlets needs to be conducted on a more granular level.

A.3.2. *Literature meta analysis on the abstract level*

To identify the optimal amount of clusters in our literature research, we utilized the elbow criterion (Thorndike, 1953). This method measures the identified performance metric for different numbers of groups, plots them against each other, and identifies points that are knee or elbow of a curve. The possible metrics for clustering could be an intra- or inter-cluster variance, the Davies–Bouldin, and Silhouette scores. Since these metrics might produce contradictory results, we decided to utilize only one of them — The Davies–Bouldin score. This score (Davies and Bouldin, 1979) shows the average similarity measure of each cluster with its most similar cluster. Figure A2 displays the Davies–Bouldin score, where similarity is the ratio of within-cluster distances to between-cluster distances. It evaluates intra-cluster similarity and inter-cluster differences. Applying the elbow criterion to these diagnostic plots leads us to a value around

14 — one of the first *elbows* of the plot, as we prefer rather lower values of the Davies–Bouldin score and the lower amounts of topics an-ease the interpretability. In Figures A3 and A4, you can find the 10 most important words for each one of these 14 topics.

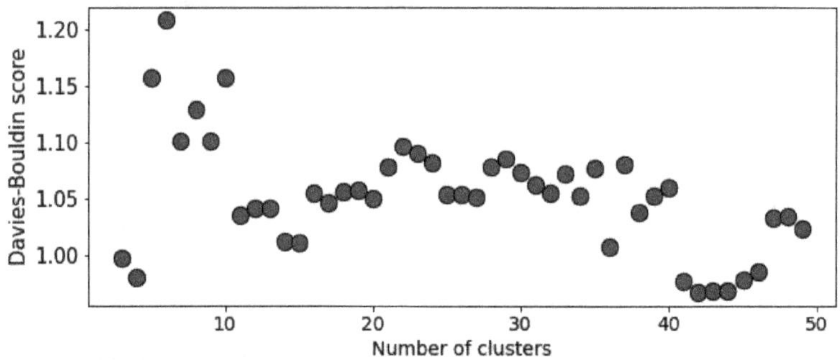

Figure A2. Identification of optimal number of groups using elbow-curve method with Davies–Bouldin score.

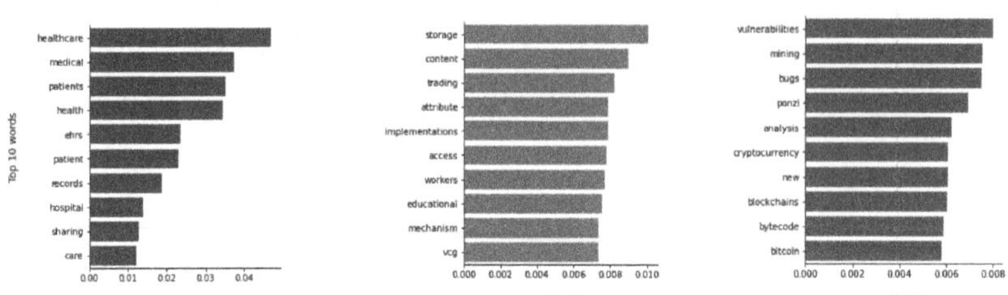

(a) Healthcare/medicine (b) Implementation/Storage (c) Vulnerabilities/Ponzi

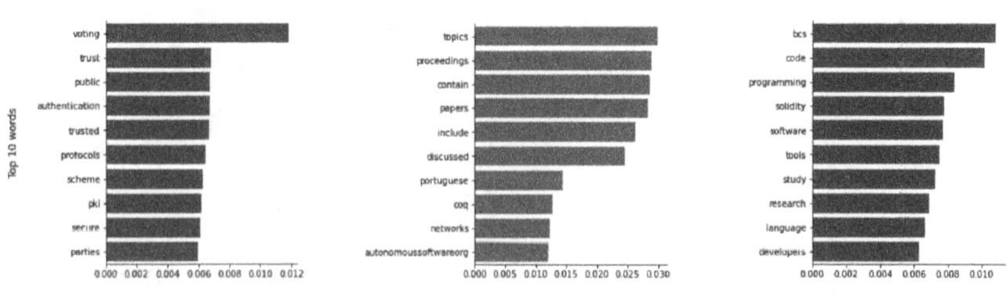

(d) Voting/Trust (e) Research/Categories of Research (f) Programming language/ Solidity/Software Development

Figure A3. Top 10 the most important words per topic identified in the existing SC research (Part 1).

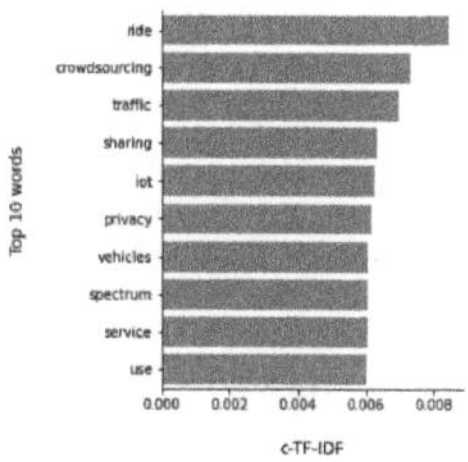

(g) Crowdsourcing/Sharing

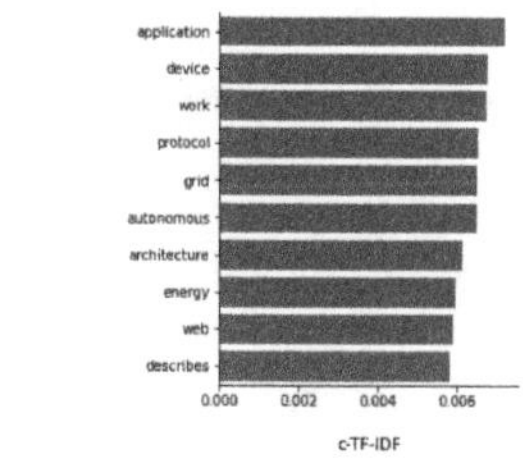

(h) Applications/Development

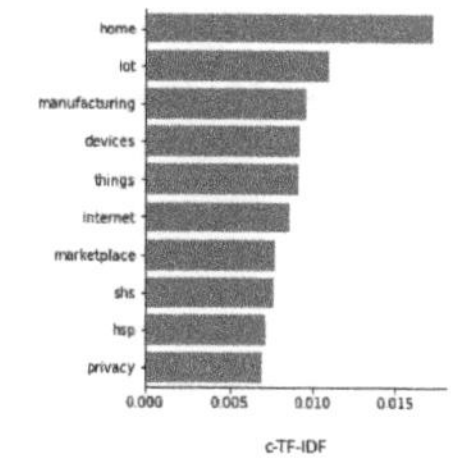

(i) IOT/Smart devices

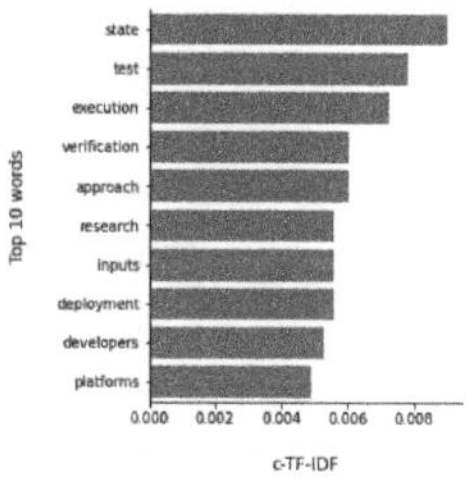

(j) Verification/Deployment

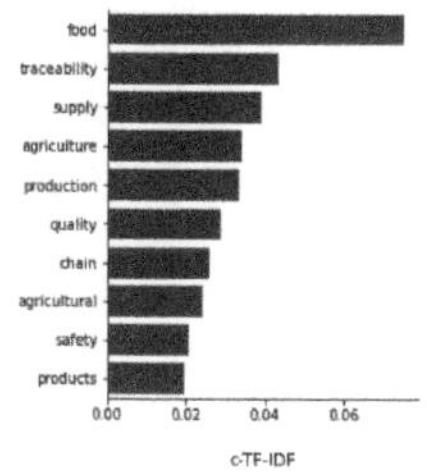

(k) Food/Agriculture

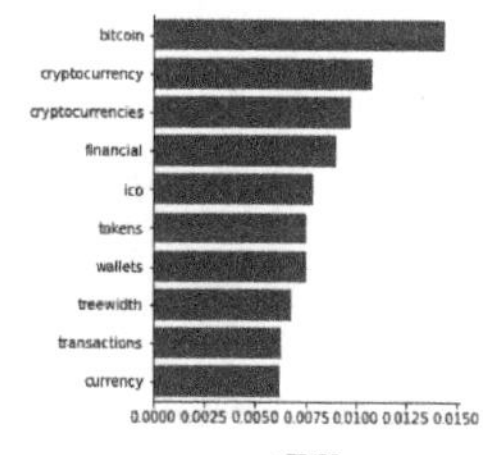

(l) BTC/Finance/ICO

Figure A3. (*Continued*)

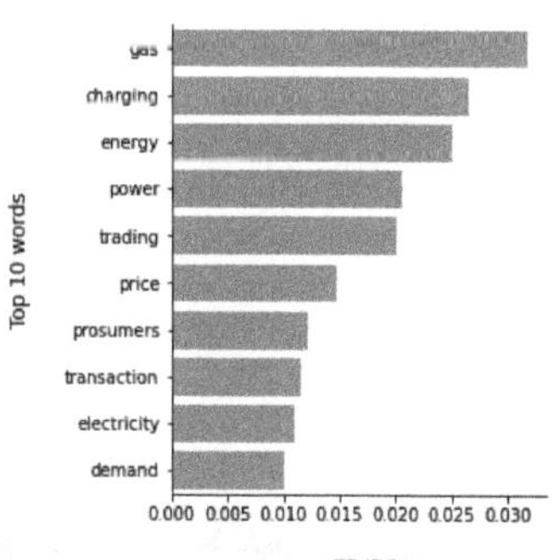

(a) Energy/Electricity/Gas

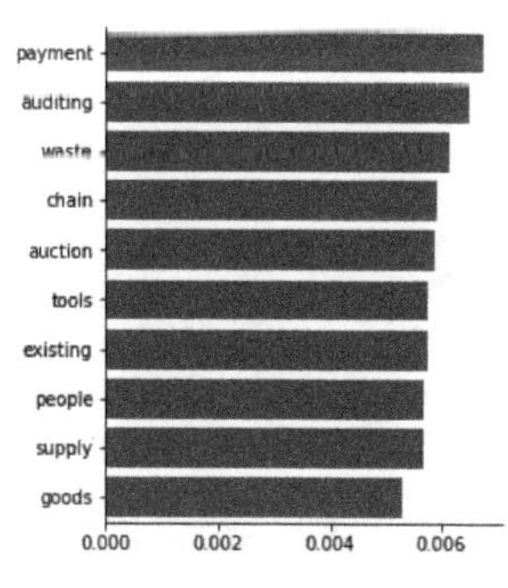

(b) Payments/Audit

Figure A4. Top 10 the most important words per topic identified in the existing SC research (Part 2).

A.4. Cryptocurrency Dynamics

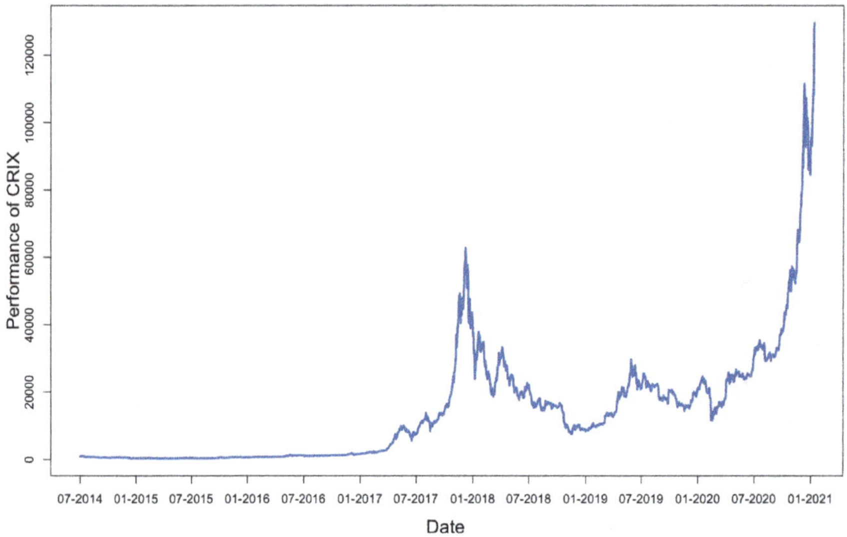

CRyptocurrency IndeX CRIX, 20140731-20210211.

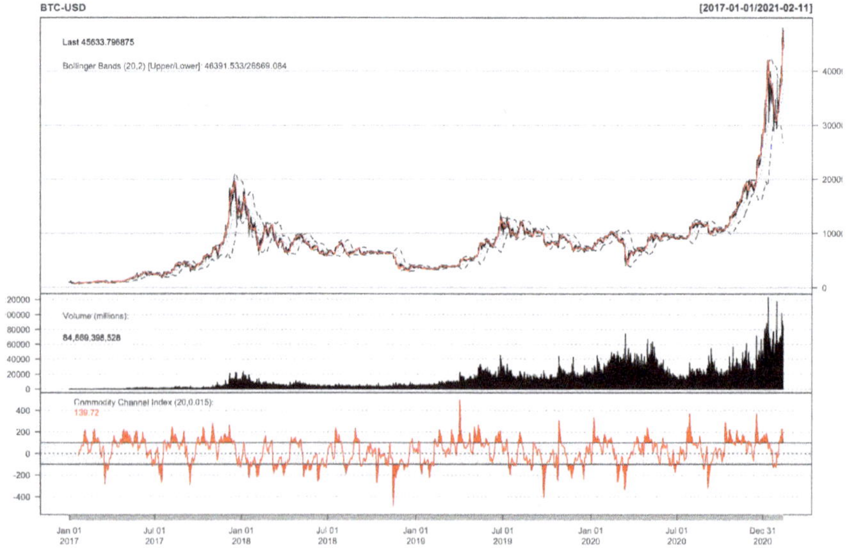

BTC-USD, 20170101-20210211.

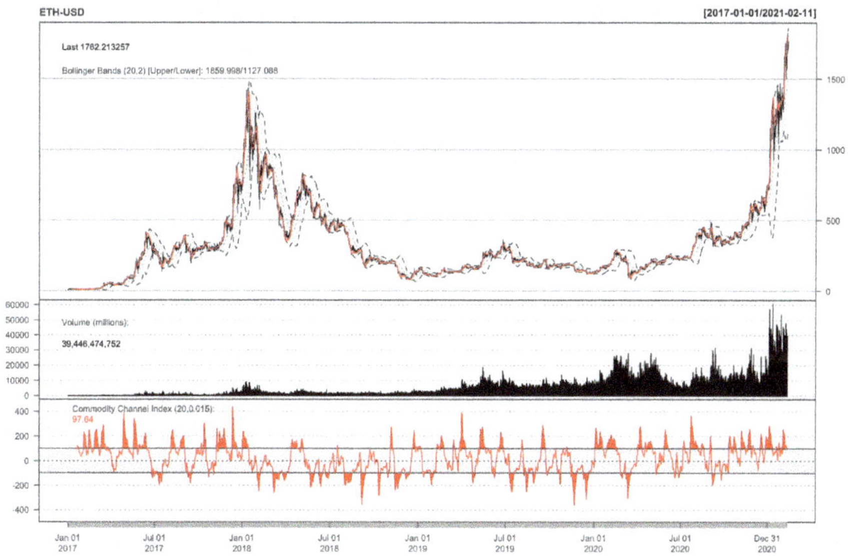

ETH-USD, 20170101-20210211.

A.5. ETH Value Denominations

Unit	Wei Value	Wei
Wei	1 wei	1
Kwei (babbage)	1e3 wei	1,000
Mwei (lovelace)	1e6 wei	1,000,000
Gwei (shannon)	1e9 wei	1,000,000,000
Microether (szabo)	1e12 wei	1,000,000,000,000
Milliether (finney)	1e15 wei	1,000,000,000,000,000
Ether	1e18 wei	1,000,000,000,000,000,000

Further units and globally available variables used in solidity can be accessed through Ethereum — Read the Docs.

A.6. Elliptic Curve Digital Signature Algorithm

Asymmetric cryptography is used to create accounts in ETH in three steps: Firstly, the private key associated with an EOA is randomly generated as SHA256 output and could look like this: b032ac4de581a6f65c41889f2c90b3a629dc80667bf7167611f8b5575744f 818 — a random 256 bit/32 bytes big and 64 hex character long output. Secondly, the public key is derived from the private key via the Elliptic Curve Digital Signature Algorithm (secp256k1 ECDSA) and could then look like this: fc2921c35715210aeb0f2fffeaad94 d906aaf2feda8a71e52c5d0a0da8ada4a44099e8ea65e3ec214b66861892 55bba2373bd2ee6b05 520dfd4dc571b682ccc3 — a 512 bits/64 bytes big and 128 hex character long output. The public key is therefore subsequently calculated from the private key, but as we are dealing with a *trapdoor function*, this is not possible vice versa being an irreversible calculation. A private key is therefore kept non-public, whereas the public key is used to derive, in a third step — via Keccak-256 hashing of that public key, which results in a bytestring of length 32, from which the first 12 bytes are removed and result in a bytestring of length 20 — the individual ETH *address*, that could look like 0x9255bba2373BD2Ee6B05520DfD4dC571B682b349 — a 160 bits/20 bytes big and 40 hex character long output (leaving out the 0x prefix). A public key can hence be used to determine, that the given signature of the information at hand is genuine, that means created with the respective public key and address of the interactor, without requiring the private key to be divulged (see further Section A.7 and Buchanan, 2020).

A.7. Zero-Knowledge Proofs

The standard notion of a mathematical proof can be related to the definition of an nondeterministic polynomial (NP) time complexity class of decision problems. That is, to prove that a statement is true one provides a sequence of symbols on a piece of paper, and a verifier checks that they represent a valid proof. Usually, though, some additional knowledge, other than the sole fact that a statement is true, is gained as a byproduct of the proof. Zero-knowledge proofs were introduced as a way to circumvent that, i.e., to convey no additional knowledge beyond proving the validity of an assertion. Goldwasser *et al.* (1989) first described zero-knowledge proofs as interactive proof systems.

As the term itself suggests, interactive zero-knowledge proofs require some interaction between a prover and a verifier. Intuitively, a proof system is considered zero-knowledge if whatever the verifier can compute, while interacting with the prover, it can compute by itself without going through the protocol (Goldreich and Oden, 1994). Formally they can be defined as follows, as per Boaz and Arora (2009).

Given an interactive proof system, or an interactive protocol (P, V), where P and V can be seen as interactive probabilistic polynomial-time (PPT) Turing machines symbolizing a Prover and a Verifier, for a formal NP-language $L \subset \{0, 1\}^*$ and an input x, the *output* of V on x at the end of interaction between P and V can be written as

$$out_V[P(x), V(x)].$$

(P, V) is called a zero-knowledge protocol for L if the following three conditions hold:

Completeness:

$$\forall x \in L, u \in \{0, 1\}^*, \qquad Pr[out_V[P(x, u), V(x)]] \geq 2/3,$$

where u is a certificate for the fact that $x \in L$. In other words the prover can convince the verifier of $x \in L$ if both follow the protocol properly.

Soundness: If $x \notin L$, then

$$\forall P^*, u \in \{0, 1\}^*, \qquad Pr[out_V[P^*(x, u), V(x)]] \leq 1/3.$$

That is, the prover cannot fool the verifier, except with small probability.

Perfect Zero-Knowledge: For every strategy V^* there exists an expected PPT simulator S^* such that

$$\forall x \in L, u \in \{0, 1\}^*, \qquad out_{V^*}[P(x, u), V * (x)] \equiv S^*(x).$$

The last condition prevents the verifier from learning anything new from the interaction, even if she does not follow the protocol but rather uses some other strategy V^*. Otherwise she could have learned the same thing by just running the simulator S^* on the publicly known input x. S^* is called the simulator for V^*, as it simulates the outcome of V^*'s interaction with the prover without any access to such an interaction.

A.8. Understanding Smart Contracts' Network

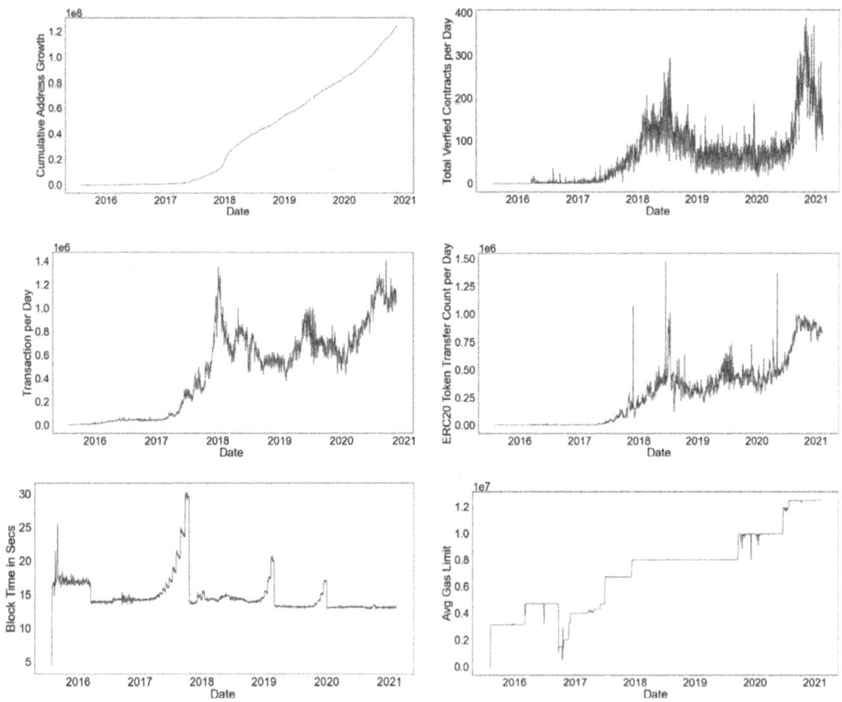

Network parameter time series, 20150630-20210211.

A.9. t-SNE (t-Distributed Stochastic Neighbor Embedding)

t-SNE is a nonlinear technique for dimension reduction and data visualization it allows to preserve the local structure and is proposed by van der Maaten and Hinton (2008). It aims to design an embedding of high-dimensional input to low-dimensional map while preserving much of a significant structure. In Algorithm 1, the reader can find the pseudocode of the t-SNE computation.

$$X = \{x_1, x_2, \ldots, x_n\} \to Y = \{y_1, y_2, \ldots, y_n\},$$

Algorithm 1: t-SNE Pseudocode

Data: data set $\chi = \{x_1, x_2, \ldots, x_n\}$
cost function parameters: perplexity $Perp$,
optimization parameters: number of iterations T, learning rate η, momentum $\alpha(t)$
Result: low-dimensional data representation $Y^{(T)} = \{y_1, y_2, \ldots, y_n\}$
begin
  compute pairwise affinities $p_{j|i}$ with perplexity $Perp$ (using Eq. (A.1));
  set $p_{ij} = \frac{p_{j|i}+p_{i|j}}{2n}$;
  sample initial solution $Y^{(0)} = \{y_1, y_2, \ldots, y_n\}$ from $N(0, 10^{-4}I)$;
  for $t = 1$ to T **do**
    computer low-dimensional affinities q_{ij} (using Eq. (A.2)));
    compute gradient $\frac{\delta C}{\delta Y}$ (using Eq. (A.3))) ;
    set $Y^{(t)} = Y^{(t-1)} + \eta\frac{\delta C}{\delta Y} + \alpha(t)(Y^{(t-1)} - Y^{(t-2)})$
  end
end

---

x_i is the ith object in high-dimensional space.
y_i is the ith object in high-dimensional space.

$$p_{j|i} = \frac{\exp(-\|x_i - x_j\|^2/2\sigma_i^2)}{\sum_{k\neq i}\exp(-\|x_i - x_k\|^2/2\sigma_i^2)}, \tag{A.1}$$

$$q_{ij} = \frac{(1 + \|y_i - y_j\|^2)^{-1}}{\sum_{k\neq l}(1 + \|y_i - y_l\|^2)^{-1}}, \tag{A.2}$$

$$\frac{\delta C}{\delta y_i} = 4\sum_j (p_{ij} - q_{ij})(y_i - y_j)(1 + \|y_i - y_j\|^2)^{-1}. \tag{A.3}$$

A.10. UMAP Versus t-SNE

The dimensionality reduction algorithm that we are using here is the Uniform Manifold Approximation and Projection for Dimension

Reduction (UMAP) (McInnes *et al.*, 2018) and is like t-SNE — a neighbor graph algorithm. The mathematical foundations of the UMAP rely on Laplacian Eigenmaps and are very extensive. The important differences between t-SNE and the UMAP are the following. The UMAP aims to better preserve more of the global structure while requiring less computational time. As compared to the t-SNE, the UMAP relies not only on the Kullback–Leibler divergence measure, but on the cross-entropy.

$$C_{\text{UMAP}} = \sum_{i \neq j} \left\{ v_{ij} \log \left(\frac{v_{ij}}{w_{ij}} \right) + (1 - v_{ij}) \log \left(\frac{1 - v_{ij}}{1 - w_{ij}} \right) \right\}, \quad \text{(A.4)}$$

where v_{ij} are the pair-wise similarities in the high dimensional space and w_{ij} — in the low-dimensional. The optimization problem used in the UMAP is the stochastic gradient descent instead of gradient descent used in the t-SNE, which speeds up the computations and decreases the required memory resources. Moreover, UMAP does not require the distance Euclidean.

A.11. Topics in the Unlabeled Smart Contracts

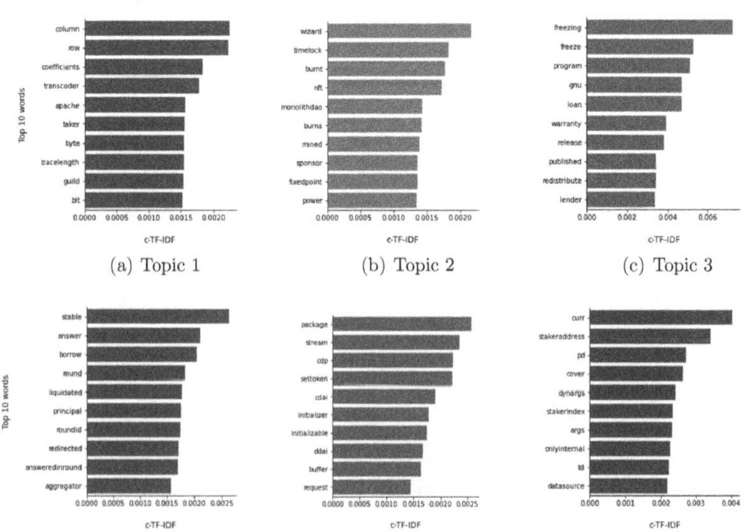

(a) Topic 1 (b) Topic 2 (c) Topic 3

(d) Topic 4 (e) Topic 5 (f) Topic 6

Top 10 the most important words per topic identified in the unlabeled SC dataset with 12 topics.

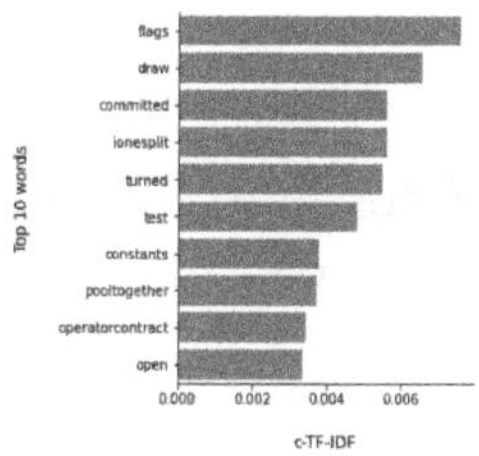

(g) Topic 7

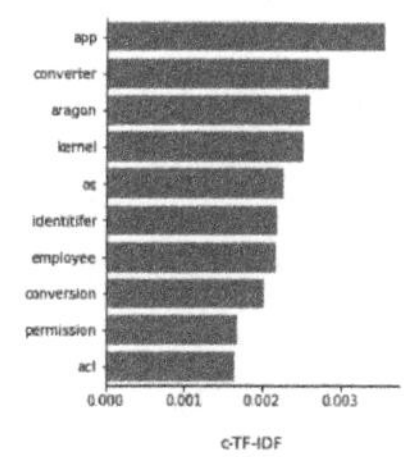

(h) Topic 8

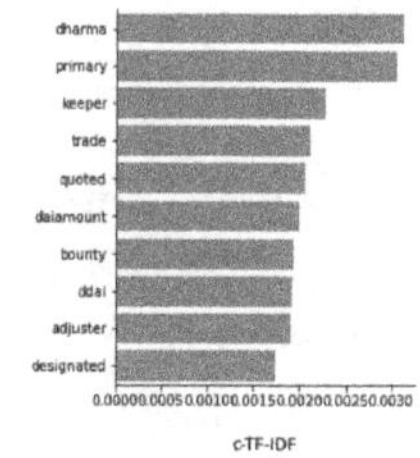

(i) Topic 9

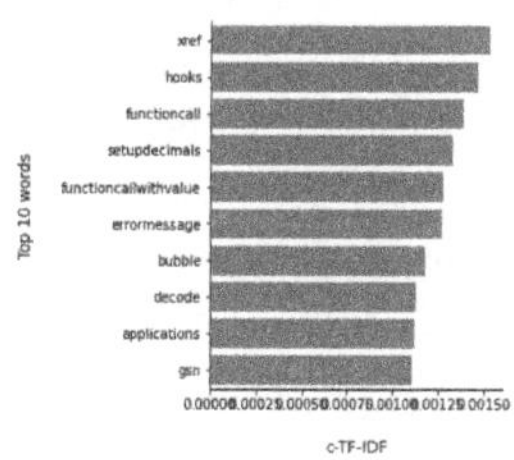

(j) Topic 10

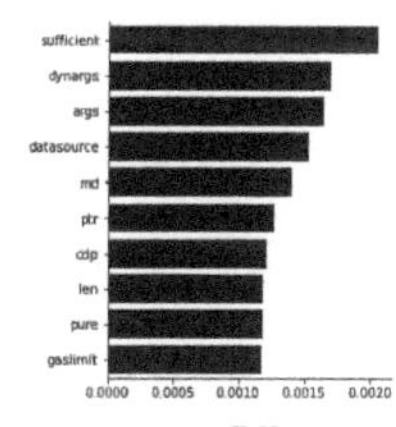

(k) Topic 11

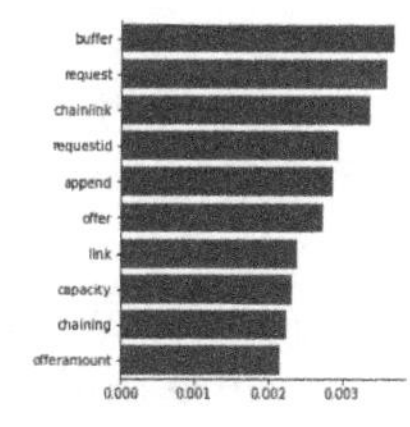

(l) Topic 12

(*Continued*)

A.12. Manual Classification of Solidity Contracts

In this section, we present our first part of the classification analysis of SCs. We randomly picked the source codes of 800 verified SCs provided by Etherscan (2019b), using the functions of random sampling in Python, and tried to group the source codes into categories by looking at the code, reading the comments, searching for titles of the SC. The nine categories that we came up with are:

- **Token creation, token sale or token creation/token sale:** SCs sole purpose is to define a token, or its crowdsale, or both.
- **Finance or token creation/finance:** Whenever an SC has an implementation of a financial product or a derivative, a bidding mechanism, a lottery, a multisignature wallet, or in general any profit-creating mechanism. A token can be implemented in a separate SC and be evoked, or defined in a Finance SC directly.
- **Airdrop or token creation/airdrop:** An implementation of a token airdrop, sometimes simultaneously with a token definition. An airdrop is a free distribution of a token, unlike a crowdsale.
- **DApp:** An implementation of an Ethereum DApp.
- **Scam:** Pyramid schemes, or financial SCs that offer, e.g., 5% daily interest.

- **Utility:** Diverse helper functions, pieces of code that are necessary for running actual SCs, extensions, libraries, etc.

Obviously, these categories are slightly different then the ones coming in the SDA data. Only the category **Finance** came up in the manual selection as well in the dataset from SDA. Moreover, just by looking at the code ourselves we were not always able to identify the category of the code or what DApp's category it belongs to. Interestingly, some of the categories were identified through meaningful comments or naming the product. Sometimes however, it required additional search to specify what the code is about. Thus, it is not always possible to accurately identify the category of the SC without using additional check up by a human-being. It requires a lot of engineering and Solidity domain expertise, which makes manual labeling more difficult or at least its scaling and outsourcing. On the other side though, it might happen that automatic classifiers would pick up the features that we do not see as a human.

A.13. Legal Documents and Their Signing

The United Nations have worked on respective measures to replicate traditional frameworks for digital societies since at last 1996, resulting in a Model Law on Electronic Signatures that is of importance due to the beforehand mentioned algorithmic uniqueness of private keys/signatures (UNICITRAL, 2001). The United States of America's Uniform Electronic Transactions Act (UETA) from 1999, and subsequently the United States Electronic Signatures in Global and National Commerce (ESIGN) Act from the year 2000, present a national legal solution to the issues raised by a digital society. They grant legal recognition to electronic signatures and records, given that the contractual parties choose to use electronic means for their agreements. Besides special requirements, such as having the intent to sign such an agreement and common consent to do business electronically, the requirements of associating the signature with continuously updated records that can be fully accessed, plays into the hand of BC-based constructions such as SCs. Under this legislation, in order to be accepted as a prima facie effective agreement, it is mandatory to have an associated record reflecting how the signature was generated or an attached proof that this agreement was reached by using electronic signatures. Moreover, the electronic signature records need to be capable of retention and accurate reproduction — once again, basic functions provided by BC-based systems as outlined in Section 3.2. We can conclude that certain legal frameworks have been established that can be used directly or in an analog way for SCs. BC users can: (1) be uniquely identified and linked to a signature, (2) have sole control over the genesis of their signatures, (3) identify accompanying signed data stored on the BC, (4) easily prove the event that the accompanying data has been changed and revoke their consent.

This leads to the possibility to also accept digital signatures of uniquely identifiable BC participants as legally valid signatures for contracts — in that sense SCs. Therefore, while certain steps towards the digitization of TCs have been accomplished, SCs can only be defined as technological means to facilitate TCs and not as contracts *sui generis*, or *authenticated agreements*.

A.14. Legal Conflicts and SC *Smartness* Versus the BC

A failsafe 'bugout' solution in the hands of a trustful third party would be a solution, which however would make it a circle argument for some governmental backing of such systems to induce trust into the *intermediary-less BC trust machine*. Plenty of legal literature and decisions are available on non-/wrong-fulfillment of any kind of agreements, ranging from, for example, an automobile being delivered in the (partially) wrong color, to not having the expected quality of lacquer, etc. These fine nuances are not representable by SCs unless the contractual parties agree *post id factum* to alter the SC — which is unfortunately only safely possible by deactivating the initial SC and by redeploying an altered one as a different instance. The fundamental problem of *legal effectiveness* of a *particular* contract also has to be taken into consideration, like for example, the legal age or a mental illness of a party, or if digital signatures can be accepted au lieu de physical signatures in a given case. However, these discussions revolve more about the regulation of oracles and, therefore, data service providers — a field that is not linked to SCs, but to classic service contract law for which a plethora of literature exists. It is *not* necessary to create yet another legal framework, as

SCs are trying to be technological portrayals of their legal counterparts — a rental contract will still be a rental contract, just in a different presentation.

This serves to underline the redundancy of an elaborated exegesis of fulfillment problems in the context of SCs, as there are more legal problems that may hinder SCs to be classified as actual and effective contracts in their legal meaning. While an aficionado may certainly be able to write a technically effective smart 'contract', it does not mean that this 'contract' is legally effective, leave alone legally enforceable. Depending on respective legal constructions, a contract may also only be partially effective, i.e., the obligation to fulfill the contract may be ineffective, yet the transfer of ownership/property part of *the* contract may be effective. Also, the contract needs to follow a certain phenotype, like being in a certain language — where it can be up to discussion, if a programming language can be chosen given the envisioned type of agreement. In the end, this is defined by the already existing respective national limits of contractual freedom. Once again we recurse on the fact that a third party — possibly governmentally backed system is needed to solve problems if an agreement should *ex tunc* be deemed as *ineffective* as BC-based actions are considered to be eternal. This is a question primarily referring to technical solutions to make such constructions post factum editable (hence against the initial idea of BC), as having, for example, illegal content on a BC could potentially invalidate it completely for further usage.

The solution to fork the BC before this event and to abandon the 'illegal BC' is highly problematic given governmental power and activity structures on such a system. The idea of ETH's SCs to grant different *states* (stages of contractual fulfillment so to say, see Section 3.2) proposes a solution if a *fallback function* to a given previous state or *reverse TX* can be coded. Courts often use the 'doctrine of reasonable expectations' as a fallback function and justification for invalidating parts or all of a given agreement: the weaker party will not be held to adhere to contract terms that are beyond what the weaker party would have reasonably expected from the contract, even if what the party reasonably expected was outside the strict letter of agreement. The necessary ambiguity in the TC and SC situation alike arises when there are plausible and competing interpretations of a certain term. Given that the contractual parties can choose the language of the agreement in certain legal frameworks — may it be French, Chinese, or Solidity — it is important to note that this exemplary doctrine is not a rule granting substantive rights to any party if there is no doubt about the meaning of the used terms. Respectively, *clickwrap/-through agreements* can pose considerable sources for problems, especially when thinking of *adhesion clickwrap.* In a traditional context, these can be invalidated, which is not as easy to do in SC/BC software code cases. As the parties agreed to use a particular language, both parties are seen as being able to understand what is written in the agreement. The limit of freedom of contract, however, is obviously reached when the counterparty does not understand the given agreement at all and is respectively exploited. Unlike natural language on physical paper, it is harder to hide nefarious proceedings in standardized code forms (see further Section 3.1), as both parties can de facto read the source code in any font they want and can check for all functions present to not be of disadvantage for them. Unless the disadvantageous party can prove to have been in a state of mental distress or similar while agreeing to this code, the only way out would be through *bona fides* rulings — which in itself are not helping the idea of legal security and may infringe on the freedom of contract.

As long as this level of *smartness* is not present with SCs, the solution to most of these problems is not to employ an armada of legal scholars and practitioners to forcibly create completely new legal frameworks but to employ the already existing legal knowledge analogously rewritten as these have proven their efficiency to eventually serve as *ius consuetudinis* with specialized international courts. Given the scope of applicability and the inherent nature of these agreements, we can obviously observe that unfair and surprising outcomes, lack of notice or understanding of clauses can cause problems especially, when considering SCs as replacements for TCs. There exists a potential for unconscionability if the TC and SC do not represent equal information. However, such an event of discrepancy and ambiguity will be resolved contra proferentem against the party drafting the contract and its mean of execution — again, there is no need to specialized codices. The European Union most notably works around these classic issues, for example, in the Rome I and Rome II regulations (see further discussion, e.g., Rühl, 2021).

A.15. Legal Example

As a hands-on-example, let us look at a SC as a mean to execute a long-term flat rental TC under German law: Landlord (L) and Tenant (T) sign a TC on renting an unrenovated ground floor road-view flat at BC-wonderland Berlin 'X-Berg's' Tourist and Club area, i.e., EUR 2.000 — gross warm rent for 45 square meters, on 1 August 2021. The flat sports a well maintained and shiny smart-lock belonging and connected to a dedicated and extremely hyped Berlin-Startup (S) BC system that runs exclusively for such businesses — obviously L and T agree in the TC to have an SC to manage respective value flows, as this is portrayed as saving them money and time, instead of making a musty repeating standing order via online banking.

After they have forwarded all their contractual, professional, and private information, besides creditworthiness, etc. to the service provider to set up the SC, the complete heating system collapses on 01 November 2021 and is not fixed for the whole month. This is the first time that T realizes that the SC has no function coded for any kind of such rent reduction due to heating shortages — the smart meters on the heating devices are not linked to the SC via an Oracle to cut on respective costs, as it is expected that lodgers in this area will always be hot. T declares to L a rental reduction of 100% for the month of November, as he was not able to use the flat accordingly — a shortcoming in the sense of § 536 Par. 1 S. 1 Bürgerliches Gesetzbuch (BGB; German Civil Code). As the L does not react and the service provider S is not reachable, T addresses his credit institute — from where the SC automatically deducted the full rent as advised repeatedly — to cancel the permission to have any funds going off toward this address. Meanwhile, T tries to reach L and S, the SC is unable to automatically deduct the rent from the banking account of T on 1 December and locks T out of the flat via a coded command to the smart-lock. After T — who suspected a typical Berlin-esque 'Digital Advancement' technical error — had the door broken open by a locksmith and having the smart-lock replaced by a conventional lock, the S tries to call T why the data-stream from the device has broken off — just seconds before the L also tries to call T after having received an automatic alert message, that T has not paid the rent.

The days pass — S has gone bankrupt in the meantime due to an overflow of unpaid marketing bills — and L prompts T — who has now access to the flat via the installed traditional lock-key-system and transfers the rent via a classic standing order — to pay the missing rent for October 2021 on the firsts of December 2021, January and February 2022. Eventually, L files a lawsuit against T in March 2022 to pay the rent for October 2021 stating that the SC is an exhaustive and final provision regarding the rights and obligations of this rental contract. T eventually terminates the TC properly and moves back to his Uckermark home village in April 2022 after not becoming a successful Avantgarde fashion designer.

In the following, we provide a rough sketch on how this case of interaction between SC and TC would be handled legally in Germany and programmatically respectively in adjacent legal system constructions:

```
I. Admissibility of the lawsuit of L against T to pay the rent
for November 2021

1. Jurisdiction
    Given the TC and missing any contradicting information - - - the SC is
        ↪ completely irrelevant
    - - - the Amtsgericht Tempelhof- Kreuzberg is factually and locally responsible
          for this case,
    § 23 Nr. 2a Gerichtsverfassungsgesetz (GVG; Courts Constitution Act) in
        ↪ conjunction with
    § 29a Par. 1 Zivilprozessordnung (ZPO; German Code of Civil Procedure).

2. Defensible Interest
    In case one should see an SC as a fully viable replacement for a TC, then one
        ↪ could argue,
    that there could be an easier way of justice than going to the courts and have
        ↪ a lengthy
    process. As we do not see SCs as equal to TC,
        but merely as a mean of execution, we do not
    need to discuss "self executing and enforcing justice".


II. Reasonableness of the lawsuit of L against T to pay the rent
for November 2021
    Conditioned that L's claim to pay the rent for October 2021 based on the
        ↪ rental TC holds.
```

```
1. Contractual Base
   Again, we do not consider an SC to be a contract in the legal sense, hence
       ↪ only the TC is
   important here with no contradicting information regarding issues with the TC.
       ↪ The SC is
   just a mean of execution of the TC. Therefore the plead of L, that the SC is
       ↪ an exhaustive
   and final provision is meaningless.

   Thinking of an SC of being just a mere mean on execution, problems regarding
       ↪ a potentially
   required written form of an agreement are of redundant nature. Importantly, it
       ↪ is commonly
   agreed, that eMails, Telefaxes, or Computerfaxes do not hold up to fulfill the
       ↪ required
   written form.

   On the other hand, if one would think of an SC being a replacement of a TC,
       ↪ one would pay
   attention to respective regulations on the way the agreement is presented, i.e.,
       ↪ the written
   form requirement of § 126 Par. 1 BGB for a contract in the sense of § 550 S. 1
       ↪ BGB can
   be replaced according to § 126 Par. 3 BGB given that respective signatures in
       ↪ the sense of
   § 126a BGB are given (recall our multiple hints towards the importance of
       ↪ signatures in a
   technical (digital signature) and legal (electronic signature) sense~- - -
       ↪ nevertheless a missing
   written form according to § 550 S. 1 BGB does not provoke a nullity according
       ↪ to § 125 S. 1
   BGB, but just an indefinite rental period of time in this particular case).

   The full legal reference of §§ 126a, 126 Par. 3, 127 Par. 1 and 3 BGB however
       ↪ hints towards
   the border of the freedom of contract in the sense of §§ 13, 125 BGB, as a
       ↪ given law may
   define this otherwise. Examples would be the §§ 484 Par. 1 S. 2, 492 Par. 1 S.
       ↪ 2,
   623 Half- S. 2, 766 S. 2 BGB, or the § 780 S. 2, 781 S. 2 BGB.


2. Rights based on Irregularity In Contractual Performance
   Rights resulting from an irregularity in contractual performance can be called
       ↪ given that a
```

```
   contractual performance is not or not as owed given.

   In this case, the T owes the L to rent for November 2021. We could consider
       ↪ that T exercised
   his right to set-off this obligation according to § 389 BGB with the rent of
       ↪ October 2021
   given that he has a right to reduction.

   The SC itself does not have any other function besides checking for cash flows
       ↪ and
   smart- lock data stream - it is obviously not that smart as it will never be able
       ↪ to represent
   the status of the rental flat, unless that flat if full of sensors and these are
       ↪ connected
   flawlessly to a respectively coded SC. This, however, does not change anything
       ↪ in the rights a
   tenant has by law. Here, as T was unable to live in the flat for the month of
       ↪ November 2021,
   he has the right to reduce the rent of November 2021 by 100% according to
   § 536 Par. 1 BGB and to set- off this position according to § 389 BGB. L can
       ↪ not demand
   the rent for November 2021.

   L's statement, that the SC is an exhaustive and final provision is on one hand
       ↪ irrelevant, as
   they also signed a TC for which the SC is only the mean of execution, and the
       ↪ rights given by
   law to T are not of a dispositive nature. In general, any contractual agreement
       ↪ needs to stand
   up to the questions of, for example, if they stand up against control towards
       ↪ their legality.


3. Cancellation of Contract
   The right to exercise the termination of a contract is a right to influence a
       ↪ legal relationship
   just like a contestation, a revocation, or others besides § 134 BGB. As outlined
       ↪  beforehand, if
   an SC should be seen as a complete surrogate for TCs, there can be issues if a
       ↪ respective
   cancellation is not coded or not coded properly.

   Given that an SC is not coded properly, the respective legal rights are not
       ↪ superseded by them
```

```
missing in an "exhaustive and final provision" as outlined above regarding the
    ↪ reduction of
the rent or the extraordinary termination of the agreement. In our example
    ↪ case, the T could
have terminated the TC immediately in December when the smart-lock did not
    ↪ let T in the
flat which represents an important issue according to § 543 Par. 1 & Par. 2 S.
    ↪ 1 BGB, as the
respective requirements for locking a tenant out of a flat via a forced eviction
    ↪ or clearance
order according to § 940a ZPO were missing.


III. Conclusion
 The abovehand outlined case would be admissible to the courts, but it can not
    ↪ be seen as
 being reasonable.

 Should one see an SC as a replacement for a TC, without a given legal
    ↪ foundation that
 identifies this equally, then one could argue, that in the case of problems
    ↪ arising the people
 utilizing this framework willingly let go of their otherwise existing frameworks
    ↪ of
 rights - - -
 caveat emptor. One can compare that to illicit employment or moonlighting to
    ↪ save on taxes
 and issues resulting from a normally given warranty for defects or in the case of
    ↪ the customers
 insolvency. Using surrogate systems to circumvent the existing regulated
    ↪ system does not
 deserve to be protected.

 At least the German legal system is not in need of a specialized BC- law or
    ↪ similar lex
 cryptographia creatures, as it is an effective tool given its abstractness to adapt
    ↪ to a given
 case, as well as given its neutrality toward any kind of technological advances,
    ↪ may they have
 been electronic signatures in the past or BC- systems at the given time of this
    ↪ writing.
```

With this rudimentary example — we are not going deeper into any claims of T against L (e.g., § 231 BGB due to being locked out — beyond §§ 858 ff. BGB), or of L against S (e.g., consequential damage in the sense of § 280 Par. 1 BGB due to a primitively coded SC), or of S against L and/or T (e.g., due to the willingly damaged smart-lock in the sense of the civil and penal law), etc. — we can quite easily present the frictions between the 'vision' and the reality of SC in other realms than being a financial vehicle like peer-to-peer lending or data transmitter in areas such as say renewable energy Prosumer situations.

We want to underline, that law enforcement and legal security do not work in the SC-framework we have at hand at the time of writing this — especially when thinking about, for example, §§ 273, 320, 229, 230, 539 Par. 2, 997 BGB, or §§ 765a, 811 ZPO. Hence (nearly) every thinkable contractual construction will run into problems when being pushed in an SC application. Gravely, the exclusive right of courts to rule on what is eventually right or wrong is circumvented and can lead to unjust overenforcement, like locking the tenant out of the flat in the above shown example. Legal systems all over the world, and to our knowledge especially such coming from a Franco-Germanic genesis, are clear enough on what individual rights are and on what these individual rights borders are — to this point, a *embedded legal knowledge* can not be represented by SCs.

A.16. Example Code

Adding to the source code review and possible use cases, we are presenting a simple *Hello World*-esque SC as provided by the Ethereum Github with explanatory adaptions to outline some of the technical complexity that has a grave impact on every adjacent structure. We have observed many non-technical outlets — especially Blogs and the such — discussing a theme, that they have apparently never seen as code itself — consequently, we will also keep this to a very brief overview to introduce the structures in a very simple example. Each comment starts with /** and ends with /*.

```
    /** Version control for the compiler, see Section A.6, as each Solidity version
        ↪ may have different commands that can be
    coded - - - higher versions will obviously improve efficiency of the coding and
        ↪ lead to better code controlling. /*
pragma solidity >=0.4.22 <0.6.0;

    /** "Mortal" is the name of this SC. /*
contract Mortal {
        /** Defines the variable "owner" of the type "address". /*
```

```
    address owner;

        /** The "constructor" is executed at initialization and sets the owner of
            ↪ the SC, i.e., it is executed once when the CA/SC is first deployed.
            ↪  Similar to other
        class- based programming languages, it initializes state variables to
            ↪ specified values. "msg.sender" refers to the address where the CA
            ↪  is being created from, i.e., here in the constructor setting the
        "owner" to the address of the SC creator. SCs depend on external TX/
            ↪ MSG to trigger its functions, whereas "msg" is a global variable
            ↪ that includes relevant data on the given interaction, such as the
            ↪ address of the sender and the value included in the interaction.
            ↪ This is assured by the "public" function, which can be called from
            ↪  within the CA/SC or externally via MSG's, like here getting the
            ↪ address of the interactor. "private" functions are not callable and
            ↪ can only reached by the SC itself - - - a particular source for grave
            ↪  errors, as you can not change the SC once deployed. /*
    constructor() public { owner = msg.sender; }

        /** Another important function, and source for grave errors if missing,
            ↪ follows and represents a mean to recover funds stored on the CA.
            ↪ Alternatively, calling "selfdestruct(address)" sends all of the SCs
            ↪ current balance to address specified. Remember, that once
            ↪ deployed the SC can not be changed unlike non- BC- based
            ↪ software. The only way to modify an SC is to deploy a corrected
            ↪ one - best after deactivating and recovering all funds in the
            ↪ problematic one. Interestingly, "selfdestruct" consumed "negative
            ↪ Gas", as it frees up BC/EVM space by clearing all of the CA/SCs'
            ↪ s data./*
    function kill() public { if (msg.sender == owner) selfdestruct(msg.sender); }
}


    /** After "Mortal", "Greeter" is another SC presented to visualize, that CA/
        ↪ SCs can "inherit" characteristics of CA/SCs enabling SCs to be
        ↪ written shorter and clearer. By declaring that "Greeter is Mortal", "
        ↪ Greeter" inherits all characteristics of "Mortal" and keeps the "Greeter
        ↪ " code herewith crisp and clear to to point, where is has individual
        ↪ functions to be executed. In this example, the inherited characteristic
        ↪ of "Mortal" gives, as defined beforehand in "Mortal", that "Greeter"
        ↪ can be deactivated with all locked funds being recovered. /*
contract Greeter is Mortal {

        /** Defines the variable "greeting" of the type "string", i.e., a sequence of
            ↪  characters. /*
```

```
    string greeting;

        /** This is defined as beforehand in "Mortal", whereas in this case the
            ↪ underscore in "\_greeting" is a style used to differentiate between
            ↪ function arguments and global variables. There is no semantic
            ↪ difference between "greeting" and "_greeting", whereas the latter
            ↪ one is defined as such not to shadow the first one. Here, the
            ↪ underscore differentiates between the global variable "greeting"
            ↪ and the corresponding function parameter. Strings can be stored
            ↪ in both "storage" and "memory" depending on the type of
            ↪ variable and usage. "memory" lifetime is limited to a function
            ↪ MSG and is meant to be used to temporarily store variables and
            ↪ respective values. Values stored in "memory" do not persist on
            ↪ the network (EVM & BC) after the interaction has been
            ↪ completed. /*

    constructor(string memory _greeting) public {
        greeting = _greeting;
    }

        /** Main function of the SC that returns the greeting once "greet"
            ↪ function is MSG'ed /*
    function greet() public view returns (string memory) {
        return greeting;
    }
}
```

References

Ajienka, N., Vangorp, P., & Capiluppi, A. (2020). An empirical analysis of source code metrics and smart contract resource consumption. *Journal of Software: Evolution and Process*, *32*(10), e2267.

Akyildirim, E., Corbet, S., Cumming, D., Lucey, B., & Sensoy, A. (2021). Riding the wave of crypto-exuberance: The potential misusage of corporate blockchain announcements. https://ssrn.com/abstract=3758490 [Accessed: 02 February 2021].

Arora, S., & Barak, B. (2009). *Computational Complexity: A Modern Approach*, 1st ed. Cambridge University Press, Cambridge.

Bartoletti, M., & Pompianu, L. (2017). An empirical analysis of smart contracts: platforms, applications, and design patterns. In *International Conference on Financial Cryptography and Data Security*. (pp. 494–509). Springer, Cham.

BBC (2017). Cryptokitties craze slows down transactions on ethereum. https://www.bbc.com/news/technology-42237162 [Accessed: 10 January 2021].

Bellia, A. (2002). Promises, trust, and contract law. *American Journal of Jurisprudence*, *47*, 25–40.

Borke, L., & Härdle, W. (2018). Q3-d3-lsa. In *Handbook of Big Data Analytics*. Springer-Verlag Berlin, Heidelberg.

Buchanan, W. (2020). Ethereum address generation, asecuritysite. https://asecuritysite.com/encryption/ethadd [Accessed: 10 January 2021].

Buterin, V. (2015). Merkling in ethereum. https://blog.ethereum.org/2015/11/15/merkling-in-ethereum/ [Accessed: 10 January 2021].

Buterin, V. (2020). Ethereum white paper — A next generation smart contract & decentralized application platform. https://ethereum.org/en/whitepaper/ [Accessed: 10 January 2021].

Celesti, A., Ruggeri, A., Fazio, M., Galletta, A., Villari, M., & Romano, A. (2020). Blockchain-based healthcare workflow for tele-medical laboratory in federated hospital iot clouds. *Sensors (Switzerland)*, *20*(9), Article Number 2590.

Chen, W., Zheng, Z., Cui, J., Ngai, E., Zheng, P., & Zhou, Y. (2018). Detecting ponzi schemes on ethereum: Towards healthier blockchain technology. In *Proceedings of the 2018 World Wide Web Conference'* (pp. 1409–1418).

Circle (2021). Usdc: The world's leading digital dollar stablecoin. https://www.circle.com/en/usdc [Accessed: 03 March 2021].

Cohney, S., & Hoffman, D. (2020). Transactional scripts in contract stacks. *Minnesota Law Review*, *105*, 319–386.

Coindesk (2016). Understanding the DAO attack. https://www.coindesk.com/understanding-dao-hack-journalists [Accessed: 10 January 2021].

Dapper Labs (2021). Cryptokitties. collect and breed furrever friends! https://www.cryptokitties.co/ [Accessed: 3 March 2021].

Davies, D., & Bouldin, D. (1979). A cluster separation measure. *IEEE Transactions on Pattern Analysis and Machine Intelligence*, *1*(2), 224–227.

De Vries, A. (2018). Bitcoin's growing energy problem. *Joule*, *2*(5), 801–805.

Devlin, J., Chang, M., Lee, K., & Toutanova, K. (2018). Bert: Pre-training of deep bidirectional transformers for language understanding. arXiv preprint arXiv:1810.04805.

Di Angelo, M., & Salzer, G. (2020). Assessing the similarity of smart contracts by clustering their interfaces. *Blockchain Systeme and Applications (BlockchainSys 2020)* (pp. 1–10).

Digiconomist (2021). Ethereum energy consumption index. https://digiconomist.net/ethereum-energy-consump-ion [Accessed: 26 January 2021].

Durieux, T., Ferreira, J., Abreu, R., & Cruz, P. (2019). Empirical review of automated analysis tools on 47,587 ethereum smart contracts, arXiv preprint arXiv:1910.10601.

EIP (2020). Ethereum improvement proposals — Ethereum request for comments. https://eips.ethereum.org/erc [Accessed: 10 January 2021].

Etherscan (2019a). Ethereum network utilization. https://etherscan.io/chart/networkutilization [Accessed: 10 February 2021].

Etherscan (2019b). Etherscan verified contracts. https://etherscan.io/contractsVerified [Accessed: 10 February 2021].

Factory, G. (2021). Golem. https://www.golem.network/ [Accessed: 3 March 2021].

Fawcett, T. (2006). An introduction to roc analysis, *Pattern recognition letters*, *27*(8), 861–874.

Firica, A. (2019). Decentralized apps vs web apps. https://wiredelta.com/decentralized-apps-vs-web-apps/ [Accessed: 26 January 2021].

GeeksforGeeks (2020). Mathematical operations in solidity. https://www.geeksforgeeks.org/mathematical-operations-in-solidity/ [Accessed: 26 January 2021].

Goldreich, O. & Oden, Y. (1994). Definitions and properties of zero-knowledge proof systems. *Journal of Cryptology*, *7*, 1–32.

Goldwasser, S., Micali, S., & Rackoff, C. (1989). The knowledge complexity of interactive proof systems. *SIAM Journal on Computing*, *18*, 168–298.

Greenspan, G. (2016). 7 Blockchains vs centralized databases. https://www.multichain.com/blog/2016/03/blockchains-vs-centralized-databases/ [Accessed: 10 January 2021].

Grigg, I. (2015). On the intersection of ricardian and smart contracts. https://iang.org/papers/intersection_ricardian_smart.html [Accessed: 10 January 2021].

Grigg, I. (2020). Ricardian contracts. http://www.webfunds.org/guide/ricardian.html [Accessed: 10 January 2021].

Grootendorst, M. (2020). Topic modeling with bert. https://towardsdatascience.com/topic-modeling-with-bert-779f7db187e6. [Accessed: 10 January 2021].

Halaburda, H. (2018). Staff analytical note/note analytique du personnel 2018-5. blockchain revolution without the blockchain. https://www.bankofcanada.ca/wp-content/uploads/2018/03/san2018-5.pdf [Accessed: 10 January 2021].

Härdle, W., Harvey, C., & Reule, R. (2020). Understanding Cryptocurrencies. *Journal of Financial Econometrics, 18*(2), 181–208.

Inmusik (2019). The music industry. https://inmusik.co/ [Accessed: 10 January 2021].

Justia, U. L. (2019). 2019 tennessee code title 47 — Commercial instruments and transactions chapter 10 — Uniform electronic transactions part 2 — Distributed ledger technology § 47-10-202. cryptographic signature — Electronic records and forms. https://law.justia.com/codes/tennessee/2019/title-47/chapter-10/part-2/section-47-10-202/ [Accessed: 10 January 2021].

Kaggle (2020). Ethereum blockchain. complete live historical ethereum blockchain data (bigquery). https://www.kaggle.com/bigquery/ethereum-blockchain [Accessed: on March 10, 2020].

Keilbar, G., & Zhang, Y. (2020). On cointegration and cryptocurrency dynamics. IRTG 1792 Discussion Paper. ISSN: 2568-5619. https://www.wiwi.hu-berlin.de/de/forschung/irtg/results/discussion-papers/discussion-papers-2017-1/irtg1792dp2020-012.pdf.

Khatoon, A. (2020). A blockchain-based smart contract system for healthcare management. *Electronics (Switzerland), 9*(1), Article number 94.

Kondo, M., Oliva, G., Jiang, Z., Hassan, A., & Mizuno, O. (2020). Code cloning in smart contracts: A case study on verified contracts from the ethereum blockchain platform. *Empirical Software Engineering, 25*(6), 4617–4675.

Laplante, P. (2017). *Dictionary of Computer Science, Engineering and Technology.* CRC Press, Boca Raton, Florida, US.

Ledger (2021). What is the difference between coins and tokens? https://www.ledger.com/academy/crypto/what-is-the-difference-between-coins-and-tokens [Accessed: 3 March 2021].

Lessig, L. (1999). *Code and Other Laws of Cyberspace*, 1st U.S. edition, 3rd printing edition (November 30, 1999). Basic Books, New York.

Li, A., Choi, J., & Long, F. (2020). Securing smart contract with runtime validation. In *Proceedings of the ACM SIGPLAN Conference on Programming Language Design and Implementation (PLDI)* (pp. 438–453), London, UK.

Liang, Y., & Zhu, K. (2018). Automatic generation of text descriptive comments for code blocks. In *Proceedings of the AAAI Conference on Artificial Intelligence*, Vol. 32, New Orleans, LA, USA.

Lin, M., Khowaja, K., Chen, C., & Härdle, W. (2021). Blockchain mechanism and distributional characteristics of cryptos, In *Book Series: Advances in Quantitative Analysis of Finance & Accounting (AQAFA)*, Vol. 18. Forthcoming.

MakerDao (2021). A better smarter currency. https://makerdao.com/en/ [Accessed: 3 March 2021].

McInnes, L., Healy, J., & Melville, J. (2018). Umap: Uniform manifold approximation and projection for dimension reduction. arXiv preprint arXiv:1802.03426.

Meyer, B. (1988). *Object-Oriented Software Construction.* Prentice Hall, Upper Saddle River, NJ, USA.

Mik, E. (2019). Smart contracts: A requiem. *Journal of Contract Law,* Forthcoming.

Ni, X., Härdle, W., & Xie, T. (2020). A machine learning based regulatory risk index for cryptocurrencies. Available at SSRN 3699345.

Nikolic, I., Kolluri, A., Sergey, I., Saxena, P., & Hobor, A. (2018). Finding the greedy, prodigal, and suicidal contracts at scale. arXiv. https://arxiv.org/abs/1802.06038 [Accessed: 10 January 2021].

Norvill, R., Pontiveros, B., State, R., Awan, I., & Cullen, A. (2017). Automated labeling of unknown contracts in ethereum. In *2017 26th International ICCCN* (pp. 1–6). IEEE.

Oliva, G., Hassan, A., & Jiang, Z. (2020). An exploratory study of smart contracts in the ethereum blockchain platform. *Empirical Software Engineering, 25*(3), 1864–1904.

Olsen, K. (1977). hello_world. http://www.computinghistory.org.uk/pages/3971/There-is-no-reason-anyone-would-want-a-computer-in-their-home [Accessed: 10 January 2021].

Petukhina, A., Reule, R., & Härdle, W. (2021a). Rise of the machines? intraday high-frequency trading patterns of cryptocurrencies. *The European Journal of Finance, 27*(1–2), 8–30.

Petukhina, A., Trimborn, S., Härdle, W., & Elendner, H. (2021b). Investing with cryptocurrencies — Evaluating the potential of portfolio allocation strategies. *Quantitative Finance, 21*(11), 1825–1853.

Pierro, G., Tonelli, R., & Marchesi, M. (2020). An organized repository of ethereum smart contracts source codes and metrics. *Future Internet. 12*(11), 1–15.

Pinna, A., Ibba, S., Baralla, G., Tonelli, R., & Marchesi, M. (2019). A massive analysis of ethereum smart contracts empirical study and code metrics. *IEEE Access, 7,* 78194–78213.

Quartz (2017). The ethereum network is getting jammed up because people are rushing to buy cartoon cats on its blockchain. https://qz.com/1145833/cryptokitties-is-causing-ethereum-network-congestion [Accessed: 10 January 2021].

Raval, S. (2016). *Decentralized Applications: Harnessing Bitcoin's Blockchain Technology.* O'Reilly Media, Inc. Sebastopol, CA, USA.

Reimers, N., & Gurevych, I. (2019). Sentence-bert: Sentence embeddings using siamese bert-networks. In *Proceedings of the 2019 Conference on EMNLP*, Hong Kong, China.

Rühl, G. (2021). Smart (legal) contracts, or: Which (contract) law for smart contracts? In Cappiello, B. & Carullo, G. (eds.), *Blockchain, Law and Governance.* Springer International Publishing, Cham, pp. 159–180. ISBN 978–3–030–52722–8.

Ryan, D. (2017). Calculating costs in ethereum contracts. https://hackernoon.com/ether-purchase-power-df40a38c5a2f [Accessed: 10 January 2021].

Sanh, V., Debut, L., Chaumond, J., & Wolf, T. (2019). Distilbert, a distilled version of bert: Smaller, faster, cheaper and lighter. arXiv preprint arXiv:1910.01108.

Scholten, O., Hughes, N., Deterding, S., Drachen, A., Walker, J., & Zendle, D. (2019). Ethereum crypto-games: Mechanics, prevalence, and gambling similarities. In *CHI PLAY '19: Proceedings of the Annual Symposium on Computer-Human Interaction in Play.* (pp. 379–389). Barcelona, Spain.

Shaw, G. (1917). *Annajanska, the Bolshevik Empress: A Revolutionary Romancelet.* Latest versions published by Players Press (2015); Good Press (2021).

Sklaroff, J. (2017). Smart contracts and the cost of inflexibility. *University of Pennsylvania Law Review, 166*, 263–303.

Star (2019). Multimillionaire 25-year-old crypto king vitalik buterin speaks to the star about the future of ethereum. https://www.thestar.com/business/2019/08/19/ethereums-vitalik-buterin-on-reducing-cryptocurrencys-risks.html [Accessed: 10 January 2021].

State of the DApps (2021). Explore decentralized applications. https://www.stateofthedapps.com/ [Accessed: 19 January 2021].

Steidl, D., Hummel, B., & Juergens, E. (2013). Quality analysis of source code comments. In *2013 21st International Conference on Program Comprehension (ICPC)* (pp. 83–92). IEEE.

Sun, H., Ruan, N., & Liu, H. (2019). Ethereum analysis via node clustering. In *International Conference on Network and System Security.* (pp. 114–129). Springer.

Susskind, R. (2013). *Tomorrow's Lawyers: An Introduction to Your Future.* Oxford University Press, Oxford.

Swende, M. (2019). vmstats. https://github.com/holiman/vmstats [Accessed: 26 June 2021].

Szabo, N. (1994). Smart contracts. http://www.fon.hum.uva.nl/rob/Courses/InformationInSpeech/CDROM/Literature/LOTwinterschool2006/szabo.best.vwh.net/smart.contracts.html [Accessed: 10 January 2021].

Szabo, N. (1997a). Accounting controls. http://www.fon.hum.uva.nl/rob/Courses/InformationInSpeech/CDROM/Literature/LOTwinterschool2006/szabo.best.vwh.net/accounting.html [Accessed: 10 January 2021].

Szabo, N. (1997b). The idea of smart contracts. https://nakamotoinstitute.org/the-idea-of-smart-contracts/ [Accessed: 10 January 2021].

Thorndike, R. (1953). Who belongs in the family? *Psychometrika*, *18*(4), 267–276.

Tracr (2019). The diamond industry supply chain. https://www.tracr.com/ [Accessed: 10 January 2021].

UBS (2016). Cutting through the blockchain hype. https://www.ubs.com/microsites/innovation/en/our-approach/2016/path-finding.html [Accessed: 10 January 2021].

UNICITRAL. (2001). UNCITRAL model law on electronic signatures with guide to enactment 2001. http://www.uncitral.org/pdf/english/texts/electcom/ml-elecsig-e.pdf [Accessed: 10 January 2021].

van der Maaten, L., & Hinton, G. (2008). Visualizing data using t-SNE. *Journal of Machine Learning Research*, *9*(Nov), 2579–2605.

Wang, W., Song, J., Xu, G., Li, Y., Wang, H., & Su, C. (2020). Contractward: Automated vulnerability detection models for ethereum smart contracts. *IEEE Transactions on Network Science and Engineering*, *8*(2), 1133–1144.

Wilcoxon, F. (1992). Individual comparisons by ranking methods. In *Breakthroughs in Statistics* (pp. 196–202). Springer. New York, NY.

Wöhrer, M., & Zdun, U. (2018). Design patterns for smart contracts in the ethereum ecosystem. In *2018 IEEE International Conference on Internet of Things (iThings) and IEEE Green Computing and Communications (GreenCom) and IEEE Cyber, Physical and Social Computing (CPSCom) and IEEE Smart Data (SmartData).* (pp. 1513–1520). IEEE.

Wood, G. (2021). Ethereum: A secure decentralised generalised transaction ledger. Petersburg version 3e2c089-2020-09-05. https://ethereum.github.io/yellowpaper/paper.pdf [Accessed: 10 January 2021].

Wüst, K., & Gervais, A. (2018). Do you need a blockchain? In *2018 Crypto Valley Conference on Blockchain Technology (CVCBT).* (pp. 45–54). IEEE.

Yu, B., Zhan, P., Lei, M., Zhou, F., & Wang, P. (2020). Food quality monitoring system based on smart contracts and evaluation models. *IEEE Access*, *8*, 12479–12490.

https://doi.org/10.1142/9781800612723_0002

Chapter 2

FinTech Regulation: A Macro-Structural Approach

Silvio Andrae
German Savings Banks Association,
Berlin, Germany
andrae@zedat.fu-berlin.de

Abstract

The rapid development of FinTech and BigTech is challenging existing regulatory approaches. However, the existing regulatory approaches seem to have reached their limits. The traditional micro perspective cannot adequately capture the specific characteristics of FinTech. With the rise of platformication and the emergence of ecosystems, smart regulation is not enough. In the FinTech era, the financial system is getting more extensive and more interconnected. The chapter presents a macro-structural regulatory approach. The structural developments require an adaptive, proactive, and comprehensive regulatory perspective. As finance becomes more granular and algorithm-driven, a paradigm shift in financial regulation is required. The response must be structural and systemic. Law is given precedence over technology.

Keywords: FinTech, financial regulation, financial supervision, central banking, technology.

1. Introduction

The 'FinTech revolution' is here. Responsible for this are the four technologies that can be summarized with the acronym ABCD. Zetzsche *et al.* (2020) define:

> '**A**I, **B**lockchain (including distributed ledgers and smart contracts), **C**loud, and **D**ata (big and small); or, in another iteration, AI, Big Data, Cloud, and DLT (including blockchain and smart contracts)' (p. 179).

These technologies are changing the way financial transactions are conducted. They make transactions faster, cheaper, and more convenient. A broader mass of the world's population could enter the world of digital finance in this way. In such a narrative, Fintech (financial technology) could be seen as a disruption to the financial market and as a force for social progress.

FinTech can also be viewed from a systemic perspective. With such a perspective, they turn out to be a complex and politically sensitive phenomenon. Omarova (2019) argues that behind the shiny surface of operational efficiency, there is a particular disruptive potential of FinTech. Omarova (2019) describes the potential as the 'public-private balance of powers, competencies, and roles in the financial system' (p. 735). Instead, the emergence of platform economies forms the narrative from which the FinTech rise is also analyzed. The story follows in broad strokes: with the dot-com crash of 2,000, a radical market shakeout took place. The crisis set the stage for BigTech companies like Google, Apple, Facebook, and Amazon to expand vigorously. Platforms and monopoly-like market structures got a new boost. The next step came in 2008, with the financial crisis. Excess cheap money was looking for new investment opportunities. The platform companies had a good offer. It was about capitalizing on behavior on the internet and user data.

In this way, platform companies gained influence not only economically but also socially and politically. They provide new social infrastructures. The large platforms are pushing into state and parastate areas of responsibility. The precautionary state is to be replaced by caring companies. Value creation is completed and secured by filling former government functions. Apart from that, platform companies do not compete in markets. Instead, they create markets in which companies compete. We speak of 'proprietary markets' (Staab, 2019). Platforms dictate the terms of access to the markets they control. The result is then something like Facebook's Libra project: creating their own private money and currency system.

New technologies can undoubtedly make financial services more efficient and widely accessible (Thakor, 2020). However, they can also reinforce the dysfunctional dynamics of the system. They contribute to excessive misallocation of credit and money (Hockett and Omarova, 2017). This development should naturally make legislators, regulators, and central banks uneasy. To be sure, a debate is also taking place on how best to regulate new financial technologies (e.g., Arner *et al.*, 2017; Ehrentraud *et al.*, 2020a). Financial and technology experts and policymakers discuss whether and how to develop new regulatory procedures for different FinTech products or adapt old ones (e.g., EU FinTech Action Plan). However, the debate and also the solution space take place within the existing regulatory model. The functional modalities shape the predominantly technocratic debate.

Omarova (2020a) argues:

> It is structurally compartmentalized along with the rigidly categorical 'product/entity type' lines, which enables and rewards bureaucratic specialization, deep but narrow technical expertise, and minimally invasive regulatory targeting of specifically cognizable 'market failures' within the relevant agency's jurisdiction (p. 77).

In this traditional paradigm, well-controlled phenomena and decision points are identified and regulated at the micro-level. Today's system of financial regulation is micro-transactional.

In contrast to this technology-oriented regulatory strategy, this chapter develops an overarching and normative framework of a regulatory strategy, inspired by the remarks of Omarova (2019, 2020a). FinTech is structurally changing financial markets.[1] New technologies are drastically changing the scale and scope of the financial

[1]The term 'FinTech' is inclusive at this point. It also includes the BigTech.

system. Platform capitalism is getting a new boost from the new technologies. On the one hand, this concerns the speed of financial transactions. Nevertheless, it also concerns the shift in the decision-making focus of financial markets from humans to algorithms. Finance is becoming less transparent and more complex. Traditional law-making is reaching its limits. Familiar product types, companies, or functions are becoming harder to isolate and control. It is even more challenging to assess and evaluate the effects on the system as a whole. The prevailing paradigm on which financial regulation is currently based, such as efficient markets, rational expectations, and models modeled on the natural sciences, is no longer up to date.

The macro-structural approach presented here should not be confused with the macroprudential approach to regulation. The latter approach also attempts to adopt a systemic perspective (Gai *et al.*, 2019). However, the regulatory approach remains within the traditional framework of microeconomics. Notable developments are considered exogenous shocks. It does not capture structural developments.[2]

Only a macro-structural regulatory approach captures platformication in the financial industry at the macro and meso levels. Platformication at the micro level means 'an emerging plug and play business model that allows multiple participants to connect, interact with each other via API or other mechanisms to create value'.[3] At the macro level, digital platforms are intermediary digital infrastructures. As quasi-markets, platforms organize the meeting of supply and demand. This fact is overlooked in numerous typologies of the platform economy or at least not pursued as a theoretically relevant phenomenon. Such approach covers, for example, when platforms offer digital money and thus enter into competition with the state monopoly on the money of the central banks. At the latest, with the new technologies and the high degree of interconnectedness, the financial system has crossed a threshold of complexity. The system

[2]Khiaonarong and Goh (2020) acknowledge that market structures are changing. The authors develop a regulatory framework for payments.

[3]See https://www.keycapital.eu/fintechglossary.

is evolving faster than regulators and rules can keep up (Goodhart, 2008). The challenge of complexity is not unique to finance. It also applies, for example, in the management of environmental systems, international relations, or cyberterrorism. In these application areas, this challenge was partially mastered.

The chapter is structured as follows. Section 2 describes the current micro-level regulatory approach to FinTech. At the core of this paradigm is the general division between the powers and responsibilities of private market participants on the one hand and the sovereign public in the form of various government agencies on the other. The private market participants essentially take on the primary, proactive, risk-generating role. The public sector has a secondary, reactive, risk-accommodating role. This dichotomy provides the basis for the regulation of new market entrants, such as FinTech. Regulatory requirements for financial firms are broadly divided into activity-based and entity-based regulations. The rough subdivision does not do justice to the activities of FinTech. Smart regulation seems to capture the specifics of FinTech better. However, three examples show that smart regulation also reaches its limits. Section 3 addresses structural developments. In recent years, a fusion of financial transactions, stock exchange trading, information theory, and communication technologies have taken place. The global digitization effects are due to a mutual entanglement and reinforcement of the financial and information economies. This development is due to the expansion of financial market capitalism. On this basis, new business models could be established and enforced. We are talking about the platformication of the economy. Section 4 highlights that wise regulation seems to grasp the evolution of platformication better. The macro-structural approach to regulation is at the heart of wise regulation. The unique features of FinTechs are growth, speed, trust, and transparency. Then the overarching principles of the alternative regulatory approach are listed. Developing an adaptive, proactive, structurally oriented, and participatory approach to FinTech requires a profound shift in the current understanding of the relationship between law, finance, and technology. Five regulatory measures represent the alternative regulatory approach. The measures relate to the introduction of central bank digital currency, the establishment of digital market infrastructure, the regulation of ecosystems, the regulation of technologies, and product licensing. The proposed measures meet the requirements of the favored macro approach, where the law is given priority over technology. Section 5 summarizes the chapter.

2. FinTech as a Regulatory Disruption

According to FSB (2017) FinTech stands for:

> Technology-enabled innovation in financial services that could result in new business models, applications, processes or products with an associated material effect on the provision of financial services (p. 7).

In practice, this term subsumes various digital assets, technologies, and infrastructures. Together, they are changing the way today's financial markets work. New technologies have a massive impact on how people make payments, manage investments, borrow and contract. Various technology companies are now entering the financial services market. On the one hand, there are the many thousands of small start-ups. On the other hand, there are large technology corporations such as Google, Apple, Facebook or Amazon (BigTech), which are now heavily involved in the financial sector. They are all changing the structural configuration and dynamics of the financial markets.

In general, FinTech developments are highlighted for their potential. For example, the efficiency of financial transactions increases by eliminating transaction frictions. Accelerating, simplifying, and cheapening financial transactions opens up new opportunities for financial inclusion and expands access to financial services (Philippon, 2019). FinTech seem to be able to transform financial market operations not only in terms of transaction efficiency but also in terms of the 'democratization' of finance. In the current discourse, the advantages and disadvantages of specific technological advances are assessed primarily on their potential impact on transaction partners' costs, convenience, or market access. From a supervisory perspective, the threats to financial stability, market integrity and consumer protection, the challenges to competition, data protection, and cybersecurity play an essential role.

2.1. *Technocratic view*

The rapid rise of FinTech accompanied by a multitude of legal and regulatory challenges over the past decade. Financial regulators worldwide have grappled with complex legal and policy issues arising from a variety of different FinTech applications. For example, there has been discussion about the economic functions and regulatory status of specific technology-based financial instruments such as crypto assets (BCBS, 2021). Such definitional issues culminate in extending supervisors' jurisdiction to unfamiliar products and services. Moreover, regulators are also entering new territory regarding the reliability and governance of the new type of market infrastructure. Various consumer and investor protection issues, prevention of financial crime, and enforcement of anti-money laundering regulations are also gaining importance.

In the background of legal and regulatory debates on these and other prudential issues, systemic risk and financial stability issues are increasingly on the FinTech agenda (FSB, 2017, 2019). Implications for monetary policy and structural changes in the overall economy are also on the minds of legislators and regulators.

However, the whole discussion goes within the existing technocratic paradigm of financial regulation. At the core of this paradigm is the general division between the powers and responsibilities of private market participants on the one hand and the sovereign public in the form of various government agencies on the other.[4] Omarova (2020a) states:

> Under its terms, private market actors retain control over substantive decisions on how to allocate financial capital to various productive uses — and thus the power to determine the overall volume and structure of financial claims in the system. The public, on the other hand, bears the primary responsibility for modulating credit-money aggregates and maintaining the overall stability of the financial system, in order to enable markets to function smoothly and efficiently (p. 80).

[4]Philippon (2016) argue 'that the current regulatory approach is subject to significant political economy and coordination costs, and therefore unlikely to deliver much structural change' (p. 15).

The private market participants essentially take on the primary, proactive, risk-generating role. The public sector has a secondary, reactive, risk-accommodating role. Micro-informational efficiency is the reason why private market participants take on this structural role (Shleifer, 2005). They have the information advantages 'on the ground' and can make better decisions about the risks and returns of specific financial transactions and products. Public authorities grant the ability to constrain the activities of private market participants if they lead to excessive system-wide risks.

Omarova (2020a) notes that this results in the technocratic model of financial regulation. By this, she means

> a cluster of certain core features of regulatory design and philosophy that systematically shape the substance and direction of regulatory action in the financial sector. Identifying these basic features, in turn, helps to expose the internal logic of the existing regulatory apparatus that makes certain regulatory outcomes more likely than others — and certain regulatory problems inherently more intractable than others (p. 80).

This principle of the prevailing regulatory philosophy shapes the structure and functioning of today's system of financial regulation. Figure 1 provides an overview of the development of financial regulation. These companies are authorized and supervised within the framework of clearly defined regulations. Licensing activities and supervision base on the products they offer and the activities they carry out, including the supervision of the processes in the financial companies. In perspective, regulation is changing towards ecosystems and interfaces (see Section 4).

Financial institutions (e.g., banks, securities brokers, insurers) and financial products (securities, banking products, insurance, commodity futures) are separated. The regulatory architecture consists of silos: separate authorities supervise formally separate parts of the financial sectors based on separate legal regulations (e.g., Capital Requirements Regulations for banks, Solvency for insurance companies). Within each regulatory silo, the respective supervisory authority (e.g., EBA, ESMA, EIOPA in the EU) clearly defines policy priorities. They reflect the legislative assessment of the core risks posed by the respective regulated entities and activities.

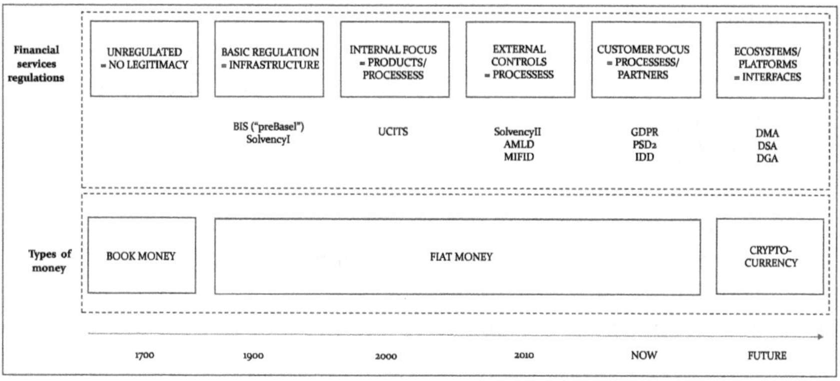

Figure 1. Evolution of financial services regulations and types of money.

Banks are subject to regulatory obligations that include minimum capital and liquidity requirements, restrictions on large exposures, and specific rules on corporate governance and remuneration schemes for decision-makers (Schmaltz *et al.*, 2014). Furthermore, banks are subject to additional regulations such as consumer protection, anti-money laundering (AML)/counter-terrorist financing (CFT), or business conduct. The rules apply to the various services offered by banks, including deposit-taking, lending, payments, and asset management.

Following the emergence of FinTech, no general adjustments have been made to the scope of the rules to reflect their activities as providers of financial services. A few exceptions introduce the category of digital banks (neo-banks) in some jurisdictions or regulations for crowdfunding platforms. The new regulatory categories for FinTech do not always aim to control the specific risks they pose but sometimes promote more competition or financial inclusion through (temporarily) lower requirements (see Section 2.3.1).

However, non-banks offering financial services (e.g., payments, loans, crowdfunding, asset management, investment advice) usually need a license. The type of license depends on the activity they carry out. For example, most large FinTech in the European Union and the US have licenses as payment service providers. In the EU, they are called payment institutions or e-money institutions, and in the US, they are called money transmitters. FinTech offering loans in the US (e.g., Quicken Loans) and China (e.g., Ant Group) have licenses as non-bank lenders. So far, FinTech and BigTech have generally not sought regular banking licenses. Exceptions exist for neo-banks (e.g., N26, Revolut, Monza). Under their current licenses, BigTech and FinTech are subject to regulatory requirements in consumer protection and AML/CFT. Sometimes the obligations also cover operational (especially cyber) resilience.

As far as competition is concerned, neither banks nor BigTech companies are subject to specific requirements that go beyond those arising from general antitrust legislation. (cf. Section 4.2.2). At the same time, some jurisdictions have adopted open banking laws to facilitate competition between banks and non-banks in the financial services market (e.g., Payment Service Directive 2 in the EU or FinTech Law in Mexico).

Banks are also increasingly realigning their business model. In this respect, a sure convergence between established banks and FinTech/BigTech is taking place. This fact refers to the concepts of open banking. Open banking defines as a service that makes consumer financial data available to third-party providers via APIs (application programming interfaces). The APIs enable consent-based data transfer of financial information, which is limited to the customer's name, account number, transaction data, and credit history. Platformication, on the other hand, is a new business model for banks (Carson *et al.*, 2021). This model drives close collaboration between traditional banks and innovative FinTech companies. The platform serves as a one-stop-shop for all financial services. The traditional pipeline business model, where the owner controls every aspect of the value chain, is replaced by the organizational structure of the platform (see Section 4). Different actors work together to fulfill a customer's need.[5]

The supervisory authorities' reluctance is currently justified because the scope of activities of FinTech is still very limited to the overall size of the financial services market. It recognizes that in some countries, there are already companies (e.g., Ant Group in China or Quicken Loans in the USA) that have already achieved

[5]See, for example, HSBC's digital banking platform.

a leading market position. Similarly, it predicts that BigTech companies may eventually achieve market dominance given significant economies of scale, data superiority, and the immense scope for network externalities.

Massive regulatory measures about the activities of BigTech in the financial sector are currently only observed in China (Frost *et al.*, 2019). According to the Chinese administration, BigTech need to avoid 'disorderly capital accumulation' to ensure China's economic and social security and enable fair competition. China has started surprisingly late to limit the market power of the BigTech. The government is now cracking down all the harder for it. The competition regulators are keeping a particularly close eye on digital financial service providers, especially the star of the industry: Ant Group, the FinTech offshoot of online retailer Alibaba. Ant Financial posed new challenges for the Chinese regulators, as many of its services do not fall within the scope of existing financial rules. At the core of the issue is whether Ant Financial should be an internet company or a bank. Ant Group must now restructure itself. Technology must not be an excuse to ignore legal, ethical, and other baselines. On the surface, it is about government control of the data the companies collect. An enormous fortune builds on this basis. Power belongs to the party, and China's internet boom has not changed that. The fact that the state monopolies remain untouched proves this. The full impact will keep the Ant leadership busy for a while. Ant Financial's other business plans, including international expansion, are on hold for now.

2.2. *Activity-based vs. entity-based regulation*

In financial regulation, social objectives such as financial stability, market integrity, or consumer protection take precedence over the promotion of competition in financial markets. The licensing requirements for these markets act as a kind of barrier to market entry. In the existing regulatory paradigm, achieving a level playing field (e.g., between banks and FinTech/BigTech) should therefore only be considered a desirable feature of the regulatory framework if other higher priority objectives are safely achieved (BCBS, 2018; Cornelli *et al.*, 2020).

Stulz (2019) believes that:

> Deregulation of banks for products supplied by non-banks as well as banks would also lead to a more level playing field. Any such evolution would reduce the regulatory cost advantage of FinTech firms (p. 92).

The regulatory requirements for financial companies roughly divide into activity-based and company-based regulations (Restoy, 2021):

- Activity-based rules consist of requirements that must be met by all institutions offering a particular service (e.g., lending, payment services, investment intermediation, investment advice).
- Enterprise-based rules consist of requirements imposed on institutions with a specific license or charter. The license or statute allows them to carry out a specific activity or combination of activities.[6]

The distinction between activity-based and company-based rules only makes sense if the companies engage in different types of regulated activities. On the other hand, if the firms engage in a combination of regulated activities and policy objectives are compromised. As a result, then the firm is subject to firm-based obligations. Most regulatory frameworks for the financial sector contain both activity-based and firm-based rules. Depending on the objectives pursued by the different regulations and activity-based, a firm-based or a mixed approach may be required (Restoy, 2021).

For example, there are areas of regulation for which an activity-based approach might be sufficient. These include, for example, consumer protection or AML/CFT. On the other hand, to the extent that risks arise from the vulnerability of an institution's balance sheets and threaten to cause distress, prudential regulation should follow a firm-based approach. The combination of activities performed by banks poses socially relevant risks that cannot fully be

[6]For example, money service providers in the United States or payment institutions in the European Union are legal entities authorized to offer a range of payment services. Similarly, institutions subject to banking supervision are called 'banks' in the US and 'credit institutions' in the EU. In both cases, these entities define in terms of institutions authorized to take deposits and make loans.

addressed by specific requirements for each service they provide. In particular, prudential regulation aims to mitigate the risks to financial stability arising from the maturity, liquidity, and other risk transformations that banks undertake through the combination of different activities. If other entities — such as FinTech and BigTech — do not engage in risk transformation, it would not be justified in the existing regulatory paradigm to require them to comply with similar prudential requirements.

However, other areas, such as operational resilience, for which an entity-based approach (in combination with activity-based rules) might be justified not only for banks but also for other financial services providers. The significance of an operational incident in a given company depends on the activity in which it is engaged.

For BigTech offering a wide range of services to a large number of players (e.g., cloud services), company-based rules could be justified. Also, for the objective of the competition, a combination of activity-based and undertaking-based rules may seem appropriate. This mix concerns the prevention of cartels, conditions for mergers and acquisitions, and controls to prevent abuse of a dominant position. It should emphasize that preventing abuse of a dominant position requires a more company-based approach (see Section 4.2.3). Anti-competitive practices can arise from the way companies combine different activities.

The central argument of the current regulatory approach is that the safety and soundness of any institution depend on all the activities carried out. To the extent that the combination of these activities also generates risks, a firm-by-firm approach is justified. There is still much hesitation about whether a stricter firm-based approach might require large non-banks (BigTech). Even in China, there is no consensus on whether an enterprise approach should apply to Alibaba and Tencent.

In particular, operational incidents on platforms offering a wide range of financial and non-financial services can cause systemic (and potentially global) disruption. Restoy (2021) states:

> This may deserve ad hoc regulatory attention and, eventually, the expansion of the notion of what is considered 'systemic', which currently applies, in practice, only to traditional financial institutions or market infrastructures so that it includes this type of firm (p. 15).

The challenge would be to monitor safeguards for operational resilience for BigTech companies with global operations. A significant strengthening of the current arrangements for cross-border regulatory and supervisory cooperation would be the result.

Specific rules for BigTech could include obligations. They range from interoperability requirements to limits on bundling services to prohibitions on eligibility criteria that unfairly discriminate against interested providers. Equally conceivable are restrictions (or even bans) on selling their products on the platforms they own. Even more complex is the issue of data use, which affects BigTech in its various activities. This extensive data availability is a source of competitive advantage over other players (such as banks) in the market for certain financial services.

Restricting the use of data would indeed ensure a high standard of data protection. Inevitably, however, this would lead to inefficiencies that may ultimately harm consumers. One approach could be to facilitate data portability. This approach is the basic idea behind open banking regulation. Specific company-based rules on the obligation to share data for large technology companies could help address the potential market failure and promote competition.

Let us come to an interim conclusion. In the existing regulatory paradigm, creating a level playing field in providing financial services is a desired outcome of the regulatory framework. This framework includes facilitating the orderly entry of new participants (FinTech and BigTech). Market entry expands consumer choice, promotes innovation, and strengthens competition. Unjustified discrepancies in regulatory obligations are to be avoided. New entrants should not jeopardize the competitive position of incumbents (such as banks).

However, promoting a level playing field is not the primary objective of financial regulation. Policy objectives such as financial stability, market integrity, and consumer protection are at the top of the priority list (Lemma, 2020). The assessment of the respective policy objectives may lead to a combination of activity-based and firm-based rules. In consumer protection or the fight against money laundering and terrorist financing, an activity-based approach may be sufficient to achieve the primary objectives. In other areas, such as financial stability, an enterprise-based approach is essential. In the third group of policy areas, such as operational resilience and competition, regulations require a combination of activity-based and firm-based rules. In these cases, it is necessary to address the specific risks that may emanate from different actors (Restoy, 2021).

2.3. *Smart regulation: Specific FinTech approaches*

If there is a discussion about the overarching principles appropriate for regulating the risks posed by FinTech, one quickly arrives at the metaphor of 'smart' regulation (Zetzsche *et al.*, 2017). Such a type of regulation describes a series of appropriate regulatory micro-optimizations or adaptations of regulatory requirements to the unique characteristics of each specific FinTech product or activity (Ehrentraud *et al.*, 2020b). In each case, the responses are transaction-oriented and guided by specific technologies. Omarova (2020b) highlights:

> This makes it an easy sell from the perspective of regulatory continuity (p. 35).

At the institutional level, cooperation between financial institutions and FinTech companies is to be promoted above all (Enriques and Ringe, 2020). According to the supervisors, this creates greater regulatory certainty.

In terms of substantive policy, various options are currently at the center of the FinTech agenda. These include, above all, regulatory experiments with sandboxes and special chartering regimes. They aim to provide FinTech firms with a steady path to complete legitimacy. The different approaches essentially follow the explanations of Omarova (2020b).

2.3.1. *The experimentation approach: Regulatory sandboxes*

The term 'regulatory sandbox' refers to programs run by regulators. Sandboxes provide a 'safe space' for FinTech firms and financial companies to test authentic products for real customers. Firms benefit from an exemption or significant relaxation of otherwise applicable regulations. Regulatory sandboxes design to support consumer-friendly financial innovation, facilitate financial inclusion, improve the efficiency and competitiveness of domestic financial institutions, and increase regulators' understanding of emerging innovative technologies. FinTech sandboxes also promote experimental learning strategies on the part of regulators. There is wide variation in the specific design and implementation of regulatory sandboxes around the world. This chapter does not have to present the regional details.

The regulatory sandbox strategy generally attracts the following criticisms. One fundamental problem is determining whether and to what extent a particular FinTech product is genuinely new or 'innovative'. This assignment justifies the preference for a regulatory sandbox. At the instrumental level, assessing the novelty and social desirability of FinTech products requires that financial regulators have sufficient breadth and depth of technical expertise. However, the financial functions of a particular FinTech product can rarely be separated from technological features (Omarova, 2020b).

Related to this is the question of how to define 'financial innovation'. It should be assessed not only from the perspective of private benefit but also as a matter of public interest. However, introducing such a macro-level perspective complicates the seemingly technical decision on whether a particular FinTech product is sufficiently innovative for the sandbox test. According to Omarova (2020b), regulators rarely conduct such normative analysis.

Another potential criticism of FinTech sandboxes points to the downside of broad regulatory discretion regarding the approval of individual companies. On the one hand, some see this as a distortion of the market and competition. The consequence would be that the financial supervisory authorities could include different firms in the sandbox. The practical result of such 'openness' would be a relaxation of existing regulatory requirements for all and thus an effective dismantling of the existing system of financial regulation.

Brown and Piroska (2021) argue:

> The sandbox approach instead of regulating FinTech, is involved in riskwashing FinTech. A sandbox engages in riskwashing to the extent that it provides a stamp of marketability for FinTech without being able to control for systemic risk, the lack of transparency of its operation creates an opportunity for framing FinTech's riskiness, and its involvement in the creation of an adequate risk-profile makes it incapable of independently evaluating that same risk-profile (p. 6).

Establishing a regulatory sandbox is an effective way to generate usable empirical data for better regulatory decisions.

However, its effectiveness depends on the specific design features of each sandbox program. Evaluation criteria for FinTech products in the sandbox would need to accurately capture the impact of these products on consumer protection, financial stability, or market integrity. This point is hardly possible. Otherwise, the data would not be a reliable indicator of how the product behaves outside the sandbox (with/without effect). Even more important is that testing the systemic effects of certain FinTech products at the macro level will hardly be possible. In this respect, the sandbox also remains only an instrument in the existing micro-regulatory framework.

2.3.2. *The incorporation approach: FinTech charters*

Another instrument of regulatory responses to FinTech innovations is the granting of special licenses to FinTech firms. This issue is a particular regulatory strategy. New market participants are to be integrated into the existing regulatory systems in this way. The instrument is mainly used in the USA. Here, many core financial activities require special authorization and supervision by one or more financial regulators. For example, no company can legally engage in the 'business of banking' without obtaining a banking license from the Office of the Comptroller of the Currency (OCC) or a federal banking regulator.

The 'FinTech charters' were first proposed by the OCC during the Obama administration. The charters aimed to allow FinTech to offer credit or payment products without insurance from the Federal Deposit Insurance Corporation (FDIC) and be under federal supervision instead of complying with state banking regulations. The OCC wants to help FinTech overcome the current requirements of securing state-level licenses with a 'special bank charter'. However, a 2019 court ruling limits the OCC's chartering ability to banks that take deposits. FinTech are currently not allowed to take deposits or seek insurance coverage from the FDIC. Although the OCC has encouraged FinTech to apply for chartering, no applications have yet been submitted. Thus, the instrument has not yet progressed beyond the conceptual level.

However, as non-deposit-taking institutions, FinTech firms with such an OCC charter would not be considered 'banks' under the Bank Holding Company Act of 1956 (BHC Act). The BHC Act significantly restricts the ability of companies to engage in non-banking activities. The BHC Act implements the US principle of separation of banking and commerce. The ability to avoid onerous restrictions on non-financial activities of the parent companies of authorized FinTech firms is therefore of particular importance to BigTech firms. Critics of FinTech charters argue that this instrument allows circumventing state regulations (e.g., interest rate caps). The potential beneficiaries of the regulatory relaxations would then include the BigTech that have already launched bank-like offerings on the market or have announced plans to do so. Allowing BigTech and other large companies to set up banks would massively change the banking landscape in the US.

The critical issue that remains open is whether financial technology companies should be regulated at the federal level. This regulation would require a very different type of regulation than if regulation were to occur at the national level. Thus, similar questions arise connected with FinTech charters as with regulatory sandboxes (cf. Section 2.3.1). It is not easy to imagine that an innovative product can be adequately assessed for systemic impact at the federal level.

Despite the promise of federal primacy and regulatory certainty, the practical benefits of OCC charters have not been apparent to date. State licenses and charters have limited legal reach. Individual states can only cover activities that affect their residents. As a result, a particular state regulatory regime offers limited benefits to FinTech firms seeking a national or global presence. The ability of technology-driven financial markets to cross territorial boundaries requires expanding the field of vision far beyond state borders (Omarova, 2020b).

However, there are also institutional concerns. The strictly subdivided US supervisory structure offers little flexibility in terms of the basic substantive requirements of the new charter types. For example, a 'special' banking license must contain certain essential elements of a traditional banking license. At the same time, incremental modification of various long-standing regulatory forms can be a proven method for incremental change. However, maintaining regulatory continuity may not always be the most effective response to changing market conditions. This fact is especially actual when it is disruptive, such as technology developments.

2.3.3. *The accommodation approach: RegTech and others*

The third category of approaches to FinTech regulation is about RegTech (regulatory technology). As with FinTech, it is about the use of innovative technology. However, RegTech focuses on the more effective and efficient mapping, fulfillment, and documentation of regulatory requirements supported by innovative technologies. Due to compliance requirements, RegTech is sometimes also referred to as CompTech (compliance technology). The term SupTech (Supervisory Technology) distinguishes it from RegTech. SupTech applications support the work of supervisory authorities. They can be understood as a counterpart to RegTech.

RegTech applications could enable companies to automate manual (sub-)processes and fulfill their regulatory requirements more precisely and with less effort. Financial institutions can not only realize speed advantages and a lower error rate with RegTech. They could also save on personnel costs. Beyond automation aspects, RegTech plays a role in the digital transformation of supervisory, control, and support functions. We currently see applications in compliance management, risk management, customer verification, fraud detection, and many other areas in practice.

Supervisors must continuously monitor RegTech developments, as the proper performance of functions requires a comprehensive understanding of relevant solutions in practice. This point is positive in the first place, as it means that the supervisor will inevitably have to deal with the new technologies. However, RegTech applications can pose a variety of risks due to technical and procedural designs. The high degree of data-drivenness of individual RegTech applications requires high data quality. Deficiencies in the data basis could lead to the derivation of inappropriate or erroneous causal representations. Risks could also arise from black-box algorithms. To the extent that companies or supervisors can no longer understand or at least comprehend how an algorithm works, there is a risk of undetectable wrong decisions. Furthermore, RegTech uses to uncover and exploit possible regulatory-supervisory loopholes in the sense of 'gaming the system'. This issue can even lead to the systematic optimization of RegTech applications to conceal reportable events.

A key feature of SupTech is that it potentially enables regulators to synchronize their data collection and supervisory monitoring with the internal data management of individual companies.

That can be done, for example, by making regulations machine-readable and by using software that is interoperable with companies' internal compliance software. This idea puts SupTech in a role where financial regulation and supervision can be made in 'real-time' in the future.

There is a lot to criticize in the application of RegTech and SupTech. The criticism starts with the complexity of financial market regulations. The cause of the high complexity of regulation does not address with these applications. Instead, the supervisors want to keep the rulebook under control with the help of technology. This point brings to mind the speech 'The Dog and the Frisbee' by Andrew Haldane (2012). He used the image of a dog trying to catch a Frisbee. The exact calculation of the trajectory requires an understanding of complex relationships.

Nevertheless, a Border Collie is quite good at catching the flying disc. The dog simply follows simple rules of thumb. Ten years on, regulation is even more complicated than it was then. Ironically, regulators today want to rely on technology to keep up with more complex regulations. Barriers to entry into the financial market are likely to be raised further, while the impact on financial stability is more than uncertain. With different technologies, authorities will not be able to manage the exploding complexity of regulation.

The process of context-specific assessment of individual companies' compliance with laws and regulations requires continuous quantitative and qualitative analysis. If this kind of holistic judgment is made through an algorithmic 'matching' of standardized micro-level data with specific machine-readable rules, there is a risk that contextual 'proportionality' would be lost. But not only that. The practical effectiveness of financial regulation and supervision also decreases dramatically. Adapting to FinTech-driven financial market developments, however, requires precisely the opposite (Omarova, 2020b).

Regulators around the world are already working on various ways to accommodate technology-driven market developments. These include, for example, the creation of national digital identity systems, which, among other things, should make it much easier for FinTech firms to comply with AML regulations. Alternatively, to mention the creation of uniform standards for different aspects of online transactions, the clarification of ambiguities through regulatory guidelines on specific topics, and the elimination of overlaps in existing legislation.

The present three approaches to FinTech regulation have shown that legislators or regulators rely mainly on existing regulatory tools and techniques (Omarova, 2020b). These instruments aim to absorb and integrate new companies and activities into the established regulatory systems (Buckley *et al.*, 2020). A focused analysis of these strategies reveals both the inherent complexity of FinTech as a subject of financial regulation. However, it also reveals the importance of regulators' ability and willingness to address the challenges.

In summary, the current model of financial regulation systematically favors technical expertise over normative engagement. The micro-transactional perspective is paramount. Working methods are based on identifying and isolating discrete micro-level phenomena and decision points and various technical tools. In this way, specific market inefficiencies are to be addressed.

Regulators are generally cautious about FinTech. They fear prematurely 'stifling' financial innovation. The provision of infrastructural support for technology-driven market developments and a more technology-friendly design of financial regulation intends to force this process. However, the authorities remain in the role of outside observers. At first glance, this cautious approach seems understandable. However, this reactive attitude can also be interpreted as the fact that the currently dominant technocratic model of financial regulation has reached its limits.

The first voices are emerging that question the existing regulatory paradigm due to BigTech platforms (e.g., Crisanto *et al.*, 2021). The focus is on four key characteristics of BigTech: network effect, gatekeeping function, number of users engaged, and level of technological investment. There is a tendency to consider specific company-based regulations for big Tech platforms that complement general competition law (see Section 4.2.2). Certain practices that could be considered anti-competitive should then be restricted ex-ante. The approach is currently discussed in the US House of Representatives, the European Union, and China (Restoy, 2021).

The unique characteristics of BigTech may justify a comprehensive policy approach. Such an approach could focus not only on individual BigTech companies and their activities. It also encompasses how individual BigTech firms work together in the background to provide services to their customers on the BigTech platform. Criteria are established that qualify a company as BigTech. In order to achieve these goals, more information about BigTech corporations is necessary. It seems that a more macro-systemic perspective is taken specifically on BigTech. Nevertheless, thinking about these companies remains in the existing model that prioritizes technical expertise and a micro-transactional perspective. The following shows that the developments of financial capitalism require a macro-structural perspective.

3. Structural Transformation of the Financial System

3.1. *Financial markets as an information standard*

For four decades, we have been observing the 'financialization' of economies, of economic and social infrastructures. The term financialization stands for a newer type of capitalism in which financial markets exert a growing influence on the real economy. However, it also reveals a gradual change in the organization of governmental techniques.

The following basic features should be emphasized. The protracted consolidation of the current financial regime cannot be grasped with the dichotomous opposition of market and state, politics, and economy. The liberalization of markets and especially financial markets, cannot be understood as a retreat of regulatory authorities. On the contrary, the demand for regulatory instruments and regulatory agencies increased proportionally to the privatization of state tasks and enterprises. The enforcement and legitimization of market mechanisms have led to a multiplicity of public, para-state, and private agencies.

Government functions have become dispersed at different levels. Market forces are forced through a proliferation of regulatory bodies. Market dynamics and actors, on the other hand, point to the densification of regulatory systems. Regulations are becoming more extensive and complex. Government functions and market-based modes of action exist in a bi-polar internal relationship to each other. This point is especially true in the financial sector. Sovereign powers, government action, and market operations intertwine. The dynamic of finance capital permeates the static of political architectures. It is breaking away from territorial ties.

Financialization catalyzes the transition from a geopolitical to a geo-economic order. The financial regime thus possesses an inter- or trans-governmental power to act. This power complements or replaces the formal authority of governments. The distinction and the previous balance between public and private are undermined. Thus, the financial regime can claim the character of a fourth power, alongside the legislative, executive, and judicial powers of government. This development has, in turn, strengthened the capacities with which the issues of the financial sphere occupy the social and political fields. However, it is too short-sighted to state a weakening of governmental practices. Instead, there is a restructuring in their goals, maxims, and procedures.

The dominance of the current financial regime cannot be explained without the symbioses and convergences between financial capital and information technologies. Financial innovations reflect in information systems. They then create the need for technological platforms. The consortium of financial economics, information theory, and technology prepare the breeding ground for maximum liquidity, optimized price discovery, and efficient data traffic. The result is the consolidation of financial markets. Information uses to link economic room for maneuver with the operational possibilities of technical systems.

We are experiencing a historic transformation in the financial markets. The currency standard (fiat money) is no longer the decisive norm but the information standard. The stabilization of the credit and money economy is no longer dependent on the conversion of book money. Instead, there is a continuous exchange between money and information. Prices on the financial markets are condensed information about assets. At the same time, they compile information about the future of prices. In payment transactions, information about money is more important than money itself. The market marks units of value as units of information. Efficient markets are markets of efficient distribution of information.[7] Competition appears as a call for informational competition. Payments and capital movements take over the function of information production.

[7]At this point, we cannot discuss the market efficient hypothesis. Markets can reduce information to the form of information itself, namely price differences. Stock exchanges and financial markets are coherently organized opinion markets. Opinion has itself become a central functional element.

This spectacular structure is not about establishing a justified knowledge of the true or fundamental value of things. Instead, it is about how valuations form from opinions. Financial markets operate as an ongoing voting process. The resonances of collective views that have coagulated into a norm circulate in prices. With each payment, a conventionalization of decision and judgment profiles takes place.

By the informatization of the financial markets, we, therefore, mean the fusion of financial transactions, stock exchange trading, information theory, and communication technologies. The global digitization effects are due to a mutual entanglement and reinforcement of the financial and information economies. This development is due to the expansion of financial market capitalism. The cheap money policy of the last decade has also created favorable opportunities for value extraction. The result was a cyclical upswing in the financial, real estate, and technology markets.

3.2. *Platformication*

The computerization of the financial sector and the financialization of the information economy created the conditions for establishing and implementing new business models. We are talking about the platform economy. Demand-oriented economies of scale characterize platform economies in information networks. They increase the effectiveness of user activities by leveraging user activities within the platform and amplify the effectiveness of pull factors and inclusion forces. The result is highly concentrated market structures. The technological and financial-economic architecture of platforms enables value-added production. The production of surplus-value takes place through external and internal access to entities that are not yet commodified. It is no more than a question of how the general availability of information products produced with minimal marginal costs can be profitably scarce.[8] Platform companies intertwine with the

---

[8]The economic principle expresses a specific theory of value. In classical economics, these reflect the economic principle of reproduction; in neoclassical economics, it is the scarcity of goods, and in Keynesian economics, the principle is expressed in the scarcity of money. These budgetary restrictions seem to have become obsolete. Now it is a question of economizing the limited availability of information goods. They form the budget constraint of financial capitalism.

current economic and financial order by implementing themselves as markets. Staab (2019) calls these proprietary markets. The goal is not maximum production but the capitalization of scarce information goods.

The data-generating applications of platform companies are proliferating. Software and hardware permeate the analog world. Search engines are expanding into hardware manufacturing, e-commerce, and financial markets. Smartphone manufacturers are entering the market with streaming and financial services. Social media offer data, information, and financial products and dabble in payment systems. A blending of industries is taking place.

Infrastructures and dependencies distribute with all these products and services. Socio-technical ecosystems or meta-platforms are emerging (cf. Section 4.2.4). These companies structure the internet as a system of hierarchized markets. Through their expansion strategies, through investments and acquisitions, they have continuously expanded the spectrum of offerings. Through network effects, a broad inclusion of users and consumers has been achieved. They mediate between producers and consumers; they manage and generate competition, and they generate profits as rents. Through the combination of proprietary infrastructures and scalable digital goods, they can expand the market function with insignificant marginal costs.

This business model of BigTech guarantees diverse information controls. They create the asymmetries that ensure the scarcity of scarce information goods (Staab, 2019):

- Data control: Extraction and appropriation of user, vendor, and market data;
- Access controls: Market participation, relating to the exclusion of competition and variation of thresholds for producers and consumers;
- Price controls: Prioritization of own offers over product copies to the personalization of purchase prices; and
- Performance controls: Evaluation and assessment procedures for products, services, or work processes.

Platform companies turn out to be standardized technical-economic systems. The decentralized coordination of network-like distributed interfaces takes place through central control. The associated machine operations such as tracking, tracing, targeting, ranking, scoring, mapping, profiling understands as elements of algorithmic management — the number of communication events on the platforms transforms into patterns. The patterns can be sorted according to significant frequencies, relationship densities, trends, or expected courses.

While liberal market theories have been struggling since the 1970s with solving and remedying asymmetric information distribution in markets (Stiglitz, 2000, 2002), they are now concerned with the systematic production of informational asymmetries. With platform business strategies, control over information and markets has become a defining productive force. These features reinforce that geo-economic order is characterized less by competing corporations than by pooled strategies of solvent financial investors.

The proprietary markets of the platform industry have nothing to do with the liberal model of supposedly neutral markets, which one wanted to understand as subjects of superior knowledge. In addition to enormous economic and political interventions (e.g., private appropriation of line networks or the abolition of net neutrality in the USA), some systemic, technological, and structural moments have made the specific control procedures of the platform companies possible. It was only in the socio-economic milieu of proprietary markets and platform business models that the concurrence of communication and control gave rise to the shape of concrete machines. With these machines, informational goods simultaneously produce efficient surveillance products. That applies to recording payment flows through payment systems and the centralization of data extraction in cloud platforms. The surveillance goods produce through control contracts — in exchange for benefits, gratifications, services, and applications of all kinds. It is not least these developments that have generated the private-public interdependencies that manifest themselves in the seamless transitions between technical, business, and governmental strategies of control. A new kind of governance is emerging. It presents itself in the form of the proliferation of new control practices or the multiple and informal mergers between public and private actors under the sign of the financial and information regime. It is also evident in the dynamics of platform companies that establish pseudo- and par-astatal structures. More or less sharp boundaries between political and state supervision and market processes are shifting into the interior of market activity.

There is a strong resemblance to an early capitalist, mercantilist consortia (Vogl, 2021).

Wie die Finanzwirtschaft von den Möglichkeiten der Informationsökonomie angezogen platform companies are now pushing into the financial business. The lucrative projects to create private payment and money systems are taking on a leading function. For example, payment service offerings have long been among the US and Chinese platform companies (Apple Pay, Google Pay, Amazon Pay, Facebook Pay, WhatsApp Pay, PayPal, Ali Pay, Wechat Pay). They offer the advantage of providing the most reliable data for the targeted placement of products and advertising. In addition, they can be used to monitor decentralized payment transactions centrally.

PayPal had already set out with the claim to create a kind of 'internet currency' to replace the dollar in international payment transactions. PayPal and others have built up various alternative payment systems in the shadow of the existing banking infrastructure. However, the build-up happened rather inconspicuously. As Katharina Pistor (2021) writes, this was both a strength and a weakness: it allowed new platforms to expand without incurring the wrath of regulators, but it also made them dependent on existing institutions and easy to copy.

Subsequently, there were always private initiatives by platform companies. One of the specifications was the creation of the Libra Association in Geneva by Facebook's subsidiary. Calibra applied for a payment system license from the Swiss financial regulator in May 2020. Even though the now renamed Diem Project in Switzerland has folded its tents, this initiative shows the way forward.[9]

Facebook, as a latecomer, hoped to use its comparative advantage as a digital platform with more than 2.3 billion users to bring digital currencies into the mainstream. Building on the fad of 'stable coins', Libra was pegged to a basket of currencies issued by countries with a reputation for stability and reliable backing from central banks. In such an ecosystem, the axis of the two-tier banking system (central banks, commercial banks) was to be bypassed. The backlash from

[9]The issuing entity has moved from Switzerland to the United States since April 2020, where it has partnered with Silvergate Bank. A token that complies with US banking regulations is now to be issued there.

regulators was swift and fierce. National authorities quickly formed a united front, clearly seeing the initiative as a threat to their monetary sovereignty. Pistor (2021) highlights: 'Above all, it is risky business to reach for the crown jewel of state sovereignty — in this case, money'.

Nevertheless, the following remains: The planned currency was not conceived and regulated as a public good. Instead, a financial ecosystem was to be established; influential capital providers would privately own that. The decentralized payment system, including the technology of distributive networks, would be re-centralized by the shareholders. Again, the argument was to make international payments more efficient. That is not just about using distributive network architecture and eliminating third parties and intermediaries. Above all, it is about a reorganization of the social contract.

The cryptographic operations used to decentrally process and authenticated the list of records or blocks have the character of smart contracts (Berg *et al.*, 2019). In the contracts, this consent of all participants or co-players is automatically documented with each transaction. This machine consensus building through transmission protocols follows a self-executing contract profile. That bypasses conventional juridical authentications. It thus comes into tension with existing national legal situations. De-state private law is automated. The currency also creates quasi-sovereign machine structures. The creation of channels for financial transactions should result in information and capital returns from Facebook. In the end, a hybrid construct would have emerged that would have vacillated between payment service, investment fund, bank, and currency system. The construct would have evaded all national and supranational control bodies. In any case, it would not have fallen within the direct remit of banking supervisory authorities.

So it is not so much the questions of financial stability, market integrity, consumer protection, money laundering, or terrorist financing at the evaluation's forefront. Instead, it is about new forms of money in the wake of large, systemically relevant social and economic platforms. They inevitably cross national borders. The relationship between payments and user data is being redefined. At stake is nothing less than the redesign of the architecture of the international monetary system and the role of state currencies.

The cartography of national currency units doubled by a geoeconomic distribution of Digital Currency Areas (DCAs). There, transactions are guaranteed with private means of payment that are valid either — as in Tencent and Ant Financial — within commercial networks. Whether Facebook, Amazon, or Alibaba — it has enormous value for platforms to introduce their tokens, for example, an Amazon dollar. The many users then only have to be persuaded to use these tokens for money transfers and payments (Cong, 2020). Combining transaction data with user behavior and consumption decisions is a trustworthy source of value creation for platforms. Platforms can screen users much more closely than banks could in the past. They can create detailed profiles because they do not just have payment data and income data but understand consumption and lifestyle. It is worth noting here that the much-discussed debate on online privacy is only made much more urgent by trends in digital money.

However, money from users is also a cheap source of funding. Under certain circumstances, platforms can use the deposits to finance investments. This source is simply cheaper than issuing bonds. Buyers of bonds charge interest in return for borrowed money. Users on the platform would probably charge lower interest or none because they receive a service in return — they get an efficient means of payment to send money back and forth.

Alternatively, as in the case of Libra/Diem, platforms may rise to form convertible or competing currencies. The horizon is opening up for digital dollarization. Private means of payment and units of account circulating on digital networks across national borders must have underlying assets to operate simultaneously in different currency systems (Brunnermeier *et al.*, 2021).

An inversion in the hierarchy of financial transactions can be observed: Payment systems are no longer dependent on intermediation between banks. Instead, traditional banking functions of financial technology are taken over by payment services and platform companies.

The term 'decentralized finance' (DeFi) should be mentioned in this context (Wharton School, 2021). This term refers to a unique ecosystem in the blockchain area that enables digital financial services (Berg *et al.*, 2019). Based mostly on the Ethereum blockchain, decentralized applications (DApps) can be explicitly created for the financial sector. The unique feature here is that these DApps can be programmed as desired. Different building blocks can be put together like in a Lego box. Once the DApp implements on the blockchain, it runs independently and decentrally, depending on its design. A DeFi DApp, an assemblage of DeFi Smart Contracts, runs completely independent of banks, is accessible 24/7, and cannot be switched off centrally. All that is required to participate in DeFi services is an internet-enabled device and a wallet. The wallet acts as a kind of bank account on which cryptocurrencies such as Bitcoin or Ethereum can be held. Each person can create as many wallets as they want.

4. Wise Regulation: A Normative Regulatory Framework

How are these structural developments to be addressed? There is not space here to develop a consistent regulatory framework in contrast to the existing regulatory paradigm, the outlines of a macro-structural framework for FinTech and BigTech to develop. In the beginning, the challenges associated with FinTech are presented (Omarova, 2020a). That follows by overarching principles of such a new paradigm. Finally, five different regulatory approaches present. They partly base on initiatives that already observe in practice to some extent.

4.1. *FinTech challenges*

4.1.1. *Growth*

The technology-driven growth in the scale and scope of the financial system brings with it a potentially dramatic increase in the scale and scope of the regulatory oversight zone. That has consequences for regulators positioned along familiar 'functional' lines to license and regulate banks, investment firms, insurance companies, fund managers, and other traditional 'financial intermediaries'. In contrast, most of the new FinTech firms do not act as financial intermediaries. The start-ups, in particular, have no established business history or organizational resources to ensure compliance with financial laws and regulations. By breaking through the regulatory fence around the financial system, FinTech are taking the task of protecting that system and ensuring proper governance to a qualitatively new level (Omarova, 2020a).

BigTech firms are causing an even more significant challenge for regulators. The dominance of BigTech in their respective markets gives them an extraordinary advantage as financial services providers. These potentially unprecedented economies of scale reinforce both the microeconomic attractiveness and the macroeconomic impact of cross-sector conglomerates.[10] Crucially, they also understand and monitor the structural power dynamics in non-financial markets, an increasingly important part of the previously narrowly specialized financial regulation and supervision (see Section 3).

Another challenge is the rapid growth in the volume and variety of technology-based financial products and services. FinTech companies are offering more and more financial apps and other products to more and more people. There is a risk of potentially abusive or fraudulent market conduct. Regulators must adapt to a much larger, more complex, and inherently fluid transaction space. In this space lurks the loss or conversion of customer funds, misuse of personal data and identity theft, money laundering, the financing of criminal activity, and numerous other problems.

The universe to be regulated is entirely digitized, data-driven, and structurally diverse. These characteristics require an increase in the legal and institutional capacity of regulators. Crucially, building FinTech-enabled regulatory capacity must be both quantitative and qualitative. More human, technological, and economic resources are needed to keep pace with market developments and enforce the game's rules under constantly changing conditions. The authorities need more extensive and flexible legal instruments and administrative powers. That is the only way to ensure that emerging systemic problems and cross-sector dependency identifies and address.

4.1.2. *Speed*

FinTech is making the financial system faster. At the macro-systemic level, the potential increase in the processing speed of financial transactions and the overall speed of trading in financial markets creates several regulatory challenges. The most significant systemic impact is the potential increase in the amplitude, suddenness, and

[10] Whether the existing antitrust laws or the European Digital Market Act are an adequate response remains to be seen (cf. Section 4.2.3).

severity of market-wide asset price fluctuations. A system based on instantaneous trading of digital assets is inherently more volatile and prone to more violent cycles (Omarova, 2020a). The developments around Bitcoin are just the tip of the iceberg. Price signals are instantaneous. Market reactions to such signals are likely to be rapid, massive, and self-reinforcing. In an entirely frictionless world of digitally controlled transactions, openly speculative trading will also become faster, cheaper, and more voluminous. That is also because access to the stock market is becoming easier and easier through broker apps such as Robinhood and Trade Republic. This issue was most recently evident at the end of January 2021, when numerous small investors joined forces and arranged to buy shares in concert. The group targeted GameStop, a stock disproportionately shorted by hedge funds. FinTech can unlock the potential for speculation in financial assets on an extraordinary scale. Given the infinitely shortened reaction time, large-scale speculative trades will effectively set the pace and direction for all trades in a given market.

The change in market dynamics also inevitably leads to a change in the role of central banks, which are responsible for safeguarding financial stability. The increased vulnerability of the financial system to sudden asset price fluctuations calls for a public market-shaping institution. Such an institution should be able to take immediate action at a truly market-wide level. Central banks need discretionary room for maneuver. Moreover, timely action in the context of smooth transactions often means acting pre-emptively and proactively (adaptive regulation and supervision). Authorities need to leave their external observer role and act directly in the relevant markets. Such an expansion of the market-safeguarding capacities of central banks and other public actors is a complex and resource-intensive undertaking. The requirement is also partly in contrast to the previous rule-bound action of most central banks.

4.1.3. *Trust*

FinTech is changing the collective understanding of the financial system as a particular form of applied information technology. That is best seen at the transaction level, where algorithms are increasingly replacing human decision-making. Financial market participants are expected to understand how a particular computer code works or trust the programmers' technical expertise and personal integrity (Finn, 2017).

The main challenge for financial regulators is to develop new methods. These methods must recognize, monitor, and potentially counteract the new dynamics of decision control and market power in the financial system. However, this challenge involves more than just writing new rules or collecting new data. It requires financial regulators and supervisors to learn to operate outside their traditional areas of expertise. The accuracy of regulatory assessments of systemic risk will increasingly depend on specific skills. These skills include understanding the assumptions and distributional preferences built into various computer programs. However, it also involves grasping the direct and indirect effects of complex technical decisions on the structure and integrity of the financial market. Supervisors need to understand, isolate and target the limitations and vulnerabilities of different complex technologies, such as their dependence on data quality and their potential to reproduce identity-based biases in decision-making. Interdisciplinary collaboration within agencies is essential (Omarova, 2020a).

Again, investments in regulatory capacity need to be made. Investments relate to technological tools to enable regulators to keep pace with market developments. Just relying on RegTechs is not enough. It also requires regulators to invest heavily in developing deep in-house expertise in computer programming, data analytics, and other technical areas (digital literacy). A more tech-centric, code-driven financial industry requires a more robust and coherent normative framework for its regulation.

4.1.4. *Transparency*

The FinTech wave continues the same trend towards an increasingly virtualized, highly fragmented, interconnected, and fragile financial market. Nonetheless, recent leaps in technological innovation reinforce these long-standing trends in financial markets and raise the associated transparency and governance issues to a qualitatively new level. ABCDs enable the potentially externally unimpeded creation, pooling, and layering of digital assets that trade on virtually infinitely scalable digital markets. That makes it more challenging to see through the many layers of financial claims in an algorithm-dependent, pyramid-like structure to assess and manage risk.

In the borderless and hyper-fast world of modern finance, the value and risk of each firm's assets and liabilities are increasingly directly dependent on systemic, market-wide dynamics. At the same time, the structural complexity and speed of contagion in technology-driven financial markets render many existing market-wide coordination and governance mechanisms potentially ineffective (see Section 3).

From a regulatory perspective, the reduced transparency and governability of the financial system pose a particularly significant challenge. Among other things, they raise the question of the limits of disclosure-based regulation. The declining effectiveness of disclosure increases the pressure on policymakers and regulators to develop an alternative — more direct and proactive — mechanisms for monitoring and intervening in the financial system. That raises the question of whether the image of a 'rational' investor can still be maintained. Regulatory instruments should therefore be fundamentally structural and not purely transactional. For example, the operations of critical structural nodes would need to be identified and monitored, such as large transaction platforms, liquidity providers, and operational standard setters and data validators (Omarova, 2020a).

4.2. *Macro-structural approach*

An effective regulatory response to this systemic change must start at a systemic level and not only at a transactional level. In the following section, various proposals of appropriate FinTech regulation present and discussed.

Improved regulatory tools must deliberately and directly address the growing difficulty of control and the increasing complexity and opacity of technocentric finance. This BigTech business model involves diverse information controls. The new instruments should seek to link financial sector regulation to the broader strategy of structurally balanced and inclusive economic development.

4.2.1. *Principles*

The current regulatory paradigm relies on narrow technical solutions to specific transaction problems. Regulators are inherently reactive: they only react when market outcomes are available. This attitude carries certain risks in case of disruptive systemic change. Micro-optimizing, technology-focused regulatory approaches are not a direct response to a fundamental disruption at the system's core. The growing power imbalance between sovereign public and private market actors increases the importance of a normative FinTech regulatory strategy (Omarova, 2020a).

The following key features characterize the regulatory strategy geared towards these policy goals.

- Regulation must follow adaptive approaches.
- A fundamentally proactive regulatory stance towards technology is required.
- The focus is on the role and importance of deliberately structural regulatory measures.
- An effective FinTech strategy includes specific instruments of direct public participation in the financial markets.

Developing an adaptive, proactive, structurally oriented, and participatory approach to FinTech requires a profound shift in the current understanding of the relationship between law, finance, and technology. Law reflects our collective normative judgments. It is the instrument for structuring social relations. Technology is reshaping the dynamics of financial market power. It reinforces the primacy of law as the primary instrument for controlling and countering potentially harmful social implications of such power shifts.

The approaches outlined in Figure 2, explicitly address the structural challenges of the financial system.

4.2.2. *Central bank digital currency*

The core concern of the state must be to ensure interoperability between platforms and non-platforms and counteract barriers to the free exchange of different types of money. Excessive exit fees and other restrictions on the disbursement of money should be prohibited. An essential requirement is the introduction of a central bank digital currency. If cash eventually disappears, a news anchor is needed to ensure the exchangeability of all different private forms of money. That is precisely the idea of a digital central bank currency. By introducing digital central bank currencies and other measures, threats to monetary sovereignty prevent by ensuring interoperability.

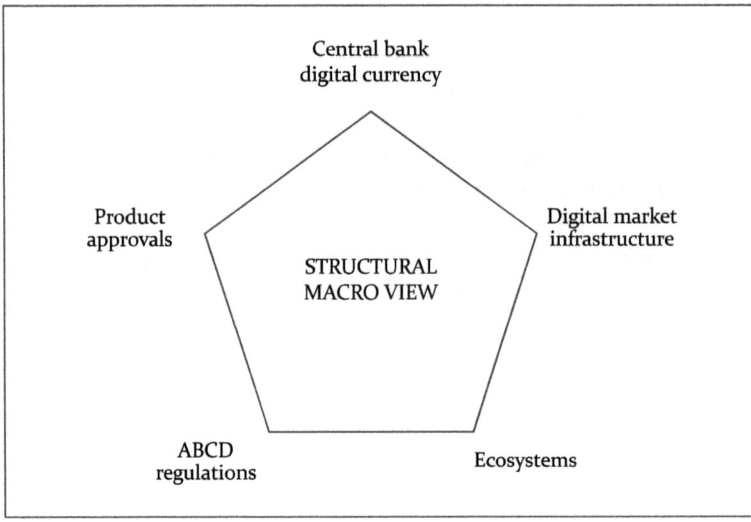

Figure 2. Financial regulation measures.

A functional CBDC would either curb privately issued cryptocurrencies, including the increasingly popular stable coins or make them far less ubiquitous in financial transactions. By eliminating multiple layers of private stable coin-driven ecosystems, CBDC would reduce the structural complexity and opacity of the financial system, thereby simplifying its oversight and internal governability. It would also prevent a potentially dangerous concentration of control over the money supply — and economic power in general — in the hands of a few large private companies like Facebook or JPMorgan.

The observation is particularly true for large currency areas. In smaller economies with weak institutions, the problem arises in a very different way. The danger of digital platforms displacing state currencies is real there.

4.2.3. *Digital market infrastructure*

A US-style FinTech charter falls far short. It does not address the challenges posed by BigTech in the financial markets and the concentration of economic and political power in the hands of a few conglomerates. Instead, the FinTech charter offers BigTech the opportunity to circumvent regulatory relief.

An alternative approach is being developed in the EU. It is the Digital Market Act (DMA). In it, an attempt is made to supplement antitrust intervention in digital markets with ex-ante regulation. It aims at platforms that are identified as 'gatekeepers'. The term gatekeeper does not refer to the entire company but a business within the conglomerate. Essential platform services are considered to be online intermediation services, online search services, social networks, video sharing, messenger services, operating systems, and cloud computing. Apart from cloud services, the financial sector does not play a role here.[11]

The basic idea is not to control the power of a monopoly infrastructure (e.g., by setting access conditions). Instead, it is to prohibit or stop behavior that intends to prevent a competitor from entering the market. The point is to create competition. The list of obligations is a catalog derived from past and current antitrust cases. They are thus aimed directly at the BigTech platforms. However, the requirements cannot be applied to other companies that also act as gatekeepers. That would require more explicit organizational principles around the platforms' business models. The need to explicitly recognize business models when designing rules for tech companies is now well established. In practice, there is wide variation in the economic characteristics and incentives of business models.[12]

4.2.4. *Ecosystems*

The business models of technology companies can best be described as ecosystems and meta-organizations (Kretschmer *et al.*, 2020; Adner, 2017). We generally distinguish between business ecosystems,

---

[11] For example, it would make sense to focus on the emerging 'super FMIs' (Financial Market Infrastructure Providers). They operate, for example, in the areas of trading and payout systems for digital assets, large MPL and other crowdfunding platforms, cloud service providers, and cryptocurrency exchanges and derivatives markets. State participation could even be considered here.

[12] Roughly three groups can be distinguished: ad-supported digital platforms, transactional or matchmaking platforms, marketplaces and exchanges, and OS ecosystem platforms. These business models differ systematically in terms of (a) the type of economies of scale they rely on; (b) the type and direction of network effects; (c) the potential for multihoming; and (d) the potential for disintermediation.

innovation ecosystems, and platform ecosystems (Jacobides *et al.*, 2018). Of particular interest for this article is the platform ecosystem. The platform ecosystem took the form of a 'hub and spoke', with many peripheral businesses connected to the central platform via common or open source technologies or technical standards. By connecting to the platform, the complementaries can produce complementary innovations and gain direct or indirect access to the platform's customers. Accordingly, platform ecosystems are seen as 'semi-regulated marketplaces' that promote entrepreneurial activity under the coordination and direction of the platform sponsor or as 'multi-sided markets' that enable transactions between different user groups (Hein *et al.*, 2019).

Ecosystems are groups of businesses that deal with either unique or supermodular complementarities. These complementarities are not generic. To create value, a specific structure of relationships and alignment is necessary. Figure 3 based on Hein *et al.* (2019) shows the individual components of a digital platform ecosystem.

The strength of ecosystems and their distinguishing feature is that they provide a structure within which complementarities (of all

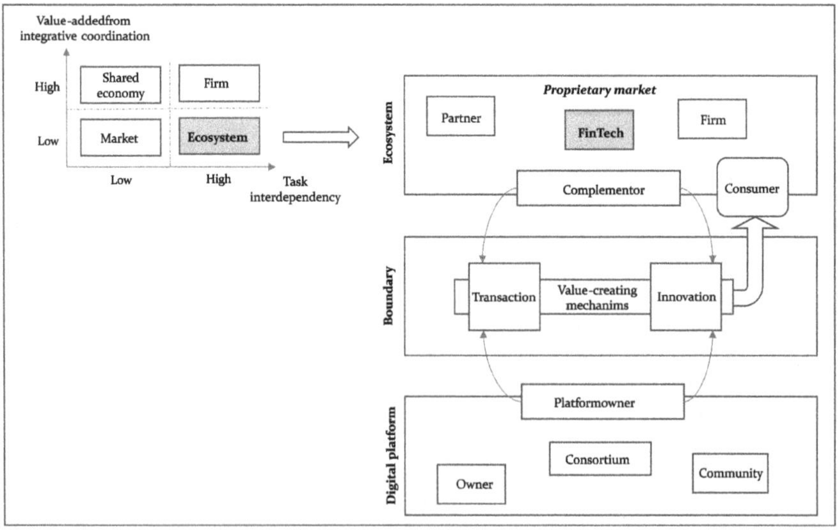

Figure 3. Digital platform ecosystem.

kinds) can be contained and coordinated without the need for vertical integration. From this perspective, ecosystems allow a certain degree of coordination without hierarchical governance. They can use some standards or baseline requirements that allow complementaries to make their own choices (in terms of design, pricing) while enabling the production of a complex, interdependent product or service.

Understanding strategic dynamics requires a clear understanding of how ecosystems are structured and governed. Behavior in an ecosystem and ultimately its success is influenced by the rules of engagement and the nature of standards and interfaces — open or closed, predetermined or emergent.

A meaningful regulatory approach must link rules to ecosystem business models and meta-organizations. However, it is challenging to formulate rules that are model-independent and work across the board. The different functions of platforms cannot be addressed with a list of rules that work across all of them. More flexibility is needed to ensure that each rule fits into each environment and is effective. With such an approach, behaviors can be captured more specifically.

4.2.5. *ABCD regulations*

A complementary option is to regulate each FinTech technology or its use. The legislators in the EU are setting different priorities here. One point concerns the topic of cloud services. Cloud computing is crucial to increasing Europe's data sovereignty as outlined in the European Commission's Data Strategy, Digital Strategy, Industrial Strategy, and the EU recovery plan. Currently, the European Commission is working on establishing a European Alliance on Industrial Data, Edge, and Cloud. Financial service providers increasingly use cloud services to remain competitive. There must be precise requirements in place for outsourcing agreements between financial entities and cloud service providers. As announced in the FinTech Action Plan, the European Commission is currently working together with stakeholders, supervisors, and regulators to define standard contractual clauses for such outsourcing agreements.

Another initiative concerns the regulation of artificial intelligence (AI). The European Commission has presented a draft AI regulation in April 2021. In it, the use of AI — and not the technology itself — is intended to be regulated. It is primarily a prohibition law that bans AI systems in specific application scenarios or depends on technical and organizational requirements. The draft regulation does not regulate civil law issues in the use of AI (e.g., liability, attribution of declarations of intent, creation of intellectual property). The draft regulation base on a broad concept of AI systems. Software must include some different AI techniques.

The significance of the draft regulation can hardly be underestimated because a tightrope walk between the protection of fundamental rights and the promotion of innovation must be mastered. Not only must potential risks caused by AI be prevented. Instead, incentives for innovation must be created or maintained at the same time. The disadvantages of an unbalanced regulation would be enormous: If protection is only incomplete, AI that endangers fundamental rights could be used. The regulations are therefore aimed at all market participants and not just specifically at FinTech and platform companies. However, they would be particularly affected by the regulation.

4.2.6. *Product approvals*

A broader, explicitly macro-structural approach to the ex-ante review of new FinTech offerings would introduce a system of mandatory pre-approval of financial products. In general, the primary purpose of introducing a general product approval system is to reduce and control the overall complexity and opacity of financial markets. If properly designed, a product approval system would provide a new procedural mechanism. It ensures that financial innovation and complex financial instruments promote productive economic entrepreneurship and provide real public benefits. Private companies must demonstrate to regulators that each complex financial product must meet various legal tests (Omarova, 2020a).

The party with the best access to this information would be responsible for assessing a particular financial product's potential risks and benefits. Such a process would indeed slow down the provision of innovative products to consumers. However, the proposal would help reduce the socially counterproductive complexity and opacity of technology-driven financial markets. The problem of the governability of digitalized finance at the system level could be addressed in this way.

5. Conclusion

Today's digital economy is built around a business model of data and wealth extraction. This development undermines the public and social value that could otherwise be derived from technological innovation.

Omarova (2020a) states:

> Technology is a tool; what to make of it is a choice. Who gets to exercise this choice, for what purposes and to what effect, is not merely a matter of technical expertise or economic efficiency — it is a matter of public policy (p. 124).

The state can solve these problems. It can only do so if it remembers its true role.

The chapter aims to present what constitutes this role and political decision in the context of FinTech. It offers starting points for an effective strategy of FinTech regulation. Given the structural changes in the financial markets, today's predominantly technocratic model of financial regulation is naturally reaching its limits. It does not do justice to the systemic challenges posed by FinTech. In the FinTech era, the financial system is getting more extensive and more interconnected. The financial system is moving faster and faster and becoming more complex. Managing risk is becoming increasingly difficult with the technocratic model. However, the emerging regulatory responses to these macro-level changes continue to operate mainly at the micro-level. Policymakers need to go further and redefine the foundations and principles on which the platform economy is based. Otherwise, regulatory efforts to date will only result in extractive practices becoming more widespread, normalizing them as inherent features of digital markets.

The chapter makes proposals at the macro and meso levels. The first proposal concerns issues related to currency and money. At the same time, the danger of a 'libraization' of society has been mitigated for the time being. The question of whether Diem and other stable coins are thus no longer (potentially) competing currencies to the dollar or euro, but merely electronic means of payment, has not been conclusively clarified. CBDC must be introduced in the major currency areas as soon as possible (BIS, 2021). With digital central bank money, the central bank would be responsible for its issuance and control as a central authority. In addition, the central bank could design the digital central bank money so that advantages of decentralization, encryption, and programmability would come into play.

Another area concerns the regulation of digital infrastructure. The proposed European Digital Markets Act would introduce ex-ante regulation for gatekeepers of the digital economy, i.e., compelling platform companies, in the form of a catalog of prohibitions on certain types of behavior. The catalog includes a wide range of typical behaviors for digital markets and is partly known from antitrust proceedings of the competition authorities. In addition, the European Commission is to be provided with instruments with which it can effectively enforce the catalog of prohibitions to identify and eliminate competition problems on digital markets in good time.

The regulation of ecosystems is also to take place partly through the DMA. However, this only succeeds to a limited extent. Uniform rules come up against the different business models of platform companies. Translating these requirements into actionable rules that people and companies can understand requires more explicit organizing principles around ecosystem business models or meta-organizations. The UK has proposed a regulation that identifies the equivalent of a gatekeeper platform. Alongside this, the proposal simultaneously creates a set of rules developed for this specific business model. The approach is better suited to capture the specific structural features of the platform undertaking.

Another option for regulation directly addresses the technologies used by FinTech and other companies. However, regulating ABCD technology is still in its infancy. The EU does have a somewhat older set of rules for regulating personal data in the form of the GDPR. However, the directive would need to be revised. The latest project concerns AI. It is a software regulation.

Finally, a product authorization procedure propose. Such a proposal contributes to reducing the socially counterproductive complexity and intransparency of technology-driven financial markets.

The structural developments require an adaptive, proactive, and comprehensive regulatory approach (Lo, 2017). As finance becomes more granular and algorithm-driven, a paradigm shift in financial regulation is required. The response must be structural and systemic. Law is given precedence over technology. If the profit motive of private parties prevails as it has in the past, the geo-economic order will consist of privatized economies. Investor groups will then replace public regulation with private governance. The result will be the replacement of the net citizen by the state's citizen — the private online state will be realized. Financial regulation would then be ineffective.

Acknowledgment

Opinions expressed are solely my own and do not express the views or opinions of my employer.

References

Adner, R. (2017). Ecosystem as structure: An actionable construct for strategy. *Journal of Management*, *43*(1), 39–58. doi:10.1177/0149206316678451.

Arner, D. W., Barberis, J. N., & Buckley, R. P. (2017). Fintech, Regtech and the reconceptualization of financial regulation. *Northwestern Journal of International Law and Business*, *37*(3), 371–413. http://scholarlycommons.law.northwestern.edu/njilb/vol37/iss3/2.

Bank for International Settlements (BIS) (2021). CBDCs: An opportunity for the monetary system. *BIS Annual Economic Report*, 2021, pp. 65–95. https://www.bis.org/publ/arpdf/ar2021e3.pdf [Accessed: 22 June 2021].

Basel Committee on Banking Supervision (BCBS) (2018). Sound practices: Implications of Fintech developments for banks and bank supervisors. https://www.bis.org/bcbs/publ/d431.pdf [Accessed: 15 January 2019].

Basel Committee on Banking Supervision (BCBS) (2021). Prudential treatment of cryptoasset exposures. https://www.bis.org/bcbs/publ/d519.pdf [Accessed: 20 June 2021].

Berg, C., Davidson, S., & Potts, J. (2019). *Understanding the Blockchain Economy: An Introduction to Institutional Cryptoeconomics*. Edward Elgar, Cheltenham.

Brown, E., & Piroska, D. (2021). Governing Fintech and Fintech as governance: The regulatory sandbox, riskwashing, and disruptive social classification. *New Political Economy*. doi:10.1080/13563467.2021.1910645.

Brunnermeier, M. K., James, H., & Landau, J.-P. (2021). *The Digitalization of Money*. BIS Working Papers No. 941. https://www.bis.org/publ/work941.pdf [Accessed: 6 June 2021].

Buckley, R. P., Arner, D. W., Zetzsche, D. A., & Weber, R. H. (2020). The road to RegTech: The (astonishing) example of the European Union. *Journal of Banking Regulation*, *21*, 26–36. doi:10.1057/s41261-019-00104-1.

Carson, B., Chakravarty, A., Koh, K., & Thomas, R. (2021). *Platform Operating Model for the AI Bank of the Future*. McKinsey & Company. https://www.mckinsey.com/industries/financial-services/our-insights/platform-operating-model-for-the-ai-bank-of- the-future [Accessed: 27 May 2021].

Cong, L.W., Li, Y., & Wang, N. (2020). *Token-based Platform Finance*. NBER Working Paper No. 27810. https://www.nber.org/papers/w27810 [Accessed: 11 November 2020].

Cornelli, G., Frost, J., Gambacorta, L., Rau, R., Wardrop, R., & Ziegler, T. (2020). *Fintech and Big Tech Credit: A New Database*. BIS Working Papers, No. 887. https://www.bis.org/publ/work887.pdf [Accessed: 4 November 2020].

Crisanto, J. C., Ehrentraud, J., & Fabian, M. (2021). *BigTechs in Finance: Regulatory Approaches and Policy Options*. Financial Stability Institute Briefs, No. 12. https://www.bis.org/fsi/fsibriefs12.pdf [Accessed: 7 April 2021].

Ehrentraud, J., Garcia Ocampo, D., & Quevedo Vega, C. (2020a). *Regulating Fintech Financing: Digital Banks and Fintech Platforms*. Financial Stability Institute Insights on policy implementation, No. 27. https://www.bis.org/fsi/publ/insights27.pdf [Accessed: 12 October 2020].

Ehrentraud, J., Garcia Ocampo, D., Garzoni, L., & Piccolo, M. (2020b) *Policy Responses to Fintech: A Cross-country Overview*. Financial Stability Institute Insights on policy implementation, No. 23. https://www.bis.org/fsi/publ/insights23.pdf [Accessed: 14 March 2020].

Enriques, L., & Ringe, W.-G. (2020). Bank-Fintech partnerships, outsourcing arrangements and the case for a mentorship regime. ECGI Law Working Paper, No. 527.

Financial Stability Board (2019). *FinTech and Market Structure in Financial Services: Market Developments and Potential Financial Stability Implications*. https://www.fsb.org/wp-content/uploads/P140219.pdf [Accessed: 21 June 2019].

Financial Stability Board (2017). *Financial Stability Implications from Fintech: Supervisory and Regulatory Issues that Merit Authorities' Attention.* https://www.fsb.org/wp-content/uploads/R270617.pdf [Accessed: 14 September 2018].

Finn, E. (2017). *What Algorithms Want: Imagination in the Age of Computing.* MIT Press, Cambridge, MA.

Frost, J., Gambacorta, L., Huang, Y., Song Shin, H., & Zbinden, P. (2019). *BigTech and the Changing Structure of Financial Intermediation.* BIS Working Papers, No. 779. https://www.bis.org/publ/work779.pdf [Accessed: 3 January 2020].

Gai, P., Kemp, M., Sánchez Serrano, A., & Schnabel, I. (2019) *Regulatory Complexity and the Quest for Robust Regulation.* ESRB Report of the Advisory Scientific Committee, No. 8. https://www.esrb.europa.eu/pub/pdf/asc/esrb.asc190604_8_regulatorycomplexityquestrobustregulation~e63a7136c7.en.pdf [Accessed: 25 October 2019].

Goodhart, C. (2008). The boundary problem in financial regulation. *National Institute Economic Review, 206*, 48–55.

Haldane, A. G. (2012). *The Dog and the Frisbee.* Speech at the Federal Reserve Bank of Kansas City's 366th economic policy symposium, 'The changing policy landscape', Jackson Hole, Wyoming, 31 August 2012.

Hein, A. *et al.* (2019). Digital platform ecosystems. *Electronic Markets*, *30*, 87–98. doi:10.1007/s12525-019-00377-4.

Hockett, R. C., & Omarova, S. T. (2017). The finance franchise. *Cornell Law Review, 102*, 1143–1218. https://scholarship.law.cornell.edu/clr/vol102/iss5/1.

Jacobides, M. G., Cennamo, C., & Gawer, A. (2018). Towards a theory of ecosystems. *Strategic Management Journal, 39*(8), 2255–2276. doi:10.1002/smj.2904.

Khiaonarong, T., & Goh, T. (2020). *Fintech and Payments Regulation: Analytical Framework.* IMF Working Paper, No. 20/75. https://www.imf.org/en/Publications/WP/Issues/2020/05/29/Fintech-and-Payments-Regulation-Analytical-Framework-49086 [Accessed: 12 February 2021].

Kretschmer, T., Leiponen, A., Schilling, M., & Vasudeva, G. (2020) Platform ecosystems as meta-organizations: implications for platform strategies. *Strategic Management Journal, 43*, 405–424. doi:10.1002/smj.3250.

Lemma, V. (2020). *FinTech Regulation: Exploring New Challenges of the Capital Markets Union.* Macmillan, London.

Lo, A. W. (2017). *Adaptive Markets: Financial Evolution at the Speed of Thought.* Princeton University Press, Princeton.

Omarova, S. T. (2019). New tech v. new deal: Fintech as a systemic phenomenon. *Yale Journal on Regulation, 36*(2), 735–793. https://www.yalejreg.com/print/new-tech-v-new-deal-fintech-as-a-systemic-phenomenon/ [Accessed: 9 April 2020].

Omarova, S. T. (2020a). Technology v technocracy: Fintech as a regulatory challenge. *Journal of Financial Regulation, 6*(1), 75–124. doi:10.1093/jfr/fjaa004.

Omarova, S. T. (2020b). Dealing with disruption: emerging approaches to FinTech regulation. *Washington University Journal of Law and Policy, 61*, 25–53. https://openscholarship.wustl.edu/law_journal_law_policy/vol61/iss1/9 [Accessed: 2 January 2021].

Philippon, T. (2016). *The Fintech Opportunity.* NBER Working Paper, No. 22476. https://www.nber.org/system/files/working_papers/w22476/w22476.pdf [Accessed: 11 August 2017].

Philippon, T. (2019). *On Fintech and financial inclusion.* NBER Working Paper, No. 26330. https://www.nber.org/system/files/working_papers/w26330/w26330.pdf [Accessed: 20 March 2020].

Pistor, K. (2021). *How not to Launch a Digital Currency.* Project Syndicate 21 May 2021. https://www.project-syndicate.org/commentary/facebook-libra-diem-failure-lessons-for-digital-currencies-by-katharina-pistor-2021-05 [Accessed: 26 May 2021].

Restoy, F. (2021). *Fintech Regulation: How to Achieve a Level Playing Field.* Financial Stability Institute Occasional Paper, No. 17. https://www.bis.org/fsi/fsipapers17.pdf [Accessed: 23 April 2021].

Schmaltz, C., Pokutta, S., Heidorn, T., & Andrae, S. (2014). How to make regulators and shareholders happy under Basel III. *Journal of Banking & Finance, 46*, 311–325. doi:10.1016/j.jbankfin.2014.05.031.

Shleifer, A. (2005). Understanding regulation. *European Financial Management, 11*(4), 439–451.

Staab, P. (2019). *Digitaler Kapitalismus. Markt und Herrschaft in der Ökonomie der Unknappheit.* Berlin, Suhrkamp.

Stiglitz, J. E. (2002). Information and the change in the paradigm in economics. *American Economic Review, 92*, 460–501.

Stiglitz, J. E. (2000). The contributions of the economics of information to twentieth century economics. *Quarterly Journal of Economics, 115*, 1441–1478.

Stulz, R. M. (2019). FinTech, BigTech, and the future of banks. *Journal of Applied Corporate Finance, 31*(4), 86–97. doi:10.1111/jacf.12378.

Thakor, A. V. (2020). Fintech and banking: What do we know? *Journal of Financial Intermediation, 41*, 100833. doi:10.1016/j.jfi.2019.100833.

Vogl, J. (2021). *Kapital und Ressentiment: Eine kurze Theorie der Gegenwart.* C.H. Beck, Berlin.

Wharton School (2021). DeFi beyond the hype. Wharton School Report. https://wifpr.wharton.upenn.edu/wp-content/uploads/2021/05/DeFi-Beyond-the-Hype.pdf [Accessed: 5 June 2021].

Zetzsche, D. A., Arner, D. W., & Buckley, R. P. (2020). Decentralized finance. *Journal of Financial Regulation*, *6*(2), 172–203. doi:10.1093/jfr/fjaa010.

Zetzsche, D. A., Buckley, R. P., Barberis, J. N., & Arner, D. W. (2017). Regulating a revolution: From regulatory sandboxes to smart regulation. *Fordham Journal of Corporate and Financial Law*, *23*(1), 31–103. https://ir.lawnet.fordham.edu [Accessed: 14 July 2018].

Part II

Cryptocurrencies: Innovation and Classification

https://doi.org/10.1142/9781800612723_0003

Chapter 3

Cryptocurrencies as a Driver of Innovation for the Monetary System

Gianna Figà-Talamanca[*,§], Sergio M. Focardi[†,¶], Davide Mazza[†,||] and Marco Patacca[‡,**]

[*]*Department of Economics, University of Perugia, via A. Pascoli 20, 06123 Perugia, Italy*

[†]*Léonard de Vinci Pôle Universitaire, Research Center, 92916 Paris La Défense Cedex, France*

[‡]*Department of Economics, University of Verona, via Cantarane 24, 37129 Verona, Italy*

[§]*gianna.figatalamanca@unipg.it*

[¶]*sergio.focardi@devinci.fr*

[||]*davide.mazza@devinci.fr*

[**]*marco.patacca@univr.it*

Abstract

In this chapter, we outline a theory of cryptocurrencies that parallels the standard theory of money. We evidence that cryptocurrencies satisfy some but not all conditions that qualify a medium of exchange as money. Specifically, the process of creation and distribution of cryptocurrencies significantly differs from that of money impacting trust and value creation. New form of cryptocurrencies, such as central bank digital currencies, are considered. We outline scenarios of future evolution of cryptocurrencies and how they might be adopted by central banks to replace cash and/or to have direct interaction with the public.

Keywords: Money, cryptocurrencies, money theory, innovation, central bank digital currencies.

1. Introduction

Since the creation of Bitcoin (Nakamoto, 2008), the first cryptocurrency appeared in 2009, cryptocurrencies, and in particular Bitcoin, have been hailed as a fundamental innovation not only in payment systems but also in the financial ones. Many have seen cryptocurrencies as an expression of entrepreneurial freedom against the control and manipulation of governments. Others, a triumph of technology that puts in the hands of individuals a financial power traditionally reserved to big centralized organizations. Still others, the victory of technology as a tool to enhance freedom against control.

The thesis of this chapter is that digital money is part of an ongoing process of profound innovation of the 'money system'. Innovation includes the introduction of a one-level central bank digital money to replace or at least complement banknotes, an ongoing process of financialization, and, possibly, a fundamental change of the role of money and of money creation in modern economic systems.

It is important to make a distinction between technological and financial aspects of currencies and payment systems. Reiss (2018) argues that, after a gradual and adaptive conversion process, money is already digital. Indeed, most money today is electronic as it is generated and distributed through electronic means, that is, computers and communication equipment. Banknotes and coins are marginal. Digital money has been a big innovation but currently is technological state of the art in any advanced economy. There are different technologies for digital money, especially insofar as transfer of money is concerned. Blockchain, or, more in general, distributed ledger technologies, are considered a major innovation as these technologies allow transfer of money without centralized control. Yet, it is essential to distinguish the benefits and risks that this technology might bring to market infrastructures and to develop a sound regulatory framework, see Guo and Liang (2016) and Priem (2020).

While digital money is a big innovation, multiple currencies have a long history. In ancient times, there were many competing coin systems. Occasionally, a specific coin such as the Florentine florin, got wide international acceptance. In modern times, almost all states took control of their currencies. State currencies acquired the role of legal tender as governments made and received payments only in the state currencies.

In parallel with the evolution of currencies, banking systems evolved. The first central bank was the Swedish central bank, the Sveriges riksbank, founded in 1668. Subsequently, all advanced economies created a central bank. Banking systems in most nations became two-level systems with a central bank and commercial banks.

Progressively, with the diffusion of electronic technology, the creation and distribution of the state money was handled by the banking systems. The vast majority of money, more than 95%, was and still is, in the form of bank deposits. But, in parallel, hundreds of alternative currencies have been created and proposed. Alternative currencies are created and distributed under a variety of different arrangements.

Creation and distribution arrangements are critical because it is clearly unfair to let a private entity to create 'money' for its own benefit. Bank money is ultimately private credit or a liability of a central bank. Banning frauds, current bank money is not issued for the profit of any entity. But alternative money could be issued for the profit of the issuers.

On the theory side, Friedrich Hayek argued in favor of private, competitive issuers of money; forcefully argued that many should not be issued by the governments but by private entities. Competition would decide which of the private currencies will prevail.

It is possible that cryptocurrencies will stay as a form of complementary currencies, but it seems unlikely that some cryptocurrency will become a major international currency independent from government control. Historically, we have witnessed many attempts to bypass or complement the state money system with private money systems. For example, in Medieval and Renaissance times, big trading companies in practice had their own financial system that bypassed controls of princes and emperors.

In modern times, the creation of two-level banking systems, with central and commercial banks, adopted by most states, has practically privatized the creation and distribution of money but still under strict government control. In fact, in modern states most banks are private enterprises while central banks have different ownership structures. Though most central banks are owned by the states, some important central banks such as that of the United States, Japan and Switzerland, are privately held.[1] Still the banking system is highly regulated; it is unlikely that modern states will allow the development of alternative unregulated, uncontrolled, large scale private money systems.

Therefore, it is critical to analyze digital money and cryptocurrencies with an engineering perspective that considers the global process of innovation of modern financial systems. Arguably, the need to address major social and environmental issues in a globalized world, such as climate changes, or health widespread emergencies, will challenge modern financial systems and will require creative financial innovation. Technology will certainly be a major actor of this process.

The practice of creating alternative currencies to the official money is not new. Though alternative currencies came to the fore in the last decade due to Bitcoin, historically, many have been created and actually used in the past. The 2006 Annual Report of the Worldwide Database of Complementary Currency Systems (DeMeulenaere, 2007) listed 150 different alternative and local currencies; most of them were based on the economic ideas of Silvio Gesell (1958), a Swiss economist and entrepreneur, who claimed that money should be used and not hoarded.

An early example of alternative currency following the idea of Gesell was attempted in the village of Wörgl, in Austria in 1932. The municipality issued a local currency in order to overcome the problems created by the economic crisis; it was guaranteed by an arrangement with a local bank and, exceptionally, could be exchanged with the official money. The experiment was very successful and gained recognition well outside Austria (Derudder, 2012). However, the Austrian central bank stopped the project after a couple of years.

The Swiss WIR, also inspired by the ideas of Silvio Gesell, was created in 1934 in Basel and it still exists as official Swiss complementary money. A WIR bank offers loans and the usual banking services. WIR circulates among a community of more than 60,000 Swiss enterprises.

[1]The blog Bank Underground https://bankunderground.co.uk/ kept by staff of the Bank of England offers many details and references on central banks' ownership and control structure.

Blanc (2018) distinguishes seven different groups or types of alternative money, one of which (the seventh) is formed by cryptocurrencies, which are the main subject of this chapter. As the author points out, most of the local or alternative currencies have been introduced to solve an economic problem of coordination of resources. This is probably not true for cryptocurrencies. Indeed, it is widely accepted that the creation of Bitcoin was based on ideological concerns on the banking system; later, the development of a huge number of alternative cryptocurrencies may have also been sustained by pure speculation.

In this chapter, we would like to discuss Bitcoin and other cryptocurrencies, so called *altcoins*, from the point of view of the Theory of Money. Since money is a human artifact, a Theory of Money is not the statement of a law of nature, but it is rather the description of how money systems work.

The definition of the nature of money is one of the main questions arising in the economic literature. A standard classification, see Mishkin (2007), states that money should represent a *unit of account*, a mean to *store value* and, finally, a *medium of exchange*. Yet, it is of strong interest to understand how money changes its value and how these changes may affect the real economy.

Money definitely represents purchasing power, and it is therefore critically important to understand how it is distributed to or transferred between agents. As forcefully remarked by Shubik (2004), money needs trust, and distribution rules are fundamental for building trust. This approach to the definition of money may be seen from an operational point of view as outlined in Focardi (2018).

To sum up, five questions are crucial within an operational perspective of the theory of money:

(1) What is money?
(2) How is it created?
(3) How is it distributed and transferred?
(4) How does it acquire, keep and change value?
(5) What is its impact on the real economy?

The anonymity of cryptocurrencies makes them the ideal candidate as a new form of money to replace cash. Therefore, it is natural that several governments and central banks are considering the possibility of issuing their own cryptocurrency; Barontini and Holden (2019) shows that 70% of central banks have started to investigate the opportunity to introduce their own crypto currencies in order to improve the payments safety, domestic efficiency and the cash changeover.

The issuing of cryptocurrencies by central banks would definitely boost their diffusion as people have more confidence in public institutions than in private firms. However, it should be clear that the issuing of a cryptocurrency by a central bank is not an example of an alternative currency. Most probably central banks will not issue alternative currencies but electronic forms complementing their own currency as revealed by pilot projects being currently monitored by Sweden, China, and Russia Central banks. Noteworthy, the issuing of such currencies is often motivated by political purposes; for instance, Russia and China may be pursuing a policy to reduce dependence on the US dollar and exert geopolitical strength.

In this framework it is important to introduce a theory of cryptocurrency and to discuss similarities and differences with traditional and alternative currencies. To this end, we answer in this chapter the above questions for the special case of cryptocurrencies. A similar, yet complementary, approach is taken in Bech and Garratt (2017) where the authors distinguish money categories according to four key properties: issuer, form, accessibility, and transfer mechanism.

First, in Section 2, we debate cryptocurrencies as real currencies or investment assets. In Section 3, we analyze the (operational) theory of money as it is currently conceived, while in Section 4, we place cryptocurrencies within the context of theory of money. In Section 5, we outline possible innovations for the monetary system and, in Section 6, we draw the future evolution of cryptocurrencies; finally, in Section 7, we provide some concluding remarks.

2. Are Cryptocurrencies Real Currencies or Investment Assets?

It is widely believed that Bitcoin and other cryptocurrencies have a dual nature as payment systems and investment assets. Nakamoto (2008) introduces Bitcoin as an open-source, peer-to-peer network where security of transactions is based on the blockchain technology without the need of trusted third parties. The main motivation of its inception was to have a deflationary[2] currency, independent of financial intermediaries and of central authorities. Over the time, the leading position acquired by web exchanges and the huge price gain obtained by the initial users attracted market speculators that have changed the Bitcoin vision from payment system to investment asset. Following this stream, Yermack (2015) concludes that Bitcoin behaves as a high volatility stock and White *et al.* (2020) investigates the nature of Bitcoin by making comparison between currency, asset class, bubble, or technology-based product.

The behavior of Bitcoin and other cryptocurrencies as investment assets has been characterized as an instance of bubbles by Nobel-Prize winners including Krugman (2018), Shiller (2014), Stiglitz (2017) and Thaler (2018).

Financial markets exhibit a long history of bubbles. Brunnermeier and Oehmke (2013) provides a thorough review of the literature on bubbles. In the entry, *Bubbles of The New Palgrave Dictionary of Economics* (Brunnermeier, 2008), Brunnermeier defines bubbles as follows: *Bubbles refer to asset prices that exceed an asset's fundamental value because current owners believe that they can resell the asset at an even higher price in the future.*

Bitcoin and other cryptocurrencies have no intrinsic value in the sense of finance, as no stream of future cash flows is associated to their ownership. This implies that any sustained increase in the price of Bitcoin or other cryptocurrencies is to be considered a bubble, as evidenced from the initial comments of the Nobel Prize winners cited before.

[2] A short but incisive illustration of deflationary nature of Bitcoin is provided by https://99bitcoins.com/bitcoin-price-and-value-deflation/. *The digital currency is actually designed to be deflationary. As a certain amount of bitcoins are produced through the process of Bitcoin mining, the amount of bitcoins that are rewarded to the miners per block is decreased. Simultaneously, as more and more bitcoins are mined, the difficulty of the hashing algorithm increases, which then requires more computing power to solve. As a result, Bitcoin mining becomes more expensive, and miners get less coins as Bitcoin mining progresses, so mining will only continue if the bitcoin rewards are worth more than the cost of the electricity that the Bitcoin mining process requires. So, deflation is literally hard-wired into the Bitcoin protocol.*

2.1. *Bubble analyses presented in the literature*

The bubbling behavior of Bitcoin has been formally analyzed with the theory of log-periodic fluctuations. Min and Zhu (2019) analyzes Bitcoin bubbles following the Log-Periodic Power Law Singularity Model (LPPLS Model) developed in Sornette (1998), Johansen *et al.* (2000); Johansen *et al.* (1999), Ide and Sornette (2002) and Sornette and Cauwels (2015).

Wheatley *et al.* (2019) shows that Bitcoin bubbles are predictable combining LPPLS models with the Metcalfe's law. Metcalfe (2013) proposed that the value of a network is proportional to the square of the number of nodes. Known as Metcalfe's Law, this rule has been applied to many technological environments. Wheatley *et al.* (2019) applied a variant of this law to determine the intrinsic value of a Bitcoin network. The fluctuations with respect to the basic valuation provided by modified Metcalfe's law can be modeled with LPPLS models. LPPLS models predict crashes as unsustainable singularities that follow supra-exponential behavior.

The above analyses suggest that investing in Bitcoin is not a sustainable investment. The behavior of Bitcoin prices can be seen as a sequence of bubbles and crashes of random amplitude on top of a kind of fundamental value. Arguably, the fundamental value is determined by the interplay of supply which is determined by the activity of miners and demand for Bitcoin as instruments of payment and transfer of value.

Nevertheless, after the bubble behavior in the end of 2017, the Bitcoin price, and consequently the whole cryptocurrency sector, seems to slowly move towards stabilization. This is fundamental to reach the store of value feature, proper for a currency. The suggestion of cryptocurrencies — either existing or future ones — as an alternative payment system, makes it interesting to describe their peculiarities through the 'lens' of the theory of money.

3. The Theory of Money

Money is a solution to the problem of facilitating exchanges, organizing economic activity, and storing value for future uses. We can say that money transmits every economic decision that results in the transfer of ownership or the fruition of services. It is therefore a fundamental tool to perform economic activities. In our analysis we look at money from an operational/engineering point of view, in line with Focardi (2018). The operational and engineering point of view is particularly important today as the financial system is going through a process of deep innovation.

Governments and central banks are studying possible changes in the monetary system and new forms of money or quasi-money are created and offered for investment and storage of value. Looking forward, it is possible not only that banknotes will be replaced or complemented by some digital money but also that the current pillars of generation and distribution of money based on credit will be complemented by other mechanisms.

An observation is in order. Payment systems, such as Visa and PayPal, are not alternative forms of money as they implement only the payment function. Indeed, they are a digital extension of the currency they are attached to; specifically, credit cards are the combination of two elements: a payment system and a credit system.

Let us therefore begin by analyzing the nature of money.

3.1. *The nature of money*

To understand the nature of money and answer the first of the above five questions, one must start from its features. Three main functions of money, see Mishkin (2007), are generally recognized:

(1) unit of account,
(2) store of value, and
(3) medium of exchange.

In the past, money had an intrinsic value as coins were made of precious metals and banknotes were linked to gold reserves stored in Central Banks. Though the notion that money should have no intrinsic value had gained general acceptance at the beginning of the 20th century (Mitchell, 1913, 1914), advanced economies abandoned the gold standard several decades after; for example, in the USA, it was abandoned in 1971 by decree of President Nixon.

Nowadays, it is widely accepted that money has no intrinsic value but rather it is a certificate, a token, which gives its holder purchasing power. Two main forms of money exist today: cash (coins and banknotes), and bank deposits. In addition, bank reserves are a special form of money used only in the relationships of commercial banks and central banks. Central banks such as the United States Federal reserve[3] and European Central Bank,[4] suggest a ranking of money aggregates; Mehrling (2012) propose a hierarchical classification of money: with the exception of the first level (cash), so-called monetary base, at each higher level money depends on the previous levels.

In modern advanced economies, the main fraction of the circulating money, is formed by commercial bank's deposits while cash represents only a small fraction, between 3% and 10%. A bank deposit has a twofold nature: it is a bank debt to the customer as the bank is committed to converting the deposit into banknotes at par; it is a certificate, generally electronic, which gives purchasing power to those who possess it.

Some modern authors, such as Ferguson (2008), Martin (2015) as well as the works Mitchell (1913, 1914) mentioned above, tend to emphasize that money is transferable credit. This conceptual position follows the line of thought favored by anthropologists, such as David Graeber, who claims in Graeber (2012) that money did not evolve from barter but from credit: money is transferable credit that one has with the rest of the community.

Though we agree that money is intrinsically related to credit, as it will become clear in the next section, we prefer to think of the true nature of money as a token that measures purchasing power, i.e., the ability to purchase goods and services. The reason is that due to financial innovation, in the future, money might not be strictly linked to credit.

3.2. *The creation, distribution, and transfer of money*

In current banking systems, the creation, distribution, and transfer of new money are strictly related processes, yet distinguished. The banking system, commercial banks plus the central bank, is

[3]https://www.federalreserve.gov/faqs/money_12845.htm.

[4]https://www.ecb.europa.eu/stats/money_credit_banking/monetary_aggregates/html/index.en.html.

responsible for the creation and transfer of money, within the legal framework of accounting and balance sheet: any flow of money corresponds to a change of stocks; any liabilities must be balanced by an asset otherwise losses occur and must be covered.

In the past, when money was formed by gold or silver coins, the creation of money was an onerous process that implied finding and exploiting gold and silver mines. Today, it relies on a complex and expensive computer and communication structure. In its essence, money as a bank deposit, is a number written in the files of an entity, a bank, whose credibility is recognized. Creating new money simply means updating computer positions. The critical points are the restrictions placed on this process. However, as the rules might change in the future, it is important to distinguish between the pure creation of money and the restrictions placed on its distribution.

New money is created and allocated primarily when a bank grants a loan to an entity and deposits are created *ex nihilo* by commercial banks. The central bank may intervene to increase or reduce the monetary base directly in two different forms: usually, by buying/selling government securities in the open market; alternatively, during financial crises, applying the so-called QE process, under which central banks buy financial assets from non-banks, e.g., pension funds. Central banks are not allowed to print money either physically or electronically without acquiring assets; these acquisitions are usually performed via intermediary commercial banks, by crediting their reserves.

The theory that banks create new money without the need to receive deposits is called *Horizontalism* and it was introduced by Moore (1988). The author did the empirical and theoretical work to show how modern banking systems work. Moore coined the term *Horizontalism* to mean endogenous generation of money where banks do not need deposits to make loans and to generate new money. The author contrasted *Horizontalism* with *Verticalism*, a term that indicates the opposite theory according to which banks need to receive deposits 'from above' in order to make new loans.

Convertibility is the main link between deposits and cash: although the creation of bank deposit does not depend on the actual deposit of cash, they can however be converted into cash, if requested. Conceptually, however, it is important to distinguish between money as a record in a computer that determines the purchasing power of a natural or legal person and money as a bank debt payable in cash. If cash is completely eliminated this distinction will become crucial.

What other financial assets can be considered money is a controversial issue. The strictest criteria to qualify a financial asset as money can be listed as follows:

- conversion at par with cash;
- liquidity;
- possibility of direct use as a means of payment;
- possibility of being used as a reserve of value.

The shadow banking system has created extreme liquid assets that convert at par, such as *Repo Funds* and *Money Market Funds*. These assets can be considered quasi-money, see Pozsar (2014).

3.3. *The value of money*

The value of money can be established only in relative terms, measuring the changes of the purchasing power of money in time. It is said that we are in a period of inflation if the amount of goods and services that can be purchased with a unit of money reduces and that we are in a period of deflation if it increases.

Inflation might seem to be a simple and intuitive concept but when trying to make the notion of inflation and the purchasing power of money quantitatively precise, difficulties are encountered:

1. many products change continuously so we cannot compare the price of the same product at different times;
2. the prices of products that are not subject to rapid qualitative changes move in different directions, due to changes in production, distribution or competition;
3. price changes are only partially linked to the characteristics of the product but also, often to a decisive extent, to its symbolic value determined by a complex network of relations.

In practice, the purchasing power of money, and therefore inflation (or deflation), is determined by calculating the change in the average value of a basket of products. In this way the Consumer Price

Index (CPI), that is the index of the prices of consumer products, is formed.[5] Each product has a weight proportional to its contribution to gross domestic product (GDP) hence baskets usually include consumer products that do not change or that change slowly overtime.

3.4. *The impact of money on the economy*

The money originated from a credit granting process has its own dynamics that can lead to imbalances and crises in real economies. The analysis of the process by which modern credit-based market economies are prone to crisis was originally conducted by Minsky (1986). Minsky noted that excessive optimism resulting from periods of robust growth can lead entrepreneurs to undertake projects that are too risky and banks to grant loans guaranteed by the future increase in value of the assets that guarantee the loan, rather than by the real ability of the debtor to generate income and to repay the debt.

The subprime crisis is considered an example of this process, with the aggravating circumstance that, due to the financialization of the US economy, the subprime problem has infected the entire financial system. Clearly, other factors of economic and financial disequilibrium in addition to the subprime problem led to the 2007–2008 crisis, but the subprime problem illustrates how the granting of loans based on the future increase in the value of certain assets can be destabilizing.

When Minsky published his analysis, the financial climate was euphoric and unprepared to hear about the crisis. The crisis of 2000 was attributed to errors in hyper-valuation of the Technology, Media, and Telecommunications (TMT) sector. It didn't help Minsky's work. The depth of the 2007–2008 crisis has instead shown how Minsky's analysis can help us understand how excess credit can generate financial crises.

[5]Different indices have been proposed, in particular the indices of Hermann Paasche, Etienne Laspeyres and Irving Fisher, defined by a different weighting scheme.

Discussing the impact of money on the economy, Focardi (2018) suggests that Minsky's analysis should be completed. If excess credit reached the economy evenly, it would create inflation as currently measured and be blocked by central authorities, always very sensitive to inflation. On the other hand, it must be recognized that financial flows selectively reach certain sectors and not the economy as a whole. The author notes that, due to the limitations to the measure of inflation, privileged financial flows to certain sectors allow the rapid expansion of financial markets and the rapid selective growth of some sectors without causing inflation detectable by the usual methods. This fact allows for the development of a crisis without prior signs, such as inflation, being observable.

4. The Monetary Theory of Cryptocurrencies

After discussing the theory of money as currently conceived, and after discussing possible innovations of the money system, let us now apply the same theoretical ideas to cryptocurrencies. It is important to refrain from defining cryptocurrencies just as digital money; indeed, in ECB (2012) among others, the authors point out the differences between:

- digital currencies;
- virtual currencies;
- cryptocurrencies.

Digital currencies are referred to as any means of electronic payment; nowadays this definition obviously includes bank deposits and therefore most money today can be viewed as digital.

Instead, *virtual currencies* are defined as a medium of exchange and as a unit of account within virtual communities such as the players of some online video-games. According to ECB (2012), 'A virtual community is to be understood as a place within cyberspace where individuals interact and follow mutual interests or goals'.

Further, *cryptocurrencies* are a specific subset of digital currencies, which are based on distributed ledger technologies, in their various forms, and obey to strict protocols agreed by the users.[6] In the last decade, cryptocurrencies have captured the imagination of the public as well the attention of professionals, banks, central banks for reasons that we will try to elucidate in the following sections. Clearly, the above definition and the properties of each cryptocurrency might change with time, according to the evolution of the technology,[7] to economic factors and to regulatory concerns of countries' authorities.

For brevity, we will use the term 'money' to denote traditional money made of bank deposits and we will use the term 'cryptocurrency' to denote digital currencies based on distributed ledger technologies.

There are speculations that Bitcoin, the first cryptocurrency implemented in 2009, was initially conceived as an *ideal money*, see Nash (2002), i.e., an international medium of exchange free from influence and manipulations by governments and other power groups. According to Nash, an *ideal money* is an international currency which has a stable value and is free from the Triffin Paradox[8] (Triffin, 1960), which arises when a currency is used as a global reserve. In his first contribution (Nash, 2002) Nash argues that the value of *ideal money* should be linked to an Industrial Consumption Price Index; in Nash (2009) the author introduces the weaker notion of an *asymptotically ideal money*, meant to achieve price stability in the long term.

George Selgin[9] discussed the problems and prospects of Bitcoin during his speech *Bitcoins: Problems and prospects* at the Hillsdale University's 2014 Free Market Forum (Selgin, 2014): while he conveyed that Bitcoin was not *good money* and possibly not money at all, at that time, he also recognized that some of the cryptocurrency's

---

[6]Protocols are initially fixed by the cryptocurrency developers but they may be changed, for most currently living cryptocurrencies, if agreed by the majority of the users.

[7]Specific features of one type of currency might simply become obsolete.

[8]The Triffin Paradox is named after the Belgian-American economist Robert Triffin.

[9]Director of the Center for Monetary and Financial Alternatives of The Cato Institute, Washington, US.

features, if suitably implemented, may lead to a form of *very good money*.

Building, most probably, on his considerations on Bitcoin, Selgin (2015) defines the concept of *synthetic commodity money*, going beyond the standard dichotomy between fiat-money and commodity-money, and argues that Bitcoin is a *semi-elastic synthetic commodity money*. Specifically, the author defines the synthetic commodity money as 'money that lacks non-monetary value but is nevertheless reproducible only at a positive and rising marginal production cost'. The term 'semi-elastic' referred to Bitcoin underlines the way in which Bitcoin specifically rules the monetary base.[10]

Research on cryptocurrencies, mostly on Bitcoin as a representative for the whole sector, has approached the relevant question, on whether they should be considered as currencies (money), commodities, or investment vehicles; yet no conclusive answer has been given to date, see Yermack (2015), Baek and Elbeck (2015), and Gregoriou (2019). Issues preventing the inclusion of cryptocurrencies among the first class are basically related to the debatable issue of them having a fundamental value, see Garcia *et al.* (2014) and Cheah and Fry (2015), or on the (in)stability of their value Yermack (2015). The former concern may be overcome by the observation that current forms of money have no intrinsic value at all, not being linked anymore to Gold reserves; the latter issue is more constraining since it completely blows up the desirable property of money to be a 'store of value'. Nevertheless, we are not focusing here on properties of existing cryptocurrencies, but rather we aim at defining a framework under which cryptocurrencies, to be possibly introduced in the future, may represent a good form of money as envisaged in Selgin (2014).

4.1. *The theory of cryptocurrencies*

In this section, we discuss the theory of cryptocurrencies using the same framework used for the theory of money. In particular, we try

[10]New Bitcoins are minted every time a block of transaction is appended to its blockchain; the amount minted is a piecewise constant function, which asymptotically decreases to zero, transforming Bitcoin from an elastic into an inelastic synthetic commodity.

to answer the five questions introduced in Section 1 for standard money:

(1) What are cryptocurrencies?
(2) How are they created?
(3) How are they distributed and transferred?
(4) How do they acquire, keep and change value?
(5) What is their impact on the real economy?

4.2. *What are cryptocurrencies?*

As already pointed out in Section 1, trust is the fundamental prerequisite of money. Economic agents accept money in exchange for their goods and services under the assumption (trust) that they will be able to exchange money for others' goods and services in the future. Nowadays, money is essentially digital, i.e., a number written in the computer of some bank. Trust in money is based on trust in the banking system. Commercial banks are private entities subject to strict Government control. In principle, money formed by bank deposits, represents a debt of the banking system towards its clients, which is payable in cash. Failure to honor convertibility of deposits in cash led to important bank failures in the past. Today, the convertibility of bank deposits in cash is not central to money operation: first, central banks stand ready to print as many banknotes as needed, then, more importantly, cash is no longer important to large clients. Instead, the critical points are the acceptance of digital money (numbers in bank databases) as equivalent to purchasing power and its transferal between accounts of different banks.

The nature of cryptocurrencies is the same as modern (digital) money; however, while bank deposits are numbers written in the computers of trusted third parties, cryptocurrencies are numbers written in computers owned by individuals.

While the generation and distribution of traditional money is perceived as susceptible to be manipulated either by the Government or by private groups, cryptocurrencies, such as Bitcoin, are perceived as free from any central authority supervision; indeed, they are a pure product of technology that free individuals from third-parties control. Differently from bank money, cryptocurrencies do not represent debts of trusted entities which are convertible in cash, but, in their present form, can be bought and sold either privately or through exchanges. No trusted third party guarantees the convertibility of cryptocurrencies in any fiat currency.[11]

4.3. *Operational characteristics of cryptocurrencies*

In this section, we try to answer the central questions about the operational properties of money for the special case of cryptocurrencies:

How is it created?
How is it distributed and transferred?
How does it acquire, keep and change value?

What distinguishes cryptocurrencies from other alternative currencies, is the method of minting money and transferring funds. The innovation of cryptocurrencies consists in using a distributed ledger implemented through the worldwide web. The fact that there is no designated controller has been hailed as a major departure from classical systems. Indeed, the creation and distribution of cryptocurrencies is done with totally different criteria and methods than money. Cryptocurrencies are embodied in network systems with built-in rules that supervise the creation and allocation of themselves. In the case of Bitcoin, the best known cryptocurrency, new tokens are created every time a block of transactions is appended to the existing blockchain and are allocated as a reward to the only *miner* who, after validating the block transactions, has solved that block; new bitcoins are therefore the remuneration of the work done in verifying the integrity of transactions.[12] *Miners*, in turn, can sell their bitcoins to the public of users in exchange of fiat money.

A fundamental difference between bank money and cryptocurrencies is that the former are created, lent to people, and then returned and destroyed[13] while, in principle, the latter are permanent.

[11]The exceptional case of stablecoins, whose value is guaranteed, will be discussed in Section 6.

[12]A complete description of the consensus protocol for appending new blocks to the cryptocurrency blockchain is beyond the scope of this chapter; see Nakamoto (2008) and Böhme *et al.* (2015) for further details.

[13]An exception to this creation-destruction cycle is when money are created through a QE monetary policy.

Indeed, once created, cryptocurrencies stay forever in the computer systems that host them. Further, new tokens are minted as a reward to entities who perform services for the network. Finally, the creation of money brings profit to its creator.

Perhaps the most important characteristic of cryptocurrencies is the process of transferring cryptocurrencies between different users which takes place in a peer-to-peer network.

If users want to transfer bitcoins to pay for some goods, they simply order the transfer to their computers. The key issue with peer-to-peer money transfers is safety. Users must not be allowed to transfer crypto-money they do not have. Cryptographic techniques, such as the Blockchain, makes it possible to implement peer-to-peer transfers by defining a consensus protocol within the network without relying on the control of any central authority. Part of the fascination with cryptocurrencies is exactly due to the fact that control on the network of users seems to emerge spontaneously through the application of the above consensus protocol. Of course, those who perform the block validation service, the so called *miners*, need to be remunerated, for instance with new coins. Since not every user is confident of leaving control on the validity of transactions to spontaneous, yet remunerated, *miners*, some cryptocurrencies delegate this task to designated entities. It can be argued that this latter situation is a kind of hybrid between the standard two-tiers banking system and the cryptocurrencies that only rely on a peer-to-peer distributed ledger system.

Cryptocurrencies are sold at market prices, following the evolution of demand and supply. When they are used to make payments, both the buyer and the seller accept the risk of changing market prices, or they convert cryptocurrencies immediately prior to a purchase or after a sale. By today, existing cryptocurrencies have shown a very volatile price, also subject to financial bubbles, see Yermack (2015), Corbet *et al.* (2018), Baur *et al.* (2018), and Cretarola and Figà-Talamanca (2020, 2021). The main conclusion is that cryptocurrencies are actually used as speculative assets rather than as alternative money, and their price is often driven by sentiment and hype, Mai *et al.* (2018), Cretarola *et al.* (2018, 2020), Eom *et al.* (2019), and Figà-Talamanca and Patacca (2019, 2020). In addition, they have been proven to be mostly market inefficient, see Almudhaf (2018), Kristoufek (2018), and Kristoufek and Vosvrda (2019).

Schilling and Uhlig (2019) have created a model of an endowment economy with two competing, but intrinsically worthless currencies (Dollar and Bitcoin). Dollars are supplied by the central bank that control inflation, while Bitcoin grows deterministically. The authors find that Bitcoins prices form a martingale in a special case and discuss policy implications. Research have mainly focused on Bitcoin and Ethereum but most qualitative results can be transferred to other cryptocurrencies once realizing the strict interconnection among the cryptocurrency sector, see Sovbetov (2018) and Figà-Talamanca *et al.* (2021a,b).

However, our research question is not to investigate whether one of the currently living cryptocurrencies may represent an alternative to money; rather, we are concerned with the ideological aspect underlying the possible issuing of new cryptocurrencies which might replace or side fiat currencies. Of course, market price stability would be an important requirement in order to make a cryptocurrency desirable as a medium of exchange.

4.4. *What is their impact on the real economy?*

The current use of cryptocurrencies for making purchases/sales is mainly justified either by ideological motivations or by a peculiar desire of secrecy. In aggregate, the desire of secrecy cannot be the only motivation. The need for secrecy is typically due to the need to hide criminal activities. But those who engage in criminal activities want to use the proceeds of their activity to buy goods and services. Therefore, it is necessary that cryptocurrencies be used primarily for normal transactions so that the proceeds of illegal activities can be used to purchase goods and services. By now, the total value of cryptocurrencies represents a very small fraction of the money in circulation, probably less than 1%, making their impact on the economy quite small.

The potential impact on economies can be appreciated by imagining scenarios of diffusion of cryptocurrencies; one main example may be the adoption by some central bank of a special cryptocurrency to side the government money. This scenario has been hypothesized several times in the recent years, e.g., by Russia Central Bank,[14] and discussed from an economic viewpoint in Selgin (2015), Raskin and Yermack (2016), Bolt and Van Oordt (2020), Mancini-Griffoli *et al.* (2018), BIS (2018). A first example of government issued cryptocurrency is the Petro, issued by Venezuela in early 2018, which is backed to oil and mineral reserves.

If a significant fraction of transactions is done through cryptocurrencies, then they will add to the global purchasing power, insofar as an increment in the volume of cryptocurrencies leaves the amount of money in circulation unchanged. Therefore, the effect of creation of cryptocurrencies is essentially the same as the creation of standard money. In-depth analysis of innovations for the monetary system and impact on the real economy given by cryptocurrencies is presented in Sections 5 and 6.

4.5. *The key differences between money and cryptocurrencies*

Summing up, the key differences between money and cryptocurrencies are the following:

1. The creation of new money is done by central and commercial banks, usually by issuing loans, while the creation of new cryptocurrencies is not performed by specialized third parties but through a reward for *miners* who guarantee the security of the network by validating transactions and following the consensus protocol of the cryptocurrency.
2. Similarly, the transfer of funds from one entity to another does depend on a trusted third party for money, while transfers occur on a peer-to-peer network (in principle), based on an open-source code and cryptographic rules.
3. New cryptocurrencies are allocated to the *miners* and later sold to the public, while money is allocated to those who sell assets to the central bank of to those who take on loans.

[14]https://www.coindesk.com/russian-central-bank-to-consider-gold-backed-cryptocurrency.

4. There is no mechanism such as credit to make cryptocurrencies directly available to the users.
5. There is no legal framework for cryptocurrencies.

5. Innovations for the Monetary System

In the previous sections, we outlined the current theory of money. Let us remark once more that a theory of money is not a law of nature, but it is a description of the working of a human artifact, the monetary system. It is likely that the current monetary system will undergo a process of fundamental innovation in the following years.

As known, innovations can be introduced either in a pushed or pulled way. It is therefore worth investigating here current limits and problems that financial and monetary systems witness today, to see whether innovations can tackle specific issues and pave the way to a solution for some of them.

Among the general drivers for innovation, two ones can be identified as mainly concerning financial systems: the introduction of a new technology, or policy, market or societal changes occurring in the economic system. In the following, we identify three possible aspects of financial systems, with a particular focus on the policies and practices of central banks, that could benefit from the wide adoption of cryptocurrency technologies and how they could improve the conduct of monetary authorities.

5.1. *Elimination of banknotes*

As we have seen, current money is hierarchical, with banknotes as base money and all other levels as packages of money of lower levels. A possible innovation, which is under study in many states, is the replacement of banknotes with digital money. Though it is unlikely, for practical reasons, that banknotes will be completely abolished, it is possible that the role of base money will be given to some kind of digital money.

Remark that a base money is necessary as a unit of value. A bank deposit is denominated in terms of a base money. If there were no base money, we would need some system to coordinate the value of bank deposits. A base money, such as banknotes, assures that a deposit at bank A in location X can be moved to bank B in location Y without any loss or gain in nominal value. In the absence of a base money, the transfer of deposits would become a matter of negotiation as if they were different currencies.

Distributed ledger technologies such as blockchain offer a natural substitute for base money; they make a digital 'currency' exchanged through a distributed ledger available to any participant. Any bank deposit can be denominated in units of that currency. With distributed ledger technologies a central bank can issue its own digital money that can freely circulate and used to coordinate the value of bank deposits.

5.2. *Credit-based money generation and distribution*

Two main ways have been identified for generating money: credit issued (by commercial banks), and purchase of assets (by central banks); both of them are based on credit.

Credit creates purchasing power given only to those who own assets as a guarantee or those who can demonstrate their ability to generate an enough stream of income in the future.

This way, the creation of money through credit has created instabilities and the creation of money through the purchase of assets by central banks has produced increase in asset prices but little effect on the real economy. In most western countries, for example, firms are net creditors while the general public is a net debtor. This situation, coupled with stagnant salaries and increased profits, is a source of systemic risk.

Debt can become unsustainable. A few proposals to create purchasing power without corresponding debts begin to appear. Governments begin to realize that there are segments of the population that have insufficient purchasing power even for mere subsistence. Therefore, it has been proposed to offer a basic transfer of money from the central bank directly to people.

Looking forward to innovative economic initiatives, we can imagine scenarios where new purchasing power is created with rules that do not entail individuals taking out debts. Of course, scenarios of this type would require a major overhaul of the banking system.

In other words, there is a possibility that money will become a 'token' of electronic nature, that creates purchasing power, but it is not strictly associated to debt: a Central Bank Digital Currency.

5.3. *A flat one-level banking system*

The replacement of banknotes with digital money can be seen as one step towards a more fundamental change of the banking system in the direction of creating a one-level banking system. Currently, the banking system is organized on two levels: central banks and commercial banks. The two-level system ensures not only controls but also orderly transfer of money. In fact, every transfer of money from one bank to another requires a corresponding transfer of bank reserves. However, if central banks begin to offer digital money with distributed ledger technologies, in practice we would see the parallel implementation of a one-level banking system. Central banks might begin to offer credit and other banking services to their digital currency clients.

Of course, today there are technological hurdles to overcome but one can predict that in the near future it will be possible to implement large scale distributed ledger technologies. Distributed ledgers might or might not be implemented with blockchain. The mechanism of independent miners to guarantee the integrity of the system might be replaced with systems under the direct control of central banks. A large-scale implementation of central bank digital money with distributed ledger technologies would imply a major change of the banking system.

6. Future Evolution of Cryptocurrencies

Many authors (like Kavuri and Milne (2020); Yermack (2019)) forecast that cryptocurrencies will be a disruptive element for banking and for finance in general.

The future of cryptocurrencies can be analyzed from different angles, like:

- The future of the blockchain technology;
- The future issue of private stablecoins;
- The adoption of Central Bank Digital Currencies (CBDCs).

The first point is related to the observation that today most money is digital, and it is based on some form of cryptographic encoding; therefore, we have to adopt a narrow definition of cryptocurrencies as currencies based on distributed ledger technology with or without permission. However, we cannot really place too much confidence in the forecast that distributed ledger technologies based on cryptographic techniques will stay for decades. Indeed, making technology forecasts has proved to be extremely difficult by now. Just to give an example, Google has just announced to have reached Quantum Supremacy, that is, they have announced to be the first to master in practice the technology of quantum computing. Google's quantum computer, called Sycamore, has only 54 qbits but, according to leaked information, is already extremely more powerful than current supercomputers. Now, the type of computing power that seems to be possible with quantum computing would place a definite challenge to any cryptographic technique. Here we have an example of two highly advertised technologies, blockchain-type, and quantum computing, both claiming to be able to have a revolutionary impact but that are basically incompatible.

As for the issue of a stable cryptocurrency (stablecoin), several large companies have advertised their interest in issuing new cryptocurrencies. For instance, Facebook is about to issue a new cryptocurrency, named Libra, having previously established the Libra Association to oversee the currency. The association includes companies from the Payment sector (e.g., Paypal, Mastercad, Visa), from web-based marketplace (e.g., Booking, eBay, Spotify) and Telecommunications (e.g., Vodafone) as well as non-profit organizations.

The belief that the future of cryptocurrencies is linked to emergence of a large issuer builds on the debate between state money and private money. Many argue that state money is governed by politics whilst private money is governed by healthy market rules and can even be thought as a truly 'democratic' tool, governed by its users. Unfortunately, this discussion is completely ill placed. First, in developed countries money is already private. Money is issued by the private banking system with rules of money generation that are essentially business rules. In fact, money is generated when private banks grant loans. Granting loans is subject to business constraints. The only large-scale intervention of central banks in the money generation process is QE, when central banks buy assets from non-banks.

The entire banking system, including the central banks, is mostly privately owned. In modern developed countries the independence of central banks, and therefore of the entire banking system, from the government is a critical political issue. Moreover, it is impossible to make forecasts on possible market reactions to the issue of such cryptocurrencies and to establish, a priori, the stability of their value over time, unless it was explicitly bind to some fiat currency (as the Thether example). Further, serious problems may arise associated to a stablecoin. Indeed, if its stability is guaranteed by an equivalent deposit in some standard currency, then large sums of money may be kept idle as bank deposits; in this case money is created (at a cost) by the banking system to be used (by the public) for buying the cryptocurrency. Further, if the equivalent deposit is invested in the financial market, then the stabilization of the cryptocurrency will be only partial, being related to market prices of the assets used as guarantee.

The monetary event with the highest impact on the current banking system and monetary policy is the possible future adoption of cryptocurrencies by central banks. In our opinion, this is the key topic when discussing the future of cryptocurrencies. According to Barontini and Holden (2019) and Mancini-Griffoli *et al.* (2018) several central banks are indeed exploring their possible use, though different purposes may be followed. Cryptocurrencies could simply be payment assets that central banks offer for sale. Further, it might be that central banks will decide to develop cryptocurrencies as money, opening accounts and letting people borrow their cryptocurrency. The introduction of such CBDCs is a subject that has come to the attention of the large public and the media after a few countries have announced plans to create their own digital money. This, in itself, would be a major disruption, since central banks would give direct access to their account to private individuals making the current two-levels banking system outdated. At this point the main question become: what are the CBDCs and how would they be implemented?

In order to answer these questions Bech and Garratt (2017) take advantage of a classification of money based on four key properties: issuer (central bank or other), form (electronic or physical), accessibility (universal or limited) and transfer mechanism (centralized or decentralized, i.e., peer-to-peer). Following this approach they

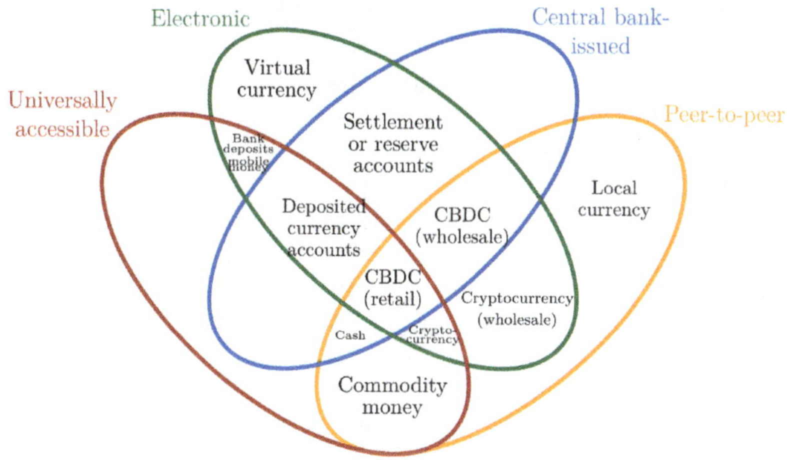

Figure 1. The money flower: A taxonomy of money.

define the CBDC[15] as 'an electronic form of central bank money that can be exchanged in a decentralized manner known as peer-to-peer, meaning that transactions occur directly between the payer and the payee without the need for a central intermediary'. The key feature that distinguishes CBDC from other forms of digital central bank money, such as reserves, is the choice of decentralization as transfer mechanism. Furthermore, defining the different accessibility level, the choice can be articulated between a universal available payment instrument (in some sense a digital cash substitute), and a restricted digital settlement for wholesale payment (a substitute for the interbank payment system). In the first case the payment system can combine the anonymity feature, that is typical of cash, with the digital form; instead, the choice of the latter option could improve the efficiency and reduce the settlement costs. Bech and Garratt (2017) propose a Venn diagram to illustrates the taxonomy of money: the *money flower*, see Figure 1.

Figure 1 underlines the retail CBDC as the only form of money that is located at the intersection of the four ellipses, that is the only

[15]In Bech and Garratt (2017) the authors use the acronym CBCC Central Bank Cryptocurrencies) instead of CBDC.

form of money that is issued by the central bank, it is electronic, it is universally accessible and guarantee peer-to-peer payments. In other word is the electronic version of cash, decentralized, and consequently anonymous, in transaction and centralized, and well identified, in supply. This form could solve the problem of high volatility price of cryptocurrencies and the potential to relieve the zero lower bound constraint on monetary policy Bech and Garratt (2017). However, the very high drawback could affect the standard commercial banks through crowding out effect, people could convert their bank deposits into CBDC Tolle (2016), and disintermediation effect. Due to these problems, the adoption of retail CBDC appears rather difficult in the short term. Distinct conclusion can be drawn for the wholesale CBDC where a technological change could lead to an improvement in the system efficiency without changing the setting of the system itself.

CPMI (2018), following the money flower scheme presented above, highlights further critical points arisen with initial exploration of CBDC; specifically the legal consideration, anti-money laundering (AML) and countering the financing of terrorism (CFT), cybersecurity and the robustness. The authors evidence that a lot of central banks do not have the authority to issue digital currencies and/or it is not clear whether a CBDC is 'legal tender'. Furthermore, it is not clear how AML/CFT requirements can be practically achieved for anonymous forms of CBDC. Let us note two facts. First, banknotes are currently sold to the public. In general, the public buys banknotes from their banks. For example, when people use an ATM machine, they receive banknotes and their bank account id debited for the same amount, a transaction which is a sale of banknotes in exchange for bank deposits. Banknotes have this paradoxical character: they are the fundamental form of money, but in practice they are sold as a commodity. Second, banknotes are anonymous. One can make a payment in banknotes without leaving any monetary trace of the transaction. Governments have already tried to recover full control of financial transactions by limiting the amount of cash that can be used and practically owned. Distributed ledger techniques such as blockchain lend themselves easily to satisfy both needs. Cryptocurrencies now in circulation are anonymous and are traded in exchange. Central banks are thinking to offer the same service. But there are a few considerations. If central banks issue CBDC the general public must have accounts with the central bank. Now, simply opening electronic accounts is not a resource-hungry operation. One can imagine that the public might have a bank account with the central bank just to order/sell CBDC. However, it has been suggested that having direct contact with the public will allow the central bank to offer full banking services including loans. This would indeed upset the banking system. First commercial banks would feel the competition from the central banks. But the central bank itself should increase staff and facilities to deal with possibly tens of millions of clients. It is difficult to imagine that this could happen on a large scale. The idea of a centralized mega-central bank in competition with the entire banking system seems to be politically unfeasible. Note that the central bank should offer on a large-scale money which is not traceable. This would make this possibility even more unlikely. As noted above, making technological or societal forecasts is always very difficult. However, it looks likely that CBDC will have a limited scope.

Finally, it must be checked whether the current distributed ledger technology guarantee a high cyber-security standard and very robust requirements for reliability, scalability, throughput and resilience. Research and development and legislative changes may require long time: according to the survey in Barontini and Holden (2019) the 70% of central bank start began to investigate the opportunity to introduce the CBDC in order to improve the payments safety, domestic efficiency and the cash changeover. However, only a few central banks consider the possibility to issue a CBDC within the next decade.

7. Concluding Remarks

In this chapter, we analyze cryptocurrencies from the point of view of the theory of money. Answering to five fundamental questions, we compare cryptocurrencies with standard money, and we evidence that cryptocurrencies satisfy some but not all conditions that qualify a medium of exchange as money. Specifically, money is created through the issue of new loans or by unilateral actions of central banks. New cryptocurrencies are typically created as a reward to miners, increasing the total amount of money in circulation, and are transferred through a peer-to-peer network without third party supervision. Typically, the value of cryptocurrencies fluctuates in function of supply and demand. An exception are stablecoins that achieve stability by freezing the corresponding amount of standard money. Among possible future scenarios, the most disruptive would be the adoption of cryptocurrencies by central banks through the issue of CBDC. CBDC might just be used to replace cash, or they might be offered together with full banking services, including loans, allowing the public to open a bank account directly with the central bank. However, the idea of a centralized huge-central-bank in competition with the traditional banking system seems to be politically unfeasible.

References

Almudhaf, F. (2018). Pricing efficiency of bitcoin trusts. *Applied Economics Letters, 25*(7), 504–508.

Baek, C., & Elbeck, M. (2015). Bitcoins as an investment or speculative vehicle? A first look, *Applied Economics Letters, 22*(1), 30–34.

Barontini, C., & Holden, H. (2019). Proceeding with caution-a survey on central bank digital currency. In *Proceeding with Caution — A Survey on Central Bank Digital Currency. (January 8, 2019).* Bank for International Settlements (BIS) paper, No. 101, Switzerland.

Baur, D. G., Hong, K., & Lee, A. D. (2018). Bitcoin: Medium of exchange or speculative assets? *Journal of International Financial Markets, Institutions and Money, 54*, 177–189.

Bech, M. L., & Garratt, R. (2017). Central bank cryptocurrencies. *BIS Quarterly Review*, September 2017, 55–70.

BIS (2018). Annual economic report 2018, Technical report, Bank for International Settlements.

Blanc, J. (2018). *Les monnaies alternatives.* La Découverte, coll. ≪ Repères économie ≫, 2018, 127 p., ISBN : 978-2-7071-8636-2.

Böhme, R., Christin, N., Edelman, B., & Moore, T. (2015). Bitcoin: Economics, technology, and governance. *Journal of Economic Perspectives, 29*(2), 213–38.

Bolt, W., & Van Oordt, M. R. (2020). On the value of virtual currencies. *Journal of Money, Credit and Banking, 52*(4), 835–862.

Brunnermeier, M. K. (2008). Bubbles. In S. Durlauf & L. Blume (Eds.), *The New Palgrave Dictionary of Economics* (2nd edn.). Palgrave Macmillan, London.

Brunnermeier, M. K., & Oehmke, M. (2013). Chapter 18 — Bubbles, financial crises, and systemic risk. In *Handbook of the Economics of Finance*, Vol. 2, Part B, pp. 1221–1288. Elsevier, North Holland.

Cheah, E.-T., & Fry, J. (2015). Speculative bubbles in bitcoin markets? An empirical investigation into the fundamental value of bitcoin. *Economics Letters, 130*, 32–36.

Corbet, S., Lucey, B., & Yarovaya, L. (2018). Datestamping the bitcoin and ethereum bubbles. *Finance Research Letters, 26*, 81–88.

CPMI (2018). Central bank digital currencies, Technical report, Committee on Payments and Market Infrastructures.

Cretarola, A., & Figà-Talamanca, G. (2020). Bubble regime identification in an attention-based model for bitcoin and ethereum price dynamics. *Economics Letters, 191*, 108831.

Cretarola, A., & Figà-Talamanca, G. (2021). Detecting bubbles in bitcoin price dynamics via market exuberance. *Annals of Operations Research, 299*(1), 459–479.

Cretarola, A., Figà-Talamanca, G., & Patacca, M. (2018). A continuous time model for bitcoin price dynamics. In *Mathematical and Statistical Methods for Actuarial Sciences and Finance.* (pp. 273–277). Springer, Cham.

Cretarola, A., Figà-Talamanca, G., & Patacca, M. (2020). Market attention and bitcoin price modeling: Theory, estimation and option pricing. *Decisions in Economics and Finance, 43*(1), 187–228.

DeMeulenaere, S. (2007). 2006 Annual Report of the worldwide database of complementary currency systems. *International Journal of Community Currency Research, 11*, 23–35.

Derudder, P. (2012). *Les monnaies locales complémentaires: pourquoi, comment?* Gap, Éditions Yves Michel, France, 256 p.

ECB (2012). Virtual currencies schemes, Technical report, European Central Bank. https://www.ecb.europa.eu/pub/pdf/other/virtualcurrencyschemes201210en.pdf

Eom, C., Kaizoji, T., Kang, S. H., & Pichl, L. (2019). Bitcoin and investor sentiment: Statistical characteristics and predictability. *Physica A: Statistical Mechanics and its Applications, 514*, 511–521.

Ferguson, N. (2008). *The Ascent of Money: A Financial History of the World.* Penguin, New York.

Figà-Talamanca, G., Focardi, S., & Patacca, M. (2021a). Common dynamic factors for cryptocurrencies and multiple pair-trading statistical arbitrages. *Decisions in Economics and Finance, 44*(2), 863–882.

Figà-Talamanca, G., Focardi, S., & Patacca, M. (2021b). Regime switches and commonalities of the cryptocurrencies asset class. *The North American Journal of Economics and Finance, 57*, 101425.

Figà-Talamanca, G., & Patacca, M. (2019). Does market attention affect bitcoin returns and volatility? *Decisions in Economics and Finance, 42*(1), 135–155.

Figà-Talamanca, G., & Patacca, M. (2020). Disentangling the relationship between bitcoin and market attention measures. *Journal of Industrial and Business Economics 47*(1), 71–91.

Focardi, S. M. (2018). *Money: What It Is, How It's Created, Who Gets It, and Why It Matters*, Routledge, London.

Garcia, D., Tessone, C. J., Mavrodiev, P., & Perony, N. (2014). The digital traces of bubbles: Feedback cycles between socio-economic signals in the bitcoin economy. *Journal of the Royal Society Interface, 11*(99), 20140623.

Gesell, S. (1958). *The Natural Economic Order.* Owen, London.

Graeber, D. (2012). *Debt: The First 5000 Years.* Penguin, UK.

Gregoriou, A. (2019). Cryptocurrencies and asset pricing. *Applied Economics Letters, 26*(12), 995–998.

Guo, Y., & Liang, C. (2016). Blockchain application and outlook in the banking industry. *Financial Innovation, 2*(1), 24.

Ide, K., & Sornette, D. (2002). Oscillatory finite-time singularities in finance, population and rupture. *Physica A, 307*, 63–106.

Johansen, A., Ledoit, O., & Sornette, D. (2000). Crashes as critical points. *International Journal of Theoretical and Applied Finance, 3*, 219–255.

Johansen, A., Sornette, D., & Ledoit, O. (1999). Predicting financial crashes using discrete scale invariance. *Risk, 1*, 5–32.

Kavuri, A. S., & Milne, A. (2020). Evolution or revolution? Distributed ledger technologies in financial services. CAMA Working Paper.

Kristoufek, L. (2018). On bitcoin markets (in)efficiency and its evolution. *Physica A: Statistical Mechanics and its Applications, 503*, 257–262.

Kristoufek, L., & Vosvrda, M. (2019). Cryptocurrencies market efficiency ranking: Not so straightforward. *Physica A: Statistical Mechanics and its Applications, 531*, 120853.

Krugman, P. (2018). Bubble, bubble, fraud and trouble. *New York Times*, 29.

Mai, F., Shan, Z., Bai, Q., Wang, X., & Chiang, R. H. (2018). How does social media impact bitcoin value? A test of the silent majority hypothesis. *Journal of Management Information Systems, 35*(1), 19–52.

Mancini-Griffoli, T., Martinez, M. S., Peria, I. A., Ari, A., Kiff, J., Popescu, A., & Rochon, C. (2018). Casting light on central bank digital currency. *IMF, Staff Discussion Note*, November.

Martin, F. (2015). *Money: The Unauthorized Biography from Coinage to Cryptocurrencies.* Vintage Books, New York.

Mehrling, P. (2012). The inherent hierarchy of money. *Social Fairness and Economics: Economic Essays in the Spirit of Duncan Foley, 169*, 394.

Metcalfe, B. (2013). Metcalfe's law after 40 years of ethernet. *Computer, 46*, 26–31.

Min, S., & Zhu, W. (2019). Real-time prediction of bitcoin bubble crashes. arXiv:1905.09647 [q-fin.ST].

Minsky, H. P. (1986). *Stabilizing an Unstable Economy*, Vol. 1. Twentieth Century Fund Report. Yale University Press, New Haven and London.

Mishkin, F. S. (2007). *The Economics of Money, Banking, and Financial Markets.* Toronto: Pearson Addison Wesley.

Mitchell, I. A. (1913). What is money? *Banking Law Journal, 30*, 377.

Mitchell, I. A. (1914). The credit theory of money. *Banking Law Journal, 31*, 151–168.

Moore, B. J. (1988). *Horizontalists and Verticalists: The Macroeconomics of credit money.* Cambridge University Press, Cambridge.

Nakamoto, S. (2008). Bitcoin: A peer-to-peer electronic cash system. White Paper.

Nash, J. F. (2002). Ideal money. *Southern Economic Journal, 69*(1), 4–11.

Nash, J. F. (2009). Ideal money and asymptotically ideal money. *Contributions to Game Theory and Management, 2*, 281–293.

Pozsar, Z. (2014). Shadow banking: The money view. Available at SSRN 2476415.

Priem, R. (2020). Distributed ledger technology for securities clearing and settlement: Benefits, risks, and regulatory implications. *Financial Innovation, 6*(1), 1–25.

Raskin, M., & Yermack, D. (2016). Digital currencies, decentralized ledgers, and the future of central banking, Technical report, National Bureau of Economic Research.

Reiss, D. G. (2018). Is money going digital? An alternative perspective on the current hype. *Financial Innovation, 4*(1), 1–6.

Schilling, L., & Uhlig, H. (2019). Some simple bitcoin economics. *Journal of Monetary Economics, 106*, 16–26.

Selgin, G. (2014). Bitcoin: Problems and Prospects. Hillsdale University's 2014 Free Market Forum. https://www.hillsdale.edu/wp-content/uploads/2016/02/FMF-2014-Bitcoin-Problems-and-Prospects.pdf

Selgin, G. (2015). Synthetic commodity money. *Journal of Financial Stability, 17*, 92–99.

Shiller, R. J. (2014). In search of a stable electronic currency. *NY Times, 1*, 04–14.

Shubik, M. (2004). *The Theory of Money and Financial Institutions*, Vol. 1. MIT Press, Cambridge, MA.

Sornette, D. (1998). Discrete-scale invariance and complex dimensions. *Physics Report, 297*, 239–270.

Sornette, D., & Cauwels, P. (2015). Financial bubbles: mechanisms and diagnostics. *Review of Behavioral Economics, 2*, 279–305.

Sovbetov, Y. (2018). Factors influencing cryptocurrency prices: Evidence from bitcoin, ethereum, dash, litcoin, and monero. *Journal of Economics and Financial Analysis, 2*(2), 1–27.

Stiglitz, J. (2017). Bitcoin ought to be out lawed. In *World Economic Forum.* https://www.weforum.org/agenda/2017/11/joseph-stiglitz-bitcoin-ought-to-be-outlawed/.

Thaler, R. (2018). The market that looks most like a bubble to me is bitcoin and its brethren. *ECO Portuguese Economy*, 22 January.

Tolle, M. (2016). Central bank digital currency: The end of monetary policy as we know it? *Bank Underground, 25.*

Triffin, R. (1960). Gold and the dollar crisis: The future of convertibility (Vol. 39). Yale University Press, New Haven.

Wheatley, S., Sornette, D., Huber, T., Reppen, M., & Gantner, R. N. (2019). Are bitcoin bubbles predictable? combining a generalized metcalfe's law and the log-periodic power law singularity mode? *Royal Society Open Science, 6*(6), 180538.

White, R., Marinakis, Y., Islam, N., & Walsh, S. (2020). Is bitcoin a currency, a technology-based product, or something else? *Technological Forecasting and Social Change, 151*, 119877.

Yermack, D. (2015). Is bitcoin a real currency? An economic appraisal. In *Handbook of Digital Currency* (pp. 31–43). Elsevier, North Holland.

Yermack, D., & Fingerhut, A. (2019). Blockchain technology's potential in the financial system. In *Proceedings of the 2019 Financial Market's Conference.*

https://doi.org/10.1142/9781800612723_0004

Chapter 4

Community Detection in Cryptocurrencies with Potential Applications to Portfolio Diversification

Jenna Gavin* and Martin Crane†

School of Computing, Dublin City University, Glasnevin, Dublin 9, Ireland

**jenna.gavin6@mail.dcu.ie*

†martin.crane@dcu.ie

Abstract

In this chapter, the cross-correlations of cryptocurrency returns are analyzed. The chapter examines one years worth of data for 146 cryptocurrencies from the period 01/01/2019 to 31/12/2019. The cross-correlations of these returns are firstly analyzed by comparing eigenvalues and eigenvector components of the cross-correlation matrix C with random matrix theory (RMT) assumptions. Results show that C deviates from these assumptions indicating that C contains genuine information about the correlations between the different cryptocurrencies. From here, Louvain community detection method is applied as a clustering mechanism and 15 community groupings are detected. Finally, Principal Component analysis (PCA) is completed on the standardized returns of each of these clusters to create a portfolio of cryptocurrencies for investment. This method selects a portfolio which contains a number of high value coins when compared back against their market ranking in the same year. In the interest of assessing continuity of the initial results, the method is also applied to a smaller dataset of the top 50 cryptocurrencies across three time periods of $T = 125$ days, which produces similar results. The results obtained in this chapter show that these methods could be useful for constructing a portfolio of optimally performing cryptocurrencies.

Keywords: Financial markets, graph theory, cryptocurrencies, correlation matrix, community structures, principal component analysis.

1. Introduction

In recent years, cryptocurrencies have become an increasingly popular investment opportunity (Alessandretti *et al.*, 2018). Since its introduction in 2009, the cryptocurrency investment market has been evolving quite quickly as it has experienced dramatic rises and falls in the space of a few years (Makarov and Schoar, 2020). Rather than investing in traditional stocks and shares, investors are now opting to invest in the thousands of cryptocurrencies that are available. Coinmarketcap,[1] shows the daily statistics on over 2,000 cryptocurrencies. With such a wide variety of currencies available for investment, an investor must choose wisely if the aim is to optimize their returns.

Throughout this chapter, cryptocurrencies are analyzed with the aim of constructing an optimal investment portfolio. Inspired by the recent work of Chaudhari and Crane (2020), we will analyze cryptocurrencies based on their groupings formed using the Louvain community detection algorithm. Chaudhari and Crane (2020) analyzed cross-correlation dynamics and community structures within 59 cryptocurrencies over 150 days. In this chapter, the methods applied in (Chaudhari and Crane, 2020) will be extended in a number of different ways. Firstly, these methods are applied to a larger dataset with over three times the amount of cryptocurrencies (146 cryptocurrencies) over a larger time period (365 days).

Secondly, the community structures are further enhanced by incorporating principal component analysis (PCA) into this study. PCA is a technique used for dimensionality reduction in data analysis. Using linear combinations of input variables, PCA reduces a large number of variables into a smaller number of factors while still maintaining most of the variability within the data (Hargreaves and Mani, 2015). In this chapter, this method is applied to the returns of cryptocurrencies based on their community groupings. The cryptocurrencies which account for the highest amount of variability within the

[1]Coinmarketcap.com.

first principal component are deemed to be the *Leading Cryptocurrency.* These *leading cryptocurrencies* are combined and analyzed to discover if these methods can be applied to construct a portfolio of best performing cryptocurrencies for investment.

Thirdly, the continuity and robustness of the methods are compared and analyzed. *Leading Cryptocurrencies* obtained are compared against market rankings to understand if these methods are useful for detecting stable cryptocurrencies which are likely to stay in a high rank after extended periods of time thus, helping to create an attractive investment portfolio.

This chapter is organized as follows: Section 2 sees a review of the relevant literature surrounding the application of topics in financial and non-financial analysis. The method of obtaining data for this analysis is detailed in Section 3. This section gives details on the pre-processing techniques used to address incomplete records included in the data. Section 4 details the methods used throughout this analysis. These methods include random matrix theory (RMT), community detection and PCA. These methods are then repeated on a smaller dataset. Finally, Section 5 looks at the results obtained and conclusions are discussed in Section 6.

2. Literature Review

Cryptocurrencies first began trading in 2009 with Bitcoin being one of the earliest coins with many more following on from it. While cryptocurrencies are still quite new on the trading market, there has already been plenty of research emerging into this relatively new area of investment in an attempt to further understand the dramatic rises and falls seen in the market and whether their co-movements could be useful (Makarov and Schoar, 2020). Stosic *et al.* (2018) consider the collective behavior of cryptocurrency price changes. They analyze the correlations between 119 cryptocurrencies over a period of 200 days and identify hierarchical structures and groupings of cryptocurrency pairs (Stosic *et al.*, 2018). Through these correlations, they discover the existence of network and community structures in the minimum spanning tree formed from the data. Stosic *et al.* (2018) conclude that these behaviors can be useful for building cryptocurrency investment portfolios (Stosic *et al.*, 2018). Liew *et al.* (2019) carry out a similar analysis, during which they consider the cross-correlation dynamics within cryptocurrencies. They also use PCA and machine learning methods to predict cryptocurrency prices. As part of their analysis, they perform tests across different numbers of cryptocurrencies and across different time periods to avoid bias in their results.

There has also been research into the effect of Bitcoin on other cryptocurrencies. Hu *et al.* (2019) utilize PCA to investigate the relationship between Altcoins (*coins alternative to Bitcoin*) and Bitcoin returns Hu *et al.* (2019). For the purpose of their analysis, they only choose currencies that have at least 2 years of time series data to ensure that only coins with sufficiently complete data is included. They show that the principal component of Altcoins daily and monthly returns is highly correlated with Bitcoin returns.

Punčeva *et al.* (2018) consider community groupings within cryptocurrencies. However, unlike other studies, they specifically consider trust communities[2] within cryptocurrencies. The data used in their study contains user ratings based on interactions with cryptocurrencies and focuses on the Bitcoin OTC and Bitcoin-Alpha networks. They find that four different community detection algorithms (*Louvain, -Infomap, -Walktrap*, and *Leading Eigenvector*) perform well and give optimal modularity. They conclude that these community structures exist and can help to decide strategies of how to interact on cryptocurrency exchange platforms (Punčeva *et al.*, 2018).

Cryptocurrencies are clearly a new class of investible instruments (Hu *et al.*, 2019), therefore one should also consider research into other financial assets available for investment. There have been similar studies on traditional stocks and shares, using PCA and community detection to build optimal investment portfolios. Hargreaves and Mani (2015) show how PCA can be used to select optimally performing stocks. They take 22 variables for over 100 stocks. Through their analysis, they reduce the 22 variables to 4 (*Return on Investment, Return on Equity, Book Value per Share* and *Revenue per Share*). These four variables were used to identify optimal stocks for investment (Hargreaves and Mani, 2015). Zahedi and Rounaghi (2015) used similar methods while analyzing stock prices in the Tehran stock

[2] *Trust communities* are created using the ratings of users after interacting with each other. These ratings are used as weights for creating such networks.

exchange. They concluded that these stock prices can be predicted using artificial neural networks and PCA.

Conlon and co-workers have also contributed to the literature in the area of portfolio analysis. In one paper, the authors explore the use of RMT for portfolio optimization of hedge funds (Conlon *et al.*, 2007). By using hedge fund returns to construct a cross-correlation matrix, it is seen that strategy information can be deduced from the deviating eigenvalues of RMT predictions. The cross-correlation matrix is cleansed using this strategy information, which improves the difference between the predicted risk and actual risk of the portfolio. Thus, they deduce that the filtered correlation matrix is useful for portfolio optimization (Conlon *et al.*, 2007). In another study, Conlon *et al.* (2009) also analyzed the cross-correlations in financial time-series data from two different stock markets. The eigenvalues of the cross-correlations, formed from random subsets of S&P equities and members of the Dow Jones Euro Stoxx 50 indices, are analyzed with various models. Using sliding windows of time intervals of 200 days, the authors analyze how the correlation matrices and eigenvalue structures change over time.

Network analysis and community detection has been researched in the area of finance and investment. Networks, such as biological, social, technological and informational, are systems which can be represented in the form of graphs where objects are represented by nodes and their interactions define how the nodes are connected (Newman, 2012). Community detection is a method of clustering networks which can give insights into natural divisions or clusters in our data (Lu *et al.*, 2015).

Fenn *et al.* (2012) investigated community dynamics within the exchange-rate market and how they can provide insight into the correlation structures and interactions between exchange-rates. Their results indicated that the exchange rates located in the centre of a community structure have strong influence on other exchange rates within the community. This can be used to show which exchange rates dominate a market at a given time (Fenn *et al.*, 2012). The authors concluded that this type of analysis could also be applied to other asset classes.

Numerous community detection algorithms have been developed. The *Louvain* method is one of which that is investigated in this chapter and is explained in more detail in Section 4.4. Louvain community detection algorithm has been previously applied in studies investigating prediction of stock prices.

Patil *et al.* (2020) explored this idea by comparing the use of graph-based deep learning models (using graph convoluted neural networks), graph-based machine learning models (using Louvain community detection algorithm) and traditional statistical approach (auto regressive integrated moving average (ARIMA)), for building a prediction model. They concluded that graph-based models outperformed a traditional statistical approach for building a prediction model. Wang and Xie (2015) used Louvain community detection while investigating the correlation structure and dynamics of international real estate securities markets. They analyzed markets from 2006–2012 and found that using Louvain community detection on planar maximally filtered graphs showed that national markets clustered together according to their geographical locations (Wang and Xie, 2015). Drozdz *et al.* (2020) and Watorek *et al.* (2021) in a comprehensive review of cryptocurrencies, detail how the asset class has developed over recent years with increased numbers of participants, turnover and transaction frequency. The authors show that, structural self-organization has led cryptocurrency markets to attain complexity characteristics comparable to those of the Forex market at the level of individual time-series. The key difference between them being that the cross-correlations between the exchange rates on cryptocurrency platforms differ. This 'stagnation' in information flow has led to the existence of more frequent arbitrage opportunities in the cryptocurrency market. The authors hold out the potential for detection of these opportunites leading to the potential for investment portfolios with reduced exposure to risk to be constructed.

Among other methods in Watorek *et al.* (2021) and, of interest to this work, the authors make use of the minimum spanning tree (MST) for the cryptocurrency market. They show that characteristics of the market appear to vary with time scale. In particular, with increasing scale, the MST structure becomes more diverse and decentralized: while Ethereum dominates at small scale, this disappears with increasing scale.

The Louvain method has also been applied in the area of health informatics. Surian *et al.* (2016) examined Twitter posts using Louvain community detection while analyzing opinions about the human papillomavirus (HPV) vaccines. They found that the use of Louvain community detection, alongside topic modeling, was a successful method to characterize Twitter communities for monitoring online opinions of public health applications. They concluded that this method could be useful in the future to identify online communities that can be easily influenced by the negative opinions about public health interventions (Surian *et al.*, 2016).

3. Data

In this study, cryptocurrency data was obtained using the *crypto* package in R. The *crypto* package retrieves historical opening, high, low and closing values for all cryptocurrencies available on the website: https://coinmarketcap.com/ (Vent, 2020).

A historical snapshot of the top 200 cryptocurrencies as at 29 December 2019 was extracted from the https://coinmarketcap.com/. The historical closing values were then extracted for these top 200 coins using the *crypto* package (Vent, 2020). A full years' worth of data was considered for this analysis in order to allow for seasonality.

Data was extracted for the top 200 coins from 1 January 2019 to 31 December 2019. In this time period, not all cryptocurrencies had been trading consistently. Coins which did not have a full years' worth of data were excluded from the dataset. This issue occurred as many of the coins in the top 200 may have only started trading in the middle of 2019 (e.g., LEO is a coin which featured 14th in our top 200 but only began trading on the 20th May). Of the 200 coins, 146 had price records for everyday of the year and the remaining coins were removed from the data.

4. Method

4.1. *Calculating the cross-correlations*

Some pre-processing must be completed on the closing prices in order to derive a correlation matrix C. Firstly, the returns of the cryptocurrencies are calculated. Let $P_i(t)$ be the closing price of cryptocurrency i at a given time t, with $i = 1, 2, \ldots, N$. Daily log returns are calculated using:

$$G_i(t) = \ln(P_i(t + \Delta t)) - \ln(P_i(t)), \tag{1}$$

where Δt is a specified time interval. As the data contains daily closing prices, $\Delta t = 1\,\text{day}$. In a similar fashion to other papers analyzing cross-correlations of price returns, normalized returns are used for constructing the cross-correlation matrix C. As the levels of volatility (i.e., standard deviations) differ between cryptocurrencies, a normalized return allows for the standardization of volatility and ensures that results are independent of varying levels of volatility Conlon *et al.* (2009), Shen and Zheng (2009). The normalized return is given by

$$g_i(t) \equiv \frac{G_i(t) - \langle G_i \rangle}{\sigma_i}, \tag{2}$$

where $\langle G_i \rangle$ refers to the average G_i over a time window T. σ_i is the standard deviation of G_i such that $\sigma_i \equiv \sqrt{\langle G_i^2 \rangle - \langle G_i \rangle^2}$. From here, the cross-correlation matrix C can be computed whose elements are of the following form:

$$C_{ij} = \langle g_i(t) g_j(t) \rangle, \tag{3}$$

where C_{ij} measures the correlation between the normalized returns of two cryptocurrencies i and j. A value of $C_{ij} = 1$ indicates a perfectly positive relationship between the normalized returns of cryptocurrencies i and j, and a value of $C_{ij} = -1$ defines a perfectly negative relationship between the normalized returns of i and j. Finally, a value of $C_{ij} = 0$ means that there is no correlation between the normalized returns of coins i and j Stosic *et al.* (2018). C is a $N \times N$ matrix where N = no. of cryptocurrencies. In our case, $N = 146$.

Figure 1 shows the distribution of correlation coefficients obtained from the correlation matrix C. From this, it can be seen that most of the correlation coefficients are positive. This would indicate that the price returns between the different cryptocurrencies more commonly tend to have positive correlations with each other than negative correlations. This right skewness of the correlation distribution indicates that the distribution is non-gaussian Wang and Xie (2015).

4.2. *Random matrix theory statistics*

The unpredictability of financial returns over time has been commented on many times (see, e.g., Mantegna, 1999). RMT is a common technique used to understand the changes in correlations of investments. RMT tests the statistics of the correlation matrix C against the properties of a random matrix R. If the properties of C deviate

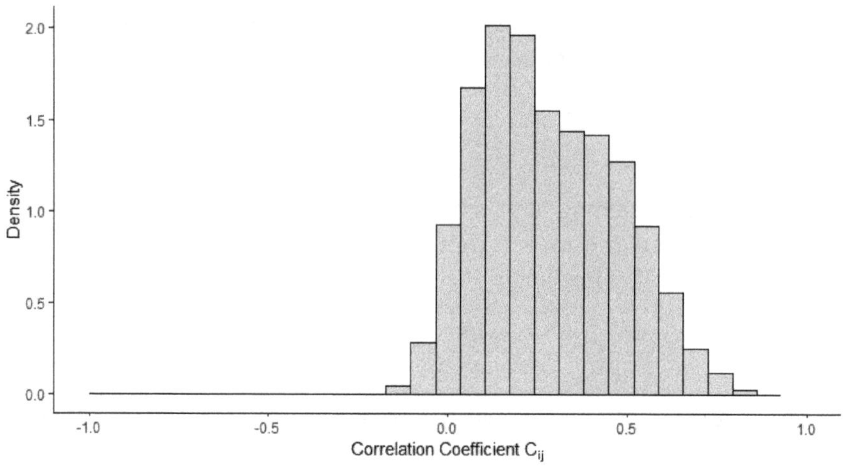

Figure 1. Distribution of correlation coefficients C_{ij}.

from those of our random matrix R, then this indicates that the correlation matrix C contains information about genuine correlations (Plerou *et al.*, 2000). The eigenvalues and eigenvectors calculated from the correlation matrix provide information about the collective behavior of the system of cryptocurrencies (Stosic *et al.*, 2018).

The use of RMT for analyzing interacting systems originated from the work of Wigner (1993) who applied it to systems of interaction while studying the energy levels of nuclei. He assumed that the components of the nucleus can be modeled as random Stosic *et al.* (2018), Plerou *et al.* (2000) such that they follow a Gaussian distribution with mean zero and unit variance. The results achieved by Wigner were later extended to financial markets by Laloux *et al.* (1999) and Plerou *et al.* (1999) who used it to analyze the cross-correlations of stock market returns. Both found that the method was useful for discovering information from the cross-correlation matrices and could be used for portfolio optimization. Since then, RMT has become a popular tool for investigating cross-correlations of financial markets Conlon *et al.* (2009) and has also been extended to the cryptocurrency markets (Chaudhari and Crane, 2020; Stosic *et al.*, 2018).

The calculated cross-correlation matrix C can be represented in the following matrix notation:

$$C = \frac{1}{T} G G^T, \tag{4}$$

where G is a matrix of size $N \times T$. As discussed by Hu *et al.* (2019), eigenvalues, λ_i, and eigenvectors, $\hat{v}_i$, are obtained from the matrix C using the following:

$$C\hat{v}_i = \lambda_i \hat{v}_i. \tag{5}$$

In order to understand if C confines to the assumptions of RMT, it is compared to the matrix R which is a random cross-correlation matrix of the following form:

$$R = \frac{1}{T} A A^T. \tag{6}$$

In which A is a $N \times T$ matrix with zero mean and unit variance Plerou *et al.* (2002). R belongs to a class of random matrices in multivariate statistics called Wishart matrices (Plerou *et al.*, 2002). One property of these matrices is that as $N \to \infty$, $T \to \infty$, with $Q \equiv T/N \geq 1$, the distribution of eigenvalues (λ_i) of R can be represented in the following form:

$$P_R(\lambda) = \frac{Q}{2\pi\sigma^2} \frac{\sqrt{(\lambda_+ - \lambda)(\lambda - \lambda_-)}}{\lambda}, \tag{7}$$

λ_+ and λ_- are the upper and lower bounds of the eigenvalues, λ_i, of R such that $\lambda_- \leq \lambda_i \leq \lambda_+$ for $i = 1, 2, \ldots, N$. $\sigma^2 = 1$ due to the normalization completed on the price returns while accounting for volatility (Laloux *et al.*, 2000; Plerou *et al.*, 2002). This give the following formula for calculating expected eigenvalue bounds of a Wishart matrix:

$$\lambda_+, \lambda_- = 1 + \frac{1}{Q} \pm 2\sqrt{\frac{1}{Q}}. \tag{8}$$

This assumed distribution is compared against the calculated eigenvalues from the correlation matrix C. The extracted data consists of $N = 146$ coins over a period of $T = 365$ days, such that the quality factor (Bouchaud and Potters, 2003), $Q = T/N = 365/146 = 2.5$. This results in eigenvalue bounds of $\lambda_- = 0.135$ and $\lambda_+ = 2.665$. Figure 2 shows the distribution of calculated eigenvalues from the correlation matrix C. Figure 2(a) shows the distribution of all eigenvalues and the second graph, Figure 2(b) shows the distribution of all eigenvalues excluding $\lambda_1 = 49.66$. From Figure 2 we can see that many of the eigenvalues fall within the range of λ_- and λ_+.

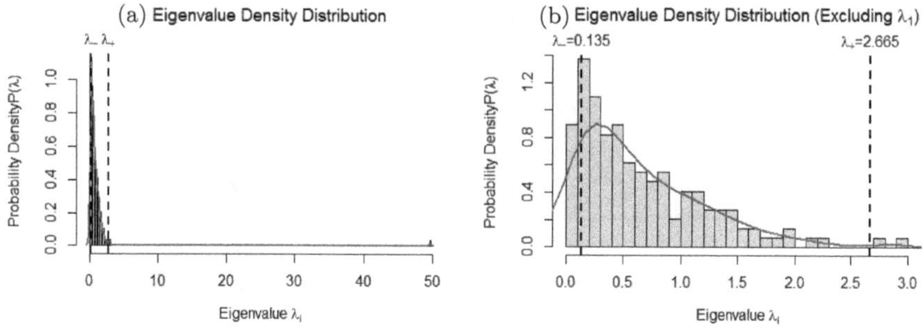

Figure 2. Eigenvector distribution.

Stosic *et al.* (2018) refer to these eigenvalues of C as 'bulk' eigenvalues such that for RMT predictions, $\lambda_i \in \lambda_{\text{bulk}}$ fall within the range $\lambda_- < \lambda_{\text{bulk}} < \lambda_+$. While this is true for the 'bulk' of the eigenvalues, we can also see there are several eigenvalues which fall outside of this range. These deviations from the predicted λ_{bulk} suggests that C contains genuine information about the correlations between the different cryptocurrencies (Plerou *et al.*, 2000).

While it has been shown that the eigenvalues of the correlation matrix C deviate from the RMT predictions, the distribution of eigenvector components must also be considered and analyzed. Plerou *et al.* (2002) explain that, under RMT, the eigenvector components $(u_l^k, l = 1, \ldots, N, k = 1, \ldots, N)$ of a correlation matrix C are expected to follow a Gaussian distribution with zero mean and unit variance such that Plerou *et al.* (2002):

$$P_{\text{RMT}(u)} = \frac{1}{\sqrt{2\pi}} \exp -\frac{u^2}{2}. \tag{9}$$

Figure 3 shows the distribution of eigenvector components corresponding to the eigenvalues, λ_i, of C. Figure 3(a) shows the distribution of the eigenvector components corresponding to the bulk eigenvalues λ_{bulk} such that $\lambda_- < \lambda_{\text{bulk}} < \lambda_+$. The second graph, Figure 3(b), shows the distribution of eigenvector components for the largest eigenvalue $\lambda_1 \notin \lambda_{\text{bulk}}$. For the graph showing the eigenvector components corresponding to the bulk eigenvalues, λ_{bulk}, we can see that these appear to conform to RMT predictions of a Gaussian distribution. However, for the largest eigenvalue λ_1, this is not the case. In Figure 3(b), we can see that its eigenvector components do not follow a similar distribution. This deviation from the predicted

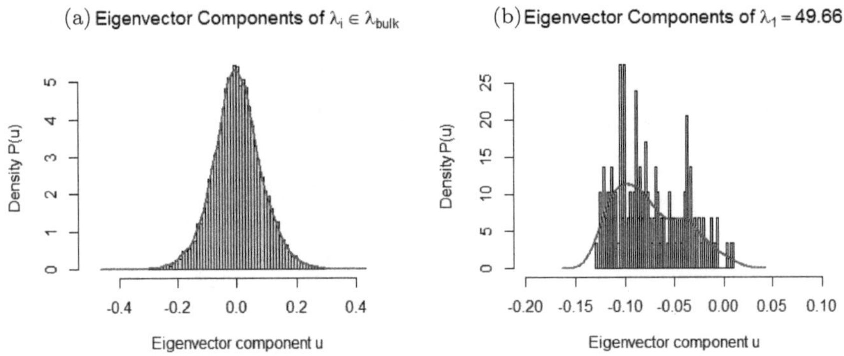

Figure 3. Eigenvector distribution.

model suggests that the cryptocurrencies 'move' together and that there exists correlations which influence the entire system Plerou *et al.* (2000).

A Kolmogorov–Smirnov (KS) test was also used to compare the eigenvector components from $\lambda_i \in \lambda_{\text{bulk}}$ and $\lambda_i \notin \lambda_{\text{bulk}}$. The KS test rejected the null hypothesis when comparing the eigenvector components from inside and outside of the eigenvalue bulk. This provides further evidence that deviating eigenvalues do not conform to the predictions of RMT.

While analyzing the components of the eigenvectors, it is also important to consider the inverse participation ratio (IPR). The IPR is used for quantifying the number of components that participate significantly in each eigenvector Conlon *et al.* (2007). It works by computing the inverse of the number of eigenvector components that contribute to each eigenvector component using the following formula:

$$I^k \equiv \sum_{l=1}^{N} [u_l^k]^4, \tag{10}$$

where u_l^k, $l = 1, \ldots, N$ are the components of eigenvector $\boldsymbol{u}^k$ (Conlon *et al.*, 2007; Plerou *et al.*, 2002). Figure 4 shows the IPR of the eigenvector components of our correlation matrix C. The graph shows the average IPR = 0.033 in which most of the eigenvalues appear to fluctuate around. As mentioned in Stosic *et al.* (2018), these fluctuations show that almost all of the cryptocurrencies contribute to these eigenvectors. This further shows that C does not conform to

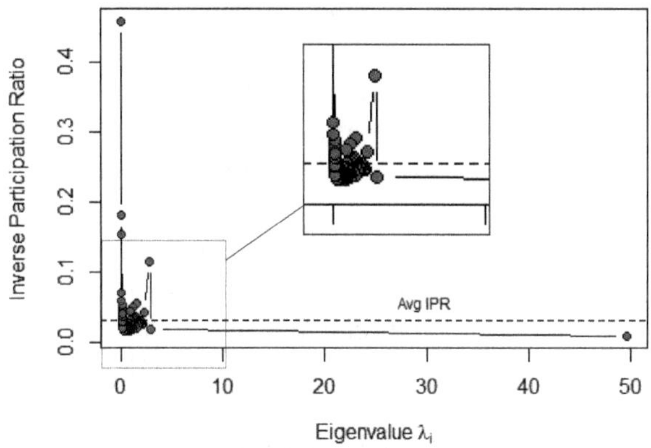

Figure 4. IPR of eigenvector components of C with (inset) eigenvalues around the average IPR = 0.033.

the RMT predictions and hence, it contains genuine information on the correlations of cryptocurrencies.

4.3. *Financial markets as network structures*

In this chapter, the interactions within financial markets are modeled using network procedures Mantegna (1999). The cryptocurrencies in this study can be represented by a network structure such that the nodes represent each cryptocurrency and the edges connecting them represent the correlations between their standardized returns (Mantegna, 1999; Namaki *et al.*, 2011).

Mantegna (1999) explains that, when forming a network using cross-correlations, it is not correct just to use correlation coefficients from the correlation matrix C to form the network as it does not fulfil the three axioms that define a metric for building networks Mantegna (1999). He further explains the method of using a distance metric, which has been applied in other studies while modeling financial returns with network structures (Chaudhari and Crane, 2020; Stosic *et al.*, 2018; Wang and Xie, 2015). The distance metric is a transformation of the correlation matrix C into a distance matrix D using the following:

$$D_{ij} = \sqrt{2(1 - C_{ij})}, \tag{11}$$

where C_{ij} and D_{ij} are the elements of the matrices C and D. The transformation of C into the distance matrix D will now fulfil the three axioms of a distance metric: 1. $D_{ij} = 0 \iff i = j$, 2. $D_{ij} = D_{ji}$, 3. $D_{ij} \leq D_{ik} + D_{kj}$ (Mantegna, 1999). This distance metric can now be used to build a network model of the cryptocurrency returns.

Following from the work of Mantegna (1999), a minimum spanning tree (MST) approach was used to form the correlation-based network of the 146 cryptocurrencies in this analysis. The idea of using MST for modeling financial markets was first introduced by Mantegna (1999) while analyzing the hierarchical structure of the US stock market and has become a commonly used network structure for analyzing the correlations in financial time series (Chaudhari and Crane, 2020). Using an $N \times N$ distance matrix D, a MST connects N nodes using $N - 1$ edges in such a way that the sum of all distances is the minimum (Mantegna, 1999; Wang and Xie, 2015). D_{ij} represents the weight on the edge connecting cryptocurrencies (nodes) i and j.

Minimum spanning trees can be implemented using different algorithms. *Prim* and *Kruskal* are commonly used algorithms for modeling hierarchical structures of financial returns. Prim's algorithm forms a minimal spanning tree by 'growing' a network from a single root node. Whereas the Kruskal algorithm forms a MST by considering the weight of every edge and 'growing' in clusters (Huang *et al.*, 2009). Huang *et al.* (2009) compared the two algorithms while studying the Shanghai and Shenzhen 300 index stock market exchange. They concluded that Kruskal was more suitable for sparse-edged network structures, whereas Prim's algorithm was more suitable for minimum spanning trees with dense edges (Huang *et al.*, 2009). As the network formed from the distance matrix D had a $N = 146$ nodes and ~10,000 vertices, Prim's algorithm was used to create the minimum spanning tree of 146 cryptocurrencies.

4.4. *Community detection*

When the MST is constructed using Prim's algorithm, the collective behavior between cryptocurrencies can be analyzed using community structures. A community structure exists in a network when the vertices can be divided into groups in such a way that the groups of vertices are compactly connected internally but the different groups are sparsely connected Wang and Xie (2015). Similar to minimum spanning trees, there are many different community detection algorithms. Following on from the methods applied in Chaudhari and Crane (2020), the *Louvain* community detection method is used for investigating the community structures within the MST of $N = 146$ cryptocurrencies.

The *Louvain* method, developed by Blondel *et al.* (2008), is a heuristic method which creates communities based on modularity optimization. Newman (2016) describes modularity as a benefit function, that is a measure of the quality of divisions of a network into communities. Every partition has a modularity value which measures the density of links inside communities compared to links between communities (Blondel *et al.*, 2008). The Louvain algorithm creates communities by initializing nodes to a community of size one. Using a 'bottom-up' approach, the clusters are sequentially combined with other clusters that produce the greatest gain in modularity (if a positive gain exists). This process is continued until there are no further gains and modularity has been optimized (Surian *et al.*, 2016).

5. Results

The Louvain community detection algorithm was applied to the MST. A total of 15 distinct communities were formed from this as shown in Figure 5. The different colors represent the 15 different communities formed. Of the 15 communities, 4 had 3 or less members belonging to them. The cryptocurrencies which made up these small communities ($<$4 members) were generally all low valued coins and can all be discounted from the next part of the analysis. The remaining communities had sizes ranging from 6 to 31.

Once the Louvain community detection method was applied, PCA was performed onto the community groupings to identify the cryptocurrency which explained the largest amount of variance within the dataset.

Using the normalized returns data calculated using Eq. (2), the dataset of 146 coins was subset into 15 groups based on their community groupings detected with the Louvain algorithm. From here, PCA was performed on each of the community groupings to determine which cryptocurrency explained the highest amount of variance

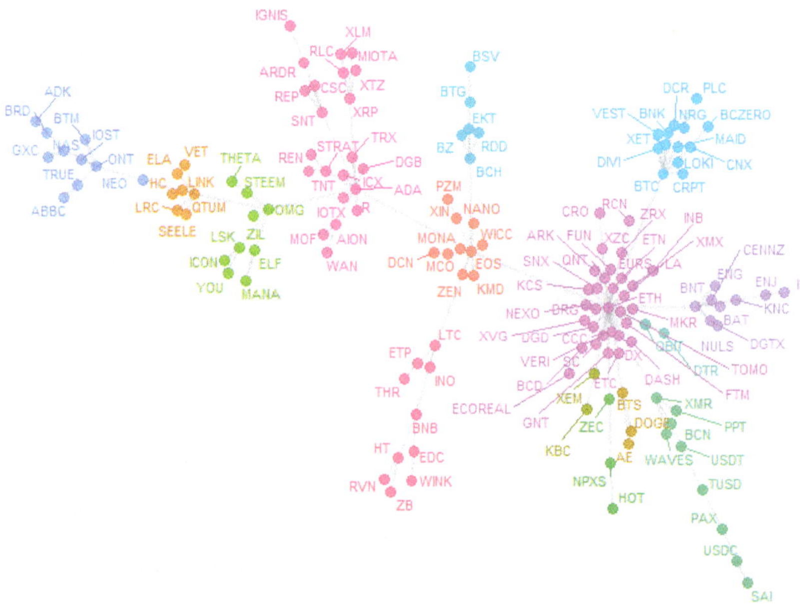

Figure 5. MST: Community detection — 15 communities.

within each of the groups of returns. The cryptocurrency which explained the highest amount of variance within the first principal component of the returns data is detailed in Table 1 as leading coin (PCA)'.

Table 1 shows details of the sizes of communities and their leading cryptocurrency from the group. The 'leading coins' were referenced back against the historical snapshot of top 200 coins as at 29 December 2019. This ranking is a historical snapshot of the coins ranking by market capitalization and is shown in the fourth column of Table 1. We can see that seven of the leading coins (*EOS, Tether, Bitcoin Cash, Bitcoin, Ethereum, Cardano, Litecoin*) lie in the top 20. *Qtum, OmiseGO, Ontology* lie between the 20 and 60 ranking and one coin, *Bancor*, was the lowest ranked leading coin from the analysis. As seven of the 11 coins lie in the top 20 leading coins by market cap, this shows that the methods applied in this chapter could be useful for creating cryptocurrency investment portfolios.

The table also shows the ranking of those coins 6 months later as at 28 June 2020. Comparing these results with their ranking 6 months

Table 1. Louvain community detection and PCA of 146 cryptocurrencies.

Community	Community size	Leading coin (PCA)	Ranking (29/12/2019)	Ranking (28/06/2020)
1	10	EOS	7	9
2	7	Qtum	41	62
5	9	OmiseGO	58	48
7	9	Tether	4	3
9	6	Bitcoin Cash	5	5
10	13	Bitcoin	1	1
11	10	Ontology	29	32
12	9	Bancor	184	105
13	31	Ethereum	2	2
14	22	Cardano	13	11
15	10	Litecoin	6	7

later, we see that the seven coins in the top 20, are remaining in the top 20 ranking. While the other coins, still stay close to the original ranking from 29 December 2019. The lack of deviations from their ranking after 6 months further shows that the methods applied in this chapter could be useful for creating cryptocurrency investment portfolios.

In order to test if there is continuity in the results obtained, the data was subdivided into a smaller dataset of the top 50 cryptocurrencies. Over three time periods of $T = 125$ days, the methods were reapplied to investigate if similar results could be obtained with a smaller dataset. With this time window, the Q factor[3] is still maintained such that $Q = 125/50 = 2.5$. The three subsets of $T = 125$ days cover the following date ranges:

(1) 01/01/2019 – 05/05/2019
(2) 01/05/2019 – 02/09/2019
(3) 29/08/2019 – 31/12/2019

[3] Q factor is the ratio of the number of observations (days) to the number of assets (Bouchaud and Potters, 2003). It is used to calculate eigenvalues bounds which are compared against eigenvalues of correlation matrix C to test RMT assumptions.

The data was pre-processed using the same methods to obtain the normalized return as detailed in Eqs. (1) and (2) and cross-correlation matrices C_1, C_2, C_3 were computed using the three sets of standardized returns.

From this, the eigenvalues and eigenvectors were calculated from each correlation matrix and analyzed using RMT statistics in a similar fashion as above. The distribution of the eigenvalues was that of what was seen for the larger dataset of $T = 365$ days. For all time periods, the majority of eigenvalues, λ_i fell within the bulk with the same eigenvalue bounds of $\lambda_- = 0.135$ and $\lambda_+ = 2.665$ such that $\lambda_- \leq \lambda_{\text{bulk}} \leq \lambda_+$. There were also deviations from this, with some eigenvalues falling outside of the bulk ($\lambda_i \notin \lambda_{\text{bulk}}$). The eigenvector components for these eigenvalues were also analyzed. Similar to our large dataset, the eigenvector components for eigenvalues within the bulk, λ_{bulk}, all appeared to conform to a Gaussian distribution. Whereas, for the eigenvalues outside of the bulk, ($\lambda_i \notin \lambda_{\text{bulk}}$), the distribution of their eigenvector components also deviated from a Gaussian normal distribution. A Kolmogorov–Smirnov (KS) test confirmed this deviation as the KS test rejected the null hypothesis when comparing the eigenvector components from inside and outside of the eigenvalue bulk for each of the three correlation matrices. Similar to the cross-correlation matrix C for $N = 146$ cryptocurrencies, this confirms that cross-correlation matrices C_1, C_2, and C_3 do not conform to RMT predictions and contain genuine information on cross-correlations of the top 50 cryptocurrencies.

As with the above methods used on $N = 146$ cryptocurrencies, three distance matrices were calculated using the cross-correlation matrices C_1, C_2, C_3, and formula (11). Louvain community detection was applied to the minimum spanning trees formed using the distance matrices and Prim's algorithm.

Table 2 shows the initial results when Louvain community detection algorithm was applied to T_1, T_2, and T_3. The algorithm detected similar numbers of communities across the time window with eight communities being detected in T_1, 7 in T_2 and 9 in T_3. Table 2 also details the number of cryptocurrencies in each community with the community sizes appearing to be similar across the three-time windows. Figures 6–8 show the graphical representation of the Louvain community detection algorithm applied to the minimum spanning trees across the three time windows T_1, T_2, and T_3. Similar to the

Table 2. Top 50 cryptocurrencies — Louvain community detection — No. of communities and their sizes.

T_1		T_2		T_3	
Community	**Size**	**Community**	**Size**	**Community**	**Size**
1	3	1	8	1	4
2	5	2	5	2	8
3	8	3	5	3	4
4	8	4	8	4	3
5	7	5	11	5	6
6	8	6	8	6	7
7	6	7	5	7	4
8	5	—	—	8	7
—	—	—	—	9	7

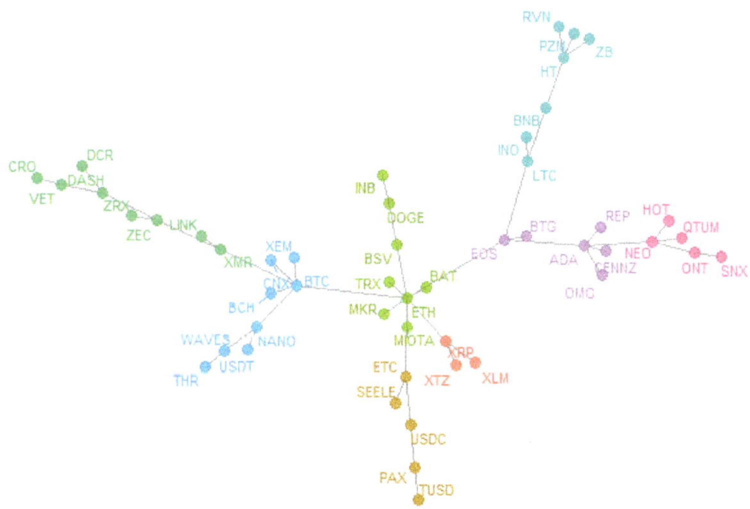

Figure 6. Minimum spanning tree with Louvain communities — Top 50 — Time window T_1.

minimum spanning tree in Figure 5, the different colors represent the different communities detected by the algorithm.

Following the same methods applied to the larger dataset of 146 cryptocurrencies, PCA was applied to the standardized returns for each of the communities detected to determine the 'leading coins' for each community.

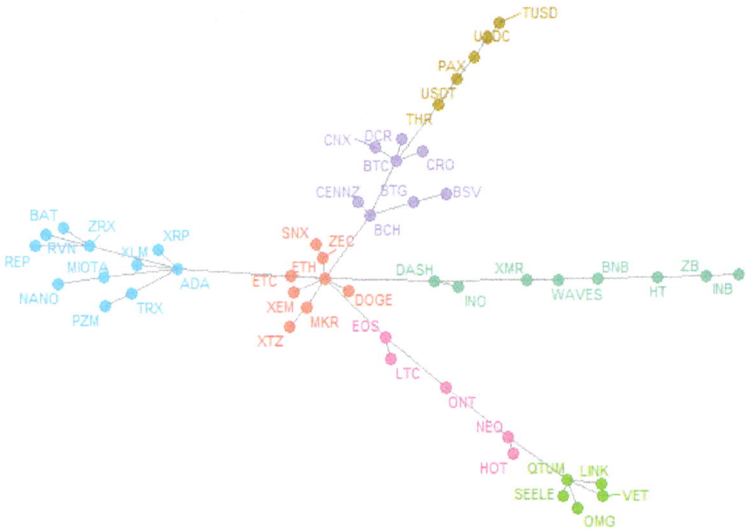

Figure 7. Minimum spanning tree with louvain communities — Top 50 — Time window T_2.

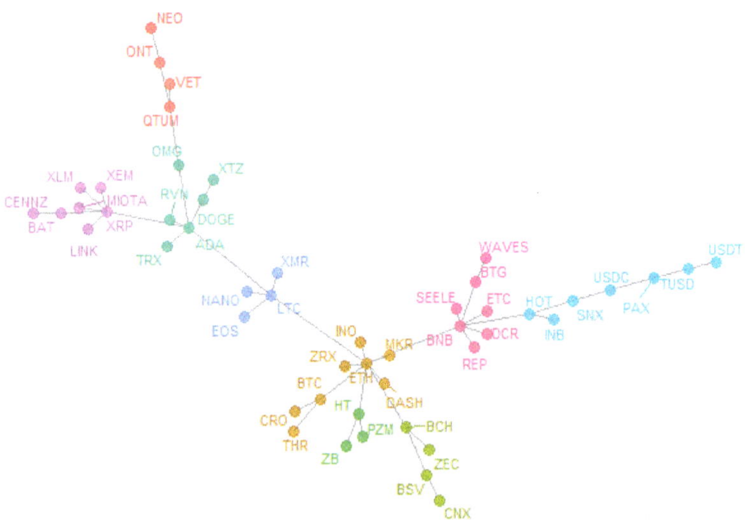

Figure 8. Minimum spanning tree with Louvain communities — Top 50 — Time window T_3.

Table 3. Results of PCA performed on Louvain communities for top 50 cryptocurrencies over three time periods.

Leading coin (PCA)	Rank* 29/12/2019	Rank* 28/06/2020	Time window T_1	T_2	T_3
Bitcoin	1	1	✓	✓	
Ethereum	2	2	✓	✓	✓
XRP	3	4	✓		✓
Bitcoin Cash	5	5			✓
Litecoin	6	7			✓
Binance Coin	8	8			✓
Cardano	13	11	✓	✓	✓
Monero	16	17		✓	
Huobi Token	17	20	✓		✓
Neo	19	21	✓		
Dash	28	23	✓		
Ontology	29	32		✓	✓
Paxos Standard	36	43	✓	✓	✓
Qtum	41	62		✓	

Notes: T_1 = Time period of $T = 125$ days from 01/01/2019 to 05/05/2019.
T_2 = Time period of $T = 125$ days from 01/05/2019 to 02/09/2019.
T_3 = Time period of $T = 125$ days from 29/08/2019 to 31/12/2019.
*Ranking refers to ranking by market capitalization.

Table 3 shows the results of the 'leading coins' obtained after applying PCA to the standardized returns of the community groupings detected across the three time windows T_1, T_2, and T_3. The table shows all leading coins and their ranking by market capitalization on 29 December 2019 and 28th June 2020. From the results of the table, we can see that the coins selected as 'leading coins' (i.e., the coins which accounted for most of the variability within the first principal component) appear to be stable in their ranking across the 6 months from December 2019 to June 2020. This shows that the method could be used in future for detecting cryptocurrencies which are deemed to be stable and are less likely to drop in ranking.

After PCA was applied to the community groupings, there were three 'leading coins' which were common across the three windows. *Ethereum*, *Cardano*, and *Paxos Standard* were all common leading coins detected when PCA was applied to the returns of the cryptocurrencies detected with Louvain community detection. Of the 14 coins detected as leading coins with PCA, seven of them appeared as leading coins in other time windows. Whereas the remaining seven only appeared as a leading coin of communities in one of the time windows. This could indicate that there may not be continuity in the methods applied in this chapter. Another interesting finding was noticed while analyzing the leading coins discovered from the community structures formed in T_3. Around seven of the nine leading coins detected in this time window are within the top 20 ranking as at 29 December 2019 and as at 28 June 2020. This could indicate that the method of using community detection and PCA could be useful for creating stock portfolios based on the data from the later part of the year.

6. Conclusion

This chapter investigates the collective behavior of 146 cryptocurrencies from 1 January 2019 to 31 December 2019. The data was pre-processed, and standardized returns were obtained in order to calculate the correlation matrix. This correlation matrix was analyzed and compared against the assumptions of RMT. The deviations from RMT predictions are in line with other research (Chaudhari and Crane, 2020; Plerou *et al.*, 2002; Stosic *et al.*, 2018) which shows that the correlation matrix contains genuine information between the interactions of cryptocurrencies. From here, the MSTs formed from the cross-correlations were analyzed using *Louvain* community detection. PCA was then used to find 'leading coins' with the aim of constructing an investment portfolio of well performing cryptocurrencies.

The results of this analysis selected several high-valued coins which continued to remain high value when their ranking was compared six months later to 28 June 2020. This shows that the methods applied in this chapter could be useful for constructing a portfolio of consistently optimal cryptocurrencies for investment.

The above methods were replicated on a smaller dataset of the top 50 cryptocurrencies of three smaller time windows of $T = 125$ days to understand if there is continuity in the results obtained on the larger dataset. The replication of the methods on the smaller datasets showed some continuity, in that several higher-valued cryptocurrencies (within the top 20 ranking) were chosen and found across the results of the other time windows. However, there was also cryptocurrencies which appeared only once as 'leading coins' across the three-time windows. This shows that further testing would be required to validate the results. Also, of the nine leading coins selected in the third window T_3, seven of them were in the top 20 ranking for December 2019 and June 2020. This result could indicate that data from the later part of the year could be more successful for selecting high-valued cryptocurrencies using the methods of this chapter.

Finally, while the methods applied in this chapter did produce some optimal results, there were also some deviations as the methods were applied over smaller time windows. For future work, these methods would need to be repeated on different time periods and time window lengths to understand if this could be a reliable method for creating investment portfolios.

Acknowledgments

This research was in part supported by the Science Foundation Ireland under Grant Agreement No. 13/RC/2106_P2 at the ADAPT SFI Research Centre at DCU. ADAPT, the SFI Research Centre for AI-Driven Digital Content Technology, is funded by the Science Foundation Ireland through the SFI Research Centres Programme.

References

Alessandretti, L., ElBahrawy, A., Aiello, L. M., & Baronchelli, A. (2018). Anticipating cryptocurrency prices using machine learning. *Complexity, 2018.* Article ID 8983590, 16 pages, https://doi.org/10.1155/2018/8983590.

Blondel, V. D., Guillaume, J.-L., Lambiotte, R., & Lefebvre, E. (2008). Fast unfolding of communities in large networks. *Journal of Statistical Mechanics: Theory and Experiment, 2008*(10), P10008.

Bouchaud, J.-P., & Potters, M. (2003). *Theory of Financial Risk and Derivative Pricing: From Statistical Physics to Risk Management.* Cambridge University Press, New York.

Chaudhari, H., & Crane, M. (2020). Cross-correlation dynamics and community structures of cryptocurrencies. *Journal of Computational Science*, *44*, 101130.

Conlon, T., Ruskin, H. J., & Crane, M. (2007). Random matrix theory and fund of funds portfolio optimisation. *Physica A: Statistical Mechanics and Its Applications*, *382*(2), 565–576.

Conlon, T., Ruskin, H. J., & Crane, M. (2009). Cross-correlation dynamics in financial time series. *Physica A: Statistical Mechanics and its Applications*, *388*(5), 705–714.

Drozdz, S., Kwapien, J., Oswiecimka, P., Stanisz, T., & Watorek, M. (2020). Complexity in economic and social systems: Cryptocurrency market at around COVID-19. *Entropy*, *22*(9), 1–25.

Fenn, D. J., Porter, M. A., Mucha, P. J., McDonald, M., Williams, S., Johnson, N. F., & Jones, N. S. (2012). Dynamical clustering of exchange rates. *Quantitative Finance*, *12*(10), 1493–1520.

Hargreaves, C. A., & Mani, C. K. (2015). The selection of winning stocks using principal component analysis. *American Journal of Marketing Research*, *1*(3), 183–188.

Hu, A. S., Parlour, C. A., & Rajan, U. (2019). Cryptocurrencies: Stylized facts on a new investible instrument. *Financial Management*, *48*(4), 1049–1068.

Huang, F., Gao, P., & Wang, Y. (2009). Comparison of prim and kruskal on shanghai and shenzhen 300 index hierarchical structure tree. In *2009 International Conference on Web Information Systems and Mining* (pp. 237–241). IEEE.

Laloux, L., Cizeau, P., Bouchaud, J.-P., & Potters, M. (1999). Noise dressing of financial correlation matrices. *Physical Review Letters*, *83*(7), 1467.

Laloux, L., Cizeau, P., Potters, M., & Bouchaud, J.-P. (2000). Random matrix theory and financial correlations. *International Journal of Theoretical and Applied Finance*, *3*(03), 391–397.

Liew, J., Li, R. Z., Budavári, T., & Sharma, A. (2019). Cryptocurrency investing examined. *The Journal of The British Blockchain Association*, *2*, 8720.

Lu, H., Halappanavar, M., & Kalyanaraman, A. (2015). Parallel heuristics for scalable community detection. *Parallel Computing*, *47*, 19–37.

Makarov, I., & Schoar, A. (2020). Trading and arbitrage in cryptocurrency markets. *Journal of Financial Economics*, *135*(2), 293–319.

Mantegna, R. N. (1999). Hierarchical structure in financial markets. *The European Physical Journal B-Condensed Matter and Complex Systems*, *11*(1), 193–197.

Namaki, A., Shirazi, A., Raei, R., & Jafari, G. (2011). Network analysis of a financial market based on genuine correlation and threshold method. *Physica A: Statistical Mechanics and its Applications, 390*(21–22), 3835–3841.

Newman, M. E. (2012). Communities, modules and large-scale structure in networks. *Nature Physics, 8*(1), 25–31.

Newman, M. E. (2016). Community detection in networks: Modularity optimization and maximum likelihood are equivalent. arXiv preprint arXiv:1606.02319.

Patil, P., Wu, C.-S. M., Potika, K., & Orang, M. (2020). Stock market prediction using ensemble of graph theory, machine learning and deep learning models. In *Proceedings of the 3rd International Conference on Software Engineering and Information Management* (pp. 85–92).

Plerou, V., Gopikrishnan, P., Rosenow, B., Amaral, L. A. N., Guhr, T., & Stanley, H. E. (2002). Random matrix approach to cross correlations in financial data. *Physical Review E, 65*(6), 066126.

Plerou, V., Gopikrishnan, P., Rosenow, B., Amaral, L. A. N., & Stanley, H. E. (1999). Universal and non-universal properties of cross correlations in financial time series. *Physical Review Letters, 83*(7), 1471.

Plerou, V., Gopikrishnan, P., Rosenow, B., Amaral, L. N., & Stanley, H. E. (2000). A random matrix theory approach to financial cross-correlations. *Physica A: Statistical Mechanics and its Applications, 287*(3-4), 374–382.

Punčeva, M., Arc, H. É., & Marina, N. (2018). Bitcoin trust communities. In *2018 10th International Congress on Ultra Modern Telecommunications and Control Systems and Workshops* (ICUMT) (pp. 1–6). IEEE.

Shen, J., & Zheng, B. (2009). Cross-correlation in financial dynamics. *EPL (Europhysics Letters), 86*(4), 48005.

Stosic, D., Stosic, D., Ludermir, T. B., & Stosic, T. (2018). Collective behavior of cryptocurrency price changes. *Physica A: Statistical Mechanics and its Applications, 507*, 499–509.

Surian, D., Nguyen, D. Q., Kennedy, G., Johnson, M., Coiera, E., & Dunn, A. G. (2016). Characterizing twitter discussions about hpv vaccines using topic modeling and community detection. *Journal of Medical Internet Research, 18*(8), e232.

Vent, J. (2020). *Crypto: Cryptocurrency Market Data*, R package version 1.1.3. https://CRAN.R-project.org/package=crypto.

Wang, G.-J., & Xie, C. (2015). Correlation structure and dynamics of international real estate securities markets: A network perspective. *Physica A: Statistical Mechanics and its Applications, 424*, 176–193.

Watorek, M., Drozdz, S., Kwapien, J., Minati, L., Oswiecimka, P., & Stanuszek, M. (2021). Multiscale characteristics of the emerging global cryptocurrency market. *Physics Reports*, *901*, 1–82. https://www.sciencedirect.com/science/article/pii/S0370157320304166.

Wigner, E. P. (1993). On a class of analytic functions from the quantum theory of collisions. In *The Collected Works of Eugene Paul Wigner* (pp. 409–440). Springer, Berlin, Heidelberg.

Zahedi, J., & Rounaghi, M. M. (2015). Application of artificial neural network models and principal component analysis method in predicting stock prices on tehran stock exchange. *Physica A: Statistical Mechanics and its Applications*, *438*, 178–187.

Part III

Machine Learning: Financial Applications

https://doi.org/10.1142/9781800612723_0005

Chapter 5

Distilling a Disruptive Disintermediary's Data: Interpretable Machine-Learning Explanations for LendingClub Customers

Thomas Conlon[*,‡] and Fearghal Kearney[†,§]

[*] *Smurfit Graduate School of Business, University College Dublin, Dublin, Ireland*

[†] *Queen's Management School, Queen's University Belfast, Belfast, UK*

[‡] *conlon.thomas@ucd.ie*

[§] *F.Kearney@qub.ac.uk*

Abstract

Machine learning may assist peer-to-peer lenders in exploiting their informational advantage through distilling large volumes of data into an evaluation of borrower credit quality. In this chapter, we use explainable artificial intelligence to pare back the opacity associated with machine learning. Using LIME (Local Interpretable Model-Agnostic Explanation) and Shapley Values, we provide a visual representation of the factors found to influence credit risk for the LendingClub peer-to-peer platform. Empirical findings indicate that FICO scores are still relevant, that experienced borrowers are less risky, that loans for credit card repayments are charged more, and that administration burdens such as verifying income leads to a higher cost of credit. Our work links to ongoing regulatory initiatives by providing a mechanism to provide meaningful interpretations from machine learning models to customers, regulators, and investors.

Keywords: Explainable artificial intelligence, financial technology, machine learning, peer-to-peer lending, prediction modeling.

1. Introduction

Financial disintermediation through peer-to-peer (P2P) lending disrupts traditional financial banking operations by facilitating effective information transmission, lowering the costs of matching counterparties, and achieving data economies of scale (Thakor, 2020). The additional information held by online P2P lenders over traditional lenders allows them to substantially reduce default rates and to increase investor returns by 12% on average (Miller, 2015). Machine learning (ML) provides a key competitive advantage to P2P platforms, allowing them to effectively exploit any informational advantage. In this chapter, we focus on the individual participants, by first illustrating how novel ML approaches can be employed to distill large volumes of information into a tractable evaluation of borrower credit quality. Building upon this, we contribute to the literature by removing the layers of opacity associated with ML using methods from interpretable ML, often referred to as *explainable artificial intelligence* (XAI). Using visual representations, as proposed by Frankel and Reid (2008), we provide clear plots of how individual features drive both the price of credit and the likelihood of default using LendingClub data.

P2P lender's use of alternative data and black box ML models help to remove layers of financial intermediation. This approach can, however, lead to an opaque business model with potential to discriminate against customers and resulting in the intermediator falling foul of the regulators. The Financial Stability Board (2017) state that a 'lack of interpretability and auditability of artificial intelligence (AI) and ML methods could become a macro risk'. The US Equal Credit Opportunity Act asserts an individual's right to be given specific reasons for a denied line of credit, while under European Union GDPR (2016) regulation automated consumer credit decisions 'should carry meaningful information about the logic involved'. At a borrower level, we propose that the use of visual representations extracted from interpretable ML procedures provides explanations appropriately adapted to the concerned unsophisticated stakeholder.

While simple models such as a linear regression or a basic regression tree may be intrinsically interpretable, more complex and less inherently interpretable models may add considerable value when dealing with economic data (Bianchi *et al.*, 2021). For the ML approaches considered here, including random forests, gradient boosting and neural network deep learning, post hoc interpretability methods are required. We employ two model agnostic approaches, Local Interpretable Model-Agnostic Explanation (LIME), proposed by Ribeiro *et al.* (2016) and SHapley Additive exPlanation (SHAP), or Shapley values, which allow us to provide a visual representation of the factors found to influence credit risk for the borrower.

Harnessing the power of large datasets and ML approaches to refine accuracy, the tractable LIME and Shapley based-plots produced equip the P2P participant with knowledge as to what and how factors are driving the cost of credit observed. In parallel, we also equip classification default models with explainability to provide participants with the ability to identify what loan attributes are driving the likelihood of default. In the illustrative application of our proposed frameworks, we make some interesting observations about the drivers of a sample of loan applications on the popular LendingClub P2P lending platform. We find that FICO scores are still relevant, that experienced borrowers are less risky, that loans for credit card repayments are charged more, and that LendingClub administration burdens such as verifying income leads to a higher cost of credit. Contrasting the XAI approaches applied, we provide evidence of some commonality among the emergent model features but highlight that differences do exist.

This research links to the fast expanding literature applying ML-based models to financial services. Applications include asset pricing (Gu *et al.*, 2020), textual analysis (Loughran and McDonald, 2016), financial fraud (Kumar *et al.*, 2019) and credit risk assessment (Khandani *et al.*, 2010).[1] Our work also links with the literature examining credit risk scoring predictive accuracy (Wang and Perkins, 2019) and to papers which show that the alternative data used by FinTech lenders leads to a fuller and more accurate picture

[1]For a detailed treatise of the core topics relating to ML in finance, see Aziz *et al.* (2019).

of credit worthiness (Jagtiani and Lemieux, 2019). The latter paper also indicates the potential for disparate treatment of borrowers and unfair lending from P2P lenders, which relates to our work in terms of trying to unveil the drivers of credit decisions. While previous literature has begun to examine the application of explainability for ML-based credit risk modeling (Bracke *et al.*, 2019; Bussmann *et al.*, 2020), this chapter focuses on a broad set of loans and provides a detailed comparison of the explanations provided by a range of interpretability techniques.

Our work also links to ongoing regulatory initiatives, such as the recent European Commission proposal for Regulation on Artificial Intelligence, by providing a mechanism to provide meaningful interpretation to customers, regulators and investors. Similarly, US lending requirements relating to discrimination, regulatory compliance and fair lending provide a further motivation for the use of XAI in consumer financial services (Hall *et al.*, 2021). The possibility for divergent interpretations emerging from the common XAI approaches applied here highlights that there is scope for further research to identify suitable interpretation objectives and unravel discriminatory model outcomes. Furthermore, XAI may have wider application across financial services in areas such as asset pricing where machine learning is becoming prominent (Adcock *et al.*, 2022).

2. Data Processing and Methodologies

In this section, we describe the data-preprocessing required and the methodologies, with a focus on the explainable AI techniques employed in the chapter.

2.1. *Filtering and processing*

As with any ML study it is imperative that one cleans and filters the dataset prior to modeling. To this end, we drop any variables where more than 10% of the observations are missing. For the remaining variables we follow imputation via medians by taking the median of each variable and using them to fill any remaining missing values. We also remove any variables that are fixed across all observations and don't have variation. We focus only on single applicant loans, thereby removing the joint application statuses. We construct a new variable (earliest_cr_line), which is the number of days prior to the loan issue date that the applicant first received a line of credit. This is done to standardize across the various years of loans being initiated.[2]

To utilize the address field (addr_state) we look at default rates by state to determine those states that have the most and least loan defaults. We filter out those states with less than 1,000 loans defaulting and find that, across the years of the in-sample analysis, 'GA' is consistently in the top 10 for most defaults and 'NV' and 'CO' are in the bottom 10. We include these three states as additional feature factors in our training and testing analysis going forward, to determine if they can help to predict loan status. Purpose is a classification provided by the borrower for the loan request. From this classification we create dummy variables for the following categories; credit card, consolidation, home improvement, house, major purchase, medical, moving, energy, small business, vacation, wedding other. We standardize annual income by funded amount, to give a proportion of how much of a borrowers annual income the loan constitutes. To reduce a number of uninformative categories we exclude home ownership entries that are listed as Any or None. This leaves us with 'renting', 'owning', and 'mortgage' options. We create dummy variables out of the employment length, as it is not a continuous variable, i.e., 0 is used for employment lengths of less than a year, and 10 is used for employment lengths of greater than 10 years.

2.2. *Methodologies*

We examine a large number of machine learning approaches to model both loan status and the level of interest rate charged. These include General Linear Models, Gradient Boosting Machines, both with and without grid searches, Regression Trees, Random Forests and Deep Learning approaches.[3] In the case of loan status we are modeling the classification, where the loan is either Fully Paid or Defaulted. In the case of the interest rate model we model the continuous

---

[2]In unreported analysis we also investigated the variation in status attributable to the month of the year for the training set. Only minimal variation is observed, so this feature is not included in the ensuing analyses.

[3]Full mathematical details of these ML techniques is beyond the scope of this chapter but can be found across a multitude of textbooks such as Lantz (2019).

interest rate that LendingClub charge for the loan using a regression type model. The interest rate and loan status, respectively, are specified as being the response when building each model. A vector of predictors are then specified using all other remaining features. LendingClub's internal grades are excluded as a predictor given that they are produced after they conduct their own internal analysis. Due to response data imbalance for loan status, with a far greater number of fully paid observations versus default observations, we implement over- and undersampling techniques to balance data class counts. Fivefold cross-validation metrics are used for early stopping in model building and to produce the model ranking shown in Tables 1 and 2.

2.2.1. *Global explanations*

To analyze what is driving the predictions emanating from these models, we utilize novel approaches that illustrate the global and individual observation drivers of the interest rate and loan status classification responses. A benefit of all the methods we employ is that they are model agnostic, allowing them to be utilized across the regression and classification ML models built and applied here. Many supervised learning algorithms can produce some measure of importance for the features used in the model, however a downside is that different and at times contrasting functions are used. The approaches that we recommend can be applied consistently across all the ML models considered. In our variable importance plots permutation features importance is used. This measures the impact on the model's error by shuffling the value of each of the features. A feature is designated as important if permuting its value increases the model error. In contrast a feature is deemed to be unimportant if permuting its value has little impact on the overall model error. For the global drivers, we show a plot of the variable importance scores highlighting the top 10 most influential features.

Permutation features importance was first introduced by Breiman (2001), who applied it to random forest models. Fisher *et al.* (2018) show it's applicability across a range of models, as we illustrate here. The advantages of these approaches are that they provide an insight into the global behavior of the models and they have an intuitive interpretation in that the model error increases when an important feature's information is destroyed during the permutation. We use these permutation features and variable importance approaches on both the training and test datasets. Also they take into account interactions with other features considered in the models, and they do not require the model to be retrained.

Permutation importance algorithm (Fisher *et al.*, 2018)
Input: A trained model f, target vector y, feature matrix X, error measure $L(y, f)$.

1. Estimate the original model error $e^{\text{orig}} = L(y, f(X))$.
2. For each feature in the set X
   (a) Generate the feature matrix X^{perm} by permuting feature j, breaking the association between feature j and true outcome y.
   (b) Estimate the updated error $e^{\text{perm}} = L(y, f(X^{\text{perm}}))$ based on the predictions of the permuted data.
   (c) Calculate the permutation feature importance using $FI^j = e^{\text{perm}}/e^{\text{orig}}$.
3. Sort features by descending FI.

2.2.2. *Individual explanations*

The approach described above allows us to produce global interpretations of the impact of each feature. However to understand what is driving the decisions made for loan applicants we must move away from aggregate global features to local individual observations. Expanding to local interpretability techniques also allows us to see the directional relationship between the input features and the outputs. We achieve this through the use of both LIME and through the use of Shapley (1953) values, a method from cooperative game theory, as adopted by Lundberg and Lee (2016) for explaining complex AI models.

LIME

We first detail the LIME approach proposed by Ribeiro *et al.* (2016). LIME is an example of a local surrogate model used to tell us why a model made individual predictions for both loan status and interest rates based on our loan attributes. LIME provides an assessment of what happens to the output if we give variations of our data to the trained model. It uses permuted samples to produce new data for the model and assesses the predictions associated with this new data. In our case these new samples are produced by perturbing each feature individually using the assumption of a normal distribution with mean and standard deviation set by each feature. An intuitively interpretable model is then trained on this new permuted dataset, with the observations closest to the original value having the largest weight of importance (using a Gower distance function) placed on it in the surrogate interpretable model.

The surrogate model implemented here is that of an intrinsically interpretable linear regression approach. For this implementation we choose $K = 5$, to focus on the five most important features, a lower K has the benefit of improving accuracy around the perturbed local observations, while also making it easier to focus on the main drivers of the observed model outputs. To aid computation we choose to split continuous variables into bins of size 4 based on the quantiles of the data when making its explanation. The LIME approach boasts many advantages. Most notably the framework produces explanations that are easy for non-AI practitioners to understand and interpret. It is model agnostic, so can be used across both the classification loan status and regression interest rate contexts that we meet in our study. A kernel width of 0.5 is specified when implementing the exponential smoothing model neighborhood around each point, however there is limited empirical guidance on a correct level to set across different applications. This motivates the use of an alternative local explanation method, namely the Shapley value explanation approach, outlined next.

Shapley

We use the game theory-based Shapley (1953) values to explain each feature's contribution to our model's predictions. In a game theory context, this is viewed as explaining a prediction by assuming that each feature value is a 'player' in a game where the output prediction is viewed as the 'payout'. The players cooperate in coalition to and receive a slice of the payout pot in return. Upon the completion of the game this payout is distributed among each of the players/features. More specifically in our context, the values of our features for a particular observation are said to cooperate to achieve the model output for that instance. The Shapley value approach then distributes the differential between this instance's prediction and that of the dataset's average across each of the features considered.

It achieves this through attempting every combination of the features. For each feature it first tests the accuracy of every combination of other features and then adds back in that feature to each combination to see how much this improves accuracy. The Shapley value is then calculated as each feature value's marginal contribution averaged across all considered combinations of coalitions. Given the excessive computational burden of directly estimating the Shapley values across all the possible coalitions we follow the Štrumbelj and Kononenko (2014) approach, which proposes an approximation using Monte-Carlo sampling. Major advantages of Shapley value explanations is that due to its theoretical grounding in game theory literature it adheres to principals of efficiency, symmetry and additivity.

The difference between the prediction and the average prediction is fairly distributed among the feature values of the instance — the efficiency property of Shapley values. This property distinguishes the Shapley value from other methods such as LIME.

3. Data

We utilize a loan dataset made publicly available by LendingClub.com. The period covers 2007 to Q3 2019. For each loan on the platform, the dataset provides us with the rate of interest charged by LendingClub for that loan and attributes about the borrower. This results in 2.6 million loan observations across 150 variables.[4] A full description of the variables available is provided in Appendix Table A1.

The dataset also provides the current loan status. From this loan status we classify loans as 'fully paid' or 'at risk'. We use a wide definition of 'at risk', namely that a loan is either listed as

[4]Ip and Lam (2020) use a tree model on accepted and rejected LendingClub loans, however this is only possible as they have so few predictors for the rejected loans. Therefore interpretability is not an issue. In our setting with a far greater number of features we highlight the need to move beyond intrinsically interpretable models such as linear regression and elementary tree structures, to improve model performance.

'Default', 'Does not meet the credit policy. Status:Charged Off', is 'In Grace Period', is associated with a 'Default Receiver', or payment is 'Late (16–30 days)' or '>Late (31–120 days)'. LendingClub loans are given for fixed periods of 36 and 60 months. We focus on 36 month loans, and those between 2007 and 2015 for our in-sample training. Loans active during the 2016–2019 are assessed as the out-of-sample testing period. These 2016–2019 period loans are chosen as they allow such loans to run their full term. To further ensure that loans have matured, we remove loans that are listed as 'Current' and have no loan status.

We seek to construct models in the spirit of how LendingClub would proceed when faced with the prospect of adding a new loan to their platform.[5] This *ex-ante* analysis means that we are including only variables that LendingClub would have available at the outset of the loan, at the point when they analyzed the likelihood of the loan to default, and on the applicable grade and associated interest rate to charge. While LendingClub assign an interest rate based upon their model-driven credit rating, we develop separate models for each, to isolate whether the determining features are common across both models.

4. Empirical Results

The ranking of models employed to understand the probability of loan default and the interest rate associated with loans are first briefly discussed. Then a global approach to explain the models is detailed. Finally, we focus on local model interpretation, examining explanations provided by LIME and Shapley values.

[5]We also have information regarding the loans made that were rejected from being listed on the platform. However, we do not include them for two reasons, firstly, LendingClub have stated that a number of these loans are erroneous/incomplete or even fraudulent applications, and secondly we only have a very small number of datapoints available for such loans so we cannot examine them in the same manner.

Table 1. Loan status leaderboard model ranking.

Model	AUC	AUC probability	Logloss	RMSE
GBM grid model 2	0.9232	0.9998	0.0065	0.0334
GBM model 1	0.9168	0.9998	0.0071	0.0337
GBM model 2	0.9125	0.9998	0.0072	0.0337
GBM grid model 1	0.9125	0.9998	0.0074	0.0334
GBM model 3	0.9104	0.9998	0.0074	0.0338
GBM model 4	0.9097	0.0998	0.0074	0.0338
GBM model 5	0.9041	0.9998	0.0078	0.0338
Stacked ensemble model	0.8895	0.9998	0.0069	0.0334
Stack ensemble best of family model	0.8882	0.9998	0.0069	0.0336
Deep learning grid model 2	0.8841	0.9998	0.2683	0.2578
Deep learning grid model 2	0.8801	0.9998	0.3669	0.2867
Distributed random forest	0.8730	0.9997	0.0129	0.0338
Extremely randomized trees	0.8618	0.9997	0.0135	0.0337

Notes: The top ranked models used to predict loan status are listed in order of Area Under the Curve (AUC). AUC probability tests the hypothesis that the AUC is equal to 0.5. The Logloss and Root Mean Squared Error (RMSE) are also provided.

4.1. *Model ranking*

A suite of different modeling approaches are taken to predict loan status and to derive the appropriate interest rate to charge on loans. Table 1 provides a ranking of the set of loan default status models by the area under the curve (AUC), which is a measure of the ability of a classification model (default or not) to distinguish between classes (Avino *et al.*, 2019). The Logloss and root mean square error (RMSE) are also detailed.

The top seven models are each variants of Gradient Boosting Machines (GBM), which involves combining multiple simple tree-based models into a single complex model. The best model consists of 67 internal trees with a mean number of leaves of 15.19. These are followed by Ensemble models, which also combine the decisions from multiple models to improve the overall performance. Deep Learning models, applied so successfully in other contexts, are found to be weak predictors of loan status, with Logloss and RMSE measures that are multiples of the other models examined.

Table 2. Interest rate model leaderboard ranking.

	Mean residual		Root mean squared	
Model	Deviance	RMSE	MAE	Log error
Stacked ensemble model	8.4941	2.9145	2.2817	0.2238
Stacked ensemble best of family model	8.4995	2.9154	2.2826	0.2239
GBM grid model 1	8.5143	2.9180	2.2889	0.2242
GBM grid model 2	8.5344	2.9214	2.2926	0.2245
GBM grid model 3	8.5549	2.9249	2.2959	0.2248
GBM grid model 4	8.5647	2.9265	2.2975	0.2250
GBM model 4	8.5793	2.9290	2.3032	0.2255
GBM model 3	8.5824	2.9257	2.3012	0.2254
GBM model 2	8.5841	2.9299	2.3001	0.2253
GBM grid model 5	8.5953	2.9318	2.3052	0.2257
GBM model 1	8.6084	2.9340	2.3043	0.2257
GBM model 5	8.7409	2.9565	2.3360	0.2285
Extremely randomized trees	9.0299	3.0050	2.3500	0.2306
Generalized linear models	9.0879	3.0146	2.3832	0.2370
Distributed random forest	9.1517	3.0252	2.3646	0.2321
Deep learning grid model 2	9.2071	3.0343	2.4193	0.2367
Deep learning grid model 1	9.2715	3.0449	2.4094	0.2378
Deep learning grid model 3	9.5898	3.0968	2.4849	0.2440

Notes: The top ranked models used to predict loan interest rates are listed in order of the mean residual deviance of the models. RMSE, mean absolute deviation (MAE) and root mean squared log error are also provided.

In Table 2, the models used to inform the interest rate to be charged on loans are ranked according to the mean residual deviation. Ensemble models provide the lowest model error. The best performing individual model for the output of interest rate is a GBM grid approach with 93 internal trees and a maximum of 975 leaves. Using a five fold cross-validated training set data we observe an RMSE value of 2.9179. As in the case of loan default predictions, Deep Learning models are found to provide the weakest forecasts among the models examined. We utilize and look to explain the best performing GBM model for each of the default and interest rate datasets.

We are not proposing that these trained models are the best available approaches, and can likely be improved further using additional refinements. Each of the best performing GBM models we later examine exhibit relatively strong levels of accuracy in terms of predicting loan status. The complexity of these models means that it is difficult to directly map how these feature inputs have impacted the output prediction we observe here. This is where our use of interpretable machine learning approaches come into play.

4.2. *Global explanations*

We begin our interpretability assessment by considering global explanations, the primary factors that influence the predictions of the models. In Figure 1, we detail the variable importance ratio (VIP) for loan status, while Figure 2 present VIP for interest rates. These are aggregated on a global basis, and therefore apply across all loan observations in our 2016 testing set.

The primary predictor of loan status is the number of mortgage accounts held, indicative perhaps of customers seeking to prevent mortgage default by taking on a more short-term loan. The same feature does not appear as an important interest rate predictor. FICO scores, a well-known third-party measure of consumer credit risk, are important determinants of both loan status and interest rates. The variation in FICO scores is found to have an asymmetric relationship, with a high FICO score associated with a high interest rate but having less influence on loan status.

The purpose of the loan has a significant association, with 'credit card' and 'undisclosed other' found to be important drivers of the interest rate charged. The 'credit card' feature is found to have less influence on loan status. Verification status, indicating whether LendingClub have verified the customer's income, is found to be a relevant determinant for both models. Focusing on the customers capacity to make debt repayments, both annual income and the customers associated debt-to-income ratio are found to be important predictors in both models. Finally, the timing of the customers earliest reported credit line is found to be influential.

These above global variable importance plots have allowed us to identify what variables are driving the model output we observe. Global variable importance does not inform how the input variables impact the output. Therefore, to understand the relationships and

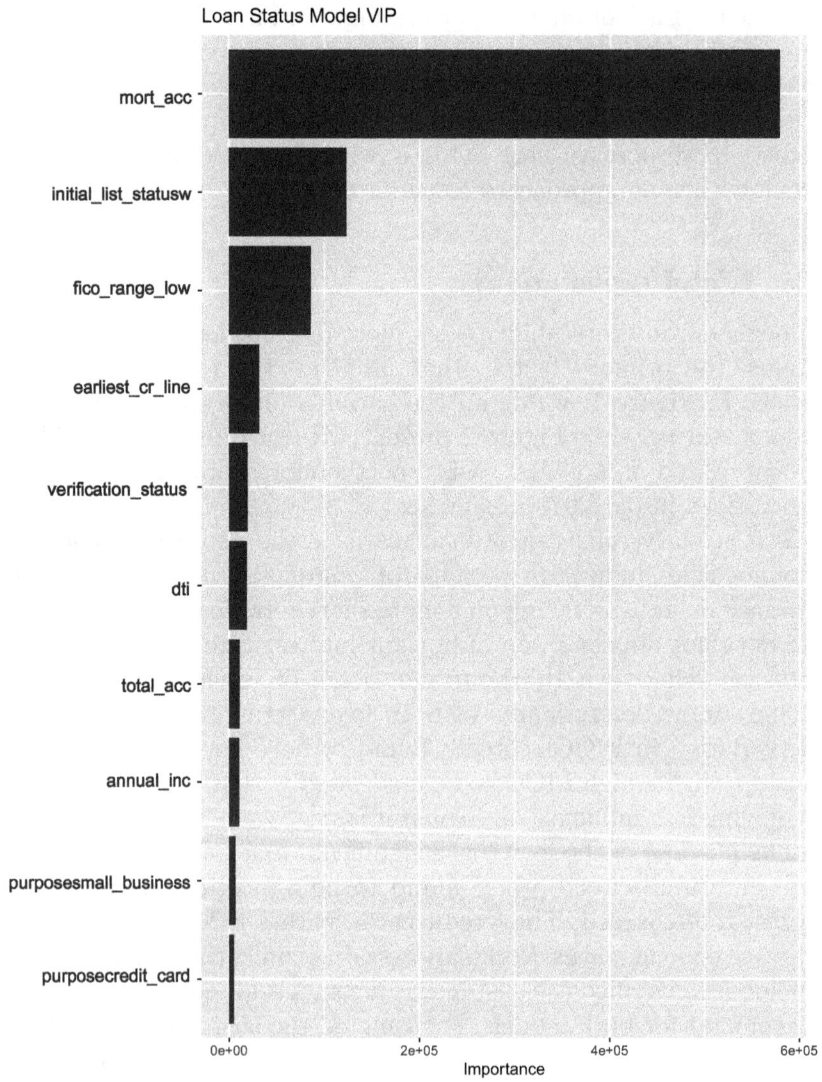

Figure 1. Loan status variable importance ratio.

Notes: Variation importance is presented for the loan status model, representing the global importance of the features from the best performing gradient boosting machine.

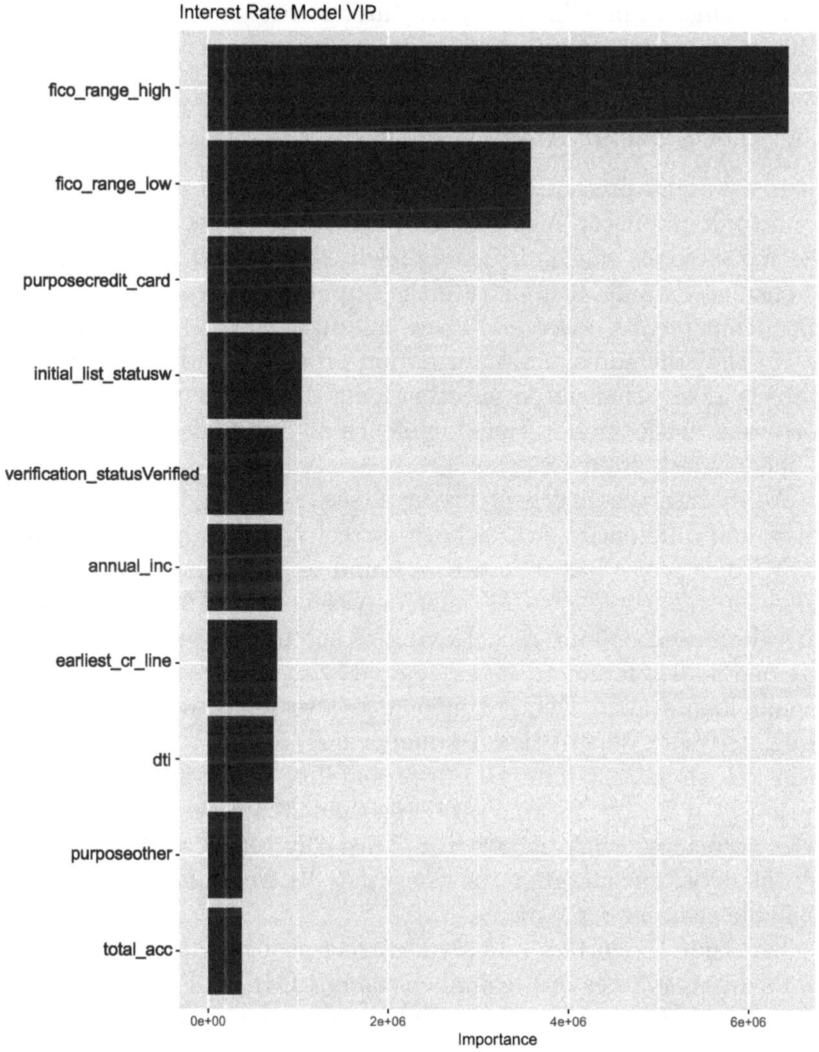

Figure 2. Interest rate variable importance ratio.

Notes: Variation importance is presented for the interest rate model, representing the global importance of the features from the best performing gradient boosting machine.

the dynamics at play in setting the interest rate and the determining default likelihood we utilize local observations.

4.3. *Local explanations — LIME*

Figures 3 and 4 present the LIME explainer plots for the case where the default predictor is correct and incorrect, respectively. We have selected six loans which ultimately resulted in default and six without an ensuing default, to illustrate the important features which drive the output results observed. These findings relate to those of Miller (2015) that the additional information provided by online P2P platforms is most beneficial in selecting loans among seemingly high risk borrowers, with the additional evidence adding little further insight to the low risk groups.

We discuss the emergent features, seeking to highlight commonalities and differences. Across both correct and incorrect predictions, a low FICO score, less than 670, is found to be a prevailing indicator of loan status, while a FICO range between 670 and 690 is associated with decreased default risk. Having either no mortgage account or just one is also found to be associated with a higher probability of default loan status. Debt to income is also found to be commonly associated with default risk. In many cases, having a debt to income ratio less than 23.3 reduces the probability of default loan status. Curiously, a debt to income ratio less than 23.3 is occasionally found to be associated with higher risk. This may relate to a disciplining role of debt, encouraging the consumer to work harder to ensure available cash for repayments.

The same six correct and six incorrect customer prediction models for interest rates are examined using LIME in Figures 5 and 6, respectively. Once again, the FICO range is found to be of central importance, with a FICO score of less than 674 often found to be associated with an increase in interest rates. For a small number of the incorrect models, a higher FICO score is associated with lower interest rates. While debt payments to income were found to be negatively associated with default loan status, they are found to have the expected positive relationship with interest rates. This highlights the prospects for unintuitive relationships underpinning machine learning-based predictions. The interest rate charged also has a negative relationship with the time since the earliest line of

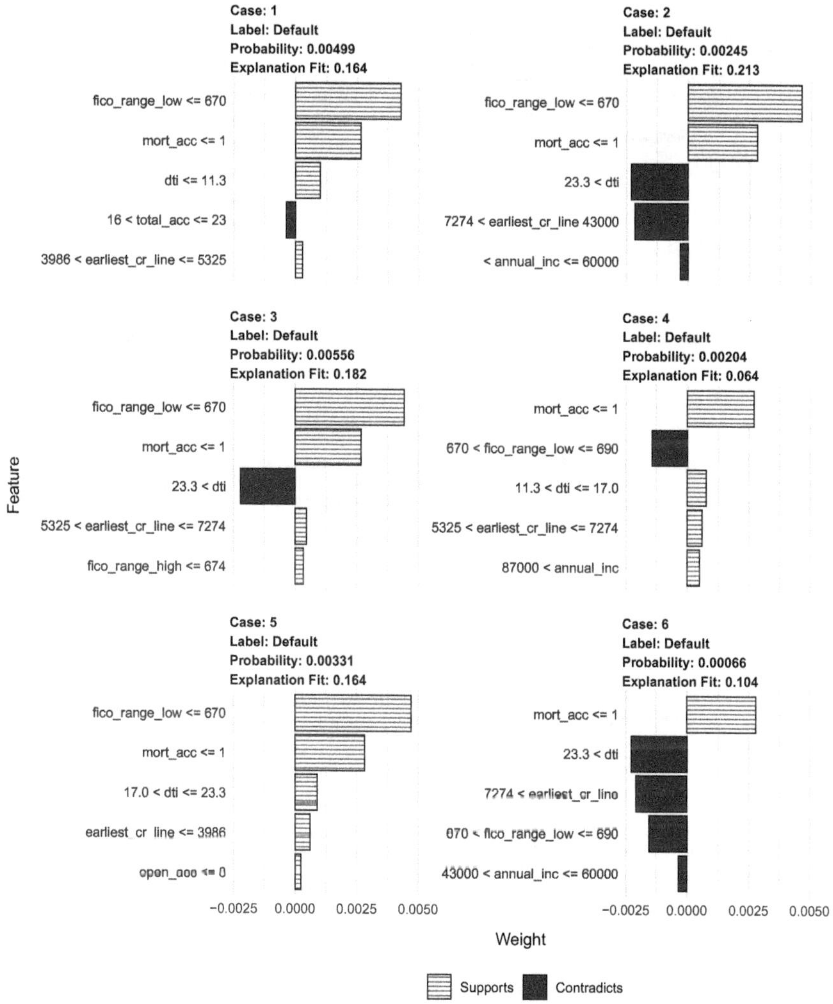

Figure 3. Lime status correct default predictions.

Notes: The top five LIME extracted features are detailed for six loan applications where the loan status prediction was correct *expost*. The six cases detailed correspond to loan application numbers 39474, 143674, 148399, 158891, 207255, and 216824, respectively.

credit was drawn. Finally, there is a distinction in interest rates for customers with high and low numbers of total accounts.

These findings indicate that LIME can be used as a mechanism to illustrate the features that influence loan status and interest rates.

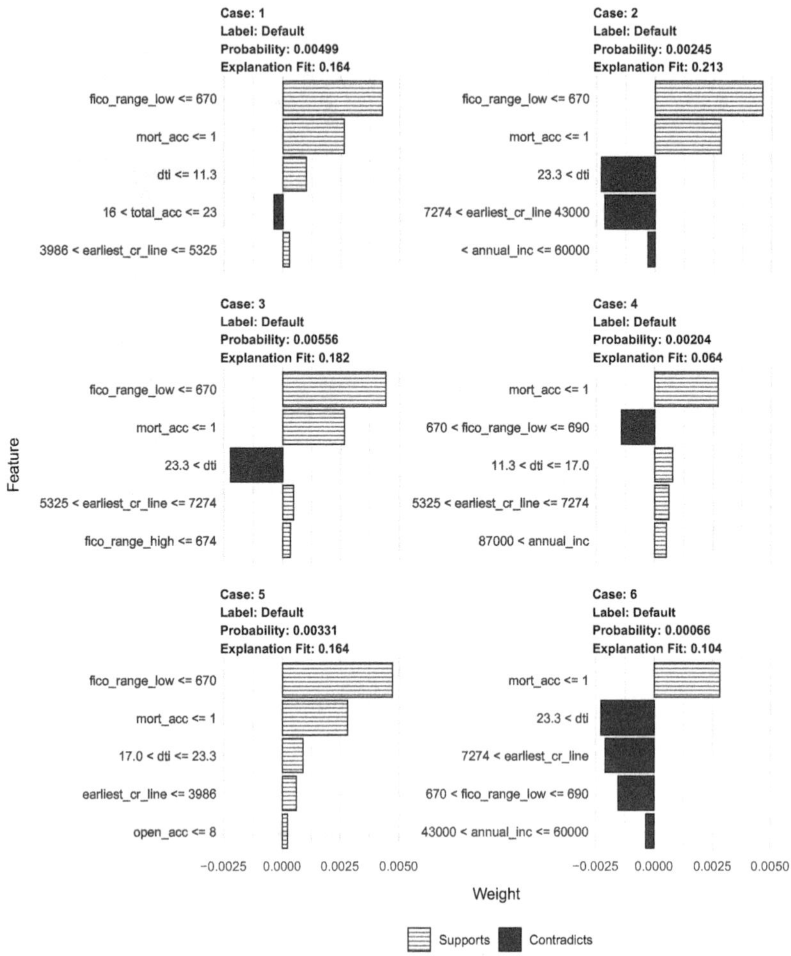

Figure 4. Lime status incorrect predictions.

Notes: The top five LIME extracted features are detailed for six loan applications where the loan status prediction was incorrect *expost*. The six cases detailed correspond to loan application numbers 14302, 59160, 109107, 161913, 168540, and 228836, respectively.

Our results indicate that, relative to the features extracted from global explanations, individual data characteristics have a significant influence on model predictions. We next examine whether an alternative local explanation method, Shapley Values, gives similar interpretations.

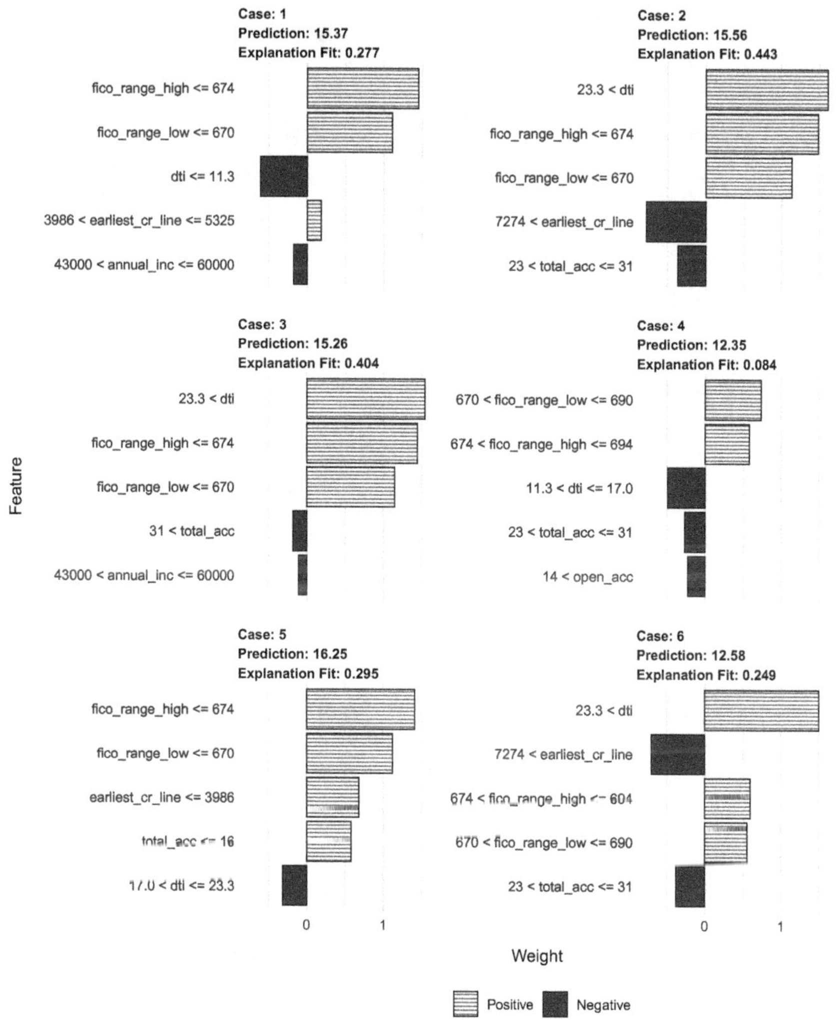

Figure 5. Lime interest rate correct predictions.

Notes: The top five LIME extracted features are detailed for six loan applications where the interest rate prediction was correct *expost*. The six cases detailed correspond to loan application numbers 39474, 143674, 148399, 158891, 207255, and 216824, respectively.

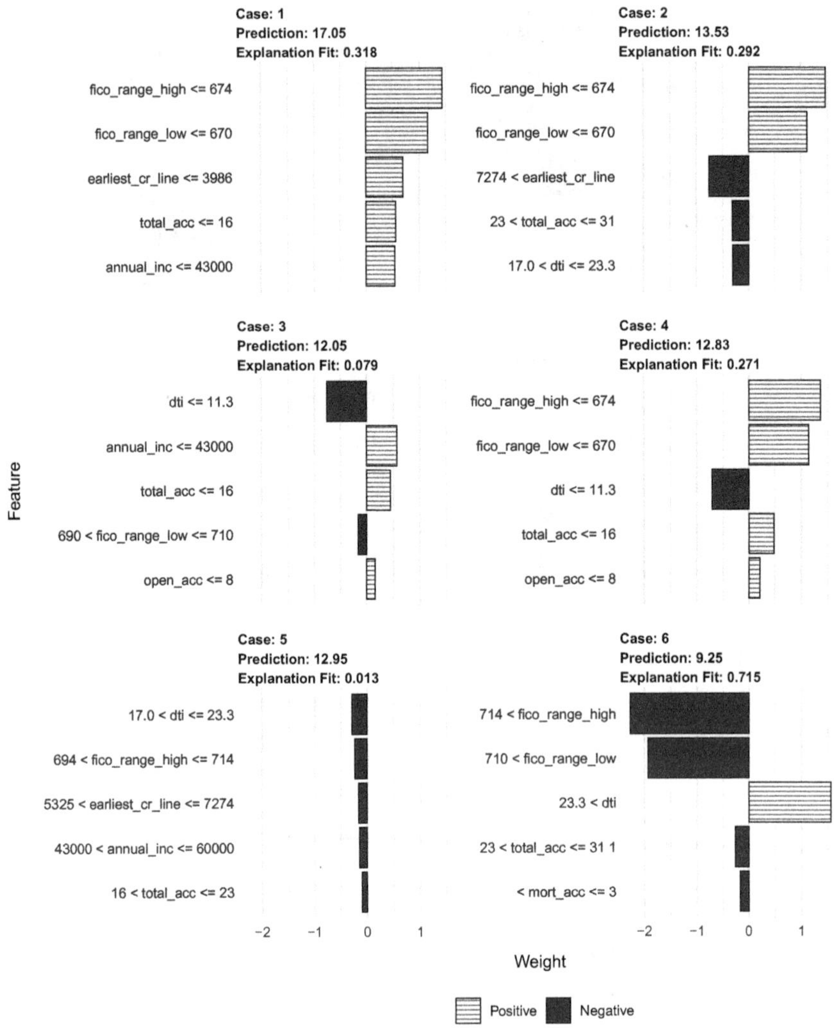

Figure 6. Lime interest rate incorrect predictions.

Notes: The top five LIME extracted features are detailed for six loan applications where the interest rate prediction was incorrect *expost*. The six cases detailed correspond to loan application numbers 14302, 59160, 109107, 161913, 168540, and 228836, respectively.

4.4. *Local explanations — Shapley values*

Using Shapley values, the contribution of each feature is assessed and the six features with highest positive value contribution and six with highest negative value contribution are detailed.[6] The range of features found to be of importance using Shapley values is much wider than those emanating from LIME.

We summarize some of the features which emerge in the case of a prediction of loan default status, as detailed in Figure 7. Where the purpose of the loan is to consolidate other outstanding debts, the probability of default is greater. Home ownership, rather than renting, is found to be associated with increased default probability. Moreover, the number of accounts held, annual income and the debt-to-income ratio are variously found to be associated with increased probability of loan default.

Considering the features which are found to be associated with a reduction in the probability of loan default, there is strong agreement. In cases where the source of income has been verified, there is an increased probability of loan status being equal to default. This may relate to a propensity to verify income in cases where the borrower is viewed as riskier. An initial loan status not equal to 'w', corresponding to the case where the loan was provided by more than one lender, is found to be associated with a reduction in risk. Similar to the verification status described, this may be a consequence of pre-validation of the borrower before deciding to lend the entire loan amount. Where the borrower only holds one mortgage account, we find that this is associated with a reduction in the probability of loan status being equal to default.

Shapley values for interest rate models are shown for the same six customers in Figure 8. Reasonable agreement is indicated in terms of the features found to explain the outcome for each customer. The FICO score is consistently associated with a higher interest rate across all customers. Curiously, while an initial list status not equal to 'w' was found to be associated with a reduction in the probability

[6]Given the LIME similarities between the emergent features for cases where forecasts are correct and incorrect, for brevity we only detail results for correct predictions here. Qualitatively similar findings are available from the authors for the incorrect predictions.

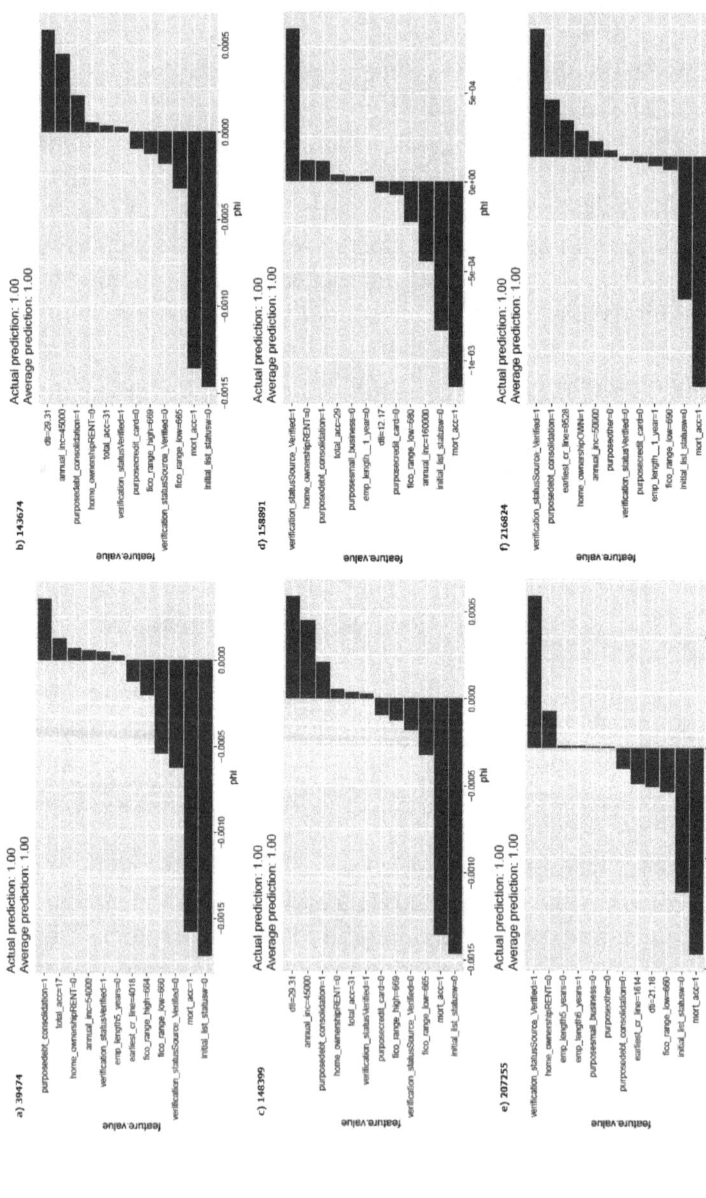

Figure 7. **Shapley values default predictions.**

Notes: The top six positive and negative features for loan status, extracted using Shapley values, are listed for loan application numbers 39474, 143674, 148399, 158891, 207255, and 216824, respectively. For each loan, the prediction was found to be correct *expost*.

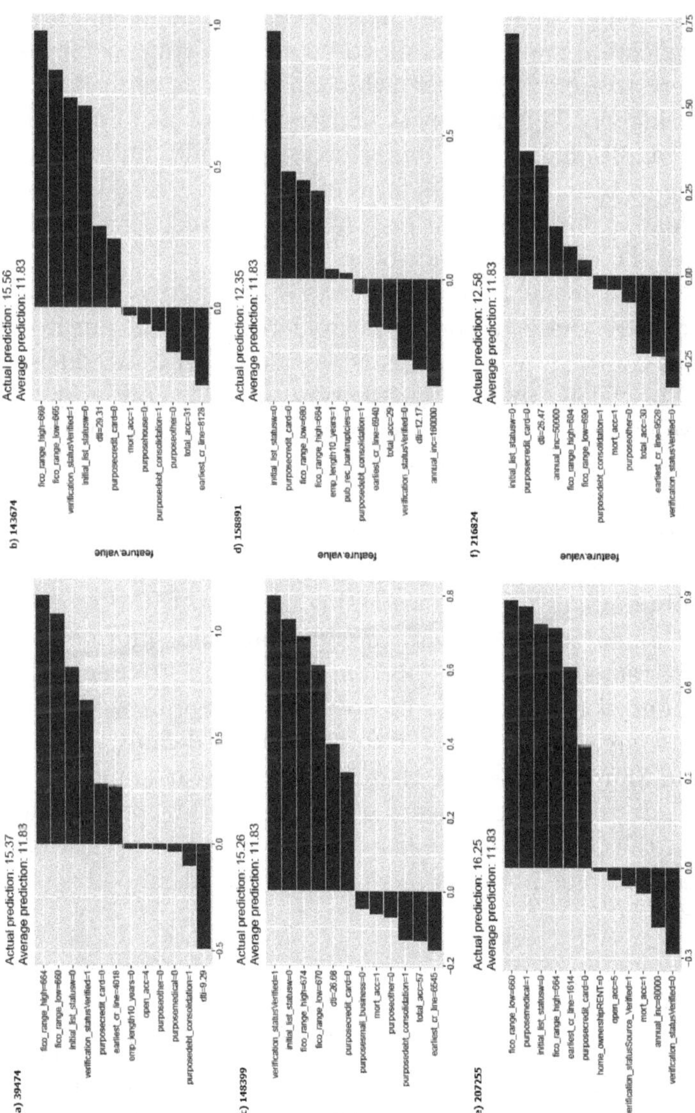

Figure 8. Shapley values interest rates predictions.

Notes: The top six positive and negative features for the interest rate model, extracted using Shapley values, are listed for loan application numbers 39474, 143674, 148399, 158891, 207255, and 216824, respectively. For each loan, the prediction was deemed to be correct *expost*.

of default, a positive link with the interest rate charged on the loan is found for all customers. This indicates that lenders are unwilling to make individual high-interest rate loans, preferring instead to split the loan among many parties, diversifying risk. Similar to findings for default, verification status is found to be an important determinant of the interest rate. In this case, where income was verified, the interest rate is higher. This may be a consequence of LendingClub passing on the additional cost of departures from fully automated decision making to borrowers in the form of increased interest rates. Finally, if the loan is not for the purpose of settling credit card debt, the interest rate is commonly found to be higher.

There is less consistency across the factors that negatively impact the interest rate to be charged. For five customers, where the purpose of the loan is to consolidate debt, this is associated with a reduced interest rate. This likely links to a reduction in the overall cost of debt from consolidation, resulting in lower risk. Cases where the customer has only one outstanding mortgage account are linked to lower interest rates for four of the customers examined. Other important factors include the number of accounts held, the month the borrowers first credit line was opened and the debt-to-income ratio.

Some overall points of note are worth highlighting. FICO scores, provided by a third party agency, provide valuable information beyond that extracted from the 'big data' available to LendingClub. The amount of requested credit does not emerge as a feature of importance, somewhat in contrast to traditional default prediction models. An unusual emergent characteristic is that home owners seem less likely to default, but are often charged higher interest rates. Similarly, the purpose of the loan is often associated with an elevated interest rate but not with increased default likelihood.

5. Conclusions and Discussion

This chapter reconsiders a major FinTech application, P2P lending, to determine whether reasonable and consistent explanations of lending decisions can be provided to customers. The distilling of explanations from model-derived decisions is important in light of the use of black-box models to inform loan adjudication and the rising regulatory requirement to provide explanations.

Global and local approaches to model explanation are assessed. Our findings indicate that, while visual representations of model-based lending decisions are possible, some heterogeneity is present between the interpretations provided by different approaches. Moreover, these explanations may not always be intuitive to the customer, perhaps raising issues regarding fairness and transparency. Our findings indicate that further research is required to determine common objectives in terms of explanations, with a particular focus on economic understanding. An assessment of partial dependency is also warranted, to identify whether feature interaction contributes significantly to model outcomes.

Our work relates to an emerging literature focusing upon the decisions underpinning and implications from P2P lending. Jagtiani and Lemieux (2019) argue that FICO scores have become less relevant in lending decisions. In contrast, our findings indicate that FICO scores are still an important determinant of both default likelihood and interest rates. Similar to Wang and Perkins (2019), we find that tree-based models provide strong accuracy. Our findings relating to the length of the customers credit history also connects to Puri *et al.* (2017), where they highlight the importance of first observing the behavior of a customer through encouraging the opening of a current or savings account before making the lending decision. While each of these papers focussed upon discussing the factors found to be statistically significant from the model, a contrast here is the focus on local interpretations which account for the specific data associated with the customer. Our work also develops the analysis of Bussmann *et al.* (2021), where Shapley were used to group predictions according to similarities in the underlying explanations.

Acknowledgments

The authors would like to thank the Editors, Daisy Chou, Conall O'Sullivan and Vassilios Papavassiliou for their help and support. Conlon acknowledges the support of Science Foundation Ireland under Grant Number 16/SPP/33 and 13/RC/2106 and 17/SP/5447.

Appendix

Table A1. Description of model features.

loan_status	Current status of the loan. From this loan status we classify loans as 'fully paid' or 'default'. We use a loose definition of default in this instance, namely that a loan is either listed as 'Default, Does not meet the credit policy. Status:Charged Off', is 'In Grace Period', is associated a 'Default Receiver', or payment is 'Late (16-30 days)', 'Late (31-120 days)'. We remove loans that are listed as 'Current' or have no loan status.
int_rate	Interest Rate on the loan.
emp_length	Employment length in years. Possible values are between 0 and 10 where 0 means less than one year and 10 means ten or more years. We create dummy variables out of the employment length, as it is not a continuous variable, i.e., 0 is used for employment lengths of less than a year, and 10 is used for employment lengths of greater than 10 years.
home_ownership	The home ownership status provided by the borrower during registration or obtained from the credit report. To reduce a number of uninformative categories we exclude home ownership entries that are listed as Any or None. Our values are: RENT, OWN, MORTGAGE, OTHER.
annual_inc	The self-reported annual income provided by the borrower during registration. We standardize annual income by funded amount, to give a proportion of how much of a borrowers annual income the loan constitutes.
verification_status	Indicates if income was verified by LC, not verified, or if the income source was verified.
purpose	A category provided by the borrower for the loan request. From this category we create dummy variables for the categories, credit card, consolidation,

Table A1. (*Continued*)

	home improvement, house, major purchase, medical, moving, other, energy, small business, vacation and wedding.
dti	A ratio calculated using the borrower's total monthly debt payments on the total debt obligations, excluding mortgage and the requested LC loan, divided by the borrower's self-reported monthly income.
earliest_cr_line	The month the borrower's earliest reported credit line was opened.
fico_range_low	The lower boundary range the borrower's loan origination FICO belongs to.
fico_range_high	The upper boundary range the borrower's loan origination FICO belongs to.
open_acc	The number of open credit lines in the borrower's credit file.
pub_rec	Number of derogatory public records.
total_acc	The total number of credit lines currently in the borrower's credit file.
initial_list_status	The initial listing status of the loan. Possible values are — W, F, referring to cases where a single investor provided the whole loan or a fraction of the loan.
application_type	Indicates whether the loan is an individual application or a joint application with two co-borrowers.
mort_acc	Number of mortgage accounts.
pub_rec_bankruptcies	Number of public record bankruptcies.
addr_state	The state provided by the borrower in the loan application. To utilize the address field we look at default rates by state to determine those states that have the most and least loan defaults. We filter out those states with less than 1,000 loans defaulting and find that across the years of the in-sample analysis the 'GA' is consistently in the top 10 for most defaults and 'NV' and 'CO' are in the bottom 10. We include these three states as additional feature factors in our training and testing analysis.

References

Adcock, C., Bessler, W., & Conlon, T. (2022). Characteristic-sorted portfolios and macroeconomic risks — An orthogonal decomposition. *Journal of Empirical Finance, 65*, 24–50.

Avino, D., Conlon, T., & Cotter, J. (2019). Credit default swaps as indicators of bank financial distress. *Journal of International Money and Finance, 94*, 132–139.

Aziz, S., Dowling, M., Hammami, H., & Piepenbrink, A. (2019). Machine learning in finance: A topic modeling approach. *European Financial Management, 28*(3), 744–770.

Bianchi, D., Büchner, M., & Tamoni, A. (2021). Bond risk premiums with machine learning. *The Review of Financial Studies, 34*(2), 1046–1089.

Bracke, P., Datta, A., Jung, C., & Sen, S. (2019). Machine learning explainability in finance: An application to default risk analysis. *Bank of England Working Paper, 816.*

Breiman, L. (2001). Random forests. *Machine learning, 45*(1), 5–32.

Bussmann, N., Giudici, P., Marinelli, D., & Papenbrock, J. (2020). Explainable AI in fintech risk management. *Frontiers in Artificial Intelligence, 3*, 26.

Bussmann, N., Giudici, P., Marinelli, D., & Papenbrock, J. (2021). Explainable machine learning in credit risk management. *Computational Economics, 57*(1), 203–216.

Financial Stability Board (2017). Artificial intelligence and machine learning in financial services: Market developments and financial stability implications. Financial Stability Board (November). http://www.fsb.org/2017/11/artificial-intelligence-and-machine-learning-in-financial-service/.

Fisher, A., Rudin, C., & Dominici, F. (2018). All models are wrong but many are useful: Variable importance for black-box, proprietary, or misspecified prediction models, using model class reliance. arXiv preprint arXiv:1801.01489, 237–246.

Frankel, F., & Reid, R. (2008). Big data: Distilling meaning from data. *Nature, 455*(7209), 30.

Gu, S., Kelly, B., & Xiu, D. (2020). Empirical asset pricing via machine learning. *The Review of Financial Studies, 33*(5), 2223–2273.

Hall, P., Cox, B., Dickerson, S., Ravi Kannan, A., Kulkarni, R., & Schmidt, N. (2021). A United States fair lending perspective on machine learning. *Frontiers in Artificial Intelligence, 4*, 78.

Ip, C., & Lam, F. (2020). AI guidance around the world. Available at SSRN 3619821.

Jagtiani, J., & Lemieux, C. (2019). The roles of alternative data and machine learning in fintech lending: evidence from the lendingclub consumer platform. *Financial Management*, *48*(4), 1009–1029.

Khandani, A., Kim, A., & Lo, A. (2010). Consumer credit-risk models via machine-learning algorithms. *Journal of Banking & Finance*, *34*(11), 2767–2787.

Kumar, G., Muckley, C., Pham, L., & Ryan, D. (2019). Can alert models for fraud protect the elderly clients of a financial institution? *The European Journal of Finance*, *25*(17), 1683–1707.

Lantz, B. (2019). *Machine Learning with R: Expert Techniques for Predictive Modeling.* Packt Publishing Ltd, London, United Kingdom.

Loughran, T., & McDonald, B. (2016). Textual analysis in accounting and finance: A survey. *Journal of Accounting Research*, *54*(4), 1187–1230.

Miller, S. (2015). Information and default in consumer credit markets: Evidence from a natural experiment. *Journal of Financial Intermediation*, *24*(1), 45–70.

Puri, M., Rocholl, J., & Steffen, S. (2017). What do a million observations have to say about loan defaults? Opening the black box of relationships. *Journal of Financial Intermediation*, *31*, 1–15.

Ribeiro, M., Singh, S., & Guestrin, C. (2016). 'Why should I trust you?' Explaining the predictions of any classifier. In *Proceedings of the 22nd ACM SIGKDD International Conference on Knowledge Discovery and Data Mining*, San Francisco, CA, USA. (pp. 1135–1144).

Shapley, L. (1953). Stochastic games. In *Proceedings of the National Academy of Sciences*, *39*(10), 1095–1100.

Štrumbelj, E., & Kononenko, I. (2014). Explaining prediction models and individual predictions with feature contributions. *Knowledge and Information Systems*, *41*(3), 647–665.

Thakor, A. (2020). Fintech and banking: What do we know? *Journal of Financial Intermediation*, *41*, 100833.

Wang, J., & Perkins, C. (2019). How magic a bullet is machine learning for credit analysis? An exploration with fintech lending data. *Federal Reserve Bank of Boston Working Paper, 19.*

https://doi.org/10.1142/9781800612723_0006

Chapter 6

Detecting Financial Statement Fraud Using Machine-Learning Methods

Xin Chen[*,§], Yang Wang[†,¶] and Yifei Zhang[‡,||]

[*]*Department of Economics, Lingnan University, Hong Kong, China*
[†]*School of Business, University of Dundee, Dundee, UK*
[‡]*School of Accounting and Finance, Faculty of Business, The Hong Kong Polytechnic University, Hong Kong, China*
[§]*xinchen5@ln.hk*
[¶]*ywang001@dundee.ac.uk*
[||]*yifei.zhang@polyu.edu.hk*

Abstract

Financial statement fraud raises substantial concerns for regulators worldwide, and regulators face severe challenges in detecting and addressing the increased incidence of this type of fraud. This chapter compares three popular machine-learning approaches based on 35 firm-level financial and linguistic features derived from annual reports. Using hand-collected financial statement fraud data in China, we aim to compare different machine-learning models and select the most accurate fraud detection model to improve fraud detection ability. In particular, we aim to assess the predictive performance of the least absolute shrinkage and selection operator (LASSO); random forest and bagging; and support vector machine (SVM) models, and compare the results with the logistic regression method. The findings suggest that the LASSO method outperforms relative to other two methods. This chapter contributes to the literature by selecting both financial and linguistic fraud predictors and contributing to an under-researched area by employing different machine-learning algorithms to detect fraud in financial statements.

Keywords: China, financial statement fraud, fraud detection, fraud factor, machine learning.

1. Introduction

Financial statement fraud has received considerable attention from the public, press, investors, business community, accounting professions, and regulators (Rezaee, 2005). A wave of high-profile financial scandals such as Enron, WorldCom, and Lehman Brothers caused significant degradation of trust in capital markets and concomitant inefficient capital allocation decisions (Throckmorton *et al.*, 2015). Financial statement fraud is a major concern for China, and Chinese regulators face severe challenges in detecting and addressing the increased incidence of this misconduct (Yang *et al.*, 2017). According to the China Securities Regulatory Commission (CSRC), they issued 310 administrative decisions against fraudulent firms in 2018, which involved monetary penalties and disgorgements amounting to US$1.49 billion (CSRC, 2019).

Financial statement fraud detection requires specific and in-depth knowledge of financial reporting standards and market trading strategies, and arguably, auditors should play an essential role in detecting financial statement fraud. However, recent empirical evidence suggests that auditors fail to detect fraudulent activities that firms committed due to lack of experience and conflicts of interests, especially given that fraud techniques have become more hidden and complex nowadays (Moore *et al.*, 2006). In addition, manual fraud detection is considered time-consuming, costly, and inaccurate (West and Bhattacharya, 2016). Consequently, the development of accurate automated fraud detection systems becomes increasingly important to address the issue of financial statement fraud. It is critical to build a robust and intelligent fraud detection system, which can provide early warning signals (i.e., red flags) that support investors' decision-making processes.

This chapter aims to develop an improved financial statement fraud detection system based on specific features derived from annual reports by comparing three popular machine-learning techniques. Financial statement fraud refers to intentional misstatements or omissions of amounts or disclosures in financial reporting to mislead financial reporting users. This leads to situations where financial reporting is not presented, in all material respects, in conformity with the Generally Accepted Accounting Principles (Wang *et al.*, 2019). Detecting financial statement fraud has proven difficult for a few reasons. One of the major reasons is that managers are often the main perpetrators, and managers can override internal control mechanisms more easily, and they tend to collude and work hard to conceal the real financial status of firms. Subsequently, it is harder to detect such fraud using traditional analytical and statistical methods (Whiting *et al.*, 2012).

A growing literature on fraud detection has begun to use the machine-learning methods to examine the fraud risk indicators and our chapter further contributes to this stream of literature from the following two aspects. First, we incorporate both linguistic and financial ratio indicators and utilize different machine-learning algorithms to detect financial statement fraud. Most previous studies only select financial variables for detecting financial statement fraud and find that firms with poor financial performance are more susceptible to fraudulent behaviors (Song *et al.*, 2014). For instance, low-profit margins encourage managers to manipulate income statements through exaggerating revenues or understating expenses (Dechow *et al.*, 2011). However, there are very limited studies that combine financial and linguistic data in predicting financial statement fraud. Subsequently, our study addresses this issue and finds that both financial and linguistic factors in annual reports are helpful for effectively detecting potential fraudulent firms.

Second, we aim to assess the predictive performance of the least absolute shrinkage and selection operator (LASSO); random forest and bagging; and support vector machine (SVM) models and compare the results with the logistic regression method. Our findings indicate that the three machine-learning methods we consider result in higher predictive accuracy than the traditional logistic estimates. In addition, we suggest that accounting professionals and regulators can pay special attention to review eleven key financial and linguistic attributes and apply the algorithm with improved accuracy to find the suspected fraudulent companies. In this regard, our findings contribute to a stream of machine-learning literature on selecting the most suitable fraud detection model with higher precision. In other words, this chapter adds to an under-researched area by employing different machine-learning algorithms for detecting fraud in financial statements. Our findings also have practical implications as the machine-learning algometric method can overcome the shortcomings of the traditional statistical analytics method by handling large datasets, particularly high dimensional data.

The remainder of the chapter is organized as follows. After this introduction, in Section 2, we review the relevant literature. Section 3 describes different machine-learning algorithms and the performance metrics. Section 4 outlines the data and variables and analyses the results. Section 5 concludes and discusses implications.

2. Literature Review

2.1. *Causes of financial statement fraud*

Financial statement fraud occurs when a firm's managers take actions to deceive investors and other users of financial reporting, which lowers market participants' confidence in audited financial reporting and damages minority shareholders' interests, particularly those who hold a firm's stocks for long-term (Conyon and He, 2016). The agency theory is often used to understand the causes of fraud. In particular, principal-agent conflicts arise when agents cannot be effectively disciplined and prioritize their own benefits above those of principals. As a result, agents (i.e., managers) behaving opportunistically at the expense of principals (i.e., shareholders) (Fama and Jensen, 1983). Agency costs associated with the separation of ownership and control are considerably higher when there are defects in corporate governance mechanisms. For instance, most independent directors in Chinese firms are *de facto* friends of the CEOs and are recruited without integrity checks. Subsequently, the recruitment process is just for 'window-dressing' the board and satisfying regulations (Clarke, 2006). This leads to ineffective monitoring of management in the financial reporting process, giving opportunities for managers to manipulate earnings. Agency conflicts not only exist between managers and shareholders but also between controlling and minority shareholders. This is particularly the case in Chinese listed firms where large controlling shareholders enable wealth to tunnel from the minority shareholders. In addition, intervention from controlling state shareholders can reduce firms' demand for high-quality external auditing. Subsequently, firms often hire local small-scale accounting firms, increasing the probability of fraud and sacrificing minority shareholders' interests (Yu and Ashton, 2015).

The existing literature on financial statement fraud also applies a fraud triangle theory from pressure, incentive, and rationalization perspectives to interpret the causes of fraud. Financial pressure generally stems from meeting third-party expectations. Third-party, such as stock exchanges and financial analysts, substantially impact investor opinion, stock price, and listing status. Their decision or forecast can put excessive pressure on managers to achieve short-term performance targets to avoid adverse stock market reactions. Subsequently, firms have strong motivations to commit financial statement fraud (Yang *et al.*, 2012).

An imperfect legal environment provides opportunities for fraud. A country's institutional and legal environment, including its process of enacting and enforcing laws and regulations, is crucial for reducing fraud. Although China has issued many regulations against fraudulent financial reporting during the past decade, investor protection remains weak (Jiang and Kim, 2015). According to a report issued by China's Supreme People's Court, some judges and court staff enjoy privileges and remain indifferent to the rights of litigants. They take bribes and deliver wrong verdicts, damaging the interests of litigants, reducing trust in the legal system, and engendering fraud (Xinhua, 2014).

Relative to some western economies, investor protection is imperfect in China. For instance, Allen *et al.* (2005) find that shareholders and creditors receive lower protection in China. The measure of anti-director rights in China is only higher than in India and Mexico but lower than in many developed economies. Katelouzou and Siems (2015) compare the development of shareholder protection among 30 countries in the last 24 years. They find that China has had the biggest increase in shareholder protection over the last 24 years. However, 'law in books' and 'law in action' can be divergent, as it is easier to enact laws than implement them. As a result, the level of legal effectiveness in China remains relatively low throughout the research period considered in this chapter. In this regard, a weak legal environment in China increases the opportunity for financial statement fraud.

The ineffectiveness of the CSRC can also result in financial statement fraud. In particular, limited regulatory resources make it difficult for regulators to deter fraud effectively. By the end of 2015, the CSRC has 3,097 staff with an annual budget of around US$160 million. In contrast, the US Securities and Exchange Commission (SEC) has 4,301 employees with an annual budget of nearly US$1,700 million. Although two regulators have a similar number of staff, the absolute budget of the CSRC is only about one-10th of that of the SEC. Even worse, the CSRC has only approximately 300 staff in the examination division involved in enforcement activities (Xu and Xu, 2020). In addition, the CSRC's budget is largely based on historical expenditure levels. The increase in the CSRC budget is not linked to the size of the stock market they need to regulate, which weakens the incentives of the enforcement staff to effectively monitor firms, thus providing opportunities for financial statement fraud (IMF, 2012).

Rationalization strategies allow offenders in a corrupt culture to view themselves as moral and ethical individuals, which frees them from any pangs of conscience that would deter them from committing fraud. If a firm develops a corrupt corporate culture at the top, employees may implement fraudulent transactions, uphold corrupt relationships and cover their tracks to protect the firm. Corrupt firms may perceive themselves as fighting a war, which leads to their taken-for-granted assumption that 'the ends justify the means'. Subsequently, employees are more likely to commit fraud (Campbell and Goritz, 2014).

Guanxi also plays an important role in Chinese corporate culture. In the Chinese language, *Guanxi* can be translated as 'relationships' or 'connections'. *Guanxi* is deeply rooted in Chinese culture and is one of the most important factors governing business success. It is necessary that members in the '*Guanxi* circle' exchange favors and meet the expectations of other members. If they fail to do so, a loss of reputation and trust will follow (Du *et al.*, 2015). Chinese firms tend to actively build *Guanxi* with regulators and local government officials to derive gains from such connections. For *Guanxi*-connected firms, they can have easier access to financial resources, e.g., loans from state-owned banks (Du *et al.*, 2017), and gain privileges in the regulatory outputs, e.g., punishments may be eased or even avoided (Chen *et al.*, 2011). *Guanxi* can also cause auditors to forgo their independence and collude with directors, and become willing participants of fraud (Guan *et al.*, 2016). Subsequently, *Guanxi*-connected firms have fewer incentives to provide high-quality financial reporting, increasing the likelihood of financial statement fraud.

2.2. *Detection of financial statement fraud*

Previous research has attempted different methods to detect financial fraud. For instance, Bell and Carcello (2000) examine the likelihood of financial statement fraud for audited clients, conditioned on the presence of different fraud-risk factors. Their findings indicate that the logistic regression model estimation is significantly more accurate and reliable than practicing auditors in evaluating the risks of financial statement fraud. Similarly, Bhattacharyya *et al.* (2011) examine the usefulness of three different methods, support vector machines, random forests, and logistic regression models, in detecting credit card fraud. They present that all three methods show sufficient credibility to model fraud, and the performance of logistic regression is similar even with varying percentages of fraud. Kirkos (2007) compares a fraudulent firm sample with a non-fraudulent firm sample and finds that the Bayesian Belief outperforms decision trees (DTs) and artificial neural networks (ANNs) in financial statement fraud detection. Pai *et al.* (2011) introduce a support vector machine-based fraud warning model to detect fraudulent financial reporting. The results support the use of this model, as it significantly reduces miscellaneous information and enables auditors to increase substantive testing during the audit process by providing more reliable and straightforward guidance.

Some recent studies compare multiple approaches and their accuracy in detecting financial statement fraud. For instance, Humpherys *et al.* (2011) examine how fraudulent firms use language differently than non-fraudulent firms in the financial markets using different machine-learning techniques, including DT, Locally Weighted Learning, Naïve Bayes, and SVM. Each machine-learning algorithm is adopted on the set of fraudulent and non-fraudulent 10-K fillings and examined using a 10-fold cross-validation technique. This is a bootstrapping technique that divides the data into ten equal sets in order to train and test the model. Their results demonstrate that the

DT and Naïve Bayes lead to classifying 136 instances correctly, yet 66 incorrectly, an overall accuracy of 67.3%. However, the Locally Weighted Learning algorithm yields a lower accuracy rate of 60.4%, with the classification of 80 instances incorrectly. In related research, Ravisankar *et al.* (2011) also use different machine-learning techniques to predict financial statement fraud. Their dataset is based on 101 fraudulent and 101 non-fraudulent firms and is analyzed using techniques including multilayer feed-forward neural network, SVM, genetic programming, group method of data handling, logistic regression, and probabilistic neural network. They find that probabilistic neural network outperforms other techniques, with an accuracy rate of 90.77% (and a sensitivity rate of 87.53%). Genetic programming comes close behind with 89.27% accuracy and 85.64% sensitivity. However, logistic regression has the lowest accuracy rate of 70.86%. Lin *et al.* (2015) have further extended Ravisankar *et al.* (2011)'s research by selecting 32 fraud risk factors based on the fraud triangle theory. The data mining approaches used in Lin *et al.* (2015)'s study includes logistic regression, DTs, and ANNs. Their results show that the ANNs technique results in a correct classification rate of 91.2%, which is 7.5% higher than that of the logistic regression technique in assessing the fraud presence. This indicates that a neural network approach not only improves the prediction accuracy, but also achieves a greater detecting power and a lower misclassification cost when comparing with a traditional commonly-used logistic regression model.

Most previous studies tend to use financial indicators taken from annual reports to identify abnormal performance and detect financial statement fraud. For instance, Dechow *et al.* (2011) analyze different financial characteristics of violation firms based on Accounting and Auditing Enforcement Releases (AAERs) issued by the US SEC and develop a model to predict financial violations. They observe that firm returns on assets are generally decreasing, yet cash sales are increasing during financial misstatement periods. In addition, firms are more likely to use operating leases to fictitiously front-load earnings and reduce reported debts during the violation period. Moreover, violating firms tend to actively raise finance during the misstatement years.

Recent empirical studies have started to use linguistic variables extracted from firm-level reports to predict financial misstatements.

Hajek and Henriques (2017) examine whether a more accurate financial fraud detection system could be developed by combining specific characteristics derived from both financial information and managerial comments in annual reports. Their samples include 311 fraudulent firms based on AAERs and are matched with 311 non-fraudulent firms. Thirty-two financial indicators relating to firm size and asset structure and eight linguistic variables are selected to develop this system. Their findings demonstrate that expected growth in revenues, growth in earnings per share (EPS), shares held by insiders, and stock price to earnings to EPS growth are the important financial variables to detect financial statement fraud. In addition, the frequency count of negative words in the managerial comment section of the annual report also shows the predictive power of financial statement fraud. Craja *et al.* (2020) further extend Hajek and Henriques (2017)'s research by including linguistic features of corporate annual reports. They have developed a hierarchical attention network (HAN) which enables the reflection of hierarchical patterns of language and find that linguistic features extracted by HAN produce promising and improved classification results, which significantly reinforce financial ratios and exhibit superior predictive power.

3. Methodology and Models

3.1. *Machine-learning algorithms*

In this chapter, we use multiple machine-learning approaches, including (1) LASSO regression estimation, (2) random forest and bagging, and (3) SVM as our fraud prediction models to investigate the impact of financial and linguistic characteristics on financial statement fraud. First, we choose LASSO regression because it improves the model interpretation by enabling the algorithm to exclude any irrelevant regressors and reduce the overfitting problems (Fonti and Belitser, 2017; Li *et al.*, 2021). Second, we incorporate the random forest method, the most popular bagging ensemble-based machine-learning algorithm, to generate powerful results whilst avoiding overfitting problems (Prasad *et al.*, 2006). Last, we include the SVM algorithm due to its good prediction ability for small, nonlinear, and high-dimensional data, which has been widely used in previous literature (Lima *et al.*, 2007; Ding *et al.*, 2008; Song *et al.*, 2014).

Before proceeding to formal predictive analytics, we split data into two random samples of equal sizes as the training and testing data. We then use the training data to train the models and generate the predictive ability of all the models based on the testing samples. We also use a logistic regression model as the benchmark performance to compare our machine-learning models against. In addition, all machine-learning algorithms in this chapter are implemented with R software.

3.1.1. *LASSO algorithm*

The LASSO regression model is a linear regression type that applies penalized terms to effectively shrink estimates towards zero relative to the traditional logistic estimates. The main objective of the LASSO regression is to improve model prediction and accuracy.[1] The shrinkage of LASSO selects only the most important predictor variables and thus avoids overfitting the model to the training data. In contrast, the logistic estimators suffer from the overfitting problem because it uses the residual sum of squares in the loss function, which can lead to overwhelming sampling characteristics especially for relatively small sample sizes. The LASSO estimator is the solution to the loss function of LASSO regression specified as follows.

$$\min_{b_1,\ldots,b_j} \left\{ \sum_{k=0}^{n} (\text{Fraud}_k - b_1 X_{k,1} - \cdots - b_j X_{k,j})^2 + \lambda \sum_{\rho=1}^{j} |b_\rho| \right\}, \quad (1)$$

where k indexes firm and the expression $\sum_{\rho=1}^{j} |b_\rho|$ in the penalty term denotes the $L_{1-\text{norm}}$ of j-vector. λ represents the regularization parameter value.

For the LASSO regression model, we also need to specify our regularization parameter λ. Following previous literature (Arlot and Celisse, 2010; Zhang and Yang, 2015), we select the best λ value and train LASSO regression in a 10-fold cross-validation framework, and conduct both the in-sample and out-of-sample tests.

[1]Noted that the LASSO-fitted penalized regression method still works reasonably well for binary outcome variables (Mullah *et al.*, 2021).

3.1.2. *Random forest and bagging algorithm*

Random forest is an ensemble-based method built on the DT algorithm, which establishes a substantial number of trees. In this study, we mainly adopt the random forest and bagging method with classification data. The random forest contains multiple single trees, each based on a random sample of the training data, and thus outperforms DT due to higher accuracy and stability. In addition, the random forest could handle the correlation across different variables and reduce the variance further, thus avoid overfitting problems.

The basic logic of random forest is to randomly select m (the number of samples chosen) in the entire sample numbers M $(m < M)$ by using a bootstrap method (Liaw and Wiener, 2002). In a similar vein, we randomly draw with the replacement of n observations from $\{(X_i, Y_i) : i = 1, \ldots, n\}$ and let $\{(X_i^*, Y_i^*) : i = 1, \ldots, n\}$ represents the resulting bootstrap sample. Then, we grow a tree T^* using $\{(X_i^*, Y_i^*) : i = 1, \ldots, n\}$. We then set $\hat{f}_{rf}^{T^*}(x)$ as the resulting estimator of $E(Y_i \mid X_i = x) = f(x)$. We repeat the previous steps to and repeat B times to produce $\hat{f}_{rf}^{T_1^*}(x), \ldots, \hat{f}_{rf}^{T_B^*}(x)$ where T_b^* is the tree grown on a bootstrap sample b. We finally average the trees over the bootstrap samples.

To achieve this, we construct a DT with the extracted sample without pruning. We can establish a large number of DTs by repeatedly conducting the previous steps and obtain a DT classification sequence. After deciding each recorded vote from the results, we can identify the final classification based on the average value, which is expressed as follows.

$$\hat{f}_{rf}^{B}(x) = \frac{1}{B} \sum_{n=1}^{B} \hat{f}_{rf}^{T_b^*}(x), \tag{2}$$

where n means the selected observations and B means the number of selecting times of the bootstrap method.

3.1.3. *SVM algorithm*

The SVM algorithm classifies data groups by learning hyperplanes that separate positive instances from negative instances (Perols, 2011). The objective is to find the optimal separating hyperplane of the two different classes, which could effectively minimize the structural risk. In particular, it specializes in nonlinear classification by mapping the inputs into high-dimensional feature outputs.

The underlying rationale of SVM classification algorithm process is presented as follows. First, we divide an initial training set $D = \{x_i y_i\}_{i=1}^{N}$ and set the input vectors $x_i = (x_i^{(1)}, \ldots, x_i^{(n)}) \in R^n$ and target labels $y_i \in \{-1, +1\}$. Then we can derive the basic SVM model listed as Eq. (3).

$$\min_{m,b} \frac{1}{2}\omega^T \omega, \tag{3}$$

where ω and b denote a weight vector and a bias value, respectively. The input vectors are mapped into a high-dimensional feature space by applying the nonlinear function ($\phi(\cdot) : R^k \to R^{nk}$). It is, therefore, a quadratic programming (QP) problem when identifying the optimal hyperplane. Following Song *et al.* (2014), we further show the following non-linear decision function.

$$y(x) = sign\left(\sum_{i=1}^{N} \alpha_i \gamma_i k(x, x_i) + b\right), \tag{4}$$

where $k(x, x_i) = \phi(x_i)^T \phi(x_j)$ is a kernel function that satisfies Mercer's condition.[2]

3.2. *Performance metrics*

In terms of the LASSO regression and the random forest methods, we use root mean squared error (RMSE) as our performance metrics to measure the model prediction error. RMSE corresponds to the average differences between the observed known values of the outcome and the predicted value of the model. In general, lower RMSE indicates better model predictive ability (Consonni *et al.*, 2010).

In addition, receiver operating characteristics (ROC) prediction graphs have been widely adopted to evaluate the predictive ability

[2]Theoretically, Mercer's condition is satisfied when a kernel function is positive definite, which guarantees the existence of an underlying map ϕ. Mercer's condition also allows us to select kernels so that ϕ could even be an infinite vector (Mercer, 1909; Graepel, 2002).

of machine-learning algorithms (Provost and Fawcett, 1997; Fawcett, 2006; Singh *et al.*, 2012). More specifically, it is a two-dimensional graph in which the y-axis denotes the true positive rate, and the x-axis corresponds to the false positive rate. According to Fawcett (2006), ROC curves depict the relative trade-offs between benefits (true positive rate) and costs (false positive rate) and visualize classifier performance without extra error costs. In other words, the area under a ROC curve is regarded as a measure of predictive quality. Therefore, we plot the ROC curves of the SVM method in comparison to the traditional logistic model to show the prediction visually. In addition to the ROC performance, we also report the single scalar values (i.e., the area under the ROC curve), also known as the AUC values (Hanley and McNeil, 1982; Bradley, 1997) of each in-sample and out-of-sample data over the two different models. Generally, higher AUC values indicate the better predictive performance of a model in distinguishing between the positive and negative classes.

4. Data and Results

4.1. *Data sources, sampling procedures, and summary statistics*

In this study, financial statement fraud data is manually collected from the official websites of the CSRC and their regional offices. Following prior literature on financial statement fraud (Beasley, 1996; Perols and Lougee, 2011), our dependent variable, *Fraud*, is a dummy variable that equals one if a firm commits financial statement fraud, and zero otherwise. Our sample period spans from 2009 to 2018, covering all reported financial statement fraud cases of publicly listed firms in China. For the candidate predictors, we include both linguistic and financial variables and enumerate the candidate factors in Table 1. Figure 1 presents the correlation plot of all the indicators used in this study.

Previous findings imply that fraudsters tend to use negative or uncertain words in financial statements. For instance, the annual reports of fraudulent firms may include three times more positive sentiment compared to truthful reports (Hajeka and Henriques, 2017). As a result, words used in the annual reports containing information such as the length and sentiment features are also analyzed.

Table 1. Definition and source of the linguistic and financial factors.[a]

Group	Factor	Variable	Source
MD&A	X1	Number of positive terms in MD&A (in thousand)	CNRDS
	X2	Number of negative terms in MD&A (in thousand)	CNRDS
	X3	Number of sentences in MD&A (in thousand)	CNRDS
	X4	Number of phrases in MD&A (in thousand)	CNRDS
	X5	Number of words in annual report (in thousand)	CNRDS
	X6	Number of phrases in annual report (in thousand)	CNRDS
	X7	Number of sentences in annual report (in thousand)	CNRDS
	X8	Number of positive terms in annual report based on L&M dictionary (in thousand)	CNRDS
	X9	Number of negative terms in annual report based on L&M dictionary (in thousand)	CNRDS
Sentiment	X10	(Number of positive terms — number of negative terms)/total number of words in annual report based on L&M dictionary	CNRDS
	X11	(Number of positive terms — number of negative terms)/total number of positive and negative terms in annual report based on L&M dictionary	CNRDS
	X12	Number of positive terms in annual report based on NTUSD	CNRDS
	X13	Number of negative terms in annual report based on NTUSD	CNRDS
	X14	(Number of positive terms — number of negative terms)/total number of positive and negative terms in annual report based on NTUSD	CNRDS
Size	X15	The natural logarithm of total assets	CSMAR

Table 1. (*Continued*)

Group	Factor	Variable	Source
	X16	Liabilities/shareholders' equity	CSMAR
	X17	Liabilities/total assets	CSMAR
Liability	X18	Long-term liabilities/total assets	CSMAR
	X19	Current assets/current liabilities	CSMAR
	X20	(Current assets-inventory-prepaid expenses)/current liabilities	CSMAR
	X21	The natural logarithm of liabilities	CSMAR
	X22	Cash/total assets	CSMAR
Asset	X23	Inventory/total assets	CSMAR
	X24	Fixed assets/total assets	CSMAR
	X25	Operating capital/total assets	CSMAR
	X26	The growth rate of accounts receivables	CSMAR
Growth	X27	The growth rate of inventory	CSMAR
	X28	The growth rate of income from principal business operations	CSMAR
	X29	Cost of principal business operation/inventory	CSMAR
Efficiency	X30	Income from principal business operation/accounts receivable	CSMAR
	X31	The natural logarithm of cost of principal business operation	CSMAR
	X32	Net earnings/total assets	CSMAR
	X33	Net earnings/fixed assets	CSMAR
Profitability	X34	Net earnings/income from principal business operation	CSMAR
	X35	Income from principal business operation/total assets	CSMAR

Notes: [a]Loughran and McDonald (2011) developed a new dictionary list specialized in financial words and sentiment analysis in the annual report. We thus make use of the financial-specific list and abbreviate it as L&M dictionary. MD&A refers to the management discussion and analysis section of a firm's annual report.

The linguistic variables in this study are collected from the Chinese Research Data Services (CNRDS) database. These linguistic factors mainly come from the management discussion and analysis section (MD&A) of a firm's annual report. In addition, the words used are identified based on rules in the L&M dictionary and the National

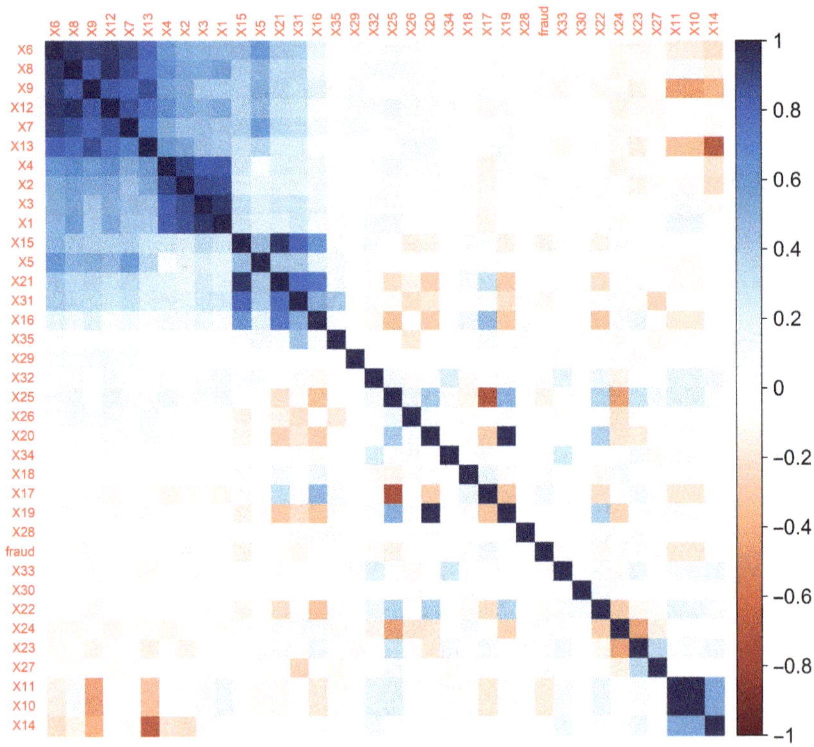

Figure 1. Correlation plot.

Note: This figure shows the correlation test between our predicted indicator, *Fraud*, and a pool of 35 linguistic and financial indicators.

Taiwan University Sentiment Dictionary (NTUSD). Our study incorporates a total of 14 linguistic variables to predict financial statement fraud.

In terms of financial performance variables, we try to incorporate exhaustive firm specifics and ratios. Following Song *et al.* (2014) and Dong *et al.* (2021), we add a pool of 20 financial variables and classify them into six sub-groups, including size, liability, asset structure, growth, efficiency, and profitability. All financial data is obtained from the China Stock Market & Accounting Research (CSMAR) Database.

Nevertheless, extant literature argues that the relation between forecasting performance and sample choice is ambiguous (McKee and Greenstein, 2000; Sun and Li, 2008; Sun *et al.*, 2014) so that many standard metrics for ML performance measurement cannot be applied in this setting. Our initial sample proportionally favors non-fraudulent firms. Subsequently, it leads to a biased ML estimator, as the non-balanced sample includes fewer fraudulent firms (Sensini, 2015). One common approach is to employ a balanced dataset by choosing the same sample size for both fraudulent and non-fraudulent firms. Therefore, following Kotsiantis *et al.* (2006) and Strobl *et al.* (2007), we randomly remove samples from the majority class (i.e., non-fraudulent firms) without replacement to alleviate this concern. After dropping missing values on all the variables, our final sample size is 812, including 406 fraudulent and 406 non-fraudulent firm-year observations. Table 2 summarizes the descriptive statistics of our financial statement fraud data and all the candidate factors based on the balanced sample.

4.2. *Main results*

We firstly present the main results in Table 3 and report the performance metrics in each model. Column (1) presents the coefficient estimates of the benchmark logistic model, and it is observed that the corresponding RMSE is 0.349. In Columns (2)–(4), we present the results of the selected variables using the LASSO method with λ selected by cross-validation based on full, in- and out-of-sample data, separately. We find that LASSO regression picks only eleven regressors and excludes the other irrelevant indicators, compared with traditional logistic regression. Interestingly, three of the eleven selected regressors are linguistic-related (X2, X4, and X10), while eight regressors are associated with financial performance (X15, X17, X23, X24, X25, X29, X30, and X33). As shown in Panel B of Table 3, the RMSE of LASSO regression is 0.2538, significantly lower relative to the logistic model. This finding suggests that linguistic factors could play an essential and non-negligible role in financial statement fraud detection. In addition, when we compare LASSO and random forest and bagging approach, we find that the RMSE value of LASSO regression is still the lowest. This suggests that the LASSO algorithm is consistently performing better as a predictor in our study. Overall, the LASSO algorithm is the best performer, amongst the methods considered, in predicting financial statement fraud with the lowest RMSE value.

Table 2. Descriptive statistics.

	Variable	Obs.	Mean	Std. dev.	Min	Max
Predicted indicator	**Fraud**	**812**	**0.5**	**0.5003**	**0**	**1**
Linguistic factors	X1	812	0.2461	0.1526	0.020	0.979
	X2	812	0.1062	0.0712	0.006	0.599
	X3	812	0.0794	0.0504	0.007	0.329
	X4	812	5.5679	4.7402	0.3905	36.5045
	X5	812	0.1437	0.0422	0.0701	0.519
	X6	812	42.9257	10.4272	18.586	90.687
	X7	812	0.0957	0.2571	0.345	2.615
	X8	812	2.9328	0.7483	1.127	6.185
	X9	812	2.9769	0.8551	1.239	8.177
	X10	812	−0.0006	0.0103	−0.0564	0.0424
	X11	812	−0.0038	0.0734	−0.3663	0.306
	X12	812	2946.671	748.1705	1028	6110
	X13	812	1143.567	399.7347	390	2826
	X14	812	0.4475	0.0860	0.1495	0.6567
Financial factors	X15	812	22.193	1.2797	18.2906	27.3178
	X16	812	0.3445	0.2018	0.0131	0.8974
	X17	812	0.5461	0.3083	0.0497	6.3477
	X18	812	0.2138	0.7932	−1.9398	21.8207
	X19	812	1.6383	1.8623	0.0834	28.0983
	X20	812	1.1815	1.7557	0.0272	27.7599
	X21	812	21.4823	1.4604	18.1684	27.0539
	X22	812	0.13526	0.10222	0.0018	0.6348
	X23	812	0.17589	0.1653	0	0.9284
	X24	812	0.2532	0.1869	0.0007	0.9363
	X25	812	0.1053	0.3053	−3.8297	0.8755
	X26	812	0.1920	0.2383	0	2.6984
	X27	812	0.7779	4.9071	0.0001	111.2262
	X28	812	4.6639	17.5847	−170.7553	306.0746
	X29	812	21.2420	236.1177	0.0025	5312.604
	X30	812	117.226	1600.391	0.3610	44258.03
	X31	812	21.2504	1.6541	14.6936	26.9197
	X32	812	0.0213	0.1262	−2.7463	0.8165
	X33	812	0.4021	6.6266	−97.3886	94.7085
	X34	812	0.0660	1.2799	−14.2198	30.9911
	X35	812	0.6944	0.7531	0.0007	10.5716

Notes: This table shows descriptive statistics of our financial statement fraud data and all the candidate factors based on the balanced sample size. Financial statement fraud data is manually collected from the official websites of the CSRC and their regional offices. The linguistic factors are mainly collected from management discussion and analysis section (MD&A) of a firm's annual report. They are identified based on two established word lists: (1) the L&M dictionary, and (2) the National Taiwan University Sentiment Dictionary. All financial data is obtained from the China Stock Market & Accounting Research (CSMAR) Database.

Table 3. Benchmark model and machine-learning approaches.

Panel A. LASSO variable selection

	Logistic		LASSO	
	Full sample	**Full sample**	**In-sample**	**Out-of-sample**
	(1)	**(2)**	**(3)**	**(4)**
X1	−0.0001			
	(0.002)			
X2	0.0132***	1.0078**	1.0053	1.0111***
	(0.003)	(0.003)	(0.004)	(0.004)
X3	0.0036			
	(0.005)			
X4	−0.0002***	1.0001	1.0001***	0.9999
	(0.001)	(0.001)	(0.001)	(0.001)
X5	−0.0001			
	(0.001)			
X6	0.0001*			
	(0.001)			
X7	−0.0008			
	(0.001)			
X8	−0.0025**			
	(0.001)			
X9	0.0018**			
	(0.001)			
X10	−52.9060	0.0256	−0.0663***	0.0236
	(140.539)	(0.025)	(0.009)	(0.033)
X11	16.4584			
	(18.187)			
X12	0.0019**			
	(0.001)			
X13	−0.0044***			
	(0.002)			
X14	−12.4470**			
	(5.207)			
X15	−1.1800**	0.7315***	0.7699***	0.7046***
	(0.548)	(0.056)	(0.075)	(0.082)
X16	−0.5252			
	(0.754)			
X17	−0.9165	2.5196	1.9483	3.6618
	(1.022)	(0.720)	(1.574)	(4.357)

(*Continued*)

Table 3. (*Continued*)

Panel A. LASSO variable selection

	Logistic		LASSO	
	Full sample	Full sample	In-sample	Out-of-sample
	(1)	(2)	(3)	(4)
X18	0.0193			
	(0.128)			
X19	−1.0279**			
	(0.435)			
X20	1.2769***			
	(0.456)			
X21	0.8819*			
	(0.535)			
X22	−0.1267			
	(1.032)			
X23	4.4953***	3.0456	0.9091	15.8573
	(1.249)	(2.079)	(0.852)	(18.938)
X24	1.0155*	1.7818	1.4015	3.0962
	(0.601)	(1.072)	(1.108)	(3.052)
X25	−1.0733	0.6672	0.8253	0.6889
	(0.782)	(0.422)	(0.699)	(0.719)
X26	0.1427			
	(0.397)			
X27	0.0181	1.0113	1.006	1.0655
	(0.023)	(0.017)	(0.017)	(0.105)
X28	0.0003			
	(0.004)			
X29	−0.0007	1.0001	1.0031	0.999*
	(0.001)	(0.001)	0.0034	(0.001)
X30	0.0001	1.0001	1.0002	0.998
	(0.001)	(0.001)	(0.001)	(0.002)
X31	−0.0349			
	(0.135)			
X32	0.4589			
	(0.671)			
X33	−0.0107	0.9797*	0.9568*	0.9774
	(0.016)	(0.011)	(0.024)	(0.017)
X34	−0.0090			
	(0.071)			
X35	0.0835			
	(0.168)			

Table 3. (*Continued*)

Panel B. Models evaluation

	Logistic	LASSO	Random forest	SVM
RMSE	0.3490	0.2538	0.4119	
AUC value$_{is}$	0.720			0.8702
AUC value$_{os}$	0.6354			0.8503
AUC value$_{full}$	0.713			0.8141

Notes: This table shows the main results and model performance using the benchmark and the machine-learning methods. In Panel A, Column (1) shows the baseline logistic results. Columns (2)–(4) indicate the results of the selected variables using LASSO method with λ selected by cross-validation based on full, in- and out-of-sample data, separately. *, **, and *** denote significance at the 10%, 5%, and 1% level, respectively. In Panel B, Columns (1)–(3) report the RMSE values using the specific methods. Columns (1) and (4) show the AUC values of both traditional logistic model and SVM algorithm based on the full, in- and out-of-sample data, respectively.

Lastly, we turn to the SVM approach and show the AUC values for both in-sample and out-of-sample tests in Columns (1) and (4) of Table 3. The results show that the AUC value of the full sample using the SVM algorithm outperforms that using the logistic regression by around 0.103. Compared with the out-of-sample test, the SVM algorithm also shows substantial predictive improvement in the logistic regression prediction value. The ROC plots are shown in Figure 2. The overall results indicate that the SVM algorithm can significantly boost predictive accuracy than the traditional logistic analysis.

4.3. *Variable importance*

We further explore the top 12 critical variables chosen by using the random forest method. Unlike the LASSO regression, the random forest method picks important regressors based on two measures: Mean Decrease Accuracy and Mean Decrease Gini. The outcomes of the two measures are shown in Figure 3. The Mean Decrease Accuracy plot indicates how much accuracy the model losses by omitting each variable. We can observe that three linguistic factors are included, and X10 is the most important among the top 12 indicators.

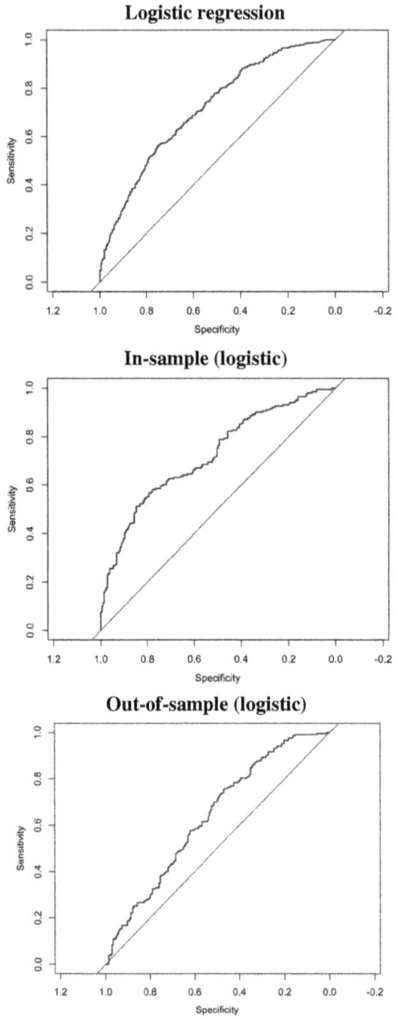

Figure 2. ROC graphs based on logistic and SVM models.
Notes: The figure compares the ROC curves of the logistic model and SVM model based on the full sample, in-, and out-of-sample analysis, respectively. The vertical axis is the true positive rate (TPR), and the horizontal axis corresponds to the false positive rate (FPR). All the 35 financial and textual factors are included to predict financial statement fraud of the Chinese listed firms.

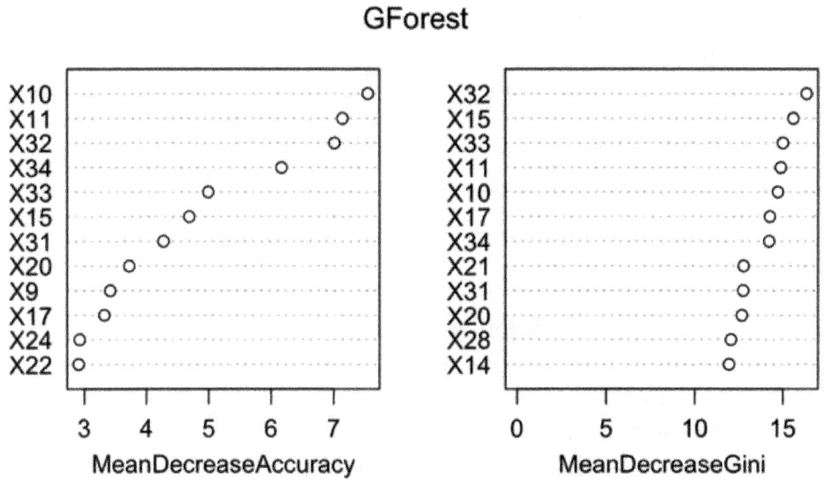

Figure 3. Variable importance using random forest method.
Notes: This figure shows the 12 most important variables using Random Forest method and the calculation is based on two selection criteria: (1) Mean Decrease Accuracy; (2) Mean Decrease Gini, respectively. The Mean Decrease Accuracy plot suggests how much accuracy the model losses by omitting each variable. The Mean Decrease in the Gini coefficient instead measures how much each variable contributes to the homogeneity of the nodes and leaves in the resulting random forest.

The Mean Decrease in the Gini coefficient measures how much each variable contributes to the homogeneity of the nodes and leaves in the resulting random forest. A higher value of Mean Decrease Gini score implies greater importance of the variable in the model. However, we find that linguistic factors (i.e., X10, X11) are relative critically scored by the Gini importance. This could be caused by the relative weakness of Gini importance index because it introduces more noise towards numeric variables and splits excessive nodes (Menze *et al.*, 2009).

5. Conclusions and Implications

This chapter investigates the application of various machine-learning approaches in financial statement fraud detection. We fit the models with the combination of 35 linguistic and financial factors of the Chinese listed companies. Moreover, we adopt three machine-learning methods and compare the differences between each model and the benchmark logistic regression. Our main results are threefold. First, we find that the LASSO model has the lowest RMSE value (0.2538) and outperforms relative to the Random Forest (bagging) approach and traditional logistic regression methods. Second, LASSO regression picks the eleven key influential factors which shrink to non-zero, and three of them are linguistic-related factors, including the pessimistic tone in MD&A, the total number of phrases in MD&A, and the net positive tone in the annual report. In addition, it is observed that the proportion of the differences between positive and negative terms in the annual report is consistently selected as one of the most important indicators when using the Random Forest and Bagging approach. Our results have important implications for regulators. Besides the traditional financial performance indicators, they should pay close attention to these linguistic indicators when developing intelligent systems to detect financial statement fraud. Third, the SVM algorithm generates a much higher AUC value than that of the logistic regression approach. Overall, our findings offer insights for regulatory agencies and independent auditors on what financial statement fraud detection and prevention methods work best. Future studies are expected to cover more high-frequency and high-dimensional datasets to identify fraudulent firms' various characteristics and improve the predictive ability of fraud.

References

Allen, F., Qian, J., & Qian, M. (2005). Law, finance, and economic growth in China. *Journal of Financial Economics, 77*(1), 57–116.

Arlot, S., & Celisse, A. (2010). A survey of cross-validation procedures for model selection. *Statistics Surveys, 4*, 40–79.

Beasley, M. S. (1996). An empirical analysis of the relation between the board of director composition and financial statement fraud. *The Accounting Review, 71*, 443–465.

Bell, T., & Carcello, J. (2000). A decision aid for assessing the likelihood of fraudulent financial reporting. *Auditing: A Journal of Practice & Theory, 19*(1), 169–184.

Bhattacharyya, S., Jha, S., Tharakunnel, K., & Westland, J. C. (2011). Data mining for credit card fraud: A comparative study. *Decision Support Systems, 50*(3), 602–613.

Bradley, A. P. (1997). The use of the area under the ROC curve in the evaluation of machine learning algorithms. *Pattern Recognition, 30*(7), 1145–1159.

Campbell, J., & Göritz, A. S. (2014). Culture corrupts! A qualitative study of organizational culture in corrupt organizations. *Journal of Business Ethics, 120*(3), 291–311.

China Securities Regulatory Commission (CSRC, 2019). CSRC 2018 annual report. Retrieved from http://www.csrc.gov.cn/csrc_en/c102063/common_list.shtml?channelid=e855fa5d4cab4ce7a9304769d9d1c4e9 [Accessed: 7th June 2022].

Chen, D., Jiang, D., Liang, S., & Wang, F. (2011). Selective enforcement of regulation. *China Journal of Accounting Research, 4*(1–2), 9–27.

Clarke, D. C. (2006). The independent director in Chinese corporate governance. *Delaware Journal of Corporate Law, 31*, 125–228.

Conyon, M. J., & He, L. (2016). Executive compensation and corporate fraud in China. *Journal of Business Ethics, 134*(4), 669–691.

Consonni, V., Ballabio, D., & Todeschini, R. (2010). Evaluation of model predictive ability by external validation techniques. *Journal of Chemometrics, 24*(3–4), 194–201.

Craja, P., Kim, A., & Lessmann, S. (2020). Deep learning for detecting financial statement fraud. *Decision Support Systems, 139*, 113421.

Dechow, P. M., Ge, W., Larson, C. R., & Sloan, R. G. (2011). Predicting material accounting misstatements. *Contemporary Accounting Research, 28*(1), 17–82.

Ding, Y. S., Song, X. P., & Zeng, Y. M. (2008). Forecasting financial condition of Chinese listed companies based on support vector machine. *Expert Systems with Applications, 34*, 3081–3089.

Dong, R., Fisman, R., Wang, Y., & Xu, N. (2021). Air pollution, affect, and forecasting bias: Evidence from Chinese financial analysts. *Journal of Financial Economics, 139*(3), 971–984.

Du, N., Ronen, J., & Ye, J. (2015). Auditors' role in China: The joint effects of Guanxi and regulatory sanctions on earnings management. *Journal of Accounting, Auditing & Finance, 30*(4), 461–483.

Du, X., Jian, W., & Lai, S. (2017). Do foreign directors mitigate earnings management? Evidence from China. *The International Journal of Accounting, 52*(2), 142–177.

Fama, E. F., & Jensen, M. C. (1983). Separation of ownership and control. *Journal of Law and Economics, 26*(2), 301–325.

Fawcett, T. (2006). An introduction to ROC analysis. *Pattern Recognition Letters, 27*(8), 861–874.

Fonti, V., & Belitser, E. (2017). Feature selection using LASSO. *VU Amsterdam Research Paper in Business Analytics, 30*, 1–25.

Graepel, T. (2002, August). Kernel matrix completion by semidefinite programming. In *International Conference on Artificial Neural Networks* (pp. 694–699). Springer, Berlin, Heidelberg.

Guan, Y., Su, L. N., Wu, D., & Yang, Z. (2016). Do school ties between auditors and client executives influence audit outcomes? *Journal of Accounting and Economics, 61*(2–3), 506–525.

Hajek, P., & Henriques, R. (2017). Mining corporate annual reports for intelligent detection of financial statement fraud — A comparative study of machine learning methods. *Knowledge-Based Systems*, *128*, 139–152.

Hanley, J. A., & McNeil, B. J. (1982). The meaning and use of the area under a receiver operating characteristic (ROC) curve. *Radiology, 143*(1), 29–36.

Humpherys, S. L., Moffitt, K. C., Burns, M. B., Burgoon, J. K., & Felix, W. F. (2011). Identification of fraudulent financial statements using linguistic credibility analysis. *Decision Support Systems*, *50*(3), 585–594.

International Monetary Fund (IMF, 2012). People's Republic of China: Detailed assessment report: Observations of IOSCO objectives and principles of securities regulation. *IMF Country Report, 12/80*, pp. 1–26.

Jiang, F., & Kim, K. A. (2015). Corporate governance in China: A modern perspective. *Journal of Corporate Finance, 32*, 190–216.

Katelouzou, D., & Siems, M. M. (2015). Disappearing paradigms in shareholder protection: Leximetric evidence for 30 countries, 1990–2013. *Journal of Corporate Law Studies, 15*(1), 127–160.

Kirkos, E., Spathis, C., & Manolopoulos, Y. (2007). Data mining techniques for the detection of fraudulent financial statements. *Expert Systems with Applications*, *32*(4), 995–1003.

Kotsiantis, S., Kanellopoulos, D., & Pintelas, P. (2006). Handling imbalanced datasets: A review. *GESTS International Transactions on Computer Science and Engineering*, *30*(1), 25–36.

Li, C., Lou, C., Luo, D., & Xing, K. (2021). Chinese corporate distress prediction using LASSO: The role of earnings management. *International Review of Financial Analysis*, *76*, 101776.

Liaw, A., & Wiener, M. (2002). Classification and regression by randomForest. *R News*, *2*(3), 18–22.

Lima, C., Coelho, A., & Zuben, F. (2007). Hybridizing mixtures of experts with support vector machines: Investigation into nonlinear dynamic systems identification. *Information Sciences, 177*, 2049–2074.

Lin, C. C., Chiu, A. A., Huang, S. Y., & Yen, D. C. (2015). Detecting the financial statement fraud: The analysis of the differences between data mining techniques and experts' judgments. *Knowledge-Based Systems*, *89*, 459–470.

Loughran, T., & McDonald, B. (2011). When is a liability not a liability? Textual analysis, dictionaries, and 10-Ks. *The Journal of Finance*, *66*(1), 35–65.

McKee, T. E., & Greenstein, M. (2000). Predicting bankruptcy using recursive partitioning and a realistically proportioned data set. *Journal of Forecasting*, *19*(3), 219–230.

Menze, B. H., Kelm, B. M., Masuch, R., Himmelreich, U., Bachert, P., Petrich, W., & Hamprecht, F. A. (2009). A comparison of random forest and its Gini importance with standard chemometric methods for the feature selection and classification of spectral data. *BMC Bioinformatics*, *10*(1), 1–16.

Mercer, J. (1909). Xvi. functions of positive and negative type, and their connection the theory of integral equations. *Philosophical Transactions of the Royal Society of London. Series A, Containing Papers of a Mathematical or Physical Character*, *209*(441–458), 415–446.

Moore, D. A., Tetlock, P. E., Tanlu, L., & Bazerman, M. H. (2006). Conflicts of interest and the case of auditor independence: Moral seduction and strategic issue cycling. *Academy of Management Review*, *31*(1), 10–29.

Mullah, M. A. S., Hanley, J. A., & Benedetti, A. (2021). LASSO type penalized spline regression for binary data. *BMC Medical Research Methodology*, *21*(1), 1–14.

Pai, P. F., Hsu, M. F., & Wang, M. C. (2011). A support vector machine-based model for detecting top management fraud. *Knowledge-Based Systems*, *24*(2), 314–321.

Perols, J. (2011). Financial statement fraud detection: An analysis of statistical and machine learning algorithms. *Auditing: A Journal of Practice & Theory*, *30*(2), 19–50.

Perols, J. L., & Lougee, B. A. (2011). The relation between earnings management and financial statement fraud. *Advances in Accounting*, *27*(1), 39–53.

Prasad, A. M., Iverson, L. R., & Liaw, A. (2006). Newer classification and regression tree techniques: Bagging and random forests for ecological prediction. *Ecosystems*, *9*(2), 181–199.

Provost, F., & Fawcett, T. (1997). Analysis and visualization of classifier performance: Comparison under imprecise class and cost distributions. In *Proceedings of the 3rd International Conference on Knowledge Discovery and Data Mining.*

Ravisankar, P., Ravi, V., Rao, G. R., & Bose, I. (2011). Detection of financial statement fraud and feature selection using data mining techniques. *Decision Support Systems, 50*(2), 491–500.

Rezaee, Z. (2005). Causes, consequences, and deterrence of financial statement fraud. *Critical Perspectives on Accounting, 16*(3), 277–298.

Sensini, L. (2015). Selection of determinants in corporate financial distress. *European Journal of Business and Management, 7*(2), 73–82.

Singh, G., Gupta, R., Rastogi, A., Chandel, M. D., & Riyaz, A. (2012). A machine learning approach for detection of fraud based on SVM. *International Journal of Scientific Engineering and Technology, 1*(3), 194–198.

Song, X. P., Hu, Z. H., Du, J. G., & Sheng, Z. H. (2014). Application of machine learning methods to risk assessment of financial statement fraud: Evidence from China. *Journal of Forecasting, 33*(8), 611–626.

Strobl, C., Boulesteix, A. L., Zeileis, A., & Hothorn, T. (2007). Bias in random forest variable importance measures: Illustrations, sources and a solution. *BMC Bioinformatics, 8*(1), 1–21.

Sun, J., & Li, H. (2008). Listed companies' financial distress prediction based on weighted majority voting combination of multiple classifiers. *Expert Systems with Applications, 35*(3), 818–827.

Sun, J., Li, H., Huang, Q. H., & He, K. Y. (2014). Predicting financial distress and corporate failure: A review from the state-of-the-art definitions, modeling, sampling, and featuring approaches. *Knowledge-Based Systems, 57*, 41–56.

Throckmorton, C. S., Mayew, W. J., Venkatachalam, M., & Collins, L. M. (2015). Financial fraud detection using vocal, linguistic and financial cues. *Decision Support Systems, 74*, 78–87.

Wang, Y., Ashton, J. K., & Jaafar, A. (2019). Money shouts! How effective are punishments for accounting fraud? *The British Accounting Review, 51*(5), 100824.

West, J., & Bhattacharya, M. (2016). Intelligent financial fraud detection: A comprehensive review. *Computers & Security, 57*, 47–66.

Whiting, D. G., Hansen, J. V., McDonald, J. B., Albrecht, C., & Albrecht, W. S. (2012). Machine learning methods for detecting patterns of management fraud. *Computational Intelligence, 28*(4), 505–527.

Xinhua (2014). China's chief justice warns of weakness in court system. Retrieved from http://www.chinadaily.com.cn/china/2014npcandcppcc/2014-03/10/content_17336392.htm [Accessed: 28 August 2021].

Xu, W., & Xu, G. (2020). Understanding public enforcement of securities law in China: An empirical analysis of the enforcement actions of the CSRC and its regional offices against informational misconduct. *International Review of Law and Economics, 61*, 105877.

Yang, D., Jiao, H., & Buckland, R. (2017). The determinants of financial fraud in Chinese firms: Does corporate governance as an institutional innovation matter? *Technological Forecasting and Social Change, 125*, 309–320.

Yang, J., Chi, J., & Young, M. (2012). A review of earnings management in China and its implications. *Asian-Pacific Economic Literature, 26*(1), 84–92.

Yu, M., & Ashton, J. K. (2015). Board leadership structure for Chinese public listed companies. *China Economic Review, 34*, 236–248.

Zhang, Y., & Yang, Y. (2015). Cross-validation for selecting a model selection procedure. *Journal of Econometrics, 187*(1), 95–112.

https://doi.org/10.1142/9781800612723_0007

Chapter 7

Artificial Intelligence and Machine Learning in Fund Performance Evaluation — A Review

Xize Guo*, Xiaolu Hu† and On Kit Tam‡

School of Economics, Finance and Marketing, College of Business and Law, RMIT University, Melbourne, Australia

**xize.guo@student.rmit.edu.au*

†xiaolu.hu@rmit.edu.au

‡onkit.tam@rmit.edu.au

Abstract

Financial technology (Fintech) has become an emerging and powerful tool that contributes to the advancement of finance research. With the recent development of Fintech, machine-learning (ML) techniques have been continuously deployed for developing more effective models in financial research. This chapter aims to provide in-depth details of ML implementation in fund performance evaluation and prediction. Building on the theoretical basics of ML, we first introduce several widely applied ML algorithms, including linear regression, least absolute shrinkage and selection operator (LASSO), ridge, K nearest neighbors (KNN), decision trees (DT), random forest (RF), support vector machine (SVM), deep learning (DL), and artificial neural networks (ANN). We then focus on each method's applicable conditions and how it contributes to forecasting and evaluating fund performance. The advantages of using ML methods over traditional methods in evaluating fund performance are also discussed.

Keywords: Mutual fund, fund performance, performance predictability, machine-learning.

1. Introduction

Since 2013, Fintech has played a vital role in financial markets and has reshaped the financial industry. The 2017 Global Findex Database shows that digital technology helps drive the development of financial services such as bank accounts and digital payments in most of the world. Fintech allows banks and firms to reach an unprecedented number of users (Demirguc-Kunt *et al.*, 2018). Apart from this, He *et al.* (2017) point out that improving profitability and fulfilling users' needs drive technological change in financial markets. The consensus of these articles is that Fintech innovations have been a vital force and have grown into a significant attraction.

ML is an important subfield of artificial intelligence (AI) and its use in the financial industry and finance research is growing enormously. ML refers to a class of methods that autonomously 'recognize and learn' general patterns from a huge set of observations and use these patterns to perform various recognition tasks or make predictions about unknown or future data. Of the four ML categories, supervised ML models are the most popular in the field of finance. By taking advantage of these ML models, finance research has experienced remarkable development.

Mutual funds have become a favored choice of wealth management for investors, especially individual investors, due to the advantages of the economics of fund scale, liquidity, professional asset management, risk diversification, and strict regulation by authorities (Bertin and Prather, 2009; King, 2002). Based on different financial investment strategies, mutual funds can be divided (roughly) into passively managed funds and actively managed funds. Since the emergence of passive funds in the US over four decades ago, there have been considerable debates over which factors may drive the performance of various funds. Further, how to assess the performance of a fund is a long-standing and inescapable topic that continues to be explored. Prior studies have developed different evaluation measurements. The most commonly used single-factor models include the Treynor ratio, Sharpe ratio, and Jensen alpha, which make it easy to access data and perform calculations (Jensen, 1968; Sharpe, 1966; Treynor and Black, 1973). As the core idea of the positive relationship between risk and return can be easily accepted and understood for individual investors with basic financial knowledge, these indicators are still widely used in the industry. However, in financial research, they have been gradually replaced by multi-factor models due to limitations such as lack of accuracy, harsh assumptions, and potentially misleading rankings (Kaur, 2013; Krimm *et al.*, 2012; Ledoit and Wolf, 2008; Scholz, 2007). Multi-factor models are constructed by identifying the essential factors that affect portfolio returns; the best known of which are the Fama and French three-factor model, the Carhart four-factor model, and the Fama and French five-factor model (Carhart, 1997; Fama and French, 1992, 1993, 2017). For nearly three decades since the Fama and French three-factor model was developed in 1992, scholars have explored other potentially important factors to improve the evaluation result and investigated whether models that contain more factors may perform better. However, testing the validity of factors by traditional methods increases exponentially in complexity with each additional artificially specified factor, not to mention larger sample sizes.

To break through the limitations of small data samples and the limited number of self-assigned factors, ML and big data techniques have been introduced, allowing the study of models evaluating fund performance to take on a new dimension in recent years. This review introduces emerging ML models used in fund performance evaluation and weighs the pros and cons of traditional and ML models. Section 2 provides an overview of the background of ML, highlighting some important concepts. We then present some ML models that are useful and worth exploring in fund performance evaluation, such as linear regression, LASSO, Ridge Regression, KNN, DT, RF, SVM, DL and ANN. We present the mechanisms and algorithmic features of these ML methods to provide technical support for the application. Section 3 begins with a comprehensive discussion of the latest research on each ML approach to fund performance assessment and prediction enhancement. It analyzes their usefulness for various types of funds and their contribution to portfolio construction and fund performance prediction in the fund market. We then provide an in-depth analysis of the advantages and disadvantages of ML measurements compared with the traditional evaluation measurements from the following four aspects: the precision and accuracy, the scale of data, the variable selection, and relationship recognition.

2. ML Models

2.1. *ML theories*

2.1.1. *Probably approximately correct learning*

In tackling problems using ML algorithms, researchers sometimes rely on multiple trials to figure out the appropriate model that fits the data, which might be costly and inefficient, not to mention the speed of computing and the errors introduced by noisy data that must be considered. Hence, computational learning theory (CLT) was invented to provide theoretical support for ML models and learning algorithms. The most fundamental of which is probably approximately correct learning (PAC-Learning) theory.

Absolute correctness does not exist since we will never know the true function of data. It is unrealistic to learn a function with an expected zero error from a limited number of training samples. Therefore, the goal of a learning algorithm is to learn an approximately correct hypothesis with a certain probability. The higher the degree of approximation, the greater the probability, the more approximately correct. The core idea of PAC-Learning is that the selected algorithm can narrow the error of the hypothesis with a high probability until it is sufficiently probably approximately correct. PAC-Learning theory can be expressed as follows:

$$P\left(\left(f(x) - h_s(x)\right) \leq \varepsilon\right) \geq 1 - \delta, \tag{1}$$

where $f(x)$ denotes the true function, $h_s(x)$ is the algorithm (or hypothesis) applied to sample data, ε is the error, and $1 - \delta$ refers to the probability that the algorithm learns an approximately correct hypothesis. Both ε and δ are relevant to the sample size. When *the* sample data size tends to infinity, the error tends to zero. That is:

$$\lim_{S \to \infty} f(x) - h_s(x) = 0. \tag{2}$$

To better understand PAC-Learning theory, we can simply divide it into two parts: 'Probably' and 'Approximately Correct'. First: 'Probably'. We expect a learning algorithm to learn an approximately correct hypothesis with a certain probability of $1-\delta$ (normally $0 < \delta < \frac{1}{2}$). That is, it is unlikely that the sample data is unrepresentative and unable to learn inner patterns (e.g., population distribution characteristics, interactions between covariates).

Next, 'Approximately Correct'. Approximately Correct is presented by error, ε (normally $0 < \varepsilon < \frac{1}{2}$). We are looking for a small error with the selected algorithm, which we hope will be smaller and smaller through multiple operations and learning rounds.

2.1.2. *Occam's Razor*

Occam's Razor is a rule of problem-solving proposed by William of Occam, a famous logician in the 14th century. It is also a general principle quoted in the field of CLT. When two models produce very similar results, the simpler one is better. The rationale for this is that, on the one hand, if a simple explanation happens to fit sample data, it is much less likely to have happened just by chance; conversely, a simple explanation may require fewer assumptions and prerequisites and less computation time (Blum, 2007). Occam's Razor is very similar to the idea of regularization in ML: simpler models may generalize better. Therefore, in the learning criterion for ML, we often introduce parameter regularization to limit the model's level of complexity and avoid overfitting.

2.2. *Overview of ML basics*

Recall that ML applies a set of techniques to autonomously 'recognize and learn' general patterns from an existing set of observations and use these patterns to make predictions about unknown/future data. The potential predictors set as inputs are considered features, and the outputs (if any) are generally considered labels or targets (Tian, 2020). Depending on the features provided by the training data and the purpose of tasks, ML algorithms generally fall into four broad categories: supervised learning, unsupervised learning, semi-supervised learning, and reinforcement learning (see Figure 1).

2.2.1. *ML categories*

2.2.1.1. Supervised learning

Supervised learning is the dominant category of ML. Typical supervised learning consists of classification and regression, where the outputs of classification are categorical, and those of regression are continuous. For example, when applied to finance, classification

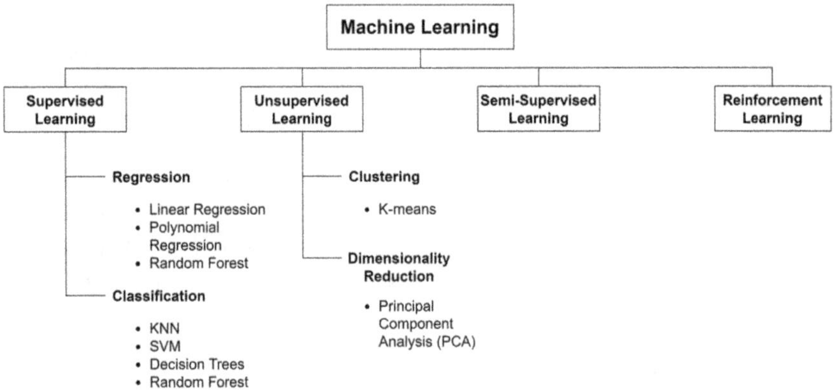

Figure 1. ML categories.
Note: Figure 1 shows the four broad categories of the ML techniques.

models such as DT can be used to forecast stock price trends (i.e., up or down) based on the stock return history and relevant financial factors (Yuan *et al.*, 2020). Regression models such as neural networks are widely used when trying to predict an output with continuous values. Again, take stocks as an example. Given historical data on market returns, market capitalization, book-to-market ratios, and other relevant stock parameters, it is possible to regress historical stock prices and predicted future stock prices based on the regression results.

2.2.1.2. Unsupervised learning

For unsupervised learning, a significant difference from supervised learning is that the inputs are investigated without the help of any labels. In some cases, unsupervised learning works as a first glimpse at the raw data set to gain a rough understanding before applying supervised learning methods to solve the problem (Chollet, 2018). Clustering and dimensionality reduction are the most representative instances of unsupervised learning. The goal of clustering is to discover inner patterns of unlabeled inputs and organize them into clusters in some way that inputs within a cluster are similar and those that belong to different clusters are dissimilar. The idea of dimensionality reduction is in line with the PCA-Learning theory, which avoids overly redundant models and eliminates unnecessary features.

2.2.1.3. Semi-supervised learning

As the name implies, semi-supervised learning is the category that falls somewhere in between the two categories mentioned above. No human-annotated labels are involved, and there are only a few desired outputs.

2.2.1.4. Reinforcement learning

Reinforcement learning is still a rapidly developing branch with great potential for development. In reinforcement learning, the machine receives information about its environment and determines a sequence of actions to maximize rewards or performance (Chollet, 2018).

2.2.2. *ML framework*

Scholars usually take the following steps when applying ML algorithms to tackle their research questions (Chollet, 2018). Regarding studies where the data is numeric rather than sounds, images, or text, we remap the following framework to ML suitable for studying financial problems (see Figure 2).

2.2.2.1. Assembling the initial dataset (data acquisition)

Identifying the type of the defined research question and decided corresponding ML algorithms. According to the hypothesis, carefully choose the output and potential inputs, and collect available data to form an initial dataset.

2.2.2.2. Data preprocessing

This stage may include feature extraction, data cleansing, and other steps to ensure that the wrangled dataset can be fed into an ML model. For example, feature extraction may be essential when the data needs to be structured to reduce its dimensionality if it is too verbose. Data cleaning includes filling missing values, removing duplicating values, data standardization, data randomization, etc.

Another important step before starting to train the model is to split data. Generally, data will be divided into three groups: training data is set to fit the model, validation data is used to tune the hyper-parameters and regularize the initial model, and test data presents the model's performance. There are some advanced ways of segmenting data when data condition is not satisfactory, such as K-fold validation.

2.2.2.3. Model training

Model training is when the algorithm, the mathematical logic, and the training data set are connected. The criteria of success should be adequately defined before applying the initial ML model (e.g., the prediction accuracy and the loss function), which is also important to further hyper-parameter tuning and model optimization. The model training process usually takes multiple rounds to achieve desirable results. The initial set of hyper-parameters will be updated for each round based on the previous round's results until the model is sharp enough to perceive and learn the patterns within the training data. However, even if the model we receive at the end of this phase fits the training data well, problems may still exist. This flaw is why model evaluation and model optimization are conducted afterward.

2.2.2.4. Model evaluation

The main task of this step is to validate the trained model by validation data obtained in data preprocessing. Since the model from the training stage performs well to the training data, validation data could evaluate whether the model has overlearned some unique patterns within the training data but not in the whole dataset, which is the overfitting issue. If the results are unsatisfactory, the ML model needs to be optimized and retrained, and this process will be repeated several times until satisfactory results are achieved. Finally, the model is expected to fit both training data and validation data. Recall that the goal of ML is to use the learned patterns to make predictions about unknown or future data. Therefore, the ML model needs a final test — the performance on the test data set that has never been recognized by the model before — and the test results will present how good the final model is.

2.2.2.5. Model optimization

The methods to improve models differ significantly from case to case. For financial research, we summarize a general process of measures to refine the model and improve accuracy. First, re-examine whether other features could be involved as inputs to the algorithm. Add these features if the accuracy increases, even if the model turns to overfit. Second, tune the hyper-parameters of the chosen algorithm to improve the model performance and tackle fitting problems. There are also particular steps for specific ML methods that can refine the model, such as dropouts in neuron networks. Last, if the model still could not meet expectations, the choice of algorithm may be reconsidered.

The framework of ML is summarized in Figure 2.

2.2.3. *Other important concepts*

2.2.3.1. Overfitting

The algorithm usually works well on the in-sample data set with model training and optimization, but this can lead to overfitting problems. The model 'over-explains' features in the training data, causing the model to incorporate unique features that belong only to the in-sample data set and not to the out-of-sample data set. Therefore, there is a trade-off between prediction accuracy on unknown data and model complexity (see Figure 3; Choi and Huang, 2021). The more particular patterns the model learns from in-sample data, the lower the prediction accuracy for out-of-sample data.

Overfitting occurs with most ML techniques. To solve this issue, a prominent and straightforward approach is to expand the sample data size so that misleading patterns can be diluted. Dividing the data into three parts (i.e., training, validation, and test data) during data preprocessing and reducing the number of features both counteract overfitting. Further, regularization plays an important role in addressing this issue.

2.2.3.2. Regularization

If all the features are useful in the algorithm, regularization, also known as the shrinkage method, should be applied to resolve the overfitting problem. The core idea of regularization is to introduce a penalty term to the loss function and shrink the size of coefficients so that the complexity of the model is discouraged (Choi and Huang, 2021; Chollet, 2018). The aim of regularization reflects

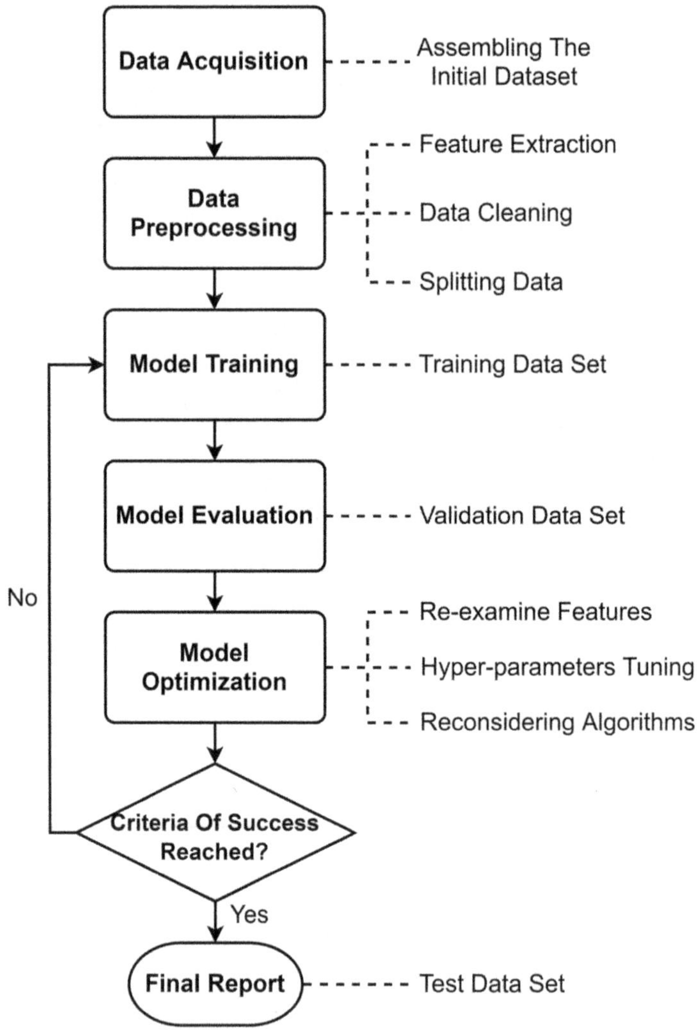

Figure 2. ML framework.
Note: Figure 2 describes the roadmap of ML framework.

Occam's Razor in ML theories; the simplest of all possible correct explanations is probably the best. The LASSO and Ridge Regression are the two most commonly used penalty functions for implementing regularization. They will be introduced in Section 2.3.2.

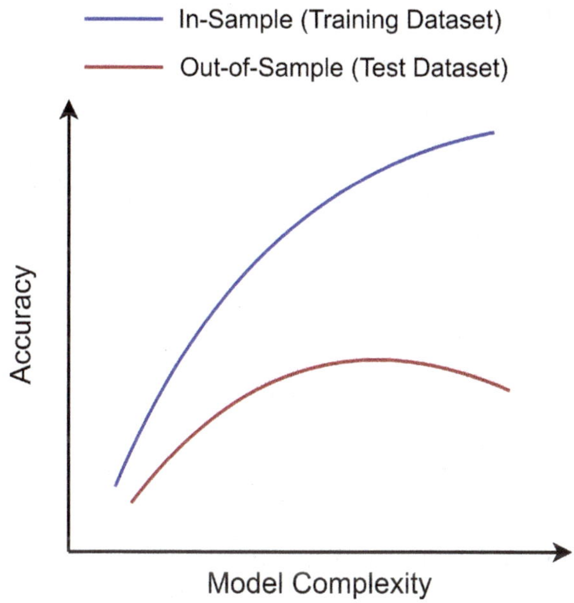

Figure 3. The trade-off between prediction accuracy and model complexity.

Note: Figure 3 describes the trade-off between prediction accuracy and model complexity, for training dataset and test dataset, respectively.

2.3. *ML techniques and models*

As discussed in Section 2.2.1, supervised learning is the dominant category of ML methods. This is also true in financial research — particularly fund performance evaluation. Next, we will introduce several ML techniques and models that have been widely used and rapidly developed in fund performance evaluation in recent years.

2.3.1. *Linear regression*

As a classical and perhaps the most familiar algorithm in statistics, linear regression is widely accepted and used in ML. In ML, a linear model is used to predict the target value (y) in the dataset or a set of features ($x_0, x_1, \ldots, x_n$). A linear model aims to find a line that can capture the general properties of the in-sample data and perform well to the out-of-sample data.

$$y = w_0x_0 + w_1x_1 + \cdots + w_nx_n + b. \tag{3}$$

To find the model that best fits the dataset, we need to minimize the error between the predicted target value $pred_i$ and the true target value y_i. This is known as the cost function J. The Mean Absolute Error (MAE) function and the Mean Squared Error (MSE) function are commonly chosen measurements.

$$MAE : J = \frac{1}{n}\sum_{i=1}^{n} |pred_i - y_i|, \tag{4}$$

$$MSE : J = \frac{1}{n}\sum_{i=1}^{n} (pred_i - y_i)^2. \tag{5}$$

To minimize cost, the gradient descent algorithm is an effective choice and is widely used in ML. Here MSE is often halved for computation convenience, as the derivative of the square function contains a two-term, and it will cancel out the $\frac{1}{2}$ term.

$$MSE : J = \frac{1}{2n}\sum_{i=1}^{n} (pred_i - y_i)^2. \tag{6}$$

Gradient descent iteratively reduces the cost by changing the weights using the derivative of the cost function until local minima are reached (see Figure 4).

Further, we can multiply the derivative with a constant called the learning rate α, to change the steps when reaching the local minima. A small learning rate can reach the minima more precisely but takes more time, while a large learning rate can be fast but may miss the local minima or even never converge.

$$w_i = w_i - \alpha\frac{\partial}{\partial w_i}J(w). \tag{7}$$

2.3.2. *LASSO and ridge regression*

As discussed in Section 2.2.3, LASSO and Ridge Regression are shrinkage methods that act as penalty functions to solve the overfitting problem.

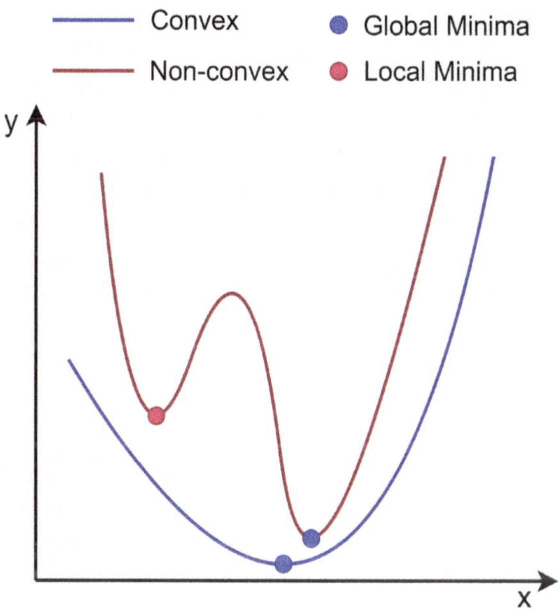

Figure 4. Gradient descent (global minima versus local minima).
Note: Figure 4 shows the difference between a convex model (blue line) and a non-convex model (red line). In a convex model (blue line), there is only one minima (a global minima, shown as blue point) that can be reached. However, in a non-convex model (red line), a local minima (red point) might be reached before reaching a global minima (blue point).

2.3.2.1. LASSO

LASSO was proposed by Tibshirani (1996) and further refined by Efron *et al.* (2004). It adds a penalty term to the original cost function, forming a new optimization algorithm. In addition to MAE and MSE, the Residual Sum of Squares is also used as a cost function when conducting LASSO.

$$RSS : J = \sum_{i=1}^{n} \left(y_i - \beta_0 - \sum_{j=1}^{p} \beta_j x_{ij} \right)^2, \tag{8}$$

$$\hat{\beta}^L = J + \lambda \sum_{j=1}^{p} |\beta_j|. \tag{9}$$

Equation 9 presents how the coefficients are calculated, where the second term on the right-hand side is the LASSO penalty, the sum of the absolute value of coefficients. Similar to the learning rate α in gradient descent, λ is a tuning parameter that reflects how much the model is penalized in LASSO. When $\lambda = 0$, there is no penalty, and the coefficients will be the same as those calculated by the cost function. However, when λ increases, the proportion of penalty term grows, and the regression coefficients shrink. It can be expected that some of the coefficients may shrink to zero when λ is large enough, and by this way, feature selection can be achieved precisely.

2.3.2.2. Ridge regression

Ridge Regression uses the sum of the square of coefficients as the Ridge penalty and adds to the cost function to form the regression (Tikhonov, 1963). Since the penalty term is a squared term, the coefficients shrink more toward zero as λ increases compared to those in LASSO. However, the coefficients obtained by Ridge could never be zero, whereas the coefficients obtained by LASSO could (Choi and Huang, 2021).

$$\hat{\beta}^R = J + \lambda \sum_{j=1}^{p} \beta_j^2. \tag{10}$$

Another point worth noting is that in using LASSO and Ridge, standardization is a must-have step. The features should be standardized to have zero means and unit variances before conducting any estimation calculation to ensure that the coefficients are penalized fairly on the same scale (Tian, 2020).

2.3.3. *K nearest neighbors (KNN)*

The KNN method is one of the most classical and mature methods in ML. Unlike other methods, KNN is also simple to understand and deploy, as it does not have a model built from the data, or we can say that the model is the data itself. The core idea of KNN is always to predict the unknown data with the majority class of KNN. Therefore, the critical point of this method is to define a distance metric to identify the KNN.

Speaking of distance metrics in a vector space, the most famous ones are the Euclidean distance and the Manhattan distance. The Minkowski distance can be considered a generalized version of these

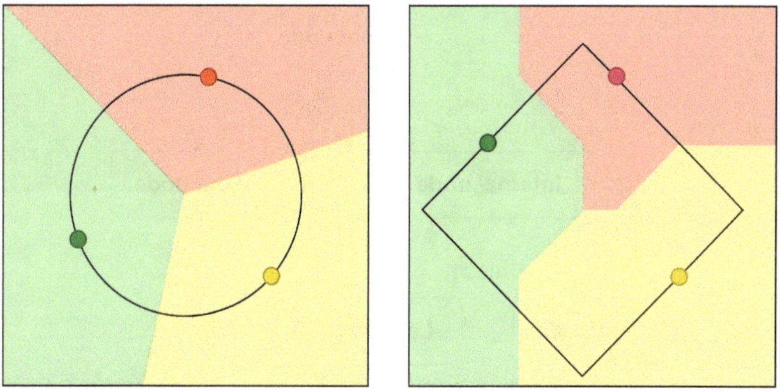

Figure 5. Different decision boundaries based on different distance metrics.
Note: Figure 5 provides an example of how different distance metrics determine the shape of decision boundaries. The left graph demonstrates the Euclidean distance and the right graph shows the Manhattan distance.

two distance metrics in a normed vector space. The Minkowski distance is based on an order p and has a form as:

$$Dis_p(x, y) = \left(\sum_{j=1}^{d} |x_j - y_j|^p \right)^{\frac{1}{p}} = ||x - y||_p, \qquad (11)$$

where $||z||_p = \left(\sum_{j=1}^{d} |z|^p \right)^{\frac{1}{p}}$ is the $p - norm$ (sometimes denoted L_p norm) of the vector z. So, we can see that the $1 - norm$ is the Manhattan distance, and the $2 - norm$ is the Euclidean distance. When order p gets larger, the distance will be increasingly dominated by the largest distance, coordinate-wise, which means $Dis_{\infty}(x, y) = \max_j(|x_j - y_j|)$, this $\infty - norm$ is also called the Chebyshev distance.

Identifying the class of unknown data is equivalent to defining the raw data's decision boundaries. Therefore, predicting the unknown data is the same as finding where the data points are. We can have different decision boundaries that lead to various prediction results based on distance metrics, so the distance metric must be carefully defined according to the data type and research objectives (see Figure 5).

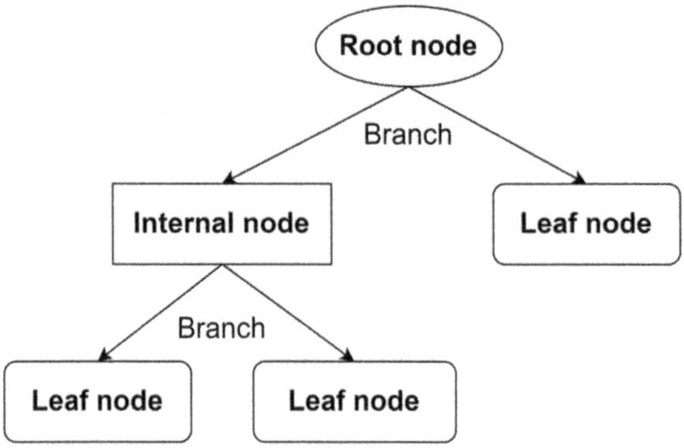

Figure 6. Decision tree framework.
Note: Figure 6 provides an example of a decision tree with two branches. There is always a root node. Each branch corresponds to an attribute value. Each internal node tests an attribute. Each leaf node assigns a classification.

2.3.4. *Decision trees (DT) and random forest (RF)*

2.3.4.1. Decision trees (DT)

DTs are popular in solving ML problems, as it is easily understandable and computationally efficient (even with large data). Despite its relatively weak predictive power compared to other complex models, it is superior in tackling both classification and regression tasks. The main logic behind DTs is divide and conquer, which means always using the most classifiable attribute (or feature) to split the data. As the name implies, the learning result of a decision tree is a tree structure, where each internal node tests an attribute, each branch corresponds to an attribute value, and each leaf node assigns a classification (see Figure 6). Hence, the question of how to find the most classifiable attribute is of great importance.

A simple way to tell if an attribute splits the data well is to measure the purity of two subsets, a measurement known as entropy. Entropy is a concept from information theory: the amount of information (in the Shannon sense) required to specify the full state of a system. It is calculated as follows:

$$Entropy(\mathrm{S}) = H(\mathrm{S}) = -\mathrm{p}_{\oplus} \log_2 \mathrm{p}_{\oplus} - \mathrm{p}_{\ominus} \log_2 \mathrm{p}_{\ominus}, \tag{12}$$

where S is a subset of training examples, $\mathrm{p}_{\oplus}$ and $\mathrm{p}_{\ominus}$ are the portion (%) of positive and negative examples in S.

In information theory, the result of Eq. 12 represents the number of bits needed to encode the system. In data science, it represents the number of bits that distinguish into which class a datum falls. So, the higher the entropy, the lower the purity of the subset. To decide which attribute has the best effect on splitting data, we need to compare the entropy drop after splitting. The concept of information gain represents the expected reduction in entropy due to sorting on some attributes:

$$Gain(S, A) = Entropy(S) - \sum_{v \in Values(A)} \frac{|S_v|}{|S|} Entropy(S_v), \quad (13)$$

where A is the tested target attribute, ν is the possible values of attribute A, S is the set of examples to split, and S is the subset of examples where $X_A = v$. As a result, the attribute with the maximum information gain is the optimal attribute to split the data.

The time for a stop is another thing to mention. Stopping too early means that the model has not fit the data well enough, leading to underfitting. Conversely, stopping too late means that the data has been split too thoroughly, resulting in overfitting. A technique called pruning is used to solve this issue, which has two different methods: pre-pruning and post-pruning. Pre-pruning stops the tree from growing when the data split is not statistically significant. For example, we can set a threshold before training for some features such as the number of leaves or the depth of the tree, then stop the training process when the threshold is met. This approach cannot avoid the underfitting problem, but it is computationally efficient (faster than post-pruning). The post-pruning process means that the complete tree is built first and pruned afterward. The reduced-error pruning is one way of post-pruning. Before the training step, we split the data into a training set and a validation set, then test the performance on the validation set after each pruning step and stop when further pruning is harmful.

2.3.4.2. Random forest (RF)

RF is a well-known technique that originated from the decision tree method, which introduces randomness into a dataset and may have better performance due to local and global minima. A decision tree is a single model built on the entire dataset, while a RF is a set of models built on a randomly selected subset of data and a randomly picked subspace of features, with prediction results based on the average or majority result of all of the tree models.

2.3.5. *Support vector machine (SVM)*

Recall that the gradient descent algorithm is applied to identify the linear decision boundaries in the linear regression model. The learning outcome may differ due to different preset parameters, such as learning rate or initial weights. In contrast, the SVM is always an optimal linear regression learning method, as it can find the maximum margin separating hyperplane (see Figure 7).

2.3.5.1. Linear SVM

The linear SVM learns a linear decision boundary by maximizing the margin. Only a few data points closest to the separation hyperplane define the margins, and these data points are called support vectors (see Figure 8).

Since the algorithm always finds the separating hyperplane with the maximum margin, it avoids overfitting. Nevertheless, it has the same limitations as the linear regression model; it can only be used

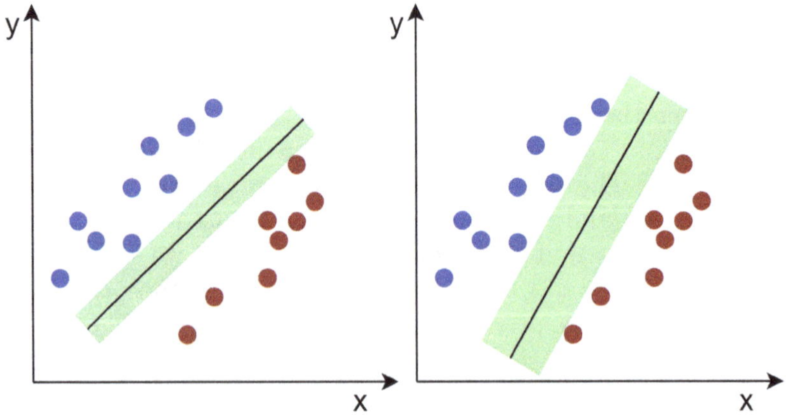

Figure 7. Different regression results for the same data set.
Note: In Figure 7, the green area indicates the different margins of different linear models. Using the same dataset, there could be different linear models that fit the data (left graph and right graph). SVM can always find the maximum margin separating hyperplane (right graph).

for linearly separable datasets. Fortunately, the linear SVM can be easily mapped into nonlinear spaces using a mathematical technique called the kernel method.

2.3.5.2. Nonlinear SVMs

As the data are represented as feature vectors, we have an original feature space Z, and the kernel method is a mapping from the original feature space Z to a new space Z' (with higher dimensions) while using computations with limited cost. This can be achieved by applying a kernel trick, using the dot production to create a new feature space. For example, a kernel trick $K(x_1, x_2) = (x_1 \cdot x_2)^2 = (x_1^2, x_2^2, \sqrt{2}x_1x_2)$ can map the original two-dimensional space into a three-dimensional space with much less computational cost (see Figure 9). After applying the kernel method, a linear SVM can be trained in the new feature space Z', which will result in a nonlinear model in the original space Z.

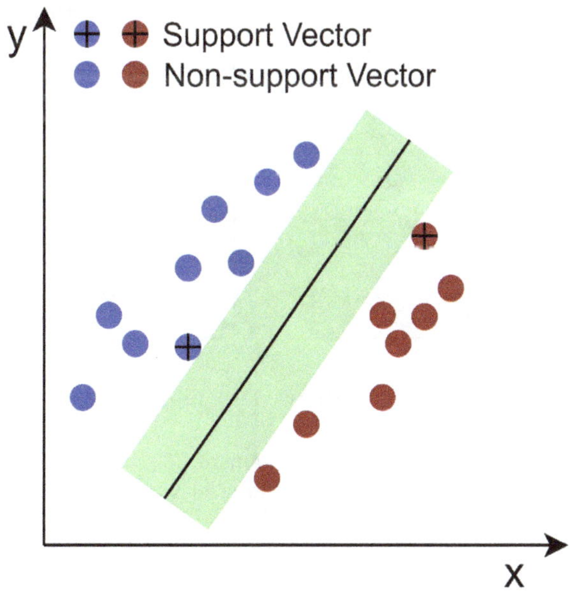

Figure 8. An example of linear SVM and support vectors.

Note: Figure 8 shows an example of support vectors (blue and red points with the crossed circle symbol) and non-support vectors (blue and red points) in a linear SVM model. Only the support vectors define the margin (green area).

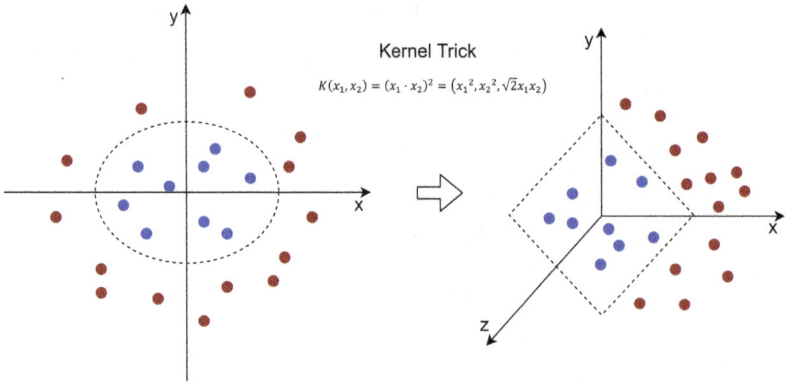

Figure 9. Example of a Kernel trick.
Note: Figure 9 demonstrates how a kernel trick turns a nonlinearly separable dataset (left) into a linearly separable dataset (right) by mapping the original two-dimensional space into a three-dimensional space.

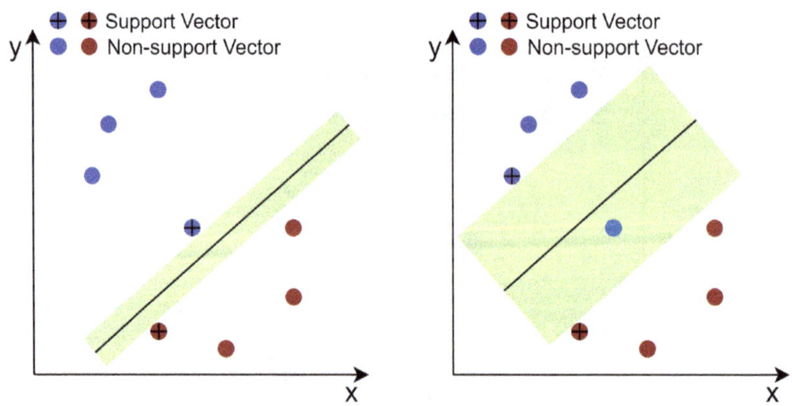

Figure 10. Higher C (Left) allows less margin error than lower C (Right).
Note: Figure 10 shows how the hyper-parameter C controls the margin errors (green area). A higher C allows less margin error (left). A lower C allows more margin error (right).

Noise data can be introduced to achieve a soft margin SVM. Margin errors are controlled by hyper-parameter C, where a high value of C means that margin errors incur a high penalty. In contrast, a low value permits more margin error (see Figure 10).

2.3.6. *Deep learning (DL), and artificial neural networks (ANN)*

2.3.6.1. Deep learning (DL)

DL is an emerging ML method that builds a prediction model with multiple layers and progressively extracts features from input data through different 'depths' of layers. For example, in image processing, lower-level layers can extract images' color features, while higher-level layers can recognize the patterns like wheels or faces. In most DL methods, ANN are used to build the prediction model.

2.3.6.2. Artificial neural networks (ANN)

In a biological neural network, information is carried by electrical pulses, and each neuron will pass the signal further to its adjacent neurons only when the signal exceeds some threshold. Besides, the connections between neurons can be empowered after the successful transmission of signals, which is thought to be the theory behind memory. An ANN is a simulation of a biological neuron network. In an ANN, each neuron takes the weighted sum of its inputs with a bias value and is then applied with an activation function. This step is similar to the threshold in biological neurons, where the output of the weighted sum can only be transmitted further when it exceeds some thresholds.

The connection of neurons in ANN consists of the output of the previous neuron along with the weights. The weights of all connections are updated using the training data set by a method called back-propagation. The mechanism is that the weights are enhanced when the prediction is correct and reduced when the prediction is wrong. This mechanism is similar to the enhancement of biological neural networks, which work as a memory process. After repeatedly learning the training data set, the parameters of the neural networks are updated to remember the correct information to accomplish the classification task. Figure 11 presents the general structure of ANN.

The number of the input nodes is N, which is defined as $\{x_1, \ldots, x_N\}$. The number of the Hidden Layer 1 nodes is p, which is defined as $\{h_{11}, \ldots, h_{1p}\}$. The number of the Hidden Layer K nodes is q, which is defined as $\{h_{K1}, \ldots, h_{Kq}\}$. The number of Output Layer nodes is M, which is defined as $\{y_1, \ldots, y_M\}$.

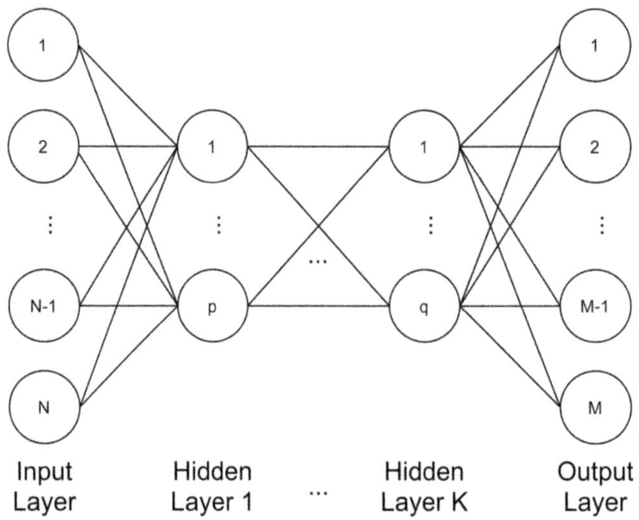

Figure 11. The general structure of an ANN.
Note: Figure 11 shows a general structure of an ANN model with an input layer, an output layer and K hidden layers.

The weight from the Input Layer nodes to the Hidden Layer 1 nodes is $W_{ij}^{1}(i = 1, \ldots, N; j = 1, \ldots, p)$, and so forth. The weight from the Hidden Layer K nodes to the Output Layer nodes is $W_{ij}^{K+1}(i = 1, \ldots, q; j = 1, \ldots, M)$. The bias term of the Input Layer is b_1 and the weight is w_{b_1}. The bias term of the Hidden Layer 1 is b_2 and the weight is w_{b_2}. The bias term of the Hidden Layer K is b_{K+1} and the weight is $w_{b_{K+1}}$.

3. ML Models in Fund Performance Evaluation

The methods for fund performance evaluation are constantly evolving. Starting with the single-factor idea since 1966, measures such as Treynor ratio, Sharpe ratio, and Jensen alpha are constructed based on the Capital Asset Pricing Model (CAPM) (Jensen, 1968; Sharpe, 1966; Treynor and Black, 1973). After adjusting for the risk premium, the obtained excess return of the fund indicates the outperformance or underperformance of the fund. To identify the sources of excess returns, multi-factor models have been proposed that include market value, book-to-market value, P/E ratio, profitability premium, investment premium, and monthly momentum factors on the assessment of fund performance, specifically the well-known Fama and French three-factor model, Carhart four-factor model, and Fama and French five-factor model (Carhart, 1997; Fama and French, 1992, 2015). Nowadays, with the recent development of Fintech, algorithms are continuously optimized to develop more effective models. The use of ML models to predict fund returns and evaluate fund performance has become one of the mainstream directions for future research. In this section, building on an overview of both traditional methods and ML methods, we further compare these two categories and discuss their advantages and disadvantages from several aspects.

3.1. *Traditional methods to evaluate fund performance*

3.1.1. *Single-factor models*

The commonly used evaluation methods of fund performance are based on the theory of CAPM and APT. The most used indicators (single-factor) are the Treynor ratio, Sharpe ratio, and Jensen alpha (Jensen, 1968; Sharpe, 1966; Treynor and Black, 1973). Treynor ratio and Sharpe ratio are both expressed by the ratio of fund returns to risks. However, compared to the Treynor ratio that only considers systematic risk, the Sharpe ratio uses the standard deviation of returns to represent the total risk of the portfolio, including systematic and non-systematic risks (Sharpe, 1966). Jensen alpha is usually obtained using CAPM regression and is used to measure the fund manager's ability to outperform the market.

$$\text{Sharpe ratio} : \text{Sharp}_i = \frac{E(r_i) - r_f}{\sigma_i}, \tag{14}$$

$$\text{Treynor ratio} : T_i = \frac{r_i - r_f}{\beta_i}, \tag{15}$$

$$\text{Jensen alpha} : R_{it} - r_{ft} = \alpha_i + \beta_i(R_{mt} - r_{ft}) + \varepsilon_{it}, \tag{16}$$

where r_i denotes the fund i's monthly net return, r_f denotes the monthly risk-free rate, β_i denotes the fund i's beta, σ_i denotes the standard deviation of the return, R_{mt} denotes the fund market return at time t.

3.1.2. *Multi-factor models*

In addition to the above single-factor models, multi-factor models have been proposed based on APT that require fewer assumptions. Fama and French (1992) propose a classic three-factor model, identifying three essential factors that influence portfolio returns: the size of firms, excess return, and Book-to-Price (B/P) value. Based on that, Carhart (1997) proposes a four-factor model that introduces the momentum factor. Later, Fama and French added two more factors to their previous three-factor model, forming the FF five-factor model (Fama and French, 2015). These three models are still hot in evaluating fund performances.

$$\begin{aligned} FF3: R_{it} - r_{ft} &= \alpha_i + \beta_i(R_{mt} - r_{ft}) + s_i SMB_t \\ &\quad + h_i HML_t + \varepsilon_{it}, \qquad (17) \\ C4: R_{it} - r_{ft} &= \alpha_i + \beta_i(R_{mt} - r_{ft}) + s_i SMB_t + h_i HML_t \\ &\quad + u_i UMD_t + \varepsilon_{it}, \qquad (18) \\ FF5: R_{it} - r_{ft} &= \alpha_i + \beta_i(R_{mt} - r_{ft}) + s_i SMB_t + h_i HML_t \\ &\quad + r_i RMW_t + c_i CMA_t + \varepsilon_{it}, \qquad (19) \end{aligned}$$

where R_{it} denotes the fund monthly net return for period t, r_f denotes the monthly risk-free rate, R_{mt} denotes the fund market return at time t, SMB_t denotes the size premium (small minus big), HML_t denotes the values premium (high minus low), RMW_t denotes the profitability premium (robust minus weak), CMA_t denotes the investment premium (conservative minus aggressive), UMD_t denotes the momentum premium.

Foye (2018) apply the FF three-factor model and FF five-factor model to investigate the effectiveness of both models in emerging markets, finding that the FF five-factor model beats the FF three-factor model in Eastern Europe and Latin America in terms of reduced intercepts. Still, the FF three-factor model wins in Asia. They agree with Lin (2017)'s explanations about why the three-factor model performs better in Asia. First, many emerging markets are bank-orientated — profitability is a better indicator. Second, firms in emerging markets might choose past investment to benefit ownership concentration and controlling shareholders, which weakens the prediction power of the investment factor (Lin, 2017).

3.2. *ML methods to evaluate fund performance*

In addition to multi-factor models, the idea of multi-factor analysis is also used to construct Fintech models in recent years. This section introduces ML methods and techniques for fund performance evaluation and shows how ML contributes to measuring and predicting fund performance.

3.2.1. *Linear regression, LASSO, and ridge regression*

The powerful calculational capabilities of ML allow researchers to go beyond the shortcomings of a limited number of factors affecting fund performance. That's where the linear regression in ML differs from traditional regression methods. However, adding variables is not boundless. The penalty term is like a weight at the other end of the scale, performing a balancing role to avoid introducing too many variables and control the model's complexity. For example, Liu and Du (2012) apply LASSO to select 14 stocks to track the CSI 300 index. They find that LASSO performs well in risk diversification and portfolio construction, which could be useful for passive investment strategy, such as quantitative analysis of passive funds. Gendreau *et al.* (2019) propose an indexation method based on LASSO to find similar conclusions. They believe the CVaR-LASSO method minimizes the risk of underperformance while also tracking the benchmark index, which aligns with the objectives of an enhanced-passive fund, especially those with high stock holdings. Roy *et al.* (2015) and Sant'Anna *et al.* (2020) both apply a combination of linear regression and LASSO methods to select stock and generate portfolios for index-tracking. Their results show that the predictive power of the LASSO linear models is enhanced, evidenced by more stable tracking performance and lower average turnover rates. Roy *et al.* (2015) also test the performance of Ridge linear regression and LASSO linear regression and find that the latter performs better within their sample.

For Ridge Regression, Xiao-Wei and Ya-Hui (2011) investigate the Chinese open-end fund market from 2004 to 2010 and analyze the investment styles of various funds. Their findings show that Ridge Regression could effectively solve the multicollinearity problem. DeMiguel *et al.* (2021) find that elastic net, where the 2-norm is a Ridge Regression, can improve the prediction power of fund performance and identify funds with positive risk-adjusted net-of-fee returns. In short, LASSO and Ridge are considered practical shrinkage methods and are widely used to replicate fund holdings, select stocks and funds, reduce tracking error, and improve investment performance.

3.2.2. *K nearest neighbors*

The core idea of KNN is always to predict the unknown data with the majority class of KNN. Therefore, it is not difficult to associate this approach with fund classification. Many scholars find that mutual funds are miscategorized in the fund market (Bams *et al.*, 2017; Chua and Tam, 2020; Kim *et al.*, 2000; Marathe and Shawky, 1999; Moreno *et al.*, 2006). Moreno *et al.* (2006) apply the KNN algorithm to classify 1,592 mutual funds in the Spanish mutual fund market. Their results show that around 40% of the mutual fund might be misclassified based on their financial attributes. They believe that over-number categories cause this misclassification. Some of the categories are separated with little difference between them, thus, making the classification less effective. Ban *et al.* (2013) extend univariate KNN to multivariate KNN to predict stocks from the S&P 500 from 2001 to 2011. They find that multivariate KNN regression works well with financial time series data and outperforms the classical univariate KNN regression. Ananthi and Vijayakumar (2021) utilize KNN regression to generate market movement signals and predict the market trend by integrating the assessment of all stocks' future performance. We believe that KNN regression models will remain useful in fund performance evaluation directly and in research areas such as fund classification and market trending. Moreover, from the perspective of fund managers and individual investors, improving the accuracy of fund classification and market trending is critical to the choice of fund investment strategy.

3.2.3. *Decision trees (DTs) and random forest (RF)*

The use of DT and RFs in fund market research has been widespread, and many studies have confirmed that DT and RF work quite well throughout mature markets and emerging markets (Arora *et al.*, 2019; Chia-Cheng *et al.*, 2020; Lohrmann and Luukka, 2019; Tan *et al.*, 2019; Wang *et al.*, 2020). Two main tasks for applying DT and

RF are classification and regression. Lohrmann and Luukka (2019) develop a classification model using the RF classifier to create a four-class classification system for S&P 500 returns. This model efficiently tells whether the return of a security is positive or negative and is strong or slight. Their results show that the accuracy is highest among KNN, naive Bayes, and the similarity classifier. This four-class classification model corresponds intuitively to the decision to buy or sell. Arora *et al.* (2019) use a decision tree model to identify the intrinsic drivers of fund managers' liquidity decisions. Compared to the classic logit model, DT and RF provide better forecasts for out-of-sample observations with an improvement of approximately 11%. Bryzgalova *et al.* (2019) extend characteristic-based sorting to DTs to propose a new asset pricing method. The asset pricing tree portfolios they construct perform well within the training set (20 years) and out-of-sample data.

In addition to this, several studies focus on the application of DT and RF on stock selection and portfolio selection and justify how the ML methods enhance trading performance. Andriyashin *et al.* (2008) construct a DT model with a series of technical variables and fundamental variables. Their new stock selection strategy significantly outperforms the market. Moritz and Zimmermann (2016) use tree-based regression models to predict future returns and find short-term returns the most important predictor in the US stock market. Tan *et al.* (2019) also observe the presence of excess returns obtained from stock selection trained by the RF training model. The stock selection process may not significantly affect the performance of passive funds, which, after all, focus more on tracking market indices. However, for active funds, identifying outperforming stocks that can diversify portfolio risk and enhance fund returns is one of the primary means by which fund managers can pursue higher excess returns and offset transaction costs.

3.2.4. *Support vector machine (SVM)*

In Section 3.2.5, we have discussed that the linear SVM can be mapped into nonlinear spaces using a mathematical technique called the kernel method. This feature gives SVM a special advantage when dealing with complex data, especially when it is not suitable for normal distribution and ordinary least squares (OLS). Abdou and

Nasereddin (2011) use the SVM approach to investigate the effect of different fund strategies on hedge fund performance. Their rationale for applying SVM is that common statistical analysis has poor predictive accuracy when hedge funds are non-normal and suffer from fat tails (Abdou and Nasereddin, 2011). The results show that SVM outperforms OLS and NN regarding the fund performance evaluation and contributes to the assessment of hedge fund strategies.

In addition to this, we also mentioned that SVM is always an optimal linear regression learning method, as it can find the maximum margin separating hyperplane. Building on this feature, Kumar and Thenmozhi (2006) find that SVM beat other traditional models in predicting the movement of the stock index. Their results are consistent with the study of Tay and Cao (2001), who examine and demonstrate the feasibility of SVM in financial time series forecasting, and the study of Kim (2003), who proves that by minimizing the upper boundary of the generalization error, SVM could show superior performance on the analysis of financial time series. Moreover, Vangara *et al.* (2018) introduce the SVM approach to the prediction of mutual fund's net asset value (NAV) using data from the Indian mutual fund market. Zamharirlou *et al.* (2020) apply SVM to analyze factors that may affect the issue and redemption of units of mutual funds. Their empirical findings show that all five variables, including fund return, fund size, market index, capital market transactions volume, and currency volatility, have significant effects on equity funds, while only the first two factors affect bond funds. In short, SVM may be an applicable choice when dealing with non-normal data or obtaining higher prediction accuracy and other factor-based analyses.

3.2.5. *Neural networks and deep learning (DL)*

In most cases, ANN and DL methods are used to build prediction models. Several studies show that NN and DL could perform best among both traditional models and other ML models. For example, Afridi *et al.* (2021) predict mutual fund performance in the US mutual fund market using the NN algorithm. Nikou *et al.* (2019) train ANN, SVM, and RF models to predict the future trend of the stock market. By comparing the prediction results of the close prices using these models, they conclude that an ANN model with a long short-term memory (LSTM) beats SVM and RF, though SVM has the highest precision. Wang and Huang (2010) implement the Fast Adaptive Neural Network Classifier (FANNC) approach proposed by Zhou *et al.* (2000) to evaluate mutual fund performance. They find that this approach could generate a better root mean square than the commonly applied backpropagation neural network model, requiring less computation time.

NN and DL methods are also used to optimize the investment behavior of mutual funds. For example, Chen *et al.* (2021) propose a DL network model to investigate the trading strategies of mutual funds. Their findings show that the proposed model considerably enhances the performance of trading strategies. Ouyang *et al.* (2019) use NN to develop a dynamic index-tracking method that achieves a smaller tracking error. Zhang (2020) innovatively forecasts mutual fund performance by investigating the textual information disclosed in mutual fund shareholder letters. The NN approach, together with a natural language processing model, makes it possible to process massive textual information of mutual funds, identifying informed funds that provide higher-than-normal returns and receive higher Morningstar ratings.

3.3. *Comparison between traditional and ML methods*

Over the past few decades, traditional methods have proven valid for fund performance evaluation, and they still have great applicability today. Relatively speaking, though the implementation of ML methods in this area is quite fresh and novel, it has demonstrated several unique advantages. In this section, we first discuss the precision and accuracy of traditional methods and ML methods. Then we compare the strengths and weaknesses of traditional methods and ML methods in detail, considering the scale of data, variable selection, and relationship recognition.

3.3.1. *Precision and accuracy*

There is debate whether the traditional indicators (i.e., Treynor ratio, Sharpe ratio, and Jensen alpha) are good enough or not. The advantage of choosing these single indicators is obvious, as it is easy for fund investors and fund managers to access data and perform calculations. Jagric *et al.* (2015) rank the mutual funds by measuring their performance using the Treynor and Sharpe ratios separately. They find that the rankings are almost the same. As the Treynor ratio only considers systematic risk and Sharpe ratio includes both systematic and non-systematic risks, similar rankings mean that idiosyncratic risks in the asset portfolio are adequately diversified. Hence, the mutual funds they choose are well diversified. Eling and Schuhmacher (2007) compare these ratios and other new measures to determine whether the choice of measurements affects fund rankings. Their results show that almost all performance measures have a high correlation, and none of the new measures displays a significant change. Therefore, they conclude that the Sharpe ratio is good enough to analyze hedge funds. Auer and Schuhmacher (2013) also provide an empirical analysis of whether fund rankings are affected by various performance measures, and they draw a similar conclusion to Eling and Schuhmacher (2007). However, Kaur (2013) holds a different view. He selects Indian equity mutual funds from 2008 to 2010 and evaluates their performance using the Treynor ratio, Sharpe ratio, and Jensen alpha. His results show that correlations between Jensen alpha and other ratios are weak, and the rank of fund performance is different from that of risk-adjusted performance. Scholz (2007) introduces an alternative refined Sharpe ratio because they find that the origin Sharpe ratio may lead to misleading rankings, especially for bear markets. Krimm *et al.* (2012) explain that under a negative market climate, the Sharpe ratio overestimates the performance of portfolios with non-systematic risks, leading to ranking bias. Ledoit and Wolf (2008) agree that the Sharpe ratio is not valid when the fund returns are far from normally distributed.

Due to limitations such as lack of accuracy, harsh assumptions, and potentially misleading rankings for single indicators, multi-factor models have gradually replaced them (i.e., FF3, C4, and FF5). Hanauer *et al.* (2014) and Taneja (2010) support the Fama and French three-factor model with empirical evidence. Their results show that the model outperforms the CAPM with a higher correlation between factors and returns, suggesting that the FF model is a good predictor for expected returns. Chen and Scholtens (2018) use Carhart's model to investigate the risk-adjusted return and investment styles of active and passive funds. The model provides explanatory power to their sample with significant R^2, allowing them to conclude that there is insufficient evidence to believe active funds beat passive funds.

However, empirical evidence shows that the accuracy of multi-factor models can be enhanced by adding new factors, as the fund market is so complex that the current factors will not fully capture the changes in fund performance. Fama and French test their new five-factor model with data from developed markets and confirm an improved description of returns in North America, Europe, and Asia Pacific (Fama and French, 2017). Busse *et al.* (2019) make some adjustments to Carhart's four-factor model. They propose a new measure for evaluating double-adjusted mutual fund performance containing factor model betas and stock benchmarks. They believe the new method could better predict the factor-alpha for as far as 9 years (Busse *et al.*, 2019). Also, the traditional models are found to output findings that may be significantly different from the same samples. For example, Li and Lin (2011) find evidence on the out-performance of active funds when using the Sharpe ratio, and the evidence disappears when they choose the multi-factor model.

Compared to the traditional approach, ML models typically perform better in terms of both precision and accuracy. Chen and Tindall (2014) investigate traditional methods such as stepwise OLS and ML techniques such as LASSO and Ridge Regression to evaluate the tracking error of replicated fund indexes. They define these shrinkage methods as non-traditional methods. They find that the non-traditional methods produce superior results in terms of reducing tracking error compared to those generated by the traditional methods. Cao *et al.* (2005) compare the predictive power of the FF three-factor model and ANN in forecasting stock prices, which helps to construct portfolios that could beat the market. The empirical results show that ANN models perform better than traditional linear regression models with significant t-scores. Chong *et al.* (2017) reach a similar conclusion by investigating stock returns and volatility in the Korean market. They find that the DL network models enhance their prediction performance and outperform the autoregressive model, as DL models can extract additional information, while the autoregressive model cannot. Tian (2020) also provides evidence on the superior performance of ML models over classic OLS regression based on data from the US mutual fund market. Their results show that the RF and gradient boost random tree models could perform better than OLS in 17 out of 20 years, and NN beat the OLS in 19 out of the 20 years (Tian, 2020).

It is worth mentioning that although the efficiency of various ML models may vary due to different characteristics in sample data, the results are generally consistent. However, as discussed above, applying different traditional evaluation models to the same data series sometimes led to very different conclusions (Kaur, 2013; Krimm *et al.*, 2012; Li and Lin, 2011; Scholz, 2007). A possible explanation for this issue is that the evaluation models are not sufficiently applicable to the selected data due to missing variables or the misspecification of models. This shortcoming happens to be fixed by ML models because they can be optimized to fit the data through the training process. Moreover, ML models can be constructed to include as many variables as possible, eliminate irrelevant terms, and retain important features during the optimization process.

3.3.2. *Scale of data*

One of the most significant advantages of ML methods is identifying and extracting features from massive data without human expertise (Chong *et al.*, 2017). The strong computational power allows the scale of sample data to become very large. In research conducted by Chia-Cheng *et al.* (2020), 1,258 S&P 500 stocks are selected and tested using RF, SVM, and ANN. Based on the well-trained models, they further evaluate the investment performance of ML models through measurements like Jensen alpha, Treynor ratio, smart beta, and Modigliani ratio. Eling and Schuhmacher (2007) use over 2,700 funds to investigate whether the choice of measurements affects rankings. Chong *et al.* (2017) apply DL algorithms to predict future stock returns in the Korean stock market. They construct three-layer neural networks based on 58,421 stock returns and find a stronger prediction power than the autoregressive model. Moritz and Zimmermann's (2016) research sample data includes monthly US stock returns for 50 years from 1963 to 2012 and firm characteristics of as many as 6,626 firms. To examine the market efficiency through prediction accuracy of stock returns, Bai and Pukthuanthong (2020) construct a data universe that contains more than 3 million monthly stock information of 26,302 common stocks. These examples are too numerous to list. The emergence of AI and ML methods has enabled research scholars and fund managers to use big data for more sophisticated computing and more robust analysis. Compared with traditional methods, data from ML methods can often span longer periods, shorter data frequencies, and more independent observations.

3.3.3. *Variable selection*

ML methods have not only greatly expanded the sample data, but the number of variables has also been increased. Traditional methods such as multi-factor models (FF3, C4, FF5) only include three to five factors. Studies based on FF models have tried to add more variables to improve prediction accuracy; however, testing the validity of factors by traditional methods increases exponentially in complexity with each additional artificially specified factor. Therefore, these traditional methods seldomly include more than 10 factors. Using ML methods makes it possible to choose dozens or even hundreds of variables as inputs to explore their relationships with the output. In this case, some potentially important variables, especially those that may have been previously overlooked and misjudged, may be identified and extracted through the process of ML.

In Section 2.2.3, we have discussed the overfitting problem that may exist in ML methods. Including too many variables may improve the performance of the training data, but it may also lead to overfitting. Remember, the objective is to maximize prediction accuracy on future data, not the training set (Dietterich, 1995). For example, Merh *et al.* (2010) and Moritz and Zimmermann (2016) observe the overfitting problem in their studies. To solve this problem, Moritz and Zimmermann (2016) add a step of averaging estimates from de-correlated models. They believe this model-averaging process could capture the true signals even if the simple model is incorrect. Therefore, the number of variables is not 'the more, the better'. Although ML techniques allow the inclusion of many variables, extra attention needs to be taken to address the overfitting issue in practical applications.

3.3.4. *Relationship recognition*

Another key advantage of ML methods is the ability to uncover nonlinear relationships. Cao *et al.* (2005) construct four models to forecast stock price movement, including two linear models and two neural network models. Based on the empirical results, they conclude that the nonlinear models outperform the linear models. Feng *et al.* (2020) design a DL model and train a neural network that allows nonlinearity and interactions on firm characteristics inputs. The findings show robust evidence in individual stock returns and out-of-sample portfolios. To investigate the nonlinear relationships between stock returns and factors, Yuan *et al.* (2020) use SVM, RF, and NN to forecast future stock prices. The results show that the RF model performs better than other models and could help investors obtain long-term returns.

There are ongoing discussions about whether nonlinear relationships work better than linear relationships. In addition to the studies mentioned above confirming better results for nonlinear relationships, empirical findings show that linear models perform better or the same as nonlinear models. Merh *et al.* (2010) investigate the hybrid models developed using neural networks and the autoregressive model and find the neural networks model performs worse for BSE 100 indices in India. Adebiyi *et al.* (2014) compare the traditional autoregressive integrated moving average model to the ANN model using daily data in the US stock market. They find that both models could provide good forecasts and the prediction results are quite close. However, the proportion of linear relationships as winners is still relatively small.

Moreover, ML methods do not reject linear relationships; they just offer more options about potential relationships. In Section 2.3, we discussed how ML models could solve problems based on an assumption of linear relationships. Approaches such as shrinkage methods and linear SVM could achieve satisfactory results. We believe that the fact that ML can uncover nonlinear relationships will provide more opportunities for research exploration. After all, reality is complex, and linear relationships are mostly relationships derived at a high level of abstraction. Hence, the implementation of AI and ML methods can contribute to the emerging literature on the use of ML to complement or replace conventional regression models.

4. Conclusion

In this chapter, we investigate the application of AI and various ML methods in fund performance evaluation and prediction. The basics of ML, including ML theories, ML categories, ML framework, and some important concepts, are introduced. Based on that, we provide a detailed overview of mostly applied ML algorithms in fund performance research, including linear regression, LASSO, Ridge, KNN, DT, and RF, SVM, DL, and ANN.

For each ML technique and algorithm, we introduce the latest research findings and applicable conditions. We analyze how these ML methods contribute to forecasting and measuring fund performance. The use of ML methods to predict fund returns and evaluate fund performance is gradually showing superiority and great potential over traditional methods. An in-depth analysis of how ML methods are superior to traditional methods is provided. In short — in terms of precision — traditional models may obtain misleading results and may come across the issue of inconsistent conclusions, thus, affecting the validity of the results. In terms of accuracy, multi-factor models have improved over single-factor models, but ML has achieved higher accuracy than multi-factor models. Moreover, we discuss how ML methods can achieve improved accuracy and precision through a larger scale of data, feature selection among numerous factors, and the capability of recognizing nonlinear relationships.

References

Abdou, K., & Nasereddin, M. (2011). The persistence of hedge fund strategies in different economic periods: A support vector machine approach. *Journal of Derivatives & Hedge Funds*, *17*(1), 2–15.

Adebiyi, A. A., Adewumi, A. O., & Ayo, C. K. (2014). Comparison of ARIMA and artificial neural networks models for stock price prediction. *Journal of Applied Mathematics*, 2014.

Afridi, S. S., Ubedulla, S., Hussain, S. A., & Nayak, R. K. (2021). Mutual fund prediction using neural network algorithms. In *International Conference on Smart Data Intelligence*.

Ananthi, M., & Vijayakumar, K. (2021). Stock market analysis using candlestick regression and market trend prediction (CKRM). *Journal of Ambient Intelligence and Humanized Computing*, *12*(5), 4819–4826.

Andriyashin, A., Härdle, W. K., & Timofeev, R. V. (2008). *Recursive Portfolio Selection with Decision Trees.* SSRN Working Paper. https://papers.ssrn.com/sol3/papers.cfm?abstract_id=2894287.

Arora, R., Fan, C., & Ouellet Leblanc, G. (2019). *Liquidity Management of Canadian Corporate Bond Mutual Funds: A Machine Learning Approach.* Bank of Canada, Staff Analytical Notes. Federal Reserve Bank of St. Louis, United States, St. Louis.

Auer, B. R., & Schuhmacher, F. (2013). Robust evidence on the similarity of Sharpe ratio and drawdown-based hedge fund performance rankings. *Journal of International Financial Markets, Institutions and Money, 24*, 153–165.

Bai, Y., & Pukthuanthong, K. (2020). Machine learning classification methods and portfolio allocation: An examination of market efficiency. https://papers.ssrn.com/sol3/papers.cfm?abstract_id=3665051.

Bams, D., Otten, R., & Ramezanifar, E. (2017). Investment style misclassification and mutual fund performance. In *28th Australasian Finance and Banking Conference.* SSRN Working Paper. https://papers.ssrn.com/sol3/papers.cfm?abstract_id=2648375.

Ban, T., Zhang, R., Pang, S., Sarrafzadeh, A., & Inoue, D. (2013). Referential kNN regression for financial time series forecasting. In *International Conference on Neural Information Processing.* Springer.

Bertin, W. J., & Prather, L. (2009). Management structure and the performance of funds of mutual funds. *Journal of Business Research, 62*(12), 1364–1369.

Blum, A. (2007). Machine learning theory. Carnegie Mellon University, School of Computer Science, 26. http://www.cs.cmu.edu/afs/cs/user/avrim/www/Talks/mlt.pdf.

Bryzgalova, S., Pelger, M., & Zhu, J. (2019). Forest through the trees: Building cross-sections of stock returns. https://papers.ssrn.com/sol3/papers.cfm?abstract_id=3493458.

Busse, J. A., Jiang, L., & Tang, Y. (2019). Double-adjusted mutual fund performance. https://papers.ssrn.com/sol3/papers.cfm?abstract_id=2516792.

Cao, Q., Leggio, K. B., & Schniederjans, M. J. (2005). A comparison between Fama and French's model and artificial neural networks in predicting the Chinese stock market. *Computers & Operations Research, 32*(10), 2499–2512.

Carhart, M. M. (1997). On persistence in mutual fund performance. *The Journal of Finance, 52*(1), 57–82.

Chen, J., Luo, C., Pan, L., & Jia, Y. (2021). Trading strategy of structured mutual fund based on deep learning network. *Expert Systems with Applications*, 115390.

Chen, J., & Tindall, M. L. (2014). Hedge fund replication using shrinkage methodologies. *The Journal of Alternative Investments, 17*(2), 26–49.

Chen, X., & Scholtens, B. (2018). The urge to act: A comparison of active and passive socially responsible investment funds in the United States. *Corporate Social Responsibility and Environmental Management, 25*(6), 1154–1173.

Chia-Cheng, C., Chun-Hung, C., & Ting-Yin, L. (2020). Investment performance of machine learning: Analysis of S&P 500 index. *International Journal of Economics and Financial Issues, 10*(1), 59.

Choi, P. M. S., & Huang, S. H. (2021). *Fintech with Artificial Intelligence, Big data, and Blockchain.* Springer, Singapore.

Chollet, F. (2018). *Deep Learning with Python.* Manning, New York.

Chong, E., Han, C., & Park, F. C. (2017). Deep learning networks for stock market analysis and prediction: Methodology, data representations, and case studies. *Expert Systems with Applications, 83*, 187–205.

Chua, A. K. P., & Tam, O. K. (2020). The shrouded business of style drift in active mutual funds. *Journal of Corporate Finance, 64*, 101667.

DeMiguel, V., Gil-Bazo, J., Nogales, F. J., & Santos, A. A. P. (2021). *Can Machine Learning Help to Select Portfolios of Mutual Funds?* Economics Working Papers: 1772. Department of Economics and Business, Pompeu Fabra University.

Demirguc-Kunt, A., Klapper, L., Singer, D., Ansar, S., & Hess, J. (2018). *The Global Findex Database 2017: Measuring Financial Inclusion and the Fintech Revolution.* The World Bank, United States, Washington, D.C.

Dietterich, T. (1995). Overfitting and undercomputing in machine learning. *ACM Computing Surveys (CSUR), 27*(3), 326–327.

Efron, B., Hastie, T., Johnstone, I., & Tibshirani, R. (2004). Least angle regression. *The Annals of Statistics, 32*(2), 407–499.

Eling, M., & Schuhmacher, F. (2007). Does the choice of performance measure influence the evaluation of hedge funds? *Journal of Banking & Finance, 31*(9), 2632–2647.

Fama, E. F., & French, K. R. (1992). The cross-section of expected stock returns. *The Journal of Finance, 47*(2), 427–465.

Fama, E. F., & French, K. R. (1993). Common risk factors in the returns on stocks and bonds. *Journal of Financial Economics, 33*, 3–56.

Fama, E. F., & French, K. R. (2015). A five-factor asset pricing model. *Journal of Financial Economics, 116*(1), 1–22.

Fama, E. F., & French, K. R. (2017). International tests of a five-factor asset pricing model. *Journal of Financial Economics, 123*(3), 441–463.

Feng, G., Polson, N., & Xu, J. (2020). Deep learning in characteristics-sorted actor models. https://papers.ssrn.com/sol3/papers.cfm?abstract_id=3243683.

Foye, J. (2018). A comprehensive test of the Fama-French five-factor model in emerging markets. *Emerging Markets Review*, *37*, 199–222.

Gendreau, B., Jin, Y., Nimalendran, M., & Zhong, X. (2019). CVaR-LASSO Enhanced Index Replication (CLEIR): Outperforming by minimizing downside risk. *Applied Economics*, *51*(52), 5637–5651.

Hanauer, M. X., Jäckel, C., & Kaserer, C. (2014). A new look at the Fama-French model: Evidence based on expected returns. https://papers.ssrn.com/sol3/papers.cfm?abstract_id=2082108.

He, M. D., Leckow, M. R. B., Haksar, M. V., Griffoli, M. T. M., Jenkinson, N., Kashima, M. M., Khiaonarong, T., Rochon, M. C., & Tourpe, H. (2017). *Fintech and Financial Services: Initial Considerations.* International Monetary Fund, United States, Washington, D.C.

Jagric, T., Podobnik, B., Strasek, S., & Jagric, V. (2015). Risk-adjusted performance of mutual funds: Some tests. *South-Eastern Europe Journal of Economics*, *5*(2), 233–244.

Jensen, M. C. (1968). The performance of mutual funds in the period 1945–1964. *The Journal of Finance*, *23*(2), 389–416.

Kaur, I. (2013). Performance, timing and selectivity skills of Indian equity mutual funds: An empirical approach. *Researchers World*, *4*(4), 87–94.

Kim, K.-J. (2003). Financial time series forecasting using support vector machines. *Neurocomputing*, *55*(1–2), 307–319.

Kim, M., Shukla, R., & Tomas, M. (2000). Mutual fund objective misclassification. *Journal of Economics and Business*, *52*(4), 309–323.

King, J. S. (2002). Mutual funds: Investment of choice for individual investors? *Review of Business*, *23*(3), 35–39.

Krimm, S., Scholz, H., & Wilkens, M. (2012). The Sharpe ratio's market climate bias: Theoretical and empirical evidence from US equity mutual funds. *Journal of Asset Management*, *13*(4), 227–242.

Kumar, M., & Thenmozhi, M. (2006). Forecasting stock index movement: A comparison of support vector machines and random forest. In *Indian Institute of Capital Markets 9th Capital Markets Conference Paper.*

Ledoit, O., & Wolf, M. (2008). Robust performance hypothesis testing with the Sharpe ratio. *Journal of Empirical Finance*, *15*(5), 850–859.

Li, N., & Lin, C. Y. (2011). Understanding emerging market equity mutual funds: The case of China. *Financial Services Review*, *20*(1), 1.

Lin, Q. (2017). Noisy prices and the Fama–French five-factor asset pricing model in China. *Emerging Markets Review*, *31*, 141–163.

Liu, R., & Du, W. (2012). Portfolio construction using variable selection: Based on LASSO method. *On Economic Problems*, *9*, 103–107.

Lohrmann, C., & Luukka, P. (2019). Classification of intraday S&P 500 returns with a Random Forest. *International Journal of Forecasting*, *35*(1), 390–407.

Marathe, A., & Shawky, H. A. (1999). Categorizing mutual funds using clusters. *Advances in Quantitative Analysis of Finance and Accounting, 7*(1), 199–204.

Merh, N., Saxena, V. P., & Pardasani, K. R. (2010). A comparison between hybrid approaches of ANN and ARIMA for Indian stock trend forecasting. *Business Intelligence Journal, 3*(2), 23–43.

Moreno, D., Marco, P., & Olmeda, I. (2006). Self-organizing maps could improve the classification of Spanish mutual funds. *European Journal of Operational Research, 174*(2), 1039–1054.

Moritz, B., & Zimmermann, T. (2016). Tree-based conditional portfolio sorts: the relation between past and future stock returns. https://papers.ssrn.com/sol3/papers.cfm?abstract_id=2740751.

Nikou, M., Mansourfar, G., & Bagherzadeh, J. (2019). Stock price prediction using DEEP learning algorithm and its comparison with machine learning algorithms. *Intelligent Systems in Accounting, Finance and Management, 26*(4), 164–174.

Ouyang, H., Zhang, X., & Yan, H. (2019). Index tracking based on deep neural network. *Cognitive Systems Research, 57*, 107–114.

Roy, S. S., Mittal, D., Basu, A., & Abraham, A. (2015). Stock market forecasting using LASSO linear regression model. In *Afro-European Conference for Industrial Advancement*. Singapore, Springer.

Sant'Anna, L. R., Caldeira, J. F., & Filomena, T. P. (2020). Lasso-based index tracking and statistical arbitrage long-short strategies. *The North American Journal of Economics and Finance, 51*, 101055.

Scholz, H. (2007). Refinements to the Sharpe ratio: Comparing alternatives for bear markets. *Journal of Asset Management, 7*(5), 347–357.

Sharpe, W. F. (1966). Mutual fund performance. *The Journal of Business, 39*(1), 119–138.

Tan, Z., Yan, Z., & Zhu, G. (2019). Stock selection with random forest: An exploitation of excess return in the Chinese stock market. *Heliyon, 5*(8), e02310.

Taneja, Y. P. (2010). Revisiting Fama French three-factor model in Indian stock market. *Vision, 14*(4), 267–274.

Tay, F. E., & Cao, L. (2001). Application of support vector machines in financial time series forecasting. *Omega, 29*(4), 309–317.

Tian, C. (2020). *Applications of Machine Learning and Reinforcement Learning in Investment and Trading.* Irvine, University of California.

Tibshirani, R. (1996). Regression shrinkage and selection via the lasso. *Journal of the Royal Statistical Society: Series B (Methodological), 58*(1), 267–288.

Tikhonov, A. N. (1963). On the solution of ill-posed problems and the method of regularization. *Doklady Akademii Nauk, 4*, 1035–1038.

Treynor, J. L., & Black, F. (1973). How to use security analysis to improve portfolio selection. *The Journal of Business*, *46*(1), 66–86.

Vangara, A., Thouseef, S., Bhat, S. S., & Rao, V. (2018). Mutual fund NAV prediction using cascaded SVM models. In *2018 3rd International Conference for Convergence in Technology (I2CT)*. IEEE.

Wang, K., & Huang, S. (2010). Using fast adaptive neural network classifier for mutual fund performance evaluation. *Expert Systems with Applications*, *37*(8), 6007–6011.

Wang, S., Li, Z., Zhu, J., Lin, Z., & Zhong, M. (2020). Stock selection strategy of A-share market based on rotation effect and random forest. *AIMS Mathematics*, *5*(5), 4563–4580.

Xiao-Wei, D., & Ya-Hui, T. (2011). Investment style analysis of open-end fund in China-based Ridge regression estimation. *Financial Theory & Practice*, *3*, 75–79.

Yuan, X., Yuan, J., Jiang, T., & Ain, Q. U. (2020). Integrated long-term stock selection models based on feature selection and machine learning algorithms for China stock market. *IEEE Access*, *8*, 22672–22685.

Zamharirlou, S., Mansourfar, G., & Ghayour, F. (2020). Explaining factors affecting the issue and redemption of mutual fund units: Comparison of the behavior of stock funds and fixed-income funds. *Financial Management Strategy*, *8*(2), 61–70.

Zhang, A. L. (2020). Uncovering mutual fund private information with machine learning. https://papers.ssrn.com/sol3/papers.cfm?abstract_id=3713966.

Zhou, Z., Chen, S., & Chen, Z. (2000). FANNC: A fast adaptive neural network classifier. *Knowledge and Information Systems*, *2*(1), 115–129.

Part IV

FinTech in Financial Services

https://doi.org/10.1142/9781800612723_0008

Chapter 8

Reimagining the Management of Outsourcing Life Cycles in the FinTech Era for Financial Services

Tristan Lim*,‡ and Patrick Thng†,§

*School of Business Management, Nanyang Polytechnic, Singapore
†School of Information Systems, Singapore Management University, Singapore
‡tris02@gmail.com, tristan_lim@nyp.edu.sg
§patrickthng@smu.edu.sg

Abstract

In today's financial services landscape, staying ahead of the innovation curve and being disciplined at enhancing core service offerings entail careful resource planning. A well-structured outsourcing arrangement can go a long way towards enhancing long term organizational strategic growth. In the post-2014 FinTech era, (i) strategic management with an innovation focus; and (ii) financial technology-associated risks, have brought about changes to outsourcing in the financial services industry. Presently, most outsourcing life cycle models in existing literature seek to provide comprehensive, yet industry-neutral guidelines lacking industry context and depth of coverage. A newly licensed financial institution deciding to embark on outsourcing but is uncertain about how to thread the increasingly complex FinTech and financial regulatory landscape, will likely find domain-specific outsourcing life cycle models useful. A more targeted financial services outsourcing life cycle approach, with a focus on strategy and risk management in today's context, can contribute more effectively to the application and review of outsourcing implementation. This chapter discusses a new Strategy-Risk outsourcing life cycle model. This is an elegant and simple-to-use end-to-end framework which can be utilized by the financial services industry to guide outsourcing decisions. The chapter also recommends areas for future research.

Keywords: FinTech, financial services, outsourcing, life cycle model, strategy-risk model.

1. Introduction

1.1. *Financial technology (FinTech)*

FinTech is the technology-enabled innovation in financial services. FinTech, a combination of the terms 'financial' and 'technology', is more aptly defined by Financial Stability Board (2017) as, *technologically enabled financial innovation that could result in new business models, applications, processes, or products with an associated material effect on financial markets and institutions and the provision of financial services* (p. 7). FinTech is not restricted to specific business models or actors; rather, it covers the full spectrum of the activities (Arner *et al.*, 2015) involving:

- The provision of enabling technology for financial services, such as artificial intelligence (AI), internet of things (IoT), distributed ledger technology and cloud computing;
- Business models, such as neo-banks, platform aggregators and data providers; and
- The activities involving the provision of innovative financial products and services, such as e-payment solutions and peer-to-peer lending.

As such, FinTech actors may broadly include financial institutions (FIs), FinTech companies (FinTechs) and BigTech companies (BigTechs). While FinTechs operate primarily in financial services, BigTechs relate to large non-financial companies who offer FinTech solutions or financial products as part of a broader set of business verticals. (Frost *et al.*, 2019). Examples of FIs are Citibank and American International Group (AIG); examples of FinTechs are Ant Financial, Stripe and Ayden; and examples of BigTechs include Amazon and Alphabet among others.

The late 1980s saw the rise of digitalization of financial services, or e-Finance (Arner *et al.*, 2015; Gomber *et al.*, 2017). It was, however, noted that the term FinTech only started gaining widespread attention from regulators, industry participants, consumers and the academia from 2014 onwards (hereon defined as FinTech era) (Arner *et al.*, 2016). Since then, there has been a (i) growing pace of diffusion of innovative FinTech solutions; (ii) emergence of more non-banks and new startups offering financial services; (iii) evolution of customer behaviors that point towards preferences to online customer engagements, lower customer loyalty, and openness towards multiple financial service providers; and (iv) growing regulatory restrictions on traditional financial service providers, consequential partly due to the financial crisis of 2007/8 (Alt *et al.*, 2018).

1.2. *Transformations in the FinTech era*

These changes in the FinTech era have brought about financial industry transformation characterized at three levels (Alt *et al.*, 2018):

- Firstly, within an organization, there is a shift towards adopting a customer-focused rapid digitalization and innovation of processes, using agile methodologies and application programming interfaces (API). (Alt and Puschmann, 2016; Ehrenfeld, 2017). These digitalization and innovation efforts are less integrated with cumbersome legacy core banking systems, easing hindrances to external collaborations.
- Secondly, at the business eco-system level, many businesses in the FinTech era have adopted a culture of openness to strategic external relationships with, for instance, new startups and BigTechs. This is a result of intense business competitions, driving lower margins and customer retention (Shim and Shin, 2016; Pousttchi and Dehnert, 2018).
- Thirdly, at the external organization level, there are increasing regulatory constraints due to the growing trials, uses and decentralization of digital infrastructure, such as payment and financing infrastructures. These infrastructures, if not well supervised, may result in systemic risks (Arner *et al.*, 2017; Lawrence, 2016; Němcová, and Dvořák, 2013). Across the financial value chain, there are reduced reliance on the

conduct of business and technology processes and activities in-house. In turn, there are increased outsourcing, innovation, specialization and diversification efforts (Alt *et al.*, 2018).

The Basel Committee on Banking Supervision (BCBS) is headquartered at the Bank of International Settlements (BIS), with memberships of 45 central bank governors from 28 jurisdictions. In 2018, the BCBS published a report detailing how FinTech may affect the financial services landscape and the activities of supervisors across the near and medium term. The report highlighted the growing use of third parties service providers, via outsourcing. In particular, the report cited increasing complexity and risks in the outsourcing value chain, due to regulatory requirements and the proliferation of innovation solutions and business models.

2. Managing Outsourcing Life Cycles for Financial Services in FinTech Era

2.1. *Outsourcing for financial services*

Outsourcing is an act through which work is contracted or delegated to an external or related entity that can be physically located at different locations, an arrangement which includes offshore outsourcing, captive offshoring, nearshoring and onshoring (Oshri *et al.*, 2015).

In the context of the financial services industry, this definition is further extended. A regulated provider of financial services, either a FI, FinTech or BigTech, that outsources its business activities, must also be able to continue its provision of financial products or services, in the event its unregulated service provider fails or becomes dysfunctional (Ng, 2007). This is so that the regulators can ensure that regulated entities comply with the necessary measures, to ensure that the integrity of the financial markets and the interests of consumers are protected (Singh, 2005). Contextualizing outsourcing to the financial services industry, BCBS (2005) defined outsourcing, *as a regulated entity's use of a third party (either an affiliated entity within a corporate group or an entity that is external to the corporate group) to perform activities on a continuing basis that would normally be undertaken by the regulated entity, now or in the future* (p. 4).

Outsourcing of business and technology processes and activities relating to financial products and service are of significant scale. Research from Information Services Group showed that the combined annual contract value of financial industry-related outsourcing, comprising of Forbes®Global 2000 companies from the banking, insurance and diversified financial sectors, grew to US$22.5B in 2017, outstripping all other industry verticals (Reynolds, 2018). This was, in part, due to the pressures for value creation, speed and agility to adapt to fast changing business conditions and regulatory environments in the financial landscape. Outsourcing allows FIs to rapidly leverage on FinTech enablers of automation, analytics, blockchain and cloud-based services (Walter, 2018).

Outsourcing in financial services can take many forms. Traditionally, these outsourcing may include, for instance, business operations such as call centre, and aspects of accounting and back-office activities; and information technology (IT), such as the development of applications and server maintenance (BCBS, 2005). Emergence of FinTech brings about outsourcing in new areas. These new outsourcing domains can include the provision of enabling FinTech, such as big data, distributed ledger technology and IoT; and the provision of FinTech activities, such as e-payment solutions, alternative credit scoring and peer-to-peer lending. One example of an outsourcing partnership is a white labeling financial product arrangement between ABN Amro, a FI headquartered in Netherlands, and solarisBank, a Berlin-based FinTech established in 2016, with a full banking license granted by the Federal Financial Supervisory Authority of Germany (BaFin). ABN Amro offers banking digital offerings through MoneYou. To increase its activity, ABN Amro partnered with solarisBank to launch a fully digital immediate instalment credit product. Although the front-end customer interface and customer ownership are with ABN Amro, the backend system processes, validation and balance sheet risk are with solarisBank. The use of solarisBank's innovative credit scoring, video identification and digital signatory systems digitalized the entire application process, brought about significant value-add, and shortened the process to 7 minutes (Glass, 2018). Another successful use case is N26, a pan-European mobile bank. N26 undertook outsourcing with a cloud banking platform, Mambu, to achieve rapid scalability through Mambu's flexible core banking cloud solution. Migration to the vendor's systems eliminated significant operating costs, and gave N26 sufficient flexibility to quickly bring new services to the market in support of its growth strategy (Mayo, 2020).

2.2. *Outsourcing for financial services in the FinTech era*

Outsourcing in the financial services industry has evolved over time:

- In the 1960s–1970s, the banking industry gained traction on the undertaking of outsourcing for facilities management and IT support, especially with the evolution of modern day data processing from mainframe centralized computers to decentralized minicomputers, facilitating the advent of technology used in electronic fund transfers, real-time point of sale terminals and automated teller machines (ATM) (Cane, 1992).
- In the 1980s–1990s, high profile successes in Merrill Lynch (today known as Bank of America) and First Fidelity Bancorp, among others, in exploiting IT outsourcing captured the imagination of many FIs (Lacity and Hirschheim, 1993; Altinkemer *et al.*, 1994). Research solely attributable to financial services outsourcing began appearing. Among many researches, Huber (1993) shared a classic successful outsourcing case study of Continental Bank (today known as JP Morgan). McLellan *et al.* (1995) discussed financial and strategic motivations pertaining to IT outsourcing, citing case studies of seven banks, where research found profound effects on cost savings, and strategic benefits such as restructuring and mitigation of technology risk. Jennings (1996) explored outsourcing opportunities in six building societies, emphasizing the need to have a formal outsourcing policy guidance and asserted the strategic benefits of outsourcing, such as cost savings, enhanced flexibility, manufacturing and maintenance of wider product portfolio ranges, and improved innovation development. Most publications in this era did not distinguish between FIs and non-FIs; rather, FIs served as useful outsourcing case studies, upon which lessons of outsourcing can be generalized and learnt by other corporations.

- Since the 2000s, financial service-related outsourcing publications have become more diversified in nature as evidenced by the nature of the journals the papers are affiliated to, and the titles of the papers. This can be attributed to the increasing familiarity and maturity of financial services outsourcing, venturing into complex arrangements such as outsourcing coalitions (Beimborn, 2008); wide functional breadths, from internal audit (Caplan *et al.*, 2007), compliance (Duck, 2006), investment banking research (Grote and Täube, 2007), to asset management (FCA, 2013); and technology areas such as big data outsourcing (Austin and Bloggs, 2018) and cloud outsourcing (FCA, 2016; Hon and Millard, 2018a, 2018b; Cristanto *et al.*, 2018; Gozman and Willcocks, 2019; Scott *et al.*, 2019). A non-exhaustive high-level summary of the multi domain nature of recent publications is highlighted in Appendix Table A1. It is apparent that these research traverse across multiple fields, including business, finance, management, IT, engineering, and legal specific in nature to financial services. In addition, publications and guidelines from regulatory bodies (e.g., central banks), and standard boards (e.g., International Standards Organization (ISO)) help provide outsourcing guidance to navigate increasingly complex outsourcing activities. For instance, the 2014 issuance of ISO37500 Guidance on Outsourcing was borne from the collective voice of outsourcing practitioners who seek a standardization of outsourcing guidelines (ISO, 2014). Pertaining to financial services, BCBS (2018) highlighted the growing importance of regulatory bodies in outsourcing supervision.
- In the post-2014 FinTech era, (i) strategic management with an innovation focus; and (ii) FinTech-associated risks, have significantly impacted outsourcing in the financial services industry. Specifically:

  A. *Strategic Management with Innovation Focus*: In the financial services industry, strategic management of outsourcing, with a focus on innovation, have increased in prevalence (Brynjolfsson and McAfee, 2014).

Arguably, the current rate of change of FinTech innovation and adoption are more rapid as compared to previous decades. When comparing the time it took to adopt different financial innovations, the adoption of ATM spanned over three decades (1960s–1980s), whereas the maturity of cryptocurrency occurred over relatively shorter period (2008 until today). Driving such strategic management efforts are a generation of digital natives bringing about widespread change — changing customer behavioral patterns and changing demand for digital financial services. These innovations are bringing about new entrants such as BigTechs and FinTechs, and high level of collaborative innovativeness to stay ahead of the innovation curve. Increasingly, the innovation, use and delivery of FinTech disruptions stem from collaborative outsourcing relationships, benefiting all actors in the financial outsourcing value chain (BCBS, 2018).

Such outsourcing strategic management efforts have proved beneficial, helping put FIs, FinTechs and BigTechs in a sustainable leadership position. Successful organizations have lowered innovation costs and risks in the order of 60–90%, while leveraging the impact of internal investments and reduced experimental cycle times in the order of ten to hundreds of times (Quinn, 2000).

B. *Emergence of FinTech-associated Risks*: As more parties are involved in an outsourcing process, ambiguity on the responsibilities of the various actors in the value chain, can lead to operational incidents. Further, if controls fail to keep pace, the expansion of the number of innovative products and services from third parties can lead to increases in such operational complexity and risks. One critical challenge is how to effectively monitor operational and risk management activities that take place at third party service providers (BCBS, 2018).

Specifically, key FinTech-associated risks (BCBS, 2018) include:

- *Operational risks*: Legacy IT systems may be an encumbrance to changes associated with the outsourcing process. The use of a greater number of third parties through outsourcing may increase sophistication and lower the transparency of operations, such as the outsourcing of cloud services. Outsourcing risk would be especially notable if some or all of the services provided by third parties were to be dominated by globally active players, resulting in a risk concentration, especially if IT interdependencies are high. Further, if specialized FinTechs are the service providers, appropriate processes to conduct appropriate due diligence, contract management and ongoing control assurance and monitoring of operations will need to be considered in order to safeguard the regulated entity. The regulated entity's need to support a third-party service provider in financial duress may be required, as it may face a termination of critical services that are required for business as usual to continue.

- *Compliance risks*: Risks facing data security, privacy, money laundering, cyber-crime and customer protection needs to be managed. This is especially so if the regulated entity does not have required standards and controls to manage those risks in an outsourcing relationship. There are increasing difficulties in meeting compliance requirements, particularly with Anti-Money Laundering/Combating the Financing of Terrorism (AML/CFT) compliance. Appropriate AML/CFT processes will need to be in place. Else, a regulated entity may suffer from conduct risk where it may be held accountable for the actions of third-party service providers if a customer suffers loss or compliance requirements are not met. For instance, in certain regulatory regimes, it may be held responsible for the authentication of customers and the covering of fraudulent transactions. Further, risks of non-compliance with data privacy laws may rise with the development of data analytics and big data, as outsourcing relationships grow between FIs, BigTechs and FinTechs relating to the use of data to derive competitive advantage.
- *Cybersecurity risks*: Outsourcing cloud computing, APIs and other new technologies can facilitate increased interconnectivity, creating benefits for both financial service providers and consumers. However, if security controls are not in place, heavy reliance on such technologies can amplify security risks, exposing large volumes of sensitive data to potential breaches. Hence, the need to promote effective management and control of cybersecurity risk cannot be overemphasized.

The factors mentioned above, that is, (A) *strategic management with innovation focus* and (B) *emergence of FinTech-associated risks* highlight complexities of outsourcing in financial services. This results in the need to utilize an industry targeted outsourcing implementation approach.

2.3. *Outsourcing life cycle management and models*

In this section, we discuss the importance of outsourcing life cycle management and introduce key models used in outsourcing life cycle management.

Most procurement activities are transactional in nature, that is, one-off or commoditized purchase of products or services such as office supplies. In contrast, outsourcing activities are partnering or collaborative in nature — with the expectation that the contract and relationship may be reviewed and renewed at the end of each term in a long-term client-vendor contractual relationship. For the latter, a life cycle approach is recommended, with the expectancy that at the end of each term, considerable effort will be applied to study various options and select the appropriate path forward. Organizations that regularly engage in complicated outsourcing deals have wisely adopted life cycle management. This is an indication of maturity in outsourcing capability, typically exhibited in organizations with experience of second- or third-generation outsourcing deals (Babin and Quayle, 2016).

Lacity *et al.* (2010) studied over a thousand peer-reviewed publications from 20 years of outsourcing research. The authors found that positive outsourcing outcomes occurred only in 60% of the cases. This appeared to persist even as buyer organizations have, across the years, developed competencies to improve the value and reduce the risk of outsourcing processes. The use of an outsourcing life cycle provides for many benefits. Among other benefits, these include: (i) reduced risks from earlier identification of problems and remediation; (ii) predictability in the sequence of activities, staff and subject matter expert requirements, and funding requirements; and (iii) common outsourcing approach in planning, oversight and anticipation of the renewal phase of the life cycle, well in advance of the end of the contractual term (Babin and Quayle, 2016). However, challenges exist in the implementation of a life cycle model. These include: (i) additional costs that may be incurred in the rolling out of a life cycle model, as the governance overhead of managing a life cycle may be 4% of the contract value, or greater (Chou and Chou, 2009; Willcocks *et al.*, 2011); and (ii) the wish to retain flexibility in the application of unique life cycle models in line with risk tolerance and profit goals of the business unit (Sullivan, 2013).

Some comprehensive non-proprietary outsourcing life cycle models have been described in publicly available academic literature, and regional or international professional organizations, and standard bodies (Cullen *et al.*, 2006; Willcocks *et al.*, 2011; IAOP, 2008; ISO, 2014; NOA, 2012). In addition, outsourcing providers and advisory firms have created proprietary life cycle models for the consistent management of outsourcing processes. This chapter will discuss the former; the latter is outside of the scope of this chapter. Comprehensive non-proprietary outsourcing life cycle models include (Babin and Quayle, 2016):

- *ISO Standard 37500* (ISO, 2014): Recognizing the importance of outsourcing, the ISO developed a public domain outsourcing guide, ISO 37500. The ISO guide proposed a four-phase model, with outsourcing governance at the heart of the model. The first phase, or the Outsourcing Strategy Analysis phase, evaluates opportunities and initiates strategies. The second phase, or the Initiation and Selection phase, provides for requirement specification, vendor selection, and establishes agreements. The third phase, or the Transition phase, establishes the change management and governance process. The final phase, or the Deliver Value phase, examines the realization and sustenance of value for both the supplier and client. The ISO guide brings standardization of life cycle model by providing a detailed industry-independent guidance on outsourcing life cycle, processes and their outputs. The standard does not provide templates or examples, and is intended to serve as a generic guideline for organizational adoption.
- *Managing Outsourcing: The Life Cycle Imperative* (Cullen *et al.*, 2006): Outsourcing implementation life cycle stages are well conceived in Cullen *et al.* (2006) and expounded in Oshri *et al.* (2015). There are four phases in this industry-independent model.

The first phase, or the Architect phase, looks to assess expectations, intelligence and insights in relation to outsourcing, determine the best organizational candidates for outsourcing, identify and assess suitable outsourcing strategies, and design appropriate outsourcing blueprint and metrics. This stage lays the groundwork for the outsourcing venture. The second phase, or the Engage phase, involves due diligence and the selection of the most fitting supplier(s), and the negotiation and contracting of the outsourcing agreement(s). The third phase, or the Operate phase, looks at rolling out appropriate organizational transition strategies to handle the outsourced function(s), and the managing of the outsourcing administration and relationship(s). The final phase, or the Regenerate phase, looks at the review of outsourcing outcomes and considers future outsourcing requirements. Post-review stage, the life cycle stages may enter into a new loop of outsourcing life cycle stages, either with new or different set of vendor(s) and/or outsourced function(s), if required. The model does not provide templates or examples, and is intended to serve as a guideline for organizational adoption.

- *The Outsourcing Life Cycle* (NOA, 2012): The National Outsourcing Association (NOA) proposed an industry-independent four-stage model of 'strategic leadership, relationship engagement, transition and change, and relationship management' that recognizes proactive governance and relationship management as vital mechanisms throughout the life cycle to maintain alignment and growth in a successful outsourcing deal. In addition, the model emphasizes the importance of effective feedback loops so that outsourcing activities are aligned with organizational leadership and strategy. However, the model is short, both in terms of having a predefined sourcing strategy, and depth in end-of-contractual-term considerations.
- *Outsourcing Professional's Body of Knowledge* (IAOP, 2008): The International Association of Outsourcing Professionals (IAOP) life cycle model is an industry-independent five-phase model of 'idea, assessment, implementation, transition, and management'. The model defines the key questions, actors, deliverables and the approximate timeline for each phase. The IAOP life cycle lacks detailed discussion regarding end-of-contractual-term considerations, and is at a higher level of abstraction when

compared with Cullen *et al.* (2006) and ISO (2014). However, the model acts as a standard for individual practitioners and its templates provide 'how-to' toolkits for practitioners' hands on execution of outsourcing processes.

It is noted that there exist other life cycle models proposed in late 1990s and early 2000s, such as Klepper and Jones (1998) and GAO (2001), based upon limited use cases (Cullen *et al.*, 2006). These models are hence not discussed in the scope of the chapter.

3. Reimagining Outsourcing Life Cycle Management for Financial Services Outsourcing: Strategy-Risk Model

3.1. *Evaluation of existing models*

In the models discussed above, all models seek to provide comprehensive industry-independent coverage of life cycles. While the life cycle models discussed earlier are relatively comprehensive, factors such as (A) *strategic management with innovation focus* and (B) *emergence of FinTech-associated risks*, which are important and critical in financial services outsourcing, require further emphasis.

Risk management are discussed in all models, however, not in the specificity and depth that is relevant to the financial services industry, in the governance of regulated entities and the management of FinTech-associated risks.

In addition, only ISO (2014) emphasized outsourcing strategic management with innovation elements, relevant to the financial services industry as an increasingly important component of outsourcing life cycles.

A financial industry related-outsourcing life cycle model, considering the nuances of financial services outsourcing in the FinTech era, is presently lacking in academic literature and industry standard guidelines.

3.2. *Introducing the strategy-risk model*

Known as the Strategy-Risk outsourcing life cycle model, an end-to-end model which can be used as a guide by the financial services industry for outsourcing decisions in the FinTech era, with emphasis on (A) *strategic management with innovation focus* (Strategy elements) and (B) *emergence of FinTech-associated risks* (Risk elements), can be used. This model builds on the life cycle model proposed in Cullen *et al.* (2006).

Figure 1 outlines the Strategy-Risk model. The lower two quadrants of the model involve outward looking (external) outsourcing planning activities, such as the collection and assessment of market intelligence, due diligence of service providers and designing of outsourcing strategic frameworks. The upper two quadrants of the model involve inward looking (internal) outsourcing execution activities, such as risk governance, contract monitoring and performance measurement.

The start point of this model commences at SR1, the Investigate node. SR1 node entering the strategy loop is read on a counter-clockwise basis; SR1 node entering the risk loop is read on a clockwise basis. The nodes loop back to starting points SR1 and a sequential iterative feedback loop ensues.

Section 3.3 and Appendix Table A2, provides details to Figure 1, by expounding on the stages of a first pass of this framework, the type of driving questions to ask for each stage (or leading driving question(s)), and the activities that can be undertaken for each stage (or leading activities). Note that the leading questions and activities are guidelines, and are by no means exhaustive in the actual implementation of the framework.

Actual implementation should be undertaken with discretion, fitting to the unique scenarios of the outsourcing situation.

Further, the Risk-Strategy model shall be read from a sequential perspective. As outsourcing contracts are typically long-term client-vendor contractual relationships, there is an expectation that the contract and relationship may be reviewed and renewed at the end of each term. The first engagement of an outsourcing partnership will be considered the 'first pass' of the Strategy-Risk model; the first renewal of this outsourcing engagement will be considered the 'second pass'; and so on.

In addition, progression across the outsourcing stages is an iterative process. This means that, if there is a need to review approaches in earlier stages, an organization can revisit earlier stages to improve the desired outcomes of outsourcing.

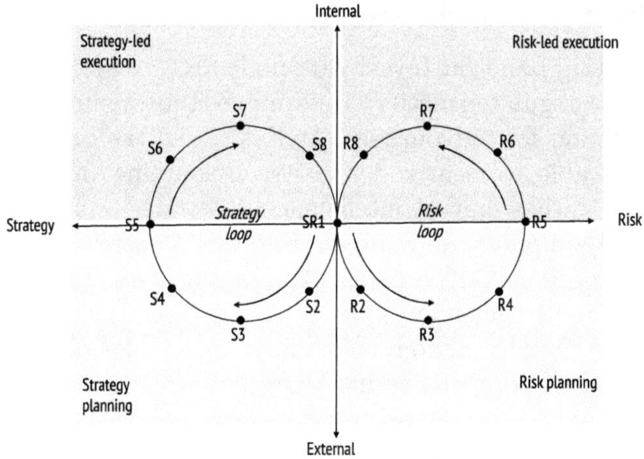

Node	Starting point	Description
SR1	Investigate	• Identify problem statement • Understand market

Node	Strategy stage	Description
S2	Opportunity	• Identify opportunity for organizational improvement
S3	Planning	• Undertake feasibility study • Define strategy
S4	Design	• Design outsourcing deal configuration
S5	Engage	• Negotiation • Contracting
S6	Monitor	• Undertake contract management
S7	Feedback	• Undertake performance measurement
S8	Innovation	• Measure value creation through innovation

Node	Risk stage	Description
R2	Relationship	• Identify stakeholders • Manage relationship dynamics
R3	Review	• Undertake due diligence
R4	Systemic Controls	• Control for organizational and industry level risk
R5	Idiosyncratic Controls	• Control for outsourced function and contract level risk

Node	Risk stage	Description
R6	Governance	• Establish guidelines for outsourcing risk management framework and governance structure
R7	Monitor	• Establish guidelines for business continuity planning (BCP) • Establish guidelines for multi-vendor monitoring • Establish guidelines for change management
R8	Feedback	• Risk audit • Regulatory compliance

Figure 1. Strategy-risk outsourcing model.

3.3. *First pass of the strategy-risk model*

At the starting point, at Investigate node SR1, the outsourcing organization (or regulated entity) determines the organizational needs and motivation for outsourcing. At this stage, the organization will need to be able to clearly define its outsourcing business requirements, and gather market intelligence on related FinTech outsourcing, related suppliers, and similar FinTech outsourcing decisions in peer organizations (Cullen *et al.*, 2005; Lacity *et al.*, 2009; Oshri *et al.*, 2015). The tools that may be used at this stage include value chain analysis and deconstruction, augmented with stakeholder interviews, and market and competitive intelligence.

3.3.1. *Stages of the strategy loop*

At the strategy loop, post Investigate node SR1, at Opportunity node S2, the outsourcing organization identifies and evaluates FinTech outsourcing opportunities for organizational improvement, such as cost reduction, operational flexibility, increased security, operational resilience, strategic growth, and/or innovation (BCBS, 2018; Lacity *et al.*, 2009). The tools that may be used at this stage include value chain and need-gap analysis, SWOT and PESTLE analysis, activity mapping, VRIO model and core competency analysis, competitor analysis, benchmarking, process improvement models, such as business process reengineering and Kanban, and innovation practices, such as design thinking, technology brokering and blue ocean strategy.

At Planning node S3, the outsourcing organization undertakes feasibility studies, defines the outsourcing strategy, and formulates the innovation practices. At this stage, the outsourcing organization develops a corporate strategy to demonstrate how FinTech outsourcing generates value, designs a detailed outsourcing life-cycle program, prepares the life-cycle communications strategy, and prepares the business case rules and the base case scenarios. In addition, the outsourcing organization may formulate an organizational innovation framework, design proactive and scalable innovation processes where innovation investments are made ahead of customer needs, and design appropriate innovation engagement methods with outsourcing partners, such as the use of agile methods (Babin, 2011; Oshri and Kotlarsky, 2011; Oshri, 2014; Oshri *et al.*, 2015). The tools that may be used at this stage include feasibility study, ROI analysis, including economic and customer value considerations, and journey mapping.

At Design node S4, the outsourcing organization designs the outsourcing deal configuration. At this stage, the outsourcing organization prepares the commercial and operating blueprint for the FinTech outsourcing project, develops balanced score metrics (including FinTech innovation measurement), drafts the service agreement and the price and contract framework, and designs the interparty relationship, the retained organization and the contract governance function (Babin, 2011; Oshri and Kotlarsky, 2011; Oshri, 2014; Oshri *et al.*, 2015). The tools that may be used at this stage include the balanced scorecard, service level agreement (SLA), and the contract and governance framework.

At Engage node S5, the outsourcing organization negotiates and contracts with the selected FinTech service provider. At this stage, the outsourcing relationships are governed by explicit and enforceable written contracts. Such contracts clearly define what activities are going to be outsourced, including appropriate service and performance levels. Contracts should neither prevent nor impede the regulated entity from meeting its respective regulatory obligations, nor the regulator from exercising its regulatory powers. Contracts should include termination clause and minimum periods to execute a termination provision, to allow the outsourced FinTech services to be transferred to another third-party service provider or to be incorporated into the regulated entity. Material issues unique to the outsourcing arrangement should be meaningfully addressed such as choice-of-law or jurisdictional provisions for adjudication of disputes. Contracts should include, where appropriate, conditions of subcontracting by the third-party service provider for all or part of an outsourced activity, with the approval of the regulated entity (BCBS, 2005). The tools that may be used at this stage include market intelligence, and outsourcing agreements, such as SLA and operational level agreement (OLA).

At Monitor node S6, the outsourcing organization undertakes contract management. At this stage, there should be close monitoring of the performance of the outsourcing service providers, including periodic working-level meetings with both the end-user groups and the supplier to review the supplier's performance. The outsourcing organization should work with thc supplier to redefine service levels as appropriate. There should be considerations for transformational outsourcing management, by developing client-provider commitment, investing in and monitoring the relationship, using diligent documentation and administration, information exchange and coordination (GAO, 2001; FDIC, 2014; Mani *et al.*, 2006). In addition, the client-provider leadership should demonstrate the following behavior: focusing on the future, transparency, problem solving, outcome-driven, spirit of togetherness, exhibit clout within own organization, swift removal of obstructions, trustworthiness, effective performance and positive chemistry (Willcocks *et al.*, 2013). The tool that may be used at this stage includes an outsourcing governance framework.

At Feedback node S7, the outsourcing organization undertakes performance measurement. At this stage, the outsourcing organization periodically undertakes studies to assess the supplier's performance, and each metric measured should logically support a requirement that is linked to a strategic goal (FFIEC, 2004; Oshri *et al.*, 2015). The tools that may be used at this stage include internal or external audit program, balanced scorecard, management report card, and need-gap analysis.

At Innovation node S8, the outsourcing organization measures value creation through innovation. For incremental innovation, at the operational and strategic level, the outsourcing organization should have developed clear measurement instruments as reference points to evaluate whether its incremental innovation targets have been met. For radical innovation, the client firm should seek both qualitative and quantitative inputs regarding performance. In terms of qualitative feedback, inputs regarding the quality of radical innovation can include periodical surveys (Oshri and Kotlarsky, 2011; Oshri, 2014). The tools that may be used at this stage include innovation audit, three horizons model, ROI analysis, benchmarking, surveys and interviews.

3.3.2. *Stages of the risk loop*

At the risk loop, post Investigate node SR1, at Relationship node R2, the outsourcing organization will need to establish who the key stakeholders are for the candidate outsourcing activities, and the stakeholders' respective aspirations and routines. It is important to understand the relationship dynamics, and figure out if there are any cultural gaps that needs to be bridged (Cullen *et al.*, 2005; Oshri *et al.*, 2015). The tools that may be used at this stage include stakeholder mapping and stakeholder interviews.

At Review node R3, the outsourcing organization will be required to conduct the relevant outsourcing due diligence. At this stage, the outsourcing organization ascertains if the FinTech service provider is qualified with the requisite domain knowledge and resources to meet the objectives of the regulated entity in the specified outsourcing activity.

It will be essential that the service provider exhibits low risk to fulfill its obligations, in particular to factors including: strength of financial condition, turnover of management and employees, ability to maintain business continuity, ability to provide accurate, relevant, and timely Management Information Systems (MIS), experience with the function outsourced, reliance on subcontractors, location (particularly if cross-border), and redundancy and reliability of communication lines. Moreover, the service provider's intangible strengths, such as their service philosophies, quality initiatives, management style, and values, should fit those of the outsourcing organization (FFIEC, 2004; BCBS, 2005). The tools that may be used at this stage include Request for Information (RFI), Request for Proposal (RFP), Request for Quotation (RFQ), Statement of Works, service providers' presentations and interviews, and market intelligence and benchmarking reports.

At Systemic Controls node R4, the outsourcing organization looks to control its organizational and industry level risk exposure. At this stage, the outsourcing organization checks if there are appropriate considerations and measures regarding risks impacting the consumers of FinTech products or services, including, data privacy, data security, continuity of financial services and the use of appropriate marketing practices. It is also appropriate to consider risk factors such as strategic and profitability risks, cyber risk, operational risk, compliance risk, money laundering risk, and liquidity risk and funding sources (BCBS, 2018). The tools that may be used at this stage include value chain analysis, scenario planning, and real options analysis.

At Idiosyncratic Controls node R5, the outsourcing organization looks to control its outsourced function and contract level risk. In terms of the outsourced function, it will be useful to understand the sensitivity of data accessed, protected, or controlled by the service provider, the volume of transactions, and its criticality to the outsourcing organization's business. In terms of risks impacting FinTech, it will be useful to understand the reliability and security of the FinTech products or services, the scalability to accommodate FinTech growth, and whether if intellectual property risk can occur. In terms of the contracted outsourcing performance, it will be useful to consider concentration risk — especially prominent if some part of the services provided by FinTech providers were to become dominated by globally active players, and/or the risk of outsourcing multiple activities exist to the same service provider. In addition, solvency risk should be considered. This is prominent if specialized young FinTechs are service providers (FFIEC, 2004; BCBS, 2018). Similarly, the tools that may be used at this stage include value chain analysis, scenario planning, and real options analysis.

At Governance node R6, the outsourcing organization establishes guidelines for outsourcing risk management framework and the outsourcing governance structure. These can include setting appropriate risk appetite and tolerance with effective thresholds to trigger prompt remedial action, identifying and assessing risks at the launch of every product, activity, process and system to ensure the timely and overarching mitigation of risks in the approval, launch and delivery of processes and systems, and appropriate exit strategies, including the maintenance of skills and expertise in-house so that outsourced functions can be taken back by the regulated firm or substituted in an orderly manner, if required (FFIEC, 2004; BCBS, 2018). The tools that may be used at this stage include risk management framework, SLA, and OLA.

At Monitor node R7, the outsourcing organization establishes guidelines for business continuity planning (BCP), multi-vendor monitoring (if any), and change management. In terms of BCP, the outsourcing organization should regularly review the BCP of the FinTech service provider to ensure any services considered 'mission critical' for the outsourcing organization could be restored within an acceptable timeframe, and the service provider's program for contingency plan testing (FFIEC, 2004). In terms of change management, an appropriate strategy should be devised comprising a transition plan, disruption minimization strategy, communication strategy, staffing arrangement, and mobilized resources, among others (Oshri *et al.*, 2015), The tools that may be used at this stage include the BCP program, OLA, transition program, and the Kotter change model.

At Feedback node R8, the outsourcing organization performs and assesses risk audit and regulatory compliance. For instance, the outsourcing organization may measure the FinTech service activity results against defined service levels, and stress test processes and technologies for day-to-day resiliency and efficacy of mission-critical functions (CBI, 2018; FDIC, 2014). The tools that may be used at this stage include internal and/or external audit programs and compliance programs.

At the end of the first round of the outsourcing contractual relationship, the organization may cease the outsourcing arrangement. In an event the outsourcing relationship is extended and renewed, we will enter a subsequent pass of the Strategy-Risk model. This will be elaborated in the next section.

3.4. *Subsequent pass of the strategy-risk model*

At the renewal phase for the outsourcing relationship, the outsourcing organization enters a new round of strategy and risk loops for the Strategy-Risk model.

At Investigate node SR1, the outsourcing organization may investigate the insights gleaned from risk audit (risk loop), and/or the insights gleaned from performance measurement and innovation (strategy loop), after the first round of working relationship with the service provider.

In the new round, at the strategy loop, at Opportunity node S2, organizations may be looking into new opportunities for organizational improvement, such as cost reduction, operational flexibility, increased security, operational resilience, strategic growth and innovation. In the subsequent stage, at Planning node S3, organizations may determine if there are appropriate design of the outsourcing policies to capture the outsourcing opportunity identified at Opportunity node S2.

In the new round, at the risk loop, at Relationship node R2, organizations may be looking into client-provider relationship management issues (e.g., when client and/or provider's staffing changes), and the tackling of contract variations and disputes, if any.

Consequently, while undertaking risk review and due diligence, at Review node R3 organizations may determine if the service provider is qualified with adequate resources to perform the outsourcing work.

The outsourcing organization continues to review and monitor the outsourcing relationship in this renewal round, in an iterative sequential manner into the subsequent stages of the strategy and risk loops.

3.5. *Cross-looping of the strategy-risk model*

In some cases, the loop may cross, such that an organization at Feedback node R8 of the risk loop can enter the strategic loop at Opportunity node S2, via Investigate node SR1. In addition, organizations at Innovation node S8 in the strategy loop can enter the risk loop at Relationship node R2, via Investigate node SR1.

The progression of stages in the Strategy-Risk model, by exiting a strategy loop and entering a risk loop, or vice versa, is termed as cross-looping. An illustration of cross-loop can be seen in Figure 2.

For instance, an invoked performance measurement penalty at Feedback node S7 of the strategy loop, may lead to a re-evaluation of the value derived from the outsourcing contract at Investigate node SR1, and trigger downstream reactions in the form of a dispute resolution in Relationship node R2 and contract review in Review node R3 of the risk loop. Less unfavorable resolutions may also lead to tighter risk controls, governance structures, closer monitoring and stringent audit and compliance checks. However, an untenable negative outcome from these node pass-throughs may lead to a termination of the contractual agreement, and consequently terminate the Strategy-Risk outsourcing model process.

In another instance, a risk audit finding at Feedback node R8 of the risk loop may identify a potential business process reengineering opportunity that may be resolved for organizational improvement. This opportunity may be a potential IT outsourcing project that can be assessed in Opportunity node S2 of the strategy loop. This reengineering opportunity, if ascertained to pass the feasibility and impact analysis in Planning node S3, can kickstart a fresh Strategy-Risk outsourcing model process.

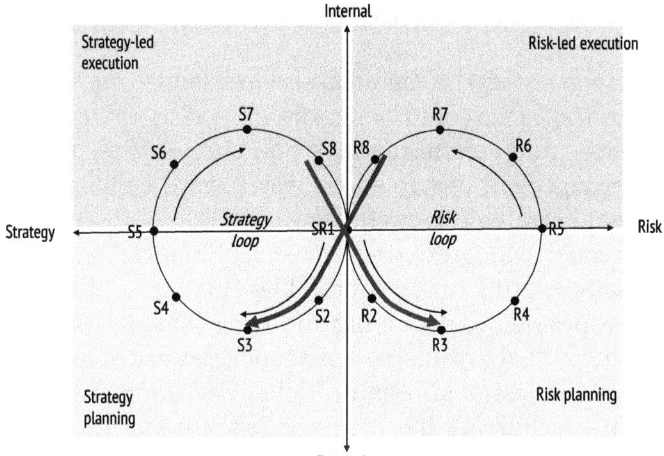

Node	Strategy stage	Description

Node	Starting point	Description
SR1	Investigate	• Identify problem statement • Understand market

Node	Strategy stage	Description
S2	Opportunity	• Identify opportunity for organizational improvement
S3	Planning	• Undertake feasibility study • Define strategy
S4	Design	• Design outsourcing deal configuration
S5	Engage	• Negotiation • Contracting
S6	Monitor	• Undertake contract management
S7	Feedback	• Undertake performance measurement
S8	Innovation	• Measure value creation through innovation

Node	Risk stage	Description
R2	Relationship	• Identify stakeholders • Manage relationship dynamics
R3	Review	• Undertake due diligence
R4	Systemic Controls	• Control for organizational and industry level risk
R5	Idiosyncratic Controls	• Control for outsourced function and contract level risk

Node	Risk stage	Description
R6	Governance	• Establish guidelines for outsourcing risk management framework and governance structure
R7	Monitor	• Establish guidelines for business continuity planning (BCP) • Establish guidelines for multi-vendor monitoring • Establish guidelines for change management
R8	Feedback	• Risk audit • Regulatory compliance

Figure 2. Cross-looping in strategy-risk outsourcing model.

4. Conclusion and Future Work

In the FinTech era in the financial services landscape, staying ahead of the innovation curve and being disciplined at enhancing core service offerings entail careful resource planning. A well-structured outsourcing arrangement can go a long way toward enhancing long term organizational strategic growth.

This chapter evaluates outsourcing for financial services, specifically in the post-2014 FinTech era. The chapter studies comprehensive non-proprietary outsourcing life cycle models that have been described in publicly available academic literature, and regional or international professional organizations, and standard bodies. Publications on outsourcing life cycle models are sparse. Many organizations are careful and reluctant to reveal outsourcing successes and failure drivers, as well as the incremental cost savings and revenue attained (Babin and Quayle, 2016). While the models studied in this chapter are relatively comprehensive, factors such as (A) *strategic management with innovation focus*; and (B) *emergence of FinTech-associated risks*, which are important and critical in financial services outsourcing, are lacking in emphasis.

This chapter looks at an elegant and simple-to-use end-to-end model which can be utilized as a guide by the financial services industry for outsourcing decisions. With emphasis on the two aforementioned factors (A) *strategic management with innovation focus* (Strategy elements); and (B) *emergence of FinTech-associated risks* (Risk elements), this model, building upon the life cycle model proposed in Cullen *et al.* (2006), is summarily known as the Strategy-Risk outsourcing life cycle model. This model proposed is a two-loop model. The strategy loop looks at, for instance, evaluating outsourcing innovation opportunities assessing market intelligence, and measuring outsourcing performance. The risk loop involves, for instance, due diligence of service providers, risk governance, and contract monitoring. The model is designed with particular relevance to outsourcing in financial services.

Actual implementation should be undertaken with discretion, fitting to the unique scenarios of the outsourcing situation. The model is sequential, as outsourcing contracts are typically long-term multi-period client-vendor contractual relationships, with the expectation that the contract and relationship may be reviewed and renewed at the end of each term. Further, progression across the outsourcing stages is an iterative process. This means that, if there is a need to review approaches in earlier stages, an organization can revisit earlier stages to improve the desired outcomes of outsourcing. The chapter also describes a cross-looping phenomenon, which allows, for instance, risk review events that arise from the risk loop to have strategic outcomes (e.g., process gap problem leading to a business reengineering opportunity), and strategic review events in the strategy loop to have risk consequences (e.g., poor performance appraisal leading to tightening of governance controls). This phenomenon provides a close mirroring of real-life outsourcing implementations.

The chapter analyzed the shortcomings of existing models and proposes a generalizable model. Limitations of this model include the possibility that evolution of this model may be required to contextualize the model to specific industry user groups or to environment changes. Future research may involve the examination of external validity:

(i) How different sub-industry groups in the financial services landscape, such as banks, hedge funds, insurance companies, and stock exchanges, can leverage on the Strategy-Risk life cycle model to provide value creation and reduce failures, through use cases and surveys.
(ii) How the model remains viable with passage of time.
(iii) How the model remains viable to specific cultural settings and regulatory jurisdictions, such as Islamic finance, in view of enhancing outsourcing outcomes.

Further, it may be worthwhile to explore variations of the Strategy-Risk model which may benefit organizations from different industries with critical risk elements and strategic focuses on innovation, such as Healthcare and MedTech.

An outsourcing partnership is successful when both vendors and clients achieve their objectives. How this success can be achieved, if well-coordinated, can lead to highly successful outcomes. FinTech and the associated risks are here to stay. Recognizing how FinTech is changing the financial services landscape and having a clear awareness of the power of outsourcing, can bring about positive giant leaps in organizations leveraging on outsourcing for growth.

Appendix

Table A1. Diversity of financial services-related outsourcing publications since 2000.

No.	Publication type	Publication author and year	Research topic
1	Business/Finance/ Management*	Beimborn (2008)	Outsourcing coalitions in banking
2	Business/Finance/ Management*	Gonzalez *et al.* (2013)	IT outsourcing in financial services
3	Business Finance/ Management*	Grote and Täube (2007)	Outsourcing pertaining to investment bank research
4	Business/Finance/ Management*	Gozman and Willcocks (2019)	Understanding outsourcing risks posed by cloud-based FinTechs
5	Business/Finance/ Management*	Clark and Monk (2013)	Insourcing, outsourcing and offshoring in FIs
6	Business/Finance/ Management*	Klus *et al.* (2019)	Motivations of outsourcing by banks and FinTechs
7	Business/Finance/ Management*	Cox and Pilbauer (2018)	Outsourcing critical financial system operations
8	Business/Finance/ Management*	Currie *et al.* (2008)	Knowledge process outsourcing in financial services
9	Business/Finance/ Management*	Caplan *et al.* (2007)	Outsourcing of internal audit function
10	Business/Finance/ Management*	Lacity *et al.* (2004)	Outsourcing of back office operations
11	Business/Finance/ Management*	Scott *et al.* (2019)	Outsourcing of cloud services in financial services
12	Business/Finance/ Management*	Folwarski (2019)	Challenges of central banks as regulators to the development of the FinTech sector
13	Information Systems/IT/ Engineering*	Gewald and Dibbern (2009)	Business process outsourcing in financial services
14	Information Systems/IT/ Engineering*	Gewald and Franke (2007)	Business process outsourcing in financial services
15	Information Systems/IT/ Engineering*	Zhu *et al.* (2017)	Outsourcing operations in banking

Table A1. (*Continued*)

No.	Publication type	Publication author and year	Research topic
16	Information Systems/IT/ Engineering*	Gutierrez and Dyson (2009)	Organizational change in IT outsourcing in banking
17	Information Systems/IT/ Engineering*	Dayasindhu (2004)	IT outsourcing in a mortgage bank
18	Information Systems/IT/ Engineering*	Smojver and Blažeković (2015)	Country-specific outsourcing of banking activities: Croatia
19	Information Systems/IT/ Engineering*	Gulla and Gupta (2012)	Country-specific outsourcing of banking activities: India
20	Information Systems/IT/ Engineering*	McCahery and de Roode (2018)	Country-specific offshoring of banking activities: Singapore
21	Information Systems/IT/ Engineering*	Tas and Sunder (2004)	Business process outsourcing in financial services
22	Information Systems/IT/ Engineering*	Braun and Winter (2005)	Classification of outsourcing phenomena in financial services
23	Information Systems/IT/ Engineering*	Austin and Bloggs (2018)	Big data outsourcing and identity verification in FinTech credit assessment
24	Legal*	Duck (2006)	Outsourcing pertaining to compliance functions of investment firms
25	Legal*	McCormack (2003)	Regulatory outsourcing policy on FIs
26	Legal*	Ozeke (2008)	Country-specific outsourcing of banking activities: Turkey
27	Legal*	Kaźmierczyk and Macholak (2014)	Country-specific outsourcing of banking activities: Poland
28	Legal*	Singh (2005)	Regulatory outsourcing policy on FIs
29	Legal*	Hon and Millard (2018a)	Outsourcing of cloud services in financial services
30	Legal*	Hon and Millard (2018b)	Outsourcing of cloud services in financial services
31	Regulator Guideline	FCA (2016)	Outsourcing pertaining to cloud and other third-party IT services by FIs

(*Continued*)

Table A1. (*Continued*)

No.	Publication type	Publication author and year	Research topic
32	Regulator Guideline	Federal Reserve (2013)	Managing outsourcing risks by FIs
33	Regulator Guideline	BCBS (2011)	Managing operational risk in outsourcing in financial services
34	Regulator Guideline	FCA (2013)	Outsourcing pertaining to asset management
35	Regulator Guideline	FFIEC (2003)	Managing outsourcing risks by FIs
36	Regulator Guideline	FDIC (2014)	Managing technology providers' performance risk by FIs
37	Regulator Guideline	CFPB (2016)	Outsourcing in compliance with federal consumer financial law
38	Regulator Guideline	OSFI (2010)	Managing outsourcing risks by FIs
39	Supervisory Body Publication	Konschalla (2013)	Comparative study of banking outsourcing
40	Supervisory Body Publication	Cristanto *et al.* (2018)	Regulating cloud outsourcing for insurance companies
41	Supervisory Body Publication	Ng (2007)	Regulatory outsourcing policy on FIs
42	Supervisory Body Publication	CBI (2018)	Regulatory outsourcing policy on FIs

Note: *Journal, Conference, Symposium, Book.

Table A2. Guidelines for strategy-risk outsourcing life cycle model.

Node	Stage (first pass)	Description	Leading driving question(s)	Leading activities
R1, S1	Investigate	1. Identify problem statement 2. Understand market	1. What are the organizational needs for outsourcing? What is the motivation for outsourcing? 2. Is the organization able to clearly define its outsourcing business requirements? 3. What is the market intelligence on related outsourcing, related suppliers, and similar outsourcing decisions in peer organizations? (Cullen *et al.*, 2005; Lacity *et al.*, 2009; Oshri *et al.*, 2015)	1. Value chain analysis and deconstruction 2. Stakeholder interviews 3. Market and competitive intelligence
R2	Relationship	1. Identify stakeholders 2. Manage relationship dynamics	1. Who are the key stakeholders? What are their aspirations and routines? 2. What are the relationship dynamics? Are there any cultural gaps that needs to be bridged? (Cullen *et al.*, 2005; Oshri *et al.*, 2015)	1. Stakeholder mapping 2. Stakeholder interviews
R3	Review	1. Undertake due diligence	1. Is the FinTech service provider qualified with domain knowledge and experience, with adequate resources to perform the outsourcing work? 2. Does the service provider understand and can meet the objectives of the regulated entity in the specified activity? 3. Does the service provider exhibit low risk to fulfill its obligations, in particular to factors including: strength of financial condition, turnover of management and employees, ability to maintain business continuity, ability to provide accurate, relevant, and timely Management Information Systems (MIS), experience with the function outsourced, reliance on subcontractors, location (particularly if cross-border), and redundancy and reliability of communication lines?	1. Request for information (RFI) 2. Request for proposal (RFP) 3. Request for quote (RFQ) 4. Statement of Works 5. Market intelligence 6. Benchmarking

(*Continued*)

Table A2. (*Continued*)

Node	Stage (first pass)	Description	Leading driving question(s)	Leading activities
			4. For servicing geographically dispersed activities, can the like-service be met by using third parties with similar reach or capability? 5. What is the economic, legal and political conditions that might adversely impact the service provider's ability to perform effectively for the regulated entity. 6. What is the provider's intangible strengths, such as their service philosophies, quality initiatives, management style and values? Do they fit those of the outsourcing organization? 7. Will the outsourcing agreement be an arms-length transaction? (FFIEC, 2004; BCBS, 2005)	
R4	Systemic Controls	1. Control for organizational and industry level risk	1. Are there appropriate considerations and measures regarding risks impacting the consumers of financial products or services, including: A. Data privacy, data security B. Discontinuity of financial service C. Appropriate marketing practices 2. Are there appropriate considerations and measures regarding risks impacting the financial services sector, including: A. Strategic and profitability risks B. Cyber risk C. Operational risk — institutional and systemic D. Compliance risk — including consumer and data protection regulation E. Money laundering — terrorism financing risk F. Liquidity risk and funding sources (BCBS, 2018)	1. Value chain analysis 2. Scenario planning 3 Real options analysis

R5	Idiosyncratic Controls	1. Control for outsourced function and contract level risk	1. Are there appropriate considerations and measures regarding risks impacting the outsourced function, including: A. Sensitivity of data accessed, protected, or controlled by the service provider B. Volume of transactions C. Criticality to the outsourcing organization's business 1. Are there appropriate considerations and measures regarding risks impacting financial technology, including: A. Reliability of FinTech products or services B. Security of FinTech products or services C. Scalability to accommodate FinTech growth D. Intellectual property risk 2. Are there appropriate considerations and measures regarding risks impacting contracted outsourcing performance, including: A. Concentration risk — prominent if some part of the services provided by FinTech providers were to become dominated by globally active players, and/or outsourcing multiple activities to the same service provider. B. Solvency risk — prominent if specialized young FinTech companies are service providers. (FFIEC, 2004; BCBS, 2018)	1. Value chain analysis 2. Scenario planning 3. Real options analysis

(*Continued*)

Table A2. (*Continued*)

Node	Stage (first pass)	Description	Leading driving question(s)	Leading activities
R6	Governance	1. Establish guidelines for outsourcing risk management framework and governance structure	1. Is the risk management framework capturing the following aspects: A. Ensuring integrated risk culture shared throughout outsourcing supply chain. B. Setting and implementing the policies, processes and systems to control risks to ensure prompt reporting, assessment and early risk mitigation for FinTech-driven risks. C. Setting appropriate risk appetite and tolerance with effective thresholds to trigger prompt remedial action using Key Risk Indicators (KRI). D. Identifying/assessing risks in all processes and systems to enhance capacity to identify, assess and mitigate risks arising from extended processes and systems in FinTech migrations. E. Assessing risks in the launch of every product, activity, process and system to ensure the timely and overarching identification, assessment of risks in the approval, launch and delivery of FinTech-driven processes and systems. F. Appropriate risk monitoring and proactive risk management to update the frequency of monitoring and reporting with appropriate escalation according to the size and nature of the risks. G. Setting 'criticality and importance of service methodology that can be applied consistently across all outsourcing decisions and is in line with relevant sectoral regulations and guidance, assessed on an ongoing basis.	1. Risk management framework 2. Service level agreement (SLA) 3. Operational level agreement (OLA)

H. Incorporating business continuity and disaster recovery plan with business disruption scenarios in FinTech-driven processes and systems.
I. Informing stakeholders of changes in banks' risk management processes and practices that reflect changes in risk profile driven by FinTech developments.
J. Adequacy of a service provider's internal and security controls, including the practicality of the service provider having an internal auditor, and the auditor's level of training and experience; service providers external auditors' training and background; and internal IT audit techniques of the service provider.
K. Appropriate exit strategies, including the maintenance of skills and expertise in-house so that functions can be taken back by the regulated firm or substituted in an orderly manner, if required.

2. Is there a SLA established to address the following issues:

A. Availability and timeliness of services; confidentiality and integrity of data; change control; security standards compliance, including vulnerability and penetration management; business continuity compliance; and help desk support.
B. SLA program and monitoring process; accountability; recourse process for non-performance; escalation process; dispute resolution process; and termination process. (FFIEC, 2004; BCBS, 2018)

(Continued)

Table A2. (*Continued*)

Node	Stage (first pass)	Description	Leading driving question(s)	Leading activities
R7	Monitor	1. Establish guidelines for business continuity planning (BCP) 2. Establish guidelines for multi-vendor monitoring 3. Establish guidelines for change management	1. Does the outsourcing organization's BCP comprise: A. Ongoing and effective business continuity and information security monitoring programs. B. Effectively management of multiple service provider relationships. C. Assessing, monitoring, and effectively controlling cross-border risks when foreign FinTech service providers are used. D. Regularly review the BCP of the FinTech service provider to ensure any services considered 'mission critical' for the outsourcing organization could be restored within an acceptable timeframe. E. Review the service provider's program for contingency plan testing. For critical services, annual or more frequent tests of the contingency plan are required. F. Assess service provider/vendor interdependencies for mission critical services and applications. 2. In a multiple supplier relationship, is the outsourcing organization monitoring the control environment through: A. Use of operational agreements between each of the service providers or stand-alone contracts. B. Use of lead service provider, who has a contractual obligation to notify the financial institution of any concerns (controls/performance) associated with any of its outsourced activities.	1. BCP program 2. Operational level agreement (OLA) 3. Transition program 4. Kotter change model

			3. Does the outsourcing organization's change management strategy comprise: A. Transition plan, disruption minimization strategy, communication strategy, staffing arrangement (transfer, redundancy, redeployment), management function (retained organization), mobilized resources (allocated training and responsibilities for transition and operational teams). (FFIEC, 2004; Oshri *et al.*, 2015)	
R8	Feedback	1. Risk audit 2. Regulatory compliance	1. Are audit and compliance procedures appropriately executed? A. Measure service activity results against defined service levels; examine measured results to identify problems and determine causes; take appropriate action to correct failed activities, functions, and/or processes; continuously guide service providers through feedback sessions based on objectively measured performance metrics. B. Test, including stress testing, of processes and technologies for day-to-day resiliency and efficacy of mission-critical functions. C. Processes for monitoring and reviewing present and new products, services or delivery channels for compliance with applicable regulatory requirements, including, as appropriate, those related to consumer protection, data protection and anti-money laundering and countering the financing of terrorism (AML/CFT). D. Ensure that for regulated firms that outsource the operational tasks of internal control functions for the monitoring and auditing of outsourcing arrangements, ensure the operational tasks are effectively performed, including receiving appropriate reports, and exercise appropriate oversight and are able to manage the risks that are created by outsourcing arrangements. (CBI, 2018; FDIC, 2014)	1. Internal/external audit program 2. Compliance program

(*Continued*)

Table A2. (*Continued*)

Node	Stage (first pass)	Description	Leading driving question(s)	Leading activities
S2	Opportunity	1. Identify opportunity for organizational improvement	1. Are there opportunities for organizational improvement through: A. Cost reduction B. Operational flexibility C. Increased security D. Operational resilience E. Strategic growth F. Innovation (BCBS, 2018; Lacity *et al.*, 2009)	1. Value chain and need-gap analysis 2. SWOT and PESTLE analysis 3. Activity map, VRIO model and core competency analysis 4. Competitor analysis, benchmarking 5. Process improvement models, e.g., business process reengineering, Kanban 6. Innovation practices, e.g., design thinking, technology brokering, blue ocean strategy

S3	Planning	1. Undertake feasibility study 2. Define strategy 3. Formulate innovation practices	1. Are there appropriate planning that will enable effective decision-making for the FinTech outsourcing process: A. Develop a corporate strategy to demonstrate how outsourcing as a management tool generates value. B. Design the detailed outsourcing life-cycle program C. Prepare the life-cycle communications strategy. D. Prepare the business case rules and the base case. E. Assess the feasibility and impact of the outsourcing on the organization. F. Strategize and assess suppliers' innovation capability. 2. Are there appropriate innovation practices in the organization to prioritize innovation: A. Formulate organizational innovation framework, e.g., bespoke design thinking. B. Design proactive and scalable innovation processes where innovation investments are made ahead of customer needs, and there are continuous and streamlined upgrading of digital capabilities. C. Design appropriate innovation engagement methods with outsourcing partners, e.g., agile. (Babin, 2011; Oshri and Kotlarsky, 2011; Oshri, 2014; Oshri *et al.*, 2015)	1. Feasibility study 2. ROI analysis, including economic and customer value considerations 3. Journey map

(*Continued*)

Table A2. (*Continued*)

Node	Stage (first pass)	Description	Leading driving question(s)	Leading activities
S4	Design	1. Design outsourcing deal configuration	1. Are there appropriate design of the FinTech outsourcing policies: A. Design corporate policies, guidelines and governance model for the use and maintenance of outsourcing as an effective management tool. B. Prepare the commercial and operating blueprint for the outsourcing project. C. Draw up innovation methodology: agree on the definition of innovation, defining a scope of the innovation project, deciding on key areas (themes) to focus on, developing an action plan for each innovation project and deciding on the governance process of the innovation program. D. Develop balanced score metrics, including innovation measurement. E. Draft the service agreement and the price and contract framework. F. Design the interparty relationship (structure, roles, authorities, etc.), the retained organization and the contract governance function. (Babin, 2011; Oshri and Kotlarsky, 2011; Oshri, 2014; Oshri *et al.*, 2015)	1. Balanced scorecard 2. Service level agreement (SLA) 3. Contract and governance framework

S5	Engage	1. Search 2. Negotiation 3. Contracting	1. Is the provider able to provide the necessary outsourced financial services solution, with demonstrated domain knowledge (e.g., programming expertise, knowledge of industry trend), related outsourcing experience, and adequate talent, financial and technology resources. 2 Are the outsourcing relationships governed by explicit and enforceable written contract: A. Clearly define what activities are going to be outsourced, including appropriate service and performance levels. The service provider's ability to meet performance requirements in both quantitative and qualitative terms should be assessable in advance. B. Contract should neither prevent nor impede the regulated entity from meeting its respective regulatory obligations, nor the regulator from exercising its regulatory powers. C. Regulated entity must ensure it has the ability to access all books, records and information relevant to the outsourced activity in the service provider. D. Contract should provide for the continuous monitoring and assessment by the regulated entity of the service provider so that any necessary corrective measures can be taken immediately. E. Include termination clause and minimum periods to execute a termination provision to allow the outsourced services to be transferred to another third-party service provider or to be incorporated into the regulated entity. Such a clause should include provisions relating to insolvency or other material changes in the corporate form, and clear delineation of ownership of intellectual property following termination, including transfers of information back to the regulated entity and other duties that continue to have an effect after the termination of the contract.	1. Market intelligence 2. Outsourcing agreement 3. Service level agreement (SLA) 4. Operational level agreement (OLA)

(Continued)

Table A2. *(Continued)*

Node	Stage (first pass)	Description	Leading driving question(s)	Leading activities
			F. Material issues unique to the outsourcing arrangement should be meaningfully addressed. For example, where the service provider is located abroad, the contract should include choice-of-law provisions and agreement covenants and jurisdictional covenants that provide for adjudication of disputes between the parties under the laws of a specific jurisdiction. G. Contract should include, where appropriate, conditions of subcontracting by the third-party service provider for all or part of an outsourced activity. In appropriate cases it should require approval by the regulated entity of the use of subcontractors by the third-party service provider for all or part of a serviced activity or activity being delivered. More generally, the contract should provide the regulated entity with the ability to maintain a similar control over the risks when a service provider outsources to other third parties as in the original direct outsourcing arrangement. (BCBS, 2005)	1. Outsourcing governance framework
S6	Monitor	1. Undertake contract management	1. Are there close monitoring of the performance of the FinTech service providers: A. Schedule periodic working-level meetings with both the end-user groups and the supplier to review the supplier's performance. B. Conduct executive-level oversight meetings with the supplier's senior management to review the supplier's performance. C. Ensure that the supplier measures and reports on performance.	

			D. Work with the supplier to redefine service levels as appropriate. E. Consider transformational against transactional outsourcing management — ascertain degree of client-provider commitment, investing in and monitoring the relationship, using diligent documentation and administration, information exchange and coordination. 2 Do the client-provider leadership demonstrate the following behavior: A. Focused on the future B. Transparency C. Problem solving D. Outcome first E. High spirit of togetherness F. High clout within own organization G. Swift removal of obstructions H. Trustworthiness I. Effective performance J. Positive chemistry (GAO, 2001; FDIC, 2014; Mani *et al.*, 2006; Willcocks *et al.*, 2013)	
S7	Feedback	1. Undertake performance measurement	1. Are there adequate performance measurements conducted on the FinTech service providers: A. Sample and audit performance data frequently enough to perform trend analysis and permit extrapolation based on historical data. B. Distribute performance data to stakeholders. C. Employees, and possibly stakeholders, to rate supplier on a regular basis using, for example, scorecards and quarterly report cards.	1. Internal/external audit program 2. Balanced scorecard, management report card 3. Need-gap analysis

(*Continued*)

Table A2. *(Continued)*

Node	Stage (first pass)	Description	Leading driving question(s)	Leading activities
			D. Trigger incentives to motivate the supplier to exceed performance requirements; consider penalties to motivate the supplier to meet performance requirements. E. Periodically undertake studies to assess how the supplier's performance compares with the value being delivered to similar clients and the extent to which the supplier's performance is improving over time (e.g., validate cost assumptions for multi-year contracts). F. Metrics should measure the performance the service provider is giving the financial institution and not be based on the performance the vendor is delivering in aggregate to all its customers. Each measurement should logically support a requirement that is linked to a strategic goal. (GAO, 2001; FDIC, 2014)	
S8	Innovation	1. Measure value creation through innovation	1. For incremental or radical FinTech innovation undertaken, are there appropriate measurement tools: A. For incremental innovation, at the operational and strategic level, client firms should have developed clear measurement instruments as reference points to evaluate whether its incremental innovation targets have been met. B. For radical innovation, the client firm should seek both qualitative and quantitative inputs regarding performance. In terms of qualitative feedback, inputs regarding the quality of radical innovation can include periodical surveys. (Oshri and Kotlarsky, 2011; Oshri, 2014)	1. Innovation audit 2. Three horizons model 3. ROI analysis 4. Benchmarking 5. Surveys and interviews

References

Alt, R., Beck, R., & Smits, M. T. (2018). FinTech and the transformation of the financial industry. *Electronic Markets, 28*, 3.

Alt, R., & Puschmann, T. (2016). *Digitalisierung der Finanzindustrie–Grundlagen der Fintech-Evolution.* Springer, Berlin/Heidelberg.

Altinkemer, K., Chaturvedi, A., & Gulati, R. (1994). Information systems outsourcing: Issues and evidence. *International Journal of Information Management, 14*(4), 252–268.

Arner, D. W., Barberis, J., & Buckley, R. P. (2015). The evolution of FinTech: A new post-crisis paradigm? *Georgetown Journal of International Law, 47*(4), 1271–1319.

Arner, D. W., Barberis, J., & Buckley, R. P. (2016). 150 years of Fintech: An evolutionary analysis. *Jassa The Finsia Journal of Applied Finance, 3*, 22.

Arner, D. W., Barberis, J., & Buckley, R. P. (2017). FinTech, RegTech and the reconceptualisation of financial regulation. *Northwestern Journal of International Law and Business, 37*(3), 371–413.

Austin, J., & Bloggs, J. (2018). Big data outsourcing and identity verification in fintech credit assessment: A case study of a microloans platform in China. In *Proceedings of Australasian Conference on Information Systems.* Sydney.

Babin, R. (2011). Best Practices in outsourcing: The Bancolombia experience — Grupo Bancolombia Case Study. In *Global Excellence in Outsourcing.* International Association of Outsourcing Professionals.

Babin, R., & Quayle, A. (2016). ISO 37500 — Comparing outsourcing lifecycle models. *Strategic Outsourcing: An International Journal, 9*(3), 271–286.

Basel Committee on Banking Supervision (BCBS). (2005). *Outsourcing in Financial Services.* Basel.

Basel Committee on Banking Supervision (BSBC). (2011). *Principles for the Sound Management of Operational Risk.* Basel.

Basel Committee on Banking Supervision (BCBS). (2018). *Sound Practices: Implications of Fintech Developments for Banks and Bank Supervisors.* Basel.

Beimborn, D. (2008). *Cooperative Sourcing: Simulation Studies and Empirical Data on Outsourcing Coalitions in the Banking Industry.* Springer Science & Business Media, Wiesbaden, Germany.

Braun, C., & Winter, R. (2005). Classification of outsourcing phenomena in financial services. *ECIS 2005 Proceedings, 2.*

Brynjolfsson, E., & McAfee, A. (2014). *The Second Machine Age: Work, Progress, and Prosperity in a Time of Brilliant Technologies.* WW Norton & Company, New York; London.

Caplan, D., Janvrin, D., & Kurtenbach, J. (2007). Internal audit outsourcing: An analysis of self-regulation by the accounting profession. *Research in Accounting Regulation, 19*, 3–34.

Cane, A. (1992). Information technology and competitive advantage: Lessons from the developed countries. *World Development, 20*(12), 1721–1736.

Central Bank of Ireland (CBI). (2018). *Outsourcing — Findings and Issues for Discussion.* Discussion Paper 8. Dublin.

Chou, D. C., & Chou, A. Y. (2009). Information systems outsourcing life cycle and risks analysis. *Computer Standards & Interfaces, 31*(5), 1036–1043.

Clark, G. L., & Monk, A. H. (2013). The scope of financial institutions: in-sourcing, outsourcing and off-shoring. *Journal of Economic Geography, 13*(2), 279–298.

Consumer Financial Protection Bureau (CFPB). (2016). *CFPB Bulletin: Service Providers.* Washington DC.

Cox, N., & Pilbauer, J. (2018). Outsourcing critical financial system operations. *Journal of Business Continuity & Emergency Planning, 11*(3), 202–210.

Cristanto, J., Donaldson, C., Ocampo, D., & Prenio, J. (2018). *Regulating and Supervising the Clouds: Emerging Prudential Approaches for Insurance Companies.* FSI Insights. Basel.

Cullen, S., Seddon, P. B., & Willcocks, L. (2006). *Managing Outsourcing: The Lifecycle Imperative.* London School of Economics and Political Science, London.

Currie, W. L., Michell, V., & Abanishe, O. (2008). Knowledge process outsourcing in financial services: The vendor perspective. *European Management Journal, 26*(2), 94–104.

Dayasindhu, N. (2004). Information technology enabled process outsourcing and reengineering: Case study of a mortgage bank. *AMCIS 2004 Proceedings, 437.*

Deloitte. (2018). *Traditional Outsourcing is Dead. Long Live Disruptive Outsourcing.* The Deloitte Global Outsourcing Survey 2018, London, UK.

Duck, T. (2006). Why outsource the compliance function? *Journal of Investment Compliance, 7*(3), 67–69.

Ehrenfeld, J. (2017). Securities market automation from standards to self-learning machines: Current state and future perspectives. *Journal of Securities Operations & Custody, 9*(3), 245–252.

Federal Deposit Insurance Corporation (FDIC). (2014). *Technology Outsourcing: Informational Tools for Community Bankers.* Washington DC.

Federal Financial Institutions Examination Council (FFIEC). (2004). *Outsourcing Technology Services IT Examination Handbook*. Virginia.

Federal Reserve. (2013). *Guidance on Managing Outsourcing Risk*. Washington DC.

Financial Conduct Authority (FCA). (2013). *TR13/10 — Outsourcing in the Asset Management Industry*. London.

Financial Conduct Authority (FCA). (2016). *FG 16/5-Guidance for Firms Outsourcing to the 'Cloud' and Other Third-Party IT Services*. London.

Financial Stability Board (FSB, 2017). *Financial Stability Implications from Fintech: Supervisory and Regulatory Issues that Merit Authorities' Attention*. Basel.

Folwarski, M. (2019). Challenges of central banks as regulators to the development of the FinTech sector. *Safe Bank*, *4*(77), 50–62.

Frost, J., Gambacorta, L., Huang, Y., Shin, H. S., & Zbinden, P. (2019). *BigTech and the Changing Structure of Financial Intermediation*. BIS Working Papers, No. 799.

Gewald, H., & Dibbern, J. (2009). Risks and benefits of business process outsourcing: A study of transaction services in the German banking industry. *Information & Management*, *46*(4), 249–257.

Gewald, H., & Franke, J. (2007). The risks of business process outsourcing: a two-fold assessment in the German banking industry. *International Journal of Electronic Finance*, *1*(4), 420–441.

Gewald, H., Wüllenweber, K., & Weitzel, T. (2006). The influence of perceived risks on banking managers' intention to outsource business processes: A study of the German banking and finance industry. *Journal of Electronic Commerce Research*, *7*, 2.

Glass, G. (2018). Outsourcing 3.0: Licensed FinTechs driving growth and efficiency for banks. PwC. https://www.finleap.com/insights/pwc-and-finleap-whitepaper-outsourcing-3-0-for-banks/ [Accessed: 16 May 2020].

Gomber, P., Koch, J.-A., & Siering, M. (2017). Digital finance and FinTech: Current research and future research directions. *Journal of Business Economics*, *87*(5), 537–580.

Gonzalez, R., Llopis, J., & Gasco, J. (2013). Information technology outsourcing in financial services. *The Service Industries Journal*, *33*(9-10), 909–924.

Government Accountability Office (GAO). (2001). *Leading Commercial Practices for Outsourcing of Services*. Washington DC.

Gozman, D., & Willcocks, L. (2019). The emerging Cloud Dilemma: Balancing innovation with cross-border privacy and outsourcing regulations. *Journal of Business Research*, *97*, 235–256.

Grote, M. H., & Täube, F. A. (2007). When outsourcing is not an option: International relocation of investment bank research — Or isn't it? *Journal of International Management, 13*(1), 57–77.

Gulla, U., & Gupta, M. P. (2012). Impact of information systems outsourcing: A study of Indian banking sector. *International Journal of Business Information Systems, 10*(2), 131–150.

Gutierrez, F., & Dyson, L. E. (2009). Managing employee expectations of organizational change: A case study of IT outsourcing at an Australian bank. *Knowledge Management and Innovation in Advancing Economies: Analyses and Solutions — Proceedings of the 13th International Business Information Management Association Conference, IBIMA.*

Hon, W. K., & Millard, C. (2018a). Banking in the cloud: Part 1 — Banks' use of cloud services. *Computer Law & Security Review, 34*(1), 4–24.

Hon, W. K., & Millard, C. (2018b). Banking in the cloud: Part 2 — regulation of cloud as 'outsourcing'. *Computer Law & Security Review, 34*(2), 337–357.

Huber, R. L. (1993). How Continental Bank outsourced its 'crown jewels'. *Harvard Business Review, 71*(1), 121–129.

International Association of Outsourcing Professionals (IAOP). (2008). *Outsourcing Professional Body of Knowledge.* Version 10. Van Haren Publishing, Zaltbommel, Netherlands.

International Association of Outsourcing Professionals (IAOP). (2014). *Outsourcing Professional Body of Knowledge.* Van Haren Publishing, Zaltbommel, Netherlands.

International Standards Organisation (ISO). (2014). *International Standard 37500 Guidance on Outsourcing.* Geneva.

Jennings, D. (1996). Outsourcing opportunities for financial services. *Long Range Planning, 29*(3), 393–404.

Kaźmierczyk, J., & Macholak, P. (2014). Outsourcing in the banking sector — The polish banking sector case. *IAFOR Journal of Politics, Economics and Law, 1*(1). https://iafor.org/journal/iafor-journal-of-politics-economics-and-law/volume-1-issue-1/article-2/.

Klepper, R., & Jones, W. O. (1998). *Outsourcing Information Technology, Systems and Services.* Prentice-Hall, New Jersey, United States.

Klus, M. F., Lohwasser, T. S., Holotiuk, F., & Moormann, J. (1998). Strategic alliances between banks and fintechs for digital innovation: Motives to collaborate and types of interaction. *The Journal of Entrepreneurial Finance, 21*(1), 1.

Konschalla, T. (2013). *Outsourcing: BaFin compares outsourcing by institutions.* BaFin, Germany. Available from: https://www.bafin.de/dok/7874416 [Accessed 25 May 2020].

Lacity, M., & Hirschheim, R. (1993). The information systems outsourcing bandwagon. *MIT Sloan Management Review, 35*(1), 73.

Lacity, M., Khan, S., & Willcocks, L. (2009). A review of the IT outsourcing literature: Insights for practice. *The Journal of Strategic Information Systems, 18*(3), 130–146.

Lacity, M., Khan, S., Yan, A., & Willcocks, L. P. (2010). A review of the IT outsourcing empirical literature and future research directions. *Journal of Information Technology, 25*(4), 395–433.

Lacity, M., & Willcocks, L. (2013). Beyond cost savings: Outsourcing business processes for innovation. *Sloan Management Review, 54*(3), 63–69.

Lacity, M., Willcocks, L., & Feeny, D. (2004). Commercializing the back office at Lloyds of London: Outsourcing and strategic partnerships revisited. *European Management Journal, 22*(2), 127–140.

Lawrence, G. B. (2016). Adaptive financial regulation and RegTech — A concept article on realistic protection for victims of bank failures. *Duke Law Journal, 66*(3), 567–604.

Mani, D., Barua, A., & Whinston, A. B. (2006). Successfully governing business process outsourcing relationships. *MIS Quarterly Executive, 5*(1), 15–29.

Mayo, D. (2020). *Enterprise Case Study: How N26 Achieved Rapid Expansion Utilizing Mambu's Cloud Banking Platform — Enabling a New Generation of Banks to Achieve Scale and Effect Change.* Informa, PLC, London, UK.

McCormack, P. (2003). The FSA approach to the supervision of outsourcing. *Journal of Financial Regulation & Compliance, 11*(2), 113.

McLellan, K., Marcolin, B. L., & Beamish, P. W. (1995). Financial and strategic motivations behind IS outsourcing. *Journal of Information Technology, 10*(4), 299–321.

National Outsourcing Association (NOA). (2012). *Outsourcing Life Cycle.* National Outsourcing Association, London.

Němcová, Z., & Dvořák, J. (2013). Technology payment cards communication with banking institutions in the field of cashless payment. *Scientific papers of the University of Pardubice. Series D, Faculty of Economics & Administration, 18*(26), 116–128.

Ng, T. (2007). The Reserve Bank's policy on outsourcing by banks. *Reserve Bank of New Zealand Bulletin, 70*, 2.

Office of the Superintendent of Financial Institutions (OSFI) (2009). Outsourcing of Business Activities, Functions and Processes. Government of Canada. Available from: https://www.osfi-bsif.gc.ca/Eng/fi-if/rg-ro/gdn-ort/gl-ld/Pages/b10.aspx [Accessed 25 May 2020].

Oshri, I. (2014). *Innovation through Outsourcing: Have You Got the Goods.* National Outsourcing Association Year Book. EOA Ltd, London, UK.

Oshri, I., & Kotlarsky, J. (2011). *Innovation in Outsourcing.* WBS White Paper for Cognizant. Warwick Business School, Coventry, UK.

Oshri, I., Kotlarsky, J., & Willcocks, L. (2015). *The Handbook of Global Outsourcing and Offshoring* (3rd ed.). Palgrave Macmillan, Basingstoke.

Ozeke, H. B. (2008). Outsourcing of banking activities. *International Financial Law Review, 27*(1), 65–68.

Pousttchi, K., & Dehnert, M. (2018). Exploring the digitalization impact on consumer decision making in retail banking. *Electronic Markets, 28*, 3.

Quinn, J. B. (2000). Outsourcing innovation: The new engine of growth. *MIT Sloan Management Review, 41*(4), 13.

Reynolds, P. (2018). ISG Momentum®Market Trends & Insights 2018 Vertical Report. Information Services Group: ISG Research. https://www.isg-one.fr/research/isg-momentum/articles/isg-momentum-market-trends-insights-2018-vertical-report [Accessed: 16 May 2020].

Scott, H. S., Gulliver, J., & Nadler, H. (2019). *Cloud Computing in the Financial Sector: A Global Perspective.* Program on International Financial Systems, Cambridge, Massachusetts, United States.

Shim, Y., & Shin, D. (2016). Analyzing China's fintech industry from the perspective of actor–network theory. *Telecommunications Policy, 40*(2–3), 168–181.

Singh, D. (2005). Outsourcing in financial services. *Journal of Banking Regulation, 6*(3), 202–204.

Smojver, S., & Blažeković, D. (2015). Information systems outsourcing in Croatian banks: Developments 2005–2012. *Economic Research-Ekonomska Istraživanja, 28*(1), 259–270.

Sullivan, J. (2013). A center of excellence is a key success factor in governing multiple outsourcing contracts, KPMG Shared Services and Outsourcing Institute. www.kpmginstitutes.com/institutes/shared-services-outsourcing-institute/articles/2013/06/governance-centers-excellence.html [Accessed: 26 May 2020].

Tas, J., & Sunder, S. (2004). Financial services business process outsourcing. *Communications of the ACM, 47*(5), 50–52.

Walter, K. (2018). ISG Provider Lens FAO Digital Outsourcing Services Quadrant Report. Information Services Group. https://research.isg-one.com/reportaction/Quadrant-FAO-Digital-Operations-Global-2018/Marketing?SearchTerms=fao [Accessed 16 May 2020].

Willcocks, L., Cullen, S., & Craig, A. (2011). *The Outsourcing Enterprise: From Cost Management to Collaborative Innovation.* Palgrave Macmillan, Basingstoke.

Willcocks, L., Lacity, M., & Craig, A. (2013). Sourcing leadership. *Professional Outsourcing, 14*, 22–25.

Zhu, N., Qiu, H., Wang, L., & Foulds, L. (2017). Outsourcing of operations in the banking industry: A case study from China. *IUP Journal of Supply Chain Management, 14*(3), 7–25.

https://doi.org/10.1142/9781800612723_0009

Chapter 9

Designing Mobile Applications for Personal Financial Management: An Exploratory User-Centered Design Study

Annisha Akosah[*,‡], Nadia Pantidi[*,†,§] and Jennifer Ferreira[*,¶]

[*]*School of Engineering & Computer Science, Te Herenga Waka — Victoria University of Wellington, Wellington, New Zealand*

[†]*Computational Media Innovation Centre, Te Herenga Waka — Victoria University of Wellington, Wellington, New Zealand*

[‡]*annisha.akosah@gmail.com*

[§]*nadia.pantidi@vuw.ac.nz*

[¶]*jennifer@ecs.vuw.ac.nz*

Abstract

As our everyday financial interactions become increasingly digital, the abundance of mobile banking applications, methods of electronic payment, and online financial services available to everyday users offer new ways of interacting with money. These digital tools have the potential to transform our understanding of how financial operations occur, as well as how we make sense of our own personal financial information. There is still limited research to guide the design of personal financial management (PFM) tools and how to better support our digital financial interactions. While existing studies provide much-needed conceptual guidance and elaboration of contextual factors, there are still few studies that derive lessons from engaging in a user-centered design process that includes the evaluation of digital prototypes and explore the interactional challenges in designing tools for the mobile context. In this chapter we present an exploratory study in which we take a user-centered approach to developing and evaluating a digital prototype mobile application for PFM. We present our design decisions, discuss the usability implications of those decisions, and suggest ways in which future tools could be enhanced.

Keywords: Personal financial management, mobile applications, user-centered design, digital prototype, usability.

1. Introduction

As digital technology and connectivity become increasingly pervasive, so too have our opportunities to pay for goods and services, and to access and interact with digital financial information. As our everyday financial interactions become more and more digital, the abundance of mobile banking applications, methods of electronic payment, and online financial services available to everyday users offer new ways of interacting with money. These digital tools have the potential to transform our understanding of how financial operations occur, as well as how we make sense of our own personal financial information.

The move towards money management and payments occurring through digital means seems to be growing for a variety of reasons, ranging from institutional imposition by banks, development of new financial services, as well as user choice (Dodgson *et al.*, 2015). There are obvious advantages in handling financial services digitally — it allows the data from our personal financial activities to be automatically recorded, manipulated and analysed. Yet, there remains a disconnect between people's needs and the tools available to them (Snow and Vyas, 2015). Further, financial data remain largely hidden or obfuscated as a result of some combination of the protections upheld by the financial institutions used for banking and payments and being in a form not easily accessible and usable for building a meaningful understanding of what people do with their finances. If people are unable to draw accurate conclusions about their finances and financial interactions, then how can they possibly gain control of their financial situations?

In this chapter we present an exploratory study in which we take a user-centered approach to developing and evaluating a digital prototype mobile application for PFM. We present how the design decisions were informed through interviews with prospective end users and discuss the usability implications of those decisions based on the usability evaluation of the developed prototype. Finally, we propose avenues for further investigations in personal and household financial contexts: (i) Further investigations into machine-learning applications and impacts of their use for pattern recognition in users' financial behavioral data, forecasting their future financial positions and classifying transactions; (ii) Building a better understanding of how to create digital tools that support collaborative financial practices between people, by effectively shifting our focus in PFM from the individual to the collective; and (iii) Identifying successful practices built into software design and development life-cycles that center ethical awareness and action.

2. Personal Financial Management (PFM): Practices and Technologies

PFM encompasses a wide range of practices that include assessing, planning, forecasting, decision-making, goal-setting, evaluating, and using financial resources such as cash, credit, savings, and investments (Deacon and Firebaugh, 1988; Chen and Volpe, 1998). Both individual and household financial management practices are typically categorized for study into four primary practices: (i) expenditure or cash-flow; (ii) savings; (iii) debt (or credit); and (iv) investment management practices (Nyamute and Maina, 2011; Hilgert *et al.*, 2003). Expenditure, or cash-flow, management is the practice of regularly comparing actual expenditures with planned expenditures via the use of a budget (O'Neill, 2002). Savings management generally involves setting aside some amount for future needs (Nyamute and Maina, 2011). Debt (or credit) management refers to strategies employed towards repaying, minimizing, or reducing debt (Nyamute and Maina, 2011). Investment management involves strategically buying and selling financial assets, such as stocks and bonds, for financial gain (Nyamute and Maina, 2011). Of these four categories, savings management has been found to be practiced to a far lesser extent in both the individual and household context while expenditure management was the most frequently undertaken finance management practice (Hilgert *et al.*, 2003; Nyamute and Maina, 2011).

Demographic characteristics, financial education, levels of wealth, and financial dispositions (e.g., materialism and willingness to take risks (Gutter and Copur, 2011)) have been found to influence PFM practices, moderating how competently and confidently they are performed, or whether they are performed at all (Brüggen *et al.*, 2017). For example, in terms of level of wealth, individuals who are cash-constrained may engage in careful expenditure management practices but may not save and invest (Hilgert *et al.*, 2003). Cultural membership and beliefs also shape our views on certain financial behaviors. For instance, Breunig *et al.* (2017) and Musharbash (2001, p. 56) have noted how the strong collective spirit and cultural obligation to support people in Australian aboriginal communities have resulted in sharing of money and denouncing money saving practices as 'selfish and stingy'.

The 'personal' in PFM is often understood to encompass households or families, and not just individuals. This is important to note as, in families or other collective circumstances, individuals have been found to negotiate, often compromise, and establish joint strategies and 'systems' to manage their everyday or long-term financials (Vyas *et al.*, 2016) — suggesting that PFM should not be treated as an outright solitary activity. Fallaw *et al.* (2020) introduced the concept of a Household Chief Financial Officer (HCFO) to highlight the complex and time-consuming nature of managing household finances–akin to the role of a chief financial officer found in organizational entities. The HCFO assigned tasks to household members or outsourced accordingly. Examples of those tasks included: paying bills or filing tax returns on time to ensure no late fees or interest charges apply, reviewing statements to ensure transaction charges are correct, research product prices before a purchase or as part of making a shopping list.

As our everyday interactions with money shift towards the digital, banks and innovators in the financial technology (or 'FinTech') industry are making more digital tools available for PFM. These tools allow users to aggregate financial transactions in one place and then use transaction and other data to help manage their money, e.g.,

Mint,[1] Quicken,[2] and Pocketsmith.[3] Many PFM tools link with users' banking institutions for ease of access to their bank transactions. While current PFM tools available appear to offer relevant money management support, research has shown that these tools are either not widely used or fall out of use after a short period. Several reasons for this have been given, including concerns about security, inconvenience, and a frustration with their mismatch against user practices and needs (Kaye *et al.*, 2014; Snow and Vyas, 2015; Vyas *et al.*, 2016).

Researchers in the field of Human Computer Interaction (HCI) are starting to investigate how people manage their personal finances with the aim of providing design guidelines and principles for improving the design of digital financial systems. From interviews conducted by Kaye *et al.* (2014) they highlight the thought and effort that people put into creating systems that make sense in their personal financial world while balancing competing demands on their time. On the basis of surveys and interviews Lewis and Perry (2019) report on patterns of activity and practices in involving physical and digital tools for money management. Studies such as these show that there is growing interest in designing digital tools that account for the highly nuanced and contextualized ways in which people manage their finances. While existing studies provide the much-needed conceptual guidance and elaboration of contextual factors, there are still few studies that derive lessons from engaging in a user-centered design process that includes the evaluation of digital prototypes for mobile PFM applications (such as that of Tandon *et al.* (2019)). In our study, we adopt an exploratory approach and engage in user-centered design to develop an early mobile PFM prototype.

3. Exploratory User-Centered Design Approach to PFM

This chapter presents our exploratory user-centered design (UCD) study in which we designed and evaluated a preliminary PFM prototype mobile application. We opted for an exploratory approach to further probe what individuals 'do' as opposed to what they 'should do'.

---

[1]https://mint.intuit.com/ Last accessed: 29 August 2021.
[2]https://www.quicken.com/ Last accessed: 29 August 2021.
[3]https://www.pocketsmith.com/ Last accessed: 29 August 2021.

Further, user-centered design (UCD) represents the techniques, processes, methods, and procedures for designing usable products and systems, but just as important, it is the philosophy that places understanding of the user needs and practices at the center of the process (Norman, 1986; Norman, 1988). By exposing the end-users' tasks and goals, we can then leverage these findings to guide design and implementation decisions with respect to the desires and requirements of the end-users (Rubin and Chisnell, 2008). For the purposes of this chapter, we present the first three phases of our study: (i) interviews with end-users; (ii) user requirements and design of a preliminary prototype; and (iii) usability evaluation of the preliminary prototype. We present the findings from these initial development phases and discuss their implications and next steps in refining the prototype.

In our exploratory UCD study, we interviewed prospective end users to learn about how they currently manage their personal finances and what they find particularly useful or challenging about their current practices. From these interviews we identified the main user requirements for a PFM application and created a preliminary prototype solution to address these requirements. Finally, we evaluated the software prototype through usability testing with a different set of end users. This study was approved by Te Herenga Waka — Victoria University of Wellington's Human Ethics Committee (HEC) in May 2020.

3.1. *Participants*

We selected candidate participants to reflect diversity, particularly with regards to age, employment status, and the presence of financial relationships such as partners, housemates, and or dependents, e.g., a child or aged parent. A total of five participants were involved in one-on-one, semi-structured interviews (see Table 1), which all took place remotely via the online meeting platform, Zoom,[4] due to COVID-19 restrictions.

We then conducted usability testing with five potential end users. One evaluation session took place remotely over Zoom and the other four were conducted in-person. Again, we selected candidate

[4]https://zoom.us/ Last accessed: 31 August 2021.

Table 1. Interview participants.

Pseudonym	Age	Gender	Employment	Experience with PFM apps
Alice	18–25	Female	Full time	Yes
Diego	18–25	Male	Student/Unemployed	Yes
Harry	26–35	Male	Full time	No
Katie	36–45	Female	Self-employed	Yes
Tom	46–55	Male	Full time	No

Table 2. Usability evaluation participants.

Pseudonym	Age	Gender	Employment	Experience with PFM apps	Evaluation type
Oliver	18–25	Male	Full time	Yes	In-person
Hannah	18–25	Female	Student/Unemployed	Yes	Remote
Felix	26–35	Male	Full time	No	In-person
Vanessa	26–35	Female	Self-employed	Yes	In-person
Andrew	36–45	Male	Full time	No	In-person

participants to reflect a diversity of age range, employment status, and the presence of financial relationships (see Table 2). All participants have been given pseudonyms to comply with confidentiality and protect their identities.

3.2. *Interviews*

We conducted one-on-one semi-structured interviews to discover participants' needs, practices and goals with regards to managing their everyday financial interactions. We asked participants to draw a map of their finances — a technique from cultural probes and used in Kaye *et al.*'s (2014) study on personal finances. We then asked participants about, (1) the different methods/systems they use to manage their finances; (2) what roles technology, apps and physical objects played in their money management; and (3) the biggest challenges they face when managing their finances. Interviews lasted on average

40 minutes, were voice recorded and transcribed. The interview data was analysed, and the resulting findings were used to inform the user requirements and the design of a preliminary prototype application.

3.3. *Design decisions and prototype development*

Interview data was analysed to identify potential themes and opportunities for design using Thematic Analysis (Braun and Clarke, 2006). Throughout this process, we repeatedly returned to the raw data in the form of the drawn financial maps and audio recordings. In Section 4, we present our findings on the main participants' concerns that were used as the foundation for our design decisions. The design process encompassed translation of the interview themes into a structured user experience in the form of an interactive mobile application. The first step was to distill functional and non-functional requirements. We settled on the following functional and non-functional requirements based on the interview data:

Functional requirements (FR):

- FR1 Log income and expenses over a given period of time. Users should have the ability to either manually input this data or set it as a fixed recurring value.
- FR2 Perform categorization of income and expenses into more granular groups (e.g., Food Drink, Entertainment).
- FR3 Visualize income and expenses using graphical representations and allow a view of different and customizable timescales.
- FR4 Auto-predict and suggest common entries when adding new transactions for faster manual logging of transactions.
- FR5 Create budgets to represent the allocation of funds to specific categories. Using the logging (FR1) and categorization (FR2) features, this should track the user's spending against the set budget. Notifying the user in the form of a push notification when they are close to the upper limit of the budget is desirable.
- FR6 Search and filter through transactions.
- FR7 Support multiple accounts as separate 'wallets' for one given user.
- FR8 User authentication and data encryption to enforce privacy and security, as well as maintaining data persistence.

Table 3. Mapping functional requirements to screens and modals.

Component/ screen	Functional requirements	Description
Add transaction modal	FR1, FR2, FR4	Component used to log new transactions
Overviews screen	FR6	Main home screen listing all transactions
Graphs screen	FR3	Screen showing visualizations of transactions
Budgets screen	FR5	Screen to create and manage budgets
Wallets screen	FR7	Screen to create and manage wallets
Login/Signup screen	FR8	Screens to let users authenticate themselves

Non-functional requirements (NFR):

- NFR1 Privacy and security.
- NFR2 Accessibility and availability.

Table 3 shows the screens and modals that were developed for the functional and non-functional requirements. The cross-platform mobile web application was built in JavaScript using the Ionic framework[5] and Firebase[6] for data storage and user authentication. Figure 1 shows the user flow through the different screens of the application.

3.4. *Usability evaluations*

Usability evaluations were structured as a cognitive walkthrough using the think-aloud protocol — a common technique used to supplement the cognitive walkthrough process in which participants are asked to verbalize their thoughts as they move through a set of tasks

[5]https://ionicframework.com/ Last accessed: 31 August 2021.
[6]https://firebase.google.com/ Last accessed: 31 August 2021.

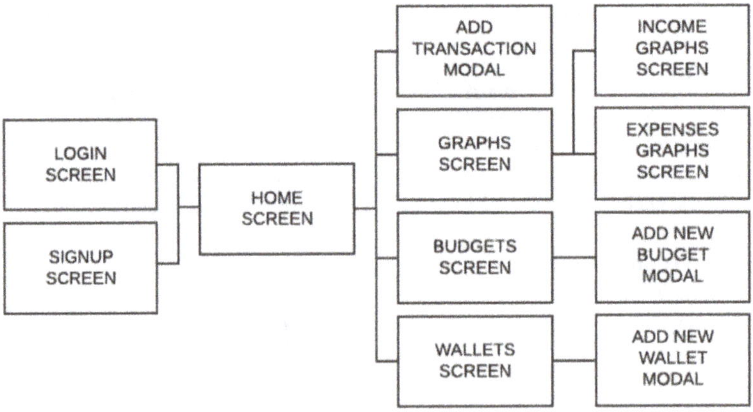

Figure 1. Flow through the screens and modals of the application.

(Mahatody *et al.*, 2010). At the end of each task, our participants were asked to assign a value from a 5-point Likert scale indicating the ease of the task, with 1 being very difficult and 5 being very easy. Evaluations were conducted both in person and remotely via Zoom. For the remote usability evaluation, the mobile application was deployed online using Firebase and made available via a public link that was shared with the participant. The participant had to additionally use the Device Mode in the Chrome[7] browser's DevTools to approximate how the web application would look and perform on a mobile device, instead of in a web browser. The screen-sharing functionality of Zoom gave the facilitator of the evaluation session a view of participants' actions as they performed the tasks. In-person evaluations were conducted in a university meeting room with the session facilitator present, and participants were given a mobile phone where the app was deployed to. All participants had access to an online Google Form specifying the tasks of the cognitive walkthrough as well as input fields for user reactions. All evaluation sessions were recorded in the form of handwritten notes to capture additional feedback from the user pertinent to the design of the prototype mobile application.

[7]https://www.google.com/chrome/ Last accessed: 31 August 2021.

4. Design Decisions Based on User Concerns with PFM Tools

In this section we examine the user concerns raised in our interviews that shaped our design decisions for the preliminary PFM prototype mobile application.

4.1. *Mobility for up-to-date personal financial management*

Our participants discussed how PFM tools that are bound to a non-mobile machine, such as a desktop computer or laptop, constrain them in performing PFM tasks — both with respect to the immediacy with which the tasks can be carried out as well as their location. Paper-based systems were also reported as 'not easy to carry around' and imposing similar constraints on users as non-mobile PFM tools. 'Spreadsheeting' — a term our participants used when referring to the use of spreadsheet software such as Microsoft Excel — was commonly performed on a desktop computer and meant that the logging of expenses could only be done on a computer stationed at home or the workplace, as opposed to logging in real-time or shortly after the transaction was completed. Our participants reported updating their spreadsheets approximately every month, which meant that between updates, the information contained in them was out of date. Participants who did not use spreadsheets, such as Diego and Tom, reported checking their bank account(s) multiple times a day, or throughout the week to keep updated with their spending and identify any unexpected transactions. For our participants, the usefulness and convenience of PFM tools was associated with mobility and accessibility to allow for transactional information to be always up to date. Based on these findings we decided to create a mobile web application, so that users could access their PFM app wherever they carried their phone.

4.2. *Stand-alone application for privacy and security*

People rank financial data as one of the most sensitive types of data (Prince and Wallsten, 2020). Similarly, our participants were concerned with how PFM tools deal with privacy issues as they acquire, transform, and share financial data. They applied expected levels of caution with respect to sharing their financial data. Both Katie and Harry expressed privacy concerns in the face of sharing financial data with a third party. However, one of our participants, Diego, expressed support for data sharing, as it 'means that you can stay on top of your money, all in one app'.

Financial data such as customer data, account data, and transaction data are closely guarded by government legislation across countries. Sharing financial data is a central tenet of Open Banking initiatives that promote the secure sharing of data between banks and third parties for increased control over financial activities and for supporting innovation in financial services (Gozman *et al.*, 2018). In this respect, PFM application developers can either seek accreditation for their PFM application (and rely on accrediting bodies to convey a sense of trustworthiness to end users) or build a stand-alone application with no data-sharing capabilities. Based on our findings, we opted to create a stand-alone mobile application that does not communicate or share data with other applications to address the privacy and security concerns reported by our interview participants.

4.3. *Full control over transaction categorization*

Accuracy of financial data and transactions in PFM tools is highly important and yet it is common for errors to occur — usually due to information not entered, entered late, or categorized incorrectly. Input and categorization of financial data can be done either manually by the user or imported and categories assigned automatically through in-built algorithms. Existing PFM tools make use of algorithmic categorization for convenience, however, our participants found that algorithmic categorization in existing tools brought several problems. For instance, Diego noted that when the algorithm of his PFM tool could not infer the category of spending, the transaction would automatically be assigned to a miscellaneous 'other' category, which soon began to heavily skew the averages and presented him with what he felt was a 'meaningless view' of his financial position. In another example, when using the import function of her PFM tool that accepts a comma-separated values (CSV) file of exported bank transactions, Katie faced the issue of having her transactions incorrectly categorized by the application's algorithm, which resulted in additional time and effort spent in manually correcting these entries.

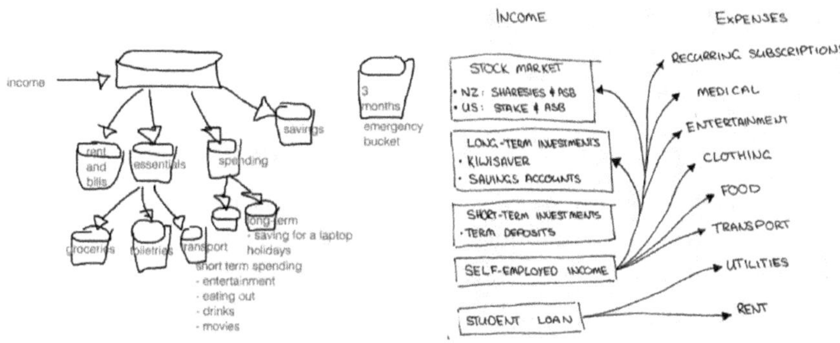

Figure 2. When asked to draw a map of their finances, Alice drew the image on the left depicting money buckets and Diego drew his income and expenses using boxes linked with arrows (right).

Another aspect of transaction categorization that holds implications for the accuracy of financial data relates to how people appropriate or personalize such categorizations based on their personal practices and mental models (Staggers and Norcio, 1993). For example, when asked to draw a map of her finances, Alice drew a chart in which her income is split into large financial 'buckets', organized by her various personal spending and saving categories. This is in line with previous findings (Zelizer, 1997) that people 'divide their money into different 'containers' or 'buckets' for different purposes', (Kaye *et al.*, 2014). Based on our interviews, it also became clear that people spend money differently depending on the source. Similarly, people's categorizations of income and expenses do not adhere to accounting discipline view on income and expenses. As can be seen in Figure 2 (right), for Diego, the student loan is considered income, because that money is available to be spent on rent and utilities.

These observations suggest that for PFM tools to better match users' mental models they should, (i) support high levels of flexibility in categorization; and (ii) be free of strict accounting rules if users wish to use personalized definitions of income and expenditure.

Based on these insights, we decided to allow users full control over the two types of categorization tasks in our prototype mobile application. Our prototype mobile application allows the user control over linking sources of incomes with outgoings through the creation of 'wallets' to manage income and expenditures within these wallets independently of others. Transactions in the prototype mobile application can also be assigned categories as created by the users.

4.4. *Constraining spending and tracking progress*

Part of managing finite financial resources is setting limits on spending and setting target amounts for accruing savings. This is typically understood as 'budgeting' wherein people self-regulate their financial activities by imposing constraints and committing to levels of savings appropriate to them. Our participants discussed how their existing PFM tools were limited in supporting budgeting functions, such as setting limits for specific categories of spending, for example, setting a target amount to save for a house deposit, or setting an amount to spend on weekly groceries. Spreadsheets were found to be more suited to these activities and so were used instead by our participants, as detailed earlier in Section 4.1. However, spreadsheets are difficult to use on a mobile device (Flood *et al.*, 2013) and tend to suffer from the limitations already discussed in Section 4.1, making it challenging for users to track real-time progress towards a set amount of expenditure or savings. For this reason, we designed budget functionality in which wallets can have various associated budgets to track actual spending against a target amount of spending. Figure 3 shows the budget functionality that was designed for the prototype mobile application. Each wallet can have one or more associated budgets which track targeted expenditure for a certain category of spending.

4.5. *Adjustable timescales for viewing financial information*

Money use has been characterized as a constant tension between saving and spending (Shefrin and Thaler, 1988; Thaler, 1990) — alternatively between fulfilling present needs and some future state. In line with this, our interviews showed that PFM tools must therefore support different views into users' current financial situation, as well as support them in planning for desired future situations. Our participants reported checking their bank account(s) multiple times a day, or throughout the week. They talked about comparing spending over different time scales (year, month, week etc.), and monitoring how their finances change over time. Participants reported being

Figure 3. The screen on the left allows new budgets to be created and added to wallets. The screen in the middle shows that the 'My Wallet' wallet has an associated 'Fun Money' budget of which 50% has already been spent. The screen on the right shows the breakdown of amounts spent in according to the categories of spending within the 'Fun Money' budget — Sports & Hobbies, Entertainment, and Food & Drink.

unable to take meaningful action on information displayed by their current PFM tools, such as the average spend/income for a given time period, or popular days for transactions in a given category. In an attempt to present potentially more useful information to the user, we created a visualization of the user's income and expenditure over time by implementing a bar graph on a timeline so that the user can compare spending/income levels across different days, weeks or years. The time period displayed can be configured as desired. The screen with the bar graph can be seen in Figure 4.

5. Usability Implications of Design Decisions

During the usability evaluations participants found the data visualizations useful for giving them a quick overview of the different aspects of their finances, such as the donut charts breaking down categories of spending and income, and the bar chart plotting

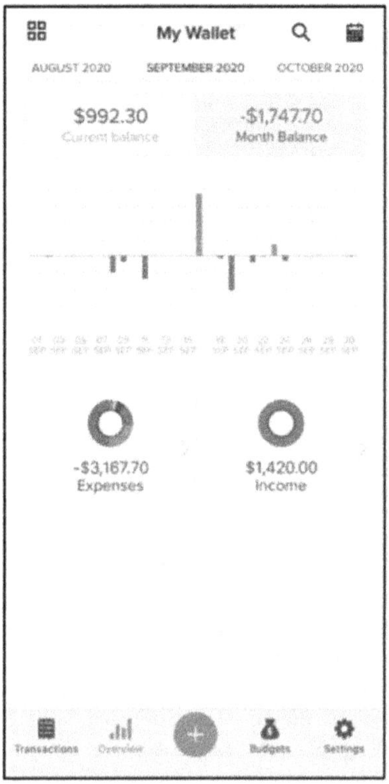

Figure 4. This screen shows the income and expenditure on a bar chart with time on the horizontal axis and dollar amount on the vertical axis and two donut charts showing the breakdown of categories of expenses and income.

expenditure and income over time. Overall, participants were very satisfied with aesthetics of the user interface and the use of color. Felix, Andrew and Hannah commented that being able to assign colors to categories helped them recognize and remember the categories in other areas of the prototype such as the visualizations. In the following sections, we report on the usability issues identified during the evaluation of the prototype mobile application.

5.1. *Limitations of small screen interactions*

The decision to develop a mobile web application for PFM was motivated by our participants' clear preference for PFM tools that are portable and their PFM information accessible to them anywhere and anytime (see Section 4.1). Further, we designed a range of visualizations to accommodate for participants' tracking of their spending and overall transactions (see Sections 4.4 and 4.5). The usability evaluations revealed the difficulties participants experienced when trying to perform certain interactions with the prototype's user interface on the small screen of the mobile phone. For example, Andrew experienced frustration caused by small touch targets, giving the impression that the prototype was unresponsive. Another concern expressed, was with regards to the scalability and presentation of expanding content. As Vanessa pointed out, as one keeps adding more custom categories of transactions, eventually it would become difficult to sort through the list to find the wanted category. This prompted participants to suggest sorting categories alphabetically.

The usability evaluations also revealed that interacting with the financial visualizations were at times hampered due to the small mobile screen size and that participants did not utilize the visualizations to their full potential. For instance, when using the bar graph, Oliver and Vanessa missed the 'hold and drag' gesture that revealed a tooltip displaying more detailed information for a given bar. Both reported that they were simply not aware of this feature. Andrew expressed frustrations with the accuracy of the 'hold and drag', especially in the monthly view when there were 30-odd bars packed in the chart. This is a limitation imposed by the lack of 'display space' on the mobile screen, but also the charting libraries used in the implementation that did not allow for interactivity (zooming and panning) around the bar graphs. To address the above issues associated with the visualization manipulation and restricted screen size of mobile phones it may be fruitful to adopt best practices for visualizing other types of data on mobile devices, such as health data (Meyer *et al.*, 2016), and on other types of small devices, such as smart watches (Islam *et al.*, 2020).

5.2. *Tedious manual input*

To address our participants' concerns and requirements around privacy and security (see Section 4.2) and to provide them with more control over categorizing transactions (see Section 4.3), we chose to create a stand-alone prototype mobile application that does not communicate or share data with other applications. A key implication of this design decision is that the user would have to log all their transactions manually. Our participants displayed varying levels of tolerance for manual data entry with our prototype, as illustrated with the example of adding a new transaction using the Add Transaction Modal. The fab button (see Figure 5) enabled access to the functionality for adding a new transaction and was placed in the center of the tab bar. On pressing the fab button, the Add Transaction Modal is presented as seen in Figure 6. Here the user is required to manually enter information about the transaction in a series of fields: the amount, a description ('Note' field), the date, set the occurrence of the transaction (if recurring) and assign a category. While Felix and Oliver found the Add Transaction Modal easy to use, Vanessa, Andrew and Hannah described it as 'overwhelming', with the components of the categorization modal AND the numerical keyboard for the transaction amount appearing at once. All participants utilized the available shortcuts for selecting common dates (yesterday/today) and recurring entries. However, participants expressed frustrations with the date input. The date field retained the previously entered date, resulting in users entering the incorrect date for their new transaction. When they became aware of the incorrect date, they said they

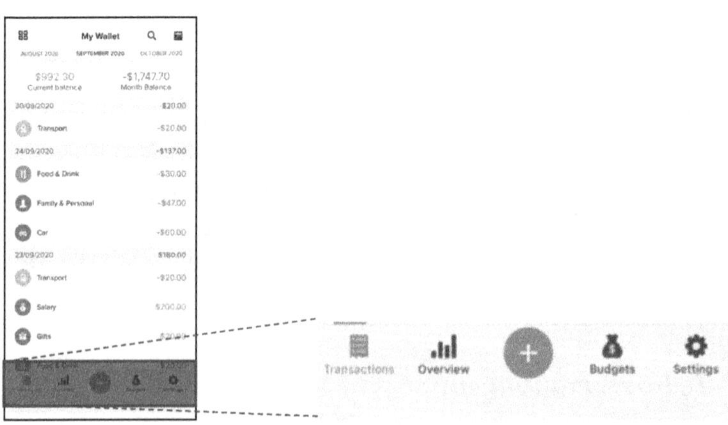

Figure 5. The highlighted area of the My Wallet screen shown on the left is zoomed in to show the fixed tab menu that appears on the bottom of each screen, with the circular floating action button in the center.

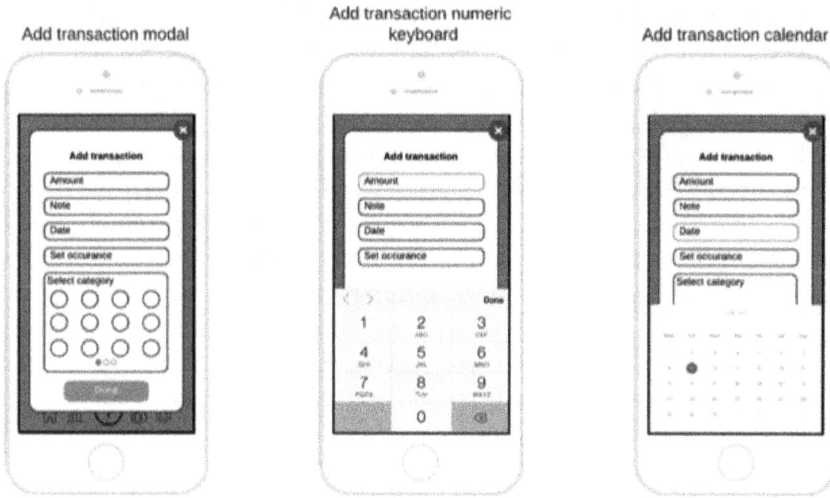

Figure 6. Logging a transaction.

had assumed the field would reset to the current date and would prefer this behavior instead. Harry expressed a preference for manually inputting and categorizing his transactions in this way, as that meant he was able to maintain the privacy of his data and control the accuracy of his logged finances; while the remaining participants, reported this type of manual input to be laborious and time consuming.

When trying to avoid the 'convenient' but often inaccurate algorithmic categorization found in existing PFM tools, creators are faced with implementing manual entry solutions. This common tradeoff between total user control and automation on the one hand allows a user freedom in how they log, categorize, and represent their transactions if they do so manually, but on the other hand, adds significantly to the effort and time required from the user. Overcoming usability issues with manual input requires alternative approaches to accessing transaction information. One possibility is automatic scanning of receipts using an optical character recognition (OCR) algorithm as proposed by (Kerber *et al.*, 2014).

5.3. *Difficulty interacting with timescales*

Our prototype included a feature that allowed users to track their finances across a timeline where they could configure the displayed time period as they wished (see Section 4.5). While the adjustable timescales feature was seen as useful by our participants, we identified a number of difficulties across several tasks in our system evaluation which were designed to assess this feature.

For the tasks involving the identification the user's balance on various timescales, most participants were successful, correctly identifying the balances of both the current period and a specified period between two dates. Participants struggled with finding the week's balance reporting it as the most difficult task. The main reason was that participants seemed to be unaware of the function that switched between different timescales and setting dates for time periods. For example, two out of five participants incorrectly identified the week's balance, as a result of failing to modify the timescales and instead reported the monthly balance which is displayed by default. When participants came to the task of adjusting the time period to two set dates, two participants only then became aware of the setting that modifies the displayed time period and the ability to switch between different timescales.

A similar problem was encountered by one participant for the task of identifying upcoming scheduled transactions, as they incorrectly set the time period when reporting the overall upcoming scheduled transactions. When it came to filtering the data by date, many participants struggled to initially find the button to configure the different timescales.

The above issues suggest the need for a clearer indication of the current time period the user is currently viewing and a reconsideration of the controls that switch between viewing different time periods.

5.4. *Cultural and mobile platform conventions*

Our usability evaluations further revealed some consistent user errors that arose from idiosyncrasies inherent in the dominant mobile platforms — iOS and Android. We believe these are noteworthy with respect to how they impact the design of PFM applications. The first involved the use of a comma (,), instead of a decimal point (·) in the numerical keyboard as the software library used for the numerical keyboard implementation in the prototype mobile application did not allow for a flexible customization of this separator. This posed a consistent error and source of confusion for our New Zealand-based participants as New Zealand currency is formatted with a decimal point separator between the dollars and cents and that is what New Zealand users would be accustomed. When asked to log the value of '$55.31', many users were puzzled with the presence of the comma separator on the numerical keyboard. The second user error related to established gesture patterns that differ between iOS and Android platforms. Users familiar with one platform may experience issues when interacting with apps or performing basic tasks on the other platform. In our case, when attempting to delete transactions all of our participants who happened to be iOS users were not aware of the 'tap and hold' gesture to delete an item, which is commonplace on Android systems. The above two errors point to the challenges with creating mobile applications that are envisioned to be used across cultures and various mobile platforms.

6. Opportunities for the Design of Mobile PFM Applications

Despite some limitations with this study — small number and range of participants, lab-based evaluation rather than in the real world — our exploratory study with an early prototype PFM application has highlighted opportunities for further investigations and refinements for future mobile PFM applications.

6.1. *Machine-learning for increased convenience, flexibility, and accuracy*

Our study has highlighted convenience, flexibility and accuracy as essential characteristics of PFM applications and echoes the findings of experiments conducted by Fatmawati and Permatasari (2019). PFM tools that inconvenience their users with onerous data entry, rigidly categories transactions according to inflexible accounting rules, and inaccurately classify their financial activities will not stand up to the fast paced, contextual, and highly nuanced ways in which people conduct their financial lives. There is great potential for PFM applications to harness machine-learning technologies for the speed at which they can carry out mundane tasks and recognize patterns in heterogeneous data. Machine-learning has seen a strong uptake by businesses and institutions involved in high frequency trading (Arévalo *et al.*, 2016), credit scoring for loans (Niu *et al.*, 2019), and fraud detection (Singh and Jain, 2020). In personal and household financial contexts we need more investigations into machine-learning applications and impacts of their use for pattern recognition in users' financial behavioral data, forecasting their future financial positions and classifying transactions.

6.2. *The social frame for collaborative financial practices*

Existing research on personal finance has started focusing on the design opportunities afforded by the social aspects of our financial lives (Snow *et al.*, 2017; Ferreira and Perry, 2019). Focusing on the social acknowledges the ways in which our financial activities affect others and are shaped by the relationships we have with those around us — whether that be our family, our household, friends or wider 'financial networks' (Vyas *et al.*, 2016) — and recognizes the variety of ways people collaborate on money use, for example, sharing household expenses, sharing payment of a restaurant meal, or as found by Collins *et al.*, 'storing' cash with friends. The value derived from using PFM tools will be determined by how well they integrate with and account for our social relationships and shared practices. We need a better understanding of how to create digital tools that support collaborative financial practices between people, by effectively shifting our focus in PFM from the individual to the collective.

6.3. *Ethical and equity considerations in digital personal financial management*

In practice, design decisions are situated trade-offs and there will be inevitable ethical reckonings for any developer of PFM tools — from decisions on whether to enable data sharing with third parties to decisions around implementing secure software features.

Experian cyber security analysts estimate the value of stolen financial data to be worth up to US$200 per record on the Dark Web (Stack, 2017). Unfortunately, traditional software development life-cycles 'do not explicitly support the reflection upon either ethical or moral issues', (Barbosa *et al.*, 2021) and secure software development life-cycle models are not widely adopted. There is a lot of work to do by scholars and practitioners in identifying successful practices built into software design and development life-cycles that center ethical awareness and action (Chivukula *et al.*, 2020).

As societies embrace cashless financial services and move services into the digital sphere we need more research into the impacts this has on offline communities, such as older populations (Vines *et al.*, 2011; Yang and Ding, 2016) and other sectors of the population whose access to digital tools may be limited (Raghavendra, 2018; Malaquias and Silva, 2020).

7. Conclusion

In this chapter we derived lessons from adopting a user-centered design approach to the development and evaluation of an early digital prototype mobile application for PFM. For our participants, the usefulness and convenience of PFM tools was associated with mobility and accessibility, privacy protections, and high levels of flexibility in managing financial transactions to match their own mental models. We encountered a tradeoff between strong privacy control and convenience, as well as the challenges of interacting with financial data visualizations on a small screen. On the foundations of this study, we propose avenues for further investigations in personal and household financial contexts: (i) Further investigations into machine-learning applications and impacts of their use for pattern recognition in users' financial behavioral data, forecasting their future financial positions and classifying transactions; (ii) Building a better understanding of how to create digital tools that support collaborative financial practices between people, by effectively shifting our focus in PFM from the individual to the collective; and (iii) Identifying successful practices built into software design and development life-cycles that center ethical awareness and action.

References

Arévalo, A., Niño, J., Hernández, G., & Sandoval, J. (2016). High-frequency trading strategy based on deep neural networks. In Huang, D., Han, K., & Hussain, A. (eds.), *ICIC 2016: 12th International Conference on Intelligent Computing Methodologies, 2–5 August 2016, Lanzhou, China* (pp. 424–436). Springer, Cham, Switzerland.

Barbosa, S. D. J., Barbosa, G. D. J., de Souza, C. S., & Leitão, C. F. (2021). A Semiotics-based epistemic tool to reason about ethical issues in digital technology design and development. In *FAccT '21: Proceedings of the 2021 ACM Conference on Fairness, Accountability, and Transparency, 3–10 March 2021, Virtual Event, Canada* (pp. 363–374). Association for Computing Machinery, New York, NY, USA.

Brüggen, E. C., Hogreve, J., Holmlund, M., Kabadayi, S., & Löfgren, M. (2017). Financial well-being: A conceptualization and research agenda. *Journal of Business Research*, *79*, 228–237.

Braun, V., & Clarke, V. (2006). Using thematic analysis in psychology. *Qualitative Research in Psychology*, *3*(2), 77–101.

Breunig, R., Hasan, S., & Hunter, B. (2019). Financial stress and indigenous Australians. *Economic Record*, *95*(308), 34–57.

Chen, H., & Volpe, R. (1998). An analysis of personal financial literacy among college students. *Financial Services Review*, *7*(2), 107–128.

Chivukula, S. S., Watkins, C. R., Manocha, R., Chen, J., & Gray, C. M. (2020). Dimensions of UX Practice that Shape Ethical Awareness. In *CHI '20: CHI Conference on Human Factors in Computing Systems, 25–30 April 2020, Honolulu, HI, USA* (pp. 1–13). Association for Computing Machinery, New York, NY, USA.

Deacon, R. E., & Firebaugh, F. M. (1988). *Family Resource Management: Principles and Applications.* Toronto, Allyn & Bacon.

Dodgson, M., Gann, D., Wladawsky-Berger, I., Sultan, N., & George, G. (2015). Managing Digital Money. *Academy of Management Journal*, *58*(2), 325–333.

Fallaw, S. S., Grable, J. E., & Kruger, M. (2020). The household CFO: Using job analysis to define tasks related to personal financial management. *Financial Planning Review*, *3*(2), e1089.

Fatmawati, I., & Permatasari, F. B. (2019). The analysis of technology acceptance model (TAM) for personal financial management on mobile application technology. In *ICOBAME 2018: Proceedings of the 2nd International Conference on Banking, Accounting, Management, and Economics, 14–15 November 2018, Yogyakarta, Indonesia* (pp. 247–255). Atlantis Press.

Ferreira, J., & Perry, M. (2019). From transactions to interactions: Social considerations for digital money. In Lynn, T., Mooney, J., Rosati, P., & Cummins, M. (eds.), *Disrupting Finance: FinTech and Strategy in the 21st Century* (pp. 121–133). Palgrave Pivot, Cham, Switzerland.

Flood, D., Harrison, R., Iacob, C., & Duce, D. (2012). Evaluating mobile applications: A spreadsheet case study. *International Journal of Mobile Human Computer Interaction (IJMHCI)*, *4*(4), 37–65.

Gozman, D., Hedman, J., & Olsen, K. S. (2018). Open banking: Emergent roles, risks & opportunities. In *ECIS2018: 26th European Conference on Information Systems, Research Papers, 23–28 June 2018, Portsmouth, UK, AIS* (p. 183). https://aisel.aisnet.org/ecis2018 \delimiter"026E30F_rp/2.

Gutter, E., & Copur, Z. (2011). Financial behaviors and financial well-being of college students: Evidence from a national survey. *Journal of Family and Economic Issues*, *32*, 699–714.

Hilgert, M. A., Hogarth, J. M., & Beverly, S. G. (2003). Household financial management: The connection between knowledge and behavior. *Federal Reserve Bulletin*, *89*(7), 309–322.

Islam, A., Bezerianos, A., Lee, B., Blascheck, T., & Isenberg, P. (2020). Visualizing information on watch faces: A survey with smartwatch users. In *VIS2020: 2020 IEEE Visualization Conference* (pp. 156–160), 23–30 October 2020, Virtual Event, USA. IEEE.

Kaye, J. J., McCuistion, M., Gulotta, R., & Shamma, D. A. (2014). Money talks: Tracking personal finances. In *CHI '14: CHI Conference on Human Factors in Computing Systems, 26 April — 1 May 2014, Toronto, Canada* (pp. 521–530). Association for Computing Machinery, New York, NY, USA.

Kerber, F., Lessel, P., Altmeyer, M., Kaltenhauser, A., Neurohr, C., & Krüger A. (2014). Towards a novel digital household account book. In *CHI EA '14: Extended Abstracts on Human Factors in Computing Systems* (pp. 1921–1926). Association for Computing Machinery, New York, NY, USA.

Lewis, M., & Perry, M. (2019). Follow the money: Managing personal finance digitally. In *CHI '19: CHI Conference on Human Factors in Computing Systems, 4–9 May 2019, Glasgow, Scotland* (pp. 1–14). Association for Computing Machinery, New York, NY, USA.

Mahatody, T., Sagar, M., & Kolski, C. (2010). State of the art on the cognitive walkthrough method, its variants and evolutions. *International Journal of Mobile Human Computer Interaction (IJMHCI)*, *26*(8), 741–785.

Malaquias, R. F., & Silva, A. F. (2020). Understanding the use of mobile banking in rural areas of Brazil. *Technology in Society*, *62*, 101260.

Meyer, J., Kazakova, A., Büsing, M., & Boll, S. (2016). Visualization of complex health data on mobile devices. In *Proceedings of the 2016 ACM Workshop on Multimedia for Personal Health and Health Care, 16 October 2016, Amsterdam, The Netherlands* (pp. 31–34). Association for Computing Machinery, New York, NY, USA.

Musharbash, Y. (2001). *Indigenous Families and the Welfare System: The Yuendumu Community Case Study, Stage Two.* Centre for Aboriginal Economic Policy Research, The Australian National University. Report number: 217/2001. https://openresearch-repository.anu.edu.au/handle/1885/41432 [Accessed: 31 August 2021].

Niu, B., Ren, J., & Li, X. (2019). Credit scoring using machine learning by combing social network information: Evidence from peer-to-peer lending. *Information, 10*(12), 397.

Norman, D. A. (1986). Cognitive engineering. In *User-Centered System Design* (pp. 31–61). Lawrence Erlbaum Associates, Hillsdale.

Norman, D. A. (1988). *The Design of Everyday Things.* Doubleday, New York.

Nyamute, W., & Maina, J. K. M. (2011). *Effect of Financial Literacy On Personal Financial Management Practices,* School of Business, University of Nairobi. http://erepository.uonbi.ac.ke/handle/11295/9897 [Accessed: 31 August 2021].

O'Neill, B. (2002). Twelve key components of financial wellness. *Journal of Family and Consumer Sciences, 94*(4), 53–58.

Prince, J., & Wallsten, S. (2020). How much is privacy worth around the world and across platforms? In *TPRC48: The 48th Research Conference on Communication, Information and Internet Policy, 17–19 February 2020, Virtual Event, USA.* http://dx.doi.org doi: 10.2139/ssrn.3528386.

Raghavendra, N. (2018). A conceptual study on digitalisation of banking — Issues and challenges in rural India. *International Journal of Management, IT, and Engineering, 8*(6), 186–191.

Rubin, J., & Chisnell, D. (2008). *Handbook of Usability Testing: How to Plan, Design, and Conduct Effective Tests* (2nd ed.). Wiley Publishing, Inc, Indianapolis.

Shefrin, H. M., & Thaler, R. H. (1988). The behavioral life-cycle hypothesis. *Economic Inquiry, 26*(4), 609–643.

Singh, A., & Jain, A. (2020). An Empirical study of AML approach for credit card fraud detection–financial transactions. *International Journal of Computers Communications & Control, 14*(6), 670–690.

Snow, S., & Vyas, D. (2015). Fixing the alignment: An exploration of budgeting practices in the home. In *CHI EA '15: Extended Abstracts on Human Factors in Computing Systems* (pp. 2271–2276). Association for Computing Machinery, New York, NY, USA.

Snow, S., Vyas, D., & Brereton, M. (2017). Sharing, saving, and living well on less: supporting social connectedness to mitigate financial hardship. *International Journal of Human–Computer Interaction, 33*(5), 345–356.

Stack, B. (2017). Here's how much your personal information is selling for on the dark web. https://www.experian.com/blogs/ask-experian/heres-how-much-your-personal-information-is-selling-for-on-the-dark-web/ [Accessed: 31 August 2021].

Staggers, N., & Norcio, A. F. (1993) Mental models: concepts for human-computer interaction research. *International Journal of Man-Machine Studies, 38*(4), 587–605.

Tandon, U., Siri, L., Mehra, A., & O'Neill, J. (2019). Designing a financial management smartphone app for users with mixed literacies. In *ICTD '19: Proceedings of the Tenth International Conference on Information and Communication Technologies and Development, 4–7 January 2019, Ahmedabad, India* (pp. 1–5). Association for Computing Machinery, New York, NY, USA.

Thaler, R. H. (1990). Anomalies: Saving, fungibility, and mental accounts. *Journal of Economic Perspectives, 4*(1) 193–205.

Vines, J., Blythe, M., Dunphy, P., & Monk, A. (2011). Eighty something: Banking for the older old. In *Proceedings of HCI 2011 The 25th BCS Conference on Human Computer Interaction, 4–8 July 2011, Newcastle Upon Tyne, UK* (pp. 64–73). Association for Computing Machinery, New York, NY, USA.

Vyas, D., Snow, S., Roe, P., & Brereton, M. (2016). Social Organization of Household Finance: Understanding Artful Financial Systems in the Home. In *CSCW '16: Proceedings of the 19th ACM Conference on Computer-Supported Cooperative Work & Social Computing, 27 February–2 March 2016, San Francisco, CA, USA* (pp. 1777–1789). Association for Computing Machinery, New York, NY, USA.

Yang, P., & Ding, X. (2016). Today's lifestyle and yesterday's life experiences: A study of financial practices of retirees in China. In *CSCW '16: Proceedings of the 19th ACM Conference on Computer-Supported Cooperative Work & Social Computing, 27 February–2 March 2016, San Francisco, CA, USA* (pp. 441–444). Association for Computing Machinery, New York, NY, USA.

Zelizer, V. A. (1997). *The Social Meaning of Money: Pin Money, Paychecks, Poor Relief and Other Currencies.* Princeton University Press, Princeton.

https://doi.org/10.1142/9781800612723_0010

Chapter 10

Estonian FinTech Evolution: The Past, Present, and Future

Maria Nemilentseva*, Bahar Bahramian Dehkordi† and Keira Nicole Soutar‡

School of Engineering Science, LUT University, Lappeenranta, Finland
**maria.Nemilentseva@lut.fi*
†bahar.Bahramian.Dehkordi@lut.fi
‡keira.Soutar@lut.fi

Abstract

Estonia has become one of the best known digital societies through its advanced FinTech industry. It is one of the top-ranking nations for internet accessibility, with 91% of its population using the internet. Estonians' lives are influenced by information technology through the range of various digital solutions available for both individuals and businesses. This chapter elaborates on the story of Estonia's Fintech evolution from the post-Soviet era to modern times with governmental cooperation and considers possible future development that will allow Estonia to continue its FinTech evolution. It also describes the foundation of technological development for its existing financial services offerings, and it forecasts future trends. The research is built on conceptual theoretical findings, secondary data on FinTech development in the Baltic countries and empirical insights from interviews conducted in 2021 with three Estonian FinTech experts. From these interviews and exploration of the historical evolution of FinTech in the country, it is shown that Estonia's success comes from the country's past, as trust in the government was still a large part of the people's culture at the time. Estonia has succeeded in its transformation due to the support of the government towards information technology. This can also be seen in the current evolutionary turn point whereby the push for the finalization of a regulatory framework for the FinTech ecosystem can allow further transparency. There are, however, limitations with any advancement towards the future.

Keywords: Fintech, Estonia, digital transformation, FinTech ecosystem, financial industry, financial services, digital products and services.

1. Introduction

The popularity of FinTech as an academic term and practical business concept for innovation and technology in the financial sector (from its development to the use of financial services) has grown enormously in the last decade (Schueffel, 2016). The incentives for FinTech come from both financial and tech influences. FinTech itself is not only about the use and implementation of technologies for providing and delivering financial solutions (Wojcik, 2021), but it can be referred to as 'an umbrella term for innovative technology-enabled financial services and the business models that accompany those services' (Mention, 2019, p. 59). FinTech solutions are able not only to attract different customers and reach underserved people but are able to disrupt the traditional banking industry due to their more user-centric focus, cost-effective solutions, better service models and flexible approach to service development.

Some of FinTech's best practices come from relatively small economies that have shown success in building digital societies and advanced FinTech industries. This can be directly demonstrated from the last 5 years, as innovative solutions have been applied in other Baltic countries[1] for the successful development of FinTech products and services and have since become well known (Furber, 2018). Over 530 FinTech companies are active in the Baltic states, and these account for almost 7% of all FinTech companies in Estonia, Latvia and Lithuania.

The Baltic region is considered a FinTech hub that provides successful companies with a solid financial market. Governmental support mechanisms, including regulatory frameworks, and the innovative culture, ability and willingness of companies to implement

[1]Latvia, Lithuania, Estonia.

new technologies are among the key factors of the success of companies within this region. The vast amount of innovative work there has promoted the interest in conducting further studies about the Baltic countries. Despite the fact that the majority of Baltic FinTech companies are based in Lithuania, in this chapter, we will focus on the experience of Estonia, as it is the forerunner in the creation of an overarching digital society (Aalto Capital, 2021; e-Estonia, 2021b).

A small Baltic country, Estonia is notable for its digital approach and fast implementation of new technologies. Nowadays, it is considered to be one of the most technological countries in the world, despite its small size of 1.3 million citizens. In Estonia, the technology sector plays a significant role and is in fact one of the most influential sources of growth for the country's economy and society. Based on reports from the World Bank, around 15% of Estonia's GDP comes from high-tech industries (de Carlos Sola, 2018).

To gain a better understanding of the FinTech situation in Estonia, we conducted three interviews with experts working in different FinTech companies and operating within the market there. Our respondents were from different levels within their companies, namely a co-founder and business developer for private companies and a COO of a multinational company.

Addressing the idea that FinTech exists to solve problems within the financial sector (Findexable, 2019; Mention, 2019) through the development implementation of technologies, we explore the Estonian FinTech evolutionary process from the past to the future. In this chapter, we introduce trends in the Estonian FinTech sector, illustrate the main triggers for its rapid development and current service offerings and look into how the future of Estonia in the case of FinTechs, technology evolution, risks and opportunities will potentially advance. The main insights from our interviews will be incorporated into the themes discussed above.

2. Past: From Independence to COVID-19

Estonia's technological development was brought to the surface by the government's reform of the 1900s that aimed to transform its society into a digital one (The New Economy, 2019). Estonians have succeeded in their transformation due to the support of the government towards information technology (IT), despite the fact that it was not easy to build either their own economy or their own identity after Estonia's long history of being a part of the Soviet Union. Because of this history, trust in the government has remained a large part of popular culture and can be seen as one positive cultural impact that has helped Estonian society in its willingness to accept innovations due to the conveniences they bring. Another reason why the FinTech seed market has grown at such a fast rate is that people in Nordic countries enjoy equal access to innovative digital products and services (Anthes, 2015). This section provides a brief overview of the history of FinTech in Estonia.

2.1. *Estonian's route to Tech and the digital society*

Kemp (2021) placed Estonia among the highest-ranked countries for internet accessibility. Indeed 1.2 million Estonia, out of the total population of 1.33 million, are internet users DataReportal — Global Digital Insights, 2021). This amounts to 91% of the country's entire population. As experts have mentioned, even though the population is small, its concentration has allowed for easier networking, collaboration and connections across different industries, including the FinTech sector. Additionally, life as an Estonian, broadly speaking, is heavily influenced by IT, due to popular trust in IT solutions. In Estonia, over 99% of financial transactions happen digitally; therefore, it can be considered a cashless society.

In many FinTech applications, digital IDs and blockchain technology are used broadly in solutions for increased transaction security whilst creating a more secure way of user authentication and ultimately streamlining transactions for financial services (Fanning and Centers, 2016). As a global centre of excellence for FinTech, Estonia boasts more than 80 FinTech firms, including startups such as Wise, NS blockchain leader Guardtime (Invest in Estonia, n.d.). Many experts, including our respondents, agree that the momentum started when Estonia gained independence in 1991, and the country has since been forging its own path to become a technology-orientated country supported by its authorities. This started with the first draft of 'Principles of Estonian Information Policy' in 1994 (e-Estonia, 2021b). The business developer of the Estonian FinTech firm said in an interview that *the Estonian government introduced and committed to a digital governance model early on*. A wide range of different digital solutions available for businesses and individuals has made Estonia one of the best known digital societies in the world. Moreover, Estonia is furthermore recognized for its e-government and e-tax systems (Tirmaste *et al.*, 2019).

The development of FinTech companies in Estonia started at the beginning of the century, and within the last 2 years, they have been developing quickly not only locally but also globally (Laidroo *et al.*, 2021). These new financial market players are changing and improving the way people pay, send, borrow, lend and invest money and are transforming the financial sector (Chishti and Barberis, 2016). In recent years, there have been changes in legislation on the national and European Union levels (Laidroo *et al.*, 2021). These changes to the regulatory framework will lead to better control over the FinTech sector, investments and other instruments that were not previously regulated.

2.2. *Main triggers for FinTech sector's development in Estonia*

After Estonia's independence in 1991, its economic growth was mainly due to foreign trade and foreign direct investment. However, focus on the development of the technology and information and communication technology sectors began to shift through a transition to an innovative state. Becoming a part of the European Union (EU) in 2004 served as an additional step in boosting Estonia's capacities and shifting towards a market economy. The need for fast and effective reformation by benchmarking other countries' best practices and models led to liberalization of the economy and monetary, structural and institutional reforms (Lumiste *et al.*, 2008).

During the transformation of Estonia's economy, the government made it a priority to provide **support for businesses**. The evolution of the IT industry was mainly based on the needs of the public sector in the 1990s. By the end of the century, the government had launched e-government services through the internet. Additionally, educational institutions were equipped with computers (Lumiste *et al.*, 2008). This helped the younger generation to become accustomed to modern technologies while also producing **well-educated specialists** and creating the basis for further transformations in different industries. As the co-founder of a private FinTech firm mentioned:

> Estonians have been ... really lucky and they've been good in getting some of the well-known ID companies into the international markets. (They are) well-recognized, globally, including Skype, Tranferwise, or Wise as they are called today — and even Wolt. (These are) very big companies, if we think of the population of the country of Estonia. This has helped in many cases, as the IT companies are well accepted ... Many are well accepted of foreign players due to Skype and other companies. So, in general, they (Estonians) have good quality companies and technology wise, and workers.

Another interviewee said:

> Our company started at university. We talked and thought let's do ... an interdisciplinary kind of a team ... Some tech people, some business people, all students — let's see what they will do.

In addition to government support for technology development, Laidroo *et al.* (2021) highlighted the importance of the ease of informal communication caused by the small size of the home market. Sometimes, the development of an industry can be provided by joint efforts, but this is not always feasible, as many companies see a lack of collaboration. Currently in Estonia there are more than 200 FinTech companies (Laidroo *et al.*, 2021). In 2018, there was a boom in establishing FinTech companies with an emphasis on digital asset exchanges. According to the Estonian FinTech Report (2021), the older Estonian FinTech companies are operating on enterprise technology provisioning, credit and data analysis and InsurTech, while the younger ones are mostly involved in RegTech, digital custody and digital identity groups. This is due to the trends of increased security, prevention of fraud and the need for Know Your Customer (KYC) procedures and risk management, etc. Representatives of the sector reflected that a 'smaller set of minds in companies allows for direct communication to stay close to merchants and customers. This has created a rare environment for collaboration whilst developing offerings.

Estonia has a unique approach to digital services, shown by the development and launch of 'e-Estonia', which provides citizens with complete digital access to anything from health to banking services completely digital. Blockchain technology has been used by Estonia since 2008, which 'has created a high-level functional financial system from scratch'. The co-founder of a company operating in Estonia and Finland is convinced that:

> (Estonians) were digital forerunners ... since around 2000, when they launched the Estonian ID card which all ... authentication needs are based on, that and it was great.

The latest advancement of this concept is that of 'e-Residency', which is based on blockchain technology. It allows talented people in any country to gain a government-issued digital identity and status that provide access to Estonia's transparent business environment. It helps attract young specialists to the country from all over the world. Because of these modern digital service advancements, *Wired* magazine has classified Estonia as one of 'the most advanced digital societies in the world' where an accurate online ecosystem of different public services has been established for a truly digital future (e-Estonia, 2021b). To allow this ecosystem to thrive beyond a digital environment, a residence visa for 'digital nomads' was launched in 2019 that allows remote workers to live in Estonia (e-Residency, n.d.), making it the first country in the world to open its borders to e-residents. Our respondents agreed that 'Estonia is already relatively digitally advanced'. Other countries have been following the success of the digital development of government and other services with great interest, understanding that it is a sound practice (Anthes, 2015). Some neighboring countries such as Finland have adopted this approach and even launched unified databases, one of which was implemented in medical organizations and pharmacies (International Monetary Fund, 2018).

As a result, Estonia's innovative government approach has led to the synergy effect caused by providing modern technologies to talented people and creating space for innovations within different sectors. Additionally, Estonia has become a front runner in the implementation of blockchain technologies at a government level and stimulated the creation of GovTech partnerships (Heston, 2017;

The New Economy, 2019). All these transformations have formed a favorable climate for business development, and especially for the formation of the country's FinTech industry. This level of technological advancement has also enabled Estonians to provide different digital solutions to confront a range of challenges during COVID-19 pandemic (e-Estonia, 2021b).

2.3. *Overview of the development of the Estonian FinTech industry*

Traditionally, FinTech's history has three phases that are defined by forthcoming inventions or turnpoints. These are the invention of the telegraph (and its use for commercial purposes since 1838) and the first transatlantic cable (1866), Telex networks and the first cash machine 1966–1967 and the financial crisis of 2008. The term 'FinTech' first appeared in the 1990s when Citigroup[2] launched the Financial Services Technology Consortium that aimed to enhance technological cooperation. However, it was only the financial crisis at the beginning of 2000s and after the economic turndown of 2008 that the real development of the sector began. Several years later, in 2014, FinTech started attracting the attention of customers, investors and regulators (Arner *et al.*, 2016; The Iyer Report: Understanding FinTech, 2017). In this chapter, we consider the evolution of the FinTech sector of modern Estonia after its independence in 1991, and mainly following the onset of the era of the Internet and mobile phones.

One of the first Estonian FinTech companies, 'Fitek' was created in 1995 and provided customers with innovative financial' automatization and optimization solutions as a core service. Other companies during the 1990s were focused mainly in the same field. The foundation of FinTech within Estonia was actually e-Estonia, a government initiative to simplify interactions between citizens and the state by utilizing electronic solutions. To create a unique digital environment

[2]In the early 1990s, Citicorp was among the most powerful corporations in the USA, and as the largest bank in the country, it was able to become a global leader in banking. As a result of the merger of Citicorp and Travelers Group, Citigroup was formed. Today it is one the leaders among financial service providers (Tichy and Charan, 1990).

for the national plan, a collaboration was formed among financial services providers, telecom providers and the government (FinTech in Baltic, 2020). Even before this, there had been attempts to provide innovative services. One of these successful experiences was given as an example by one of our interviewees:

> This ... company Mobi was just an SMS payments service for everyone .... Because SMS payments were something that were very much connected to telephone companies (not a solo company just for payments) .... At the beginning of the 2000s, (it) was not something attainable for most (companies), because telephone companies were the superstars in the scene. And then you (a customer wanting to have SMS payments) could just go with any self-service (and) start your own mobile payment SMS payment thing ... in Estonia.

There are many well-known, high-level tech companies, in addition to some of the most innovative FinTech startups, that have been established in Estonia. Among them, Skype is one of the most famous platforms developed there. Its establishment in 2004 created a revolution in the online communication arena. In addition, one of the best known innovative startups in FinTech, Wise (formerly known as TransferWise), engaged peer-to-peer technology to simplify currency transactions between accounts all over the world and is seen as one of the most successful platforms (FinTech in Baltic, 2020; Klein *et al.*, 2017).

According to a report that explored the development of financial innovation in eastern European nations, although Estonia is a small country, it has more potential and capability to utilize novel financial products and services compared to some bigger countries that have a comparable level of ICT infrastructure but are not as highly ranked in 'financial education' and 'innovation skills' (Sumedrea, 2020).

Estonian FinTech industry development has been very active since 2014. Based on information from the Estonia Startup (Startup Estonia, 2021), the country became a leader in the number of 'newborn' FinTech startups in 2018. The data from this source covers companies registered in or after 2011 and are presented in Figure 1.

Figure 1 illustrates the main trends of sector development and market evolution. As can be seen, there were few FinTech startups

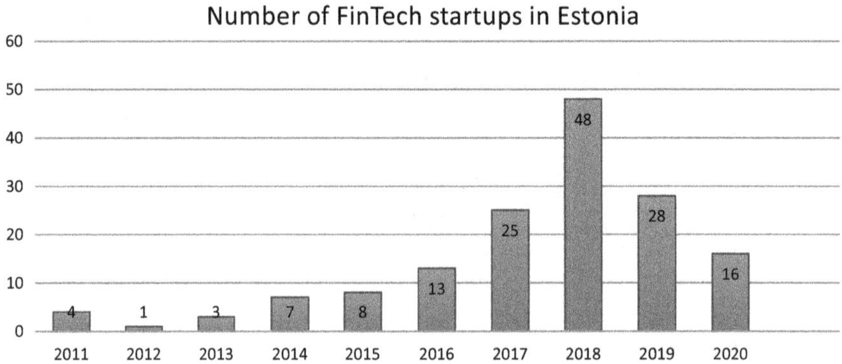

Figure 1. Estonian FinTech startups from 2011 to 2020 (based on Startup Estonia, 2021).

established in Estonia until 2016, and the main peak of the registration of FinTech companies took place from 2017–2019. The main reason for this growth is that some regulatory changes have happened since 2017 that have resulted in e-banking and e-business register development that could provide technical solutions to attract people from anywhere to open a bank account or establish companies in Estonia (e-Estonia, 2021b). Estonia was the first European country to issue licenses to companies working with virtual currencies. Together with the e-residence programme, it led to the growth of startups wishing to attain the EU license in 2017. During these 2 years, the majority of registered FinTech companies in Estonia were represented by virtual currency service providers. From 2019 onwards, the number fell, as illustrated in Figure 1. This was caused by the announcement of amendments to the Money Laundering and Terrorist Financing Prevention Act that were enacted in March 2020. According to the amendments, holders of virtual currency licenses should register their headquarters in Estonia and operate through them, and other due diligence measures were presented (Laidroo *et al.*, 2021).

In this chapter, we did not factor in the developments from 2021, but based on the same source, the number of startups registered in the first months of the year was five. The reasons for this include competition in the field, the pandemic and forthcoming changes in the regulatory framework. However, the growing interest in the field during the several years before the pandemic can be easily covered. In the following sections, we will focus on the current FinTech offerings and consider the main players in the market.

2.4. *Ecosystem development*

FinTech ecosystems consist of different actors such as policymakers, financial institutions, entrepreneurs and companies that are active in the FinTech area, including technology developers. Additionally, some researchers include financial customers (individuals and organizations) as a part of the FinTech ecosystem. When discussing innovative FinTech ecosystems, it usually follows that all parties in the system, whilst in cooperation, can create some form of a synergic effect that can result in the development of innovative and more user-friendly solutions whilst helping to overcome customer expectations. Further, the effectiveness of the dynamic ecosystem leads to better economic results and has an effect not only on the industry but also on economic development. Naturally, when we talk about the FinTech ecosystem, startups are seen as the drivers of further development and are considered to be among the founding innovation sources (Lee and Shin, 2018; Centric Digital, 2016).

Traditionally, innovations within the financial industry have been directly related to technology development. Nowadays, the evolution of FinTech and the development of FinTech ecosystems influence innovation processes and activities within the field. Customers can see significant changes that are not limited to some modifications of existing services. Technology developers, following the rise of FinTech have acquired new clients operating in the financial sector and had the opportunity to develop new offerings for banking institutions as the technology has brought value to the financial sector in many ways. This has included lowering the costs related to different processes, better time management, reducing risks and faster transactions. Additionally, banking institutions have realized the importance of newcomers to the market and attempted to implement new technologies. They were later forced to develop new services faster than before, sometimes in collaboration with FinTech companies driving the change. That makes them an inherent part of FinTech ecosystem development (Still *et al.*, 2019; Tirmaste, 2019).

As Estonia is a part of the EU, the activities of participants of the FinTech ecosystem are regulated by it. In 2019, the main financial market regulator was the Financial Supervision Authority (Financial Supervision Authority Act). This authority supervised the activity of the players in the financial market (banks, insurance companies, investment funds, etc.) and issued licenses. In addition, some segments that are not covered by the Financial Supervision Authority regulations are regulated by the Financial Intelligence Unit. These mainly operate as financial institutions, providing virtual wallet services and exchanging a virtual currency against a fiat. There is no specific regulation for FinTech companies, and at the same time, many different laws can be applied to the actors in the sector. Although the regulations can sometimes serve as an obstacle in the FinTech industry, Estonian regulations have had the most significant role in the development of the FinTech ecosystem in the country (Tirmaste *et al.*, 2019). FinTech companies cover a range of financial service providers' activities, and there is no specific law or guidelines for them. The acts that can be applied for the FinTech companies based on their activities are presented in Table 1.

Table 1. Financial regulatory framework.

Regulatory framework	Regulated companies
Credit Institutions Act Creditors and Credit Intermediaries Act	Banks and creditors, credit intermediaries, initial coin offering providers
Investment Funds Act	Initial coin providers
Payment and E-money Institutions Act	Payment and e-money service providers
Money Laundering and Terrorist Financing Prevention Act	Companies engaged in services for exchanging a virtual currency and providing virtual currency wallet services
Securities Market Act	Investment firms, credit institutions, fund managers, operators of regulated security markets, operators of securities settlement systems, initial coin offering providers
Law of Obligations Act	Initial coin offering providers

Source: Elaborated by the authors based on Laidroo *et al.* (2019).

As previously mentioned, the Estonian government has formed a conducive environment for developing new businesses and provided substantial opportunities for FinTech startups to develop their activities in Estonia, which is a result of the country's well-developed entrepreneurship ecosystem.

Since Estonia is a technologically developed country that produces talent in the field, its technology developers are able to create innovative, essential solutions and offerings for the local and global markets. The small size of the domestic market assists in faster implementation of technologies and rapid development of services for customers. A digitally savvy population is very eager to use technology novelties that can make the lives of individuals easier. Thus, the FinTech sector has financial customers who are ready not only to use new solutions but also to participate in their development. This is due to the continued development of the FinTech ecosystem in Estonia.

3. Existing at Once: Estonian FinTech Today and Tomorrow

From the point of view of customers, the pandemic has forced the rapid development of different digital services. The majority of businesses have gone online, and there has been a vast amount of changes to the business models of different organizations. Our new reality has affected consumers' behavior and preferences. This section looks more deeply at how the Estonian FinTech sector has responded to this challenge.

3.1. *Overview of the sector from 2019–2021*

Estonia has been affected by global and local changes that have taken place swiftly. These rapid developments, in addition to the recent COVID-19 crisis, have influenced the standard approach of businesses (Laidroo *et al.*, 2021). A recent interview with Taavi Tamkivi, head of the FinTech section and board member of FinanceEstonia, indicated that although the pandemic has certainly affected Estonian businesses, and FinTech companies among them, no drastic negative changes have occurred, and some companies have even used this crisis as an opportunity to grow and develop new products and services.

When the crisis hit, the main challenges and transformations were about rearranging working practices and switching to remote work (Raiffeisen Bank International in Austria 2021; Laidroo *et al.*, 2021).

Some companies in the sector have taken governmental support due to loss of profits. Some companies did not even mention losses during the global pandemic, while others identified new opportunities through necessary adaptation for the changing environment and answered the call to develop and launch innovative solutions faster (Raiffeisen Bank International in Austria, 2021). This was confirmed by one of the interviewees, who is responsible for business development in a well-known Estonian FinTech company:

> We see that the payment volumes are bigger and were significantly bigger when the pandemic first started. But now, I would say it's plateaued, or is even in decline ... The biggest boost ... was seen in e-commerce, but as we are not part of e-commerce then we didn't see that as much .... I would say it had a positive effect also on us (the company), and quite many other companies that had negative effects, but our value proposition was to direct it, to take digital payments.

A comparison of Estonian FinTech reports from 2018 to 2021 reveals Estonia's current situation in the FinTech sector. The sector has been seeing steady economic growth during recent years, since FinTech companies have been actively participating in different areas such as digital payments, enterprise technology provisioning, WealthTech and digital capital raising (Laidroo *et al.*, 2021). In other words, it can be stated that FinTech is a significant contributor in terms of employee numbers and employment tax paid. Figures show that in the FinTech segment during the first half of 2021, the average gross pay was around 2,767 Euros per month. Additionally, turnover in the FinTech sector was more than 10% of the total generated by the startup sector in the first half of 2021 (Startup Estonia, 2021). With superior infrastructure and transparency in government regulations, Estonia has become one of the most desirable countries for local and international entrepreneurs to register their companies. Estonia has more than 251 FinTech companies with a total revenue of 235 million Euros, according to reports from 2019.

As a whole, FinTech in Estonia has developed and overcome challenges during the last few years, and if its growth continues, it could attract many more FinTech concepts and companies from all over the world (Laidroo *et al.*, 2021). Since it launched the e-residence programme, interest from foreign entrepreneurs has been growing at a steady rate. It has been attracting new players and innovative models to the market. During the pandemic, the main challenge for FinTech companies was the adaptation to new remote modes of work.

3.2. *FinTech ecosystem evolvement*

The Estonian FinTech Report (2021) identified, five main players of the Estonian FinTech ecosystem: FinTech companies that 'feel they are a part of the ecosystem' (Laidroo *et al.*, 2021, p. 10); the state represented by ministries, the Financial Supervision Authority, Enterprise Estonia, and Finance Estonia and its members; incubators and accelerators; and academia and R&D organizations. Once again we highlight the ease of building relationships inside the sector and when forming the ecosystem due to the small size of the Estonian market. On the other hand, a lack of real collaboration always takes place in the reticent financial industry (Laidroo *et al.*, 2021). Figure 2 outlines the Estonian FinTech ecosystem.

All the parts of this ecosystem are interconnected. For example, technology developers are partners of FinTechs, financial institutions, the government and even some financial customers. Academia and R&D organizations usually do not directly participate in the ecosystem development process, but they can analyze its performance and provide some recommendations to different parties. While customers can give an incentive for future services development, translate their real needs and participate in service development. One of the important features of the ecosystem is the regulatory framework that has been described above.

Today in Estonia, there are different incubators and accelerators, some of which have specific programmes for FinTech startups. According to Tirmaste *et al.* (2019), two of the best known of these are Startup Wise Guys and the Lighthouse Development Programme. The Lighthouse programme, presented by SEB with Mastercard and NFT Ventures, became the first one to pursue the development of FinTech in Estonia. It supports collaboration between FinTech

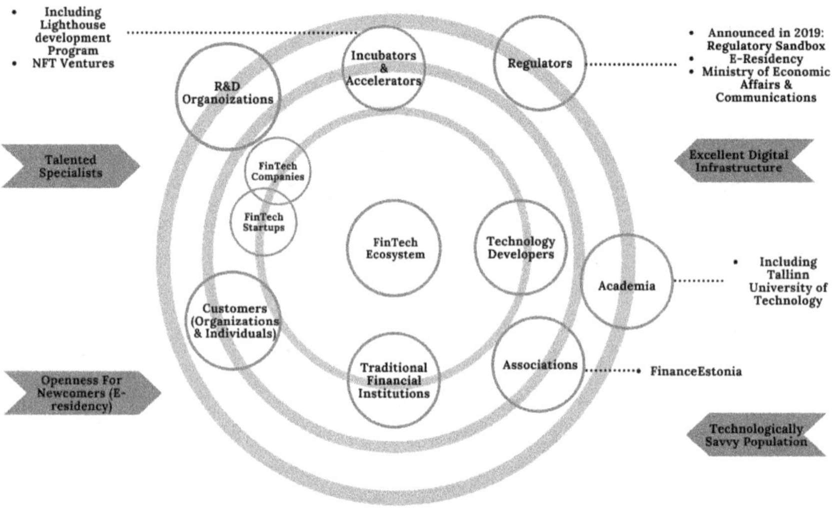

Figure 2. Estonian FinTech ecosystem.

companies, investors, advisors and banking institutions for the creation of innovative solutions across the Nordic and Baltic regions (SEB, 2019; Mastercard Lighthouse, 2020). In 2019, the Lighthouse programme announced a partnership with SEB (the official banking partner in the Baltic region). Before the start of this programme, SEB had experience in organizing hackathons and co-investments in some FinTech companies. Another reason for this partnership is the fact that the bank was interested in collaborating with FinTech companies because of its aim to become a leader in open banking (Mastercard Lighthouse, 2019). In 2020, a second programme make and scale social impact version (MASSIV) was introduced. One year later, focusing on FinTech, it was again renamed 'The financial initiative (FINITIV)'. Today this programme is presented in a digital format. Among the partners in addition to SEB are DNB, Danske Bank and Swedbank. This programme and its development reinforce the innovative potential of the region and highlight the growing interest of entrepreneurs in financial technology services (Mastercard Lighthouse, 2021). The Startup Wise Guys accelerator was established in 2012 in Estonia and has been investing in early-stage startups across different countries and industries and has a special programme launched for FinTech companies. By 2021, there were four FinTech accelerator programmes covering startups from fields such as PropTech, RegTech, InsurTech, analytics, and cybersecurity. Earlier programmes lasted 3 months, but then Startup Wise Guys launched a new format for its accelerator. Consisting of nine modules, it embraces all phases of product and company development and accelerates entrepreneurs from founders. It includes 3-day boot camps and after-program care for 25 startups selected by a committee consisting of investors, mentors and the Wise Guys FinTech team (Startup Wise Guys, 2021).

Estonia is among the top 10 FinTech countries of the world (Findexable, 2019), and the success of the development of FinTech companies in such a small country proves that for example its companies very often win the competition and participate in different startup programmes, including Lighthouse, focused on Nordic and Baltic countries. In 2020, the Baltic region was represented only by Estonian FinTech companies: out of more than 100 applications, only 15 companies were chosen, and five of them were from Estonia, representing the whole Baltic geography. Despite the fact that Lithuania is the leader of this region, as mentioned earlier in the introduction (SEB, 2020).

The head of Salv Technologies, a FinTech company well known for developing technologies that help financial institutions prevent money laundering, mentioned that it is important to develop the branding of FinTech companies, improve networking and contacts globally and learn about the world's technological trends by listening to other FinTech companies. This can happen through participation at different FinTech events that are held all over the world yearly. Therefore, 12 FinTech companies including Bankish, EstateGuru, EveryPay, GetID, Inbank, Messente Communications and Modularbank, under the support of Enterprise Estonia, took part in one of the best-known FinTech events in Europe, Money 20/20 held in Amsterdam in September 2021. This shows that the Estonian government is promoting local FinTech companies by providing different types of support and an ecosystem for potential growth in the FinTech sector (e-Estonia, 2021a).

As has been discussed previously, Estonia created a friendly entrepreneurial environment for its citizens and for foreign entrepreneurs, who can register their companies very quickly online and attain e-residence. Talented specialists and an excellent digital infrastructure create a sound basis for ecosystem evolution. In addition to financial and technology companies, one of the main actors for the development of the industry is the FinanceEstonia association, which aims to support the economy by increasing business opportunities for firms that are members, thus enhancing the internationalization of the financial industry (Mittal, 2019).

3.3. *Startup activities 2019–2020 and regulatory framework*

During 2019–2020 more than 30 FinTech startups were registered, and more than half of them commenced their activities during this period (Estonia Startup, 2021; Laidroo *et al.*, 2021). The main interest of the startups was in the digital asset exchange and digital payments sectors. Wealth technology was also attracting the attention of newcomers, as digital capital raising and lending. Based on the Estonian FinTech Report (2021), FinTech companies now, are mainly operated in the following segments: digital asset exchange, digital lending, digital payments, enterprise tech provisioning, WealthTech, digital capital raising. Additionally, InsurTech companies operating with credit and data analytics, digital custody and identity are also present in the Estonian market. Some of these companies and the sectors they are active in are listed in the summary table of FinTech companies (see Appendix Table A1).

In 2019, the European Bank for Reconstruction and Development (EBRD) started working with the Estonian Ministry of Finance aiming to form the county's first FinTech regulatory sandbox. The initiative set out to provide the FinTech sector with a supportive regulatory environment to create and shape Estonian law for FinTechs (Fintech Law, 2019). FinTech companies operating in Estonia consider this movement as an essential part of the development and are waiting for the introduction of new regulations that will allow the participants of deals to be more clear and transparent. One of the main things demanding rapid improvement in the field is the creation of guidelines based on the upcoming changes (Tirmaste, 2019).

Launched in 2019, the FinTech regulatory sandbox project united 35 representatives of startups, banks and innovators. It allowed companies not only to develop and test their ideas but also policymakers to gain knowledge about innovative companies. The authorities could see the potential of the sector and realized the need for a supportive regulatory environment that would save costs and reduce the time it took to launch innovative products and services on the market (Bell, 2019). The second part of the project set out to begin the implementation of the sandbox, based on a list of recommendations presented to the Estonian government for regulatory legislative changes (Bell, 2019; Peyton, 2019).

In March 2018, the European Commission, considering how new technologies force changes to financial service development and accessibility, realized the need to regulate the fast-developing FinTech sector. The FinTech Action Plan it presented included actions aimed at enabling innovative business models to reach EU scale, stimulating and supporting financial service innovation through the implementation of technologies and strengthening safety and consistency in the financial industry (Tirmaste *et al.*, 2019; Van de Wiele, 2018). In September 2020, the digital finance package was introduced, and it will provide a catalyst for the development of a competitive financial sector in the EU. The new rules will be in use from November 2021 (Laidroo *et al.*, 2021).

3.4. *Future: AI, collaboration, new trends*

Based on the existing trends, we have identified the possible direction the financial services market and technology evolution may take. Technology development will shape many industries, as it has been seen in the past year already. The use of machine-learning (ML) and artificial intelligence (AI) in many industries, including the FinTech sector, will continue in the near future. In 2020, many companies reviewed their working practices by attempting to optimize their business processes and adapting to the changing business environment. As we could see from the overview of the Estonian FinTech industry and the results of the interviews, the sector has adjusted to the new reality quite smoothly. Some companies had strengthened their business models even before the pandemic by implementing modern technologies (Kazmi, 2021).

The most common applications of AI and ML currently used in the financial industry are presented in Table 2.

All the main applications of AI and ML in the FinTech sector highlight how its services are customer-orientated and user-friendly.

Table 2. The most common use of AI and ML in the FinTech industry.

Use of AI and ML	Explanation
Advanced financial decision-making	FinTech apps analyze data and transform it into insights that can be used for financial decision-making.
Security and fraud detection	AI and ML monitor and reveal suspicious actions and notify users.
Asset management	New algorithms can manage bank accounts and identify how a user can reduce costs and avoid unnecessary processes.
Customer support	Bots and chatbots assist customers alongside robo advisors and automated customer support.
Insurance	Risk levels can be determined through the assessment of different factors.
Loans	Easy and faster ways of credit scoring, helping to save costs and exclude prejudice.
Forecasts	Predictive analysis with the help of different apps. Helps users to check and plan their income and spending.
Personalization	Personalization of users' financial management.

Source: Elaborated by the authors based on Kazmi (2021).

The use of AI improves financial services and allows them to be more attractive. Data science and artificial intelligence (DSAI) comprise classic AI such as logic, modeling, planning and simulation. Advanced aspects of DSAI comprise intelligent interactions and conversations, identification and authentication, advanced analytics and learning, knowledge discovery, behavior and social media analysis and, finally, deep learning, automated interactions, learning and responses, transfer learning and human-centered brain and cognitive computing all of which are entering into our lives. For the FinTech industry, in addition to the areas mentioned above, statistical and mathematical modeling is also something important to consider. With DSAI techniques, FinTechs can improve their performance, communication and collaboration with stakeholders, their existing business models and offerings, and they can provide security for operations and transactions. It is anticipated that all this will lead to customer loyalty, cost-efficiency and increased innovation (Cao *et al.*, 2021).

In addition to AI and ML, FinTech companies are increasingly focused on the co-creation of services with customers. It is well known that users are ready to trust these companies and choose their services based not only on price but also the ease of use (Blackstad and Allen, 2018). Beyond co-work with clients, the Estonian FinTech ecosystem will develop to include collaboration with established financial service providers. The need for the development of an effective regulatory framework that will support the evolution of the sector and encourage innovations in the field is crucial and demands cooperation with the government (Laidroo *et al.*, 2021).

New technologies can provide the starting point for new services. Nowadays, interest in digital wallets is still very current, and companies are ready to focus on the development of a range of payment solutions. This interest has risen because of the successful experiences of other countries with bigger FinTech ecosystems. For example, during an interview one of the respondents explained his position regarding the future of digital wallets:

> So, in five, ten years time, DCB (Direct Carrier Billing) will be … substituted for digital wallets … In our case in Europe, the digital wallet is very convenient … (Compared to) people (who) are unbanked … can reach their wallet, even without the bank. (They) can just put the cash in that special point of sale … And because of that, their adoption has been so fast.
>
> We started onboarding first wallets also during the pandemic. So, we were one or two years too late, but before we did the business analysis on the topic one year ago, or two years ago, then it was a quite interesting area, but we didn't have enough proof that it would (work). Now we have plenty … They (Indonesians) don't have any legacy maybe … this is why we are quite confident that we are not late and it's time to pursue.

Another possible trend after the pandemic could be that of mergers and acquisitions. Over the last few years, some Estonian FinTechs were bought by different foreign and domestic companies. The opportunity for such mergers and acquisitions in the future will depend heavily on the regulatory framework and its ability to stimulate the fast implementation of innovative solutions, provide firms with a clear and transparent business environment and foster collaboration between actors in the FinTech ecosystem.

4. Conclusion

Overall, this chapter shows how FinTech has been inspired in Estonia and demonstrates how it is one of the top-ranked countries in the FinTech industry. It also studies the factors that have been behind the country's success, especially in FinTech. There are many reasons why Estonia is viewed as one of the most digitally advanced societies in the world. Analyzing the past retrospective of FinTech development in Estonia provides an understanding of how it has impacted the current environment and pushed us to investigate factors that may come into play in the future of FinTech within the country to advance the digital society to a higher level.

Delving into the country's past relationship with the Soviet Union, trust in the government is still a large part of the popular culture and can be seen as one positive cultural impact that has aided Estonia's society in its willingness to accept innovations due to the conveniences they bring. The country has succeeded in its transformation due to the support of the government towards IT, even though it was not easy to build both its own economy and identity after a long history of being a part of the Soviet Union. We have also seen how solid digital platforms and competition within neighboring Nordic regions have allowed Estonia to kick-start its production of innovative digital products and services. This investigation was backed up by three professionals in the Estonian FinTech market. The insights from their interviews provided us with confirmation of an assortment of topics examined by various sources of published work.

Another driver of Estonia's success comes from its ecosystem and infrastructure, which have been developing step by step, to make the growth of FinTech startups and companies easy and smooth.

Certainly, the future of the FinTech industry in Estonia will be dependent on further local and international regulations. After the regulatory framework is finally formulated, the Estonian FinTech environment should become more transparent. These rules and laws should create the opportunity for further evolution of the FinTech ecosystem and at the same time continue to attract startups, including those wishing to become e-residents of Estonia. With every advancement must come limitations to consider. The slow adaptation and hesitancy of the financial industry can be seen as one of them. Another is the industry's need for collaboration. Although there have been some cases whereby demand for user-centeredness has been demonstrated, it is still lacking in the industry. The global pandemic has helped to bridge the gap, but only time will tell whether the industry has grasped the digital advancements needed for the users of the future.

This chapter highlights just one digitally forward country within the Baltic region. With FinTech on the rise in the development of the financial industry, investigation of other developing nations in the region poses an interesting direction of research. As we have identified already, friendly and neighborly competition already creates new innovative platforms. We have studied past trends in the region and industry with regard to policy, pandemic development and ecosystem. Although we cannot predict the future, we cannot wait to witness what the future holds, not only for the digital financial industry but for the future development of Estonian FinTech.

Appendix

Table A1. Summary of some Estonian FinTech companies and their key activities, 2008–2020.

Name (established)	Key services	Business model
Companies founded before 2008		
Fitek (1995)	• Financial processes' automatization and optimization	B2B
Fortumo (2007)	• Programming & engineering • Marketing/finding clients • Operative business/serving clients • Analytics, payments • Global monetization and growth platform for digital content merchants	B2B Commission
Iizi (2000)	• Programming & engineering • Marketing/finding clients • Operative business/serving clients • Insurance • Insurance broker, insurance	B2B, B2C SaaS Commission
Modularbank (2002)	• Offering different modules to financial institutions to build banking products • Core banking platform for financial institutions • Flexible and convenient financial services: banking as a service for financial institutions • API-first banking platform	B2B
2008–2013		
Bondora (2008)	• Programming & engineering • Analytics, deposit and lending, investment management • Online P2P lending platform for personal loans	B2C (Int) Interest Commission
Wallester (2009)	• Marketing/finding clients • Banking infrastructure, payments payment solutions, development of financial digital technology and issue of Visa cards	B2B (Int) SaaS Commission License fee

Table A1. (*Continued*)

Name (established)	**Key services**	**Business model**
Creditstar (2009)	• Marketing/finding clients • Operative business/serving clients • Deposit and lending • Lending loans	B2C Interest Commission
Aasa (2011)	• Operative business/serving clients • Deposit and lending • Credit solutions to consumers and businesses	B2C Interest Commission Trading
EveryPay (2012)	• Programming & engineering • Operative business/serving clients • Payments (digital and personal) cloud-native payment gateaway platform	B2B SaaS
Maksekeskus (2012)	• Programming & engineering • Operative business/serving clients • Payment • Payment solution company, online payments	B2B SaaS Commission
EstateGuru (2013)	• Programming & engineering • Operative business/serving clients • Deposit and lending, investment management • P2P platform for commercial real estate loans	B2B B2B2C SaaS Commission Data License fee
Big Data Scoring (2013)	• Marketing/finding clients • Operative business/serving clients • Analytics, banking infrastructure cloud-based credit decision engine that improves credit quality through the use of big data	B2B SaaS, Data
2014–2019		
Crowdestate (2014)	• Marketing/finding clients • Deposit and lending • Real estate crowdfunding platform	B2B, B2C Commission

(*Continued*)

Table A1. (*Continued*)

Name (established)	Key services	Business model
Investly (2014)	• Programming & engineering • Operative business/serving clients • Deposit and lending, investment management • P2P finance platform for SMEs for selling invoices to investors	B2B SaaS Commission License fee
Datame (2015)	• Programming & engineering • Operative business/serving clients • Analytics, banking infrastructure credit information processing and analytics; a cutting edge solution where all financial institutions including banks can share data in real time	B2B SaaS Commission data License fee
Resys (2015)	• Marketing/finding clients • Baking infrastructure, investment management • Open-source FinTech platform	B2B, SaaS Commission
Pocosys (2015)	• Programming & engineering • Banking infrastructure	B2B, SaaS License fee
Paytailor (2015)	• Marketing/finding clients • Payments; cloud-based commerce software for e-commerce, IoT and payments	B2B License fee
Change Invest (2016)	• Programming & engineering • Digital wallet for cryptocurrencies • Buy and sell bitcoin. Change app	B2C
Supplier plus (2016)	• Programming & engineering • Marketing/finding clients • Operative business/serving clients • Deposit and lending, banking infrastructure • Making invoice finance easy, fast and affordable	B2B, Trading

Table A1. (*Continued*)

Name (established)	Key services	Business model
Paytomat (2016)	• Programming & engineering • Analytic, distributed ledger • Wallet • Complete payment platform for businesses	B2B
Iuvo (2016)	• Security and high returns via contemporary peer-to-peer investment platform • Credit portfolio	
Zantepay (2017)	• Programming & engineering • Banking infrastructure, distributed ledger, payments • Multiwallet possibilities with a payment card • DeFi platform integrated with encrypted messenger email	B2B B2C Commission Trading
Crowd Coinage (2017)	• Programming & engineering • Payments	B2B, B2C SaaS Interest
Crassula (2017)	• Programming & engineering • Operative business/serving clients	B2B
Bankish (2017)	• Programming & engineering • Marketing/finding clients	B2B B2B2C
askRobin (2017)	• Programming & engineering • Marketing/finding clients	B2C B2B2C
Black Foundation (2017)	• Programming & engineering • Marketing/finding clients • Insurance	B2B Commission Data
CINDX (2017)	• Programming & engineering • Operative business/serving clients • Blockchain-based multifunctional platform for investments in the crypto market that creates a complete ecosystem for cryptocurrency trading	

(*Continued*)

Table A1. (*Continued*)

Name (established)	Key services	Business model
Xchange (2018)	• Programming & engineering • Marketing/finding clients • Operative business/serving clients • Distributed ledger, investment management, payments • Application for personal finance combining a multi-currency wallet, globally accepted payment card, and a financial services marketplace	B2C Commission Trading
Piixpay (2018)	• Programming & engineering • Operative business/serving clients • Distributed ledger, payments • Bridge between crypto and traditional money; payment solutions	B2B B2B2C
LEXIT (2018)	• Programming & engineering • Distributed ledger, banking infrastructure • All-in-one solution marketplace for buying and selling companies and assets • NFT and DeFi platform	B2B SaaS Commission License Fee
Currencii (2018)	• Marketing/finding clients • Operative business/serving clients • Banking infrastructure • Online B2B currency exchange marketplace • Karenzi is an online exchange facility that implements currency exchange on the basis of a license issued by the Central Bank of Armenia. Based out of Tallinn, Harjumaa, Estonia	B2B Commission
Envoy (2018)	• Programming & engineering • Marketing/finding clients • Online marketplace for trade financing	B2C
Salv (2019)	• Anti-money laundering, crime-fighting platform	B2B

Table A1. (*Continued*)

Name (established)	Key services	Business model
Modularbank (2019)	• Offering different modules to financial institutions to build banking products • Core banking platform for financial institutions • Flexible and convenient financial services: banking as a service for financial institutions • API-first banking platform	B2B
2020–Present		
YIELD App (2020)	• Programming & engineering • Enables people to invest in decentralized finance • DeFi banking	
Income (2020)	• Marketing/finding clients • A marketplace for investment in loans	B2B B2C
Wisora Financial Planning (2020)	• Programming & engineering	B2B B2C
ProBit Exchange (2020)	• ProBit exchange is a global Top 20 crypto exchange in real daily trading volume	B2B B2C
Polkadex (2020)	• Programming & engineering • Operative business/serving clients • Fully decentralized peer-to-peer orderbook-based cryptocurrency exchange for the DeFi ecosystem	B2C
Wert (2020)	• Programming & engineering • Operative business/serving clients	B2B, B2B2C
Landex (2021)	• Marketing/finding clients • Operative business/serving clients	B2B, B2C
2local (2021)	• Programming & engineering • Operative business/serving clients	B2B, B2C
Story Blanket (2021)	• Programming & engineering • Marketing/finding clients	C2C
Moss Estonia (2021)	• Programming & engineering • Operative business/serving clients	B2B

Sources: Tirmaste *et al.* (2019), Cledara (2021), Fybish (2021) and Tracxn (2021).

References

Aalto Capital (2021). FinTech in the Baltics. https://aaltocapital.com/wp-content/uploads/2021/08/FinTech-in-the-Baltics-Paper-FINAL-29.7.21.pdf [Accessed: 22 August 2021].

Anthes, G. (2015). Estonia: A model for e-government. *Communications of the ACM, 58*(6), 18–20.

Arner, D., Barberis, J., & Buckley, R. (2016). The evolution of FinTech: A new post-crisis paradigm? *Georgetown Journal of International Law, 47*, 1271–1278.

Bell, D. (2019). ERBD and Estonia are working on their first sandbox. https://www.ebrd.com/news/2019/moving-the-regulatory-debate-forward-ebrd-and-estonia-are-working-on-their-first-sandbox.html [Accessed: 2 September 2021].

Cao, L., Yang, Q., & Yu, P. S. (2021). Data science and AI in FinTech: An overview. *International Journal of Data Science and Analytics, 12*, 81–99.

Centric Digital (2016). How FinTech is shaping the financial services industry. https://www.centricdigital.com/blog/how-fintech-is-shaping-the-financial-services-industry [Accessed: 15 August 2021].

Chishti, S., & Barberis, J. (2016). *The Fintech Book: The Financial Technology Handbook for Investors, Entrepreneurs and Visionaries*. John Wiley & Sons, West Sussex.

Cledara (2021). The 30 hottest startups in the Baltics. https://www.cledara.com/blog/the-30-hottest-startups-in-the-baltics [Accessed: 21 August 2021].

DataReportal — Global Digital Insights (2021). Digital 2021: Estonia. https://datareportal.com/reports/digital-2021-estonia [Accessed: 25 May 2021].

de Carlos Sola, J. (2018). Process of modernization and technological development in Estonia. https://www.unav.edu/en/web/global-affairs/detalle/-/blogs/process-of-modernization-and-technological-development-in-estonia [Accessed: 15 August 2021].

e-Estonia (2021a). The trendsetters of Estonian FinTech companies at Money 20/20. https://e-Estonia.com/the-trendsetters-of-estonian-fintech-companies-at-money-20-20/ [Accessed: 1 September 2021].

e-Estonia (2021b). We have built a digital society and we can show you how. https://e-Estonia.com/ [Accessed: 29 May 2021].

e-Residency (n.d.). Digital nomad visa. https://e-resident.gov.ee/nomad visa/ [Accessed: 29 May 2021].

Fanning, K., & Centers, D. P. (2016). Blockchain and its coming impact on financial services. *Journal of Corporate Accounting & Finance,*

27(5), 53–57. https://onlinelibrary.wiley.com/doi/abs/10.1002/jcaf.22179 [Accessed: 18 June 2021].

Findexable (2019). The Global FinTech Index 2020. The global FinTech index city rankings report. https://findexable.com/wp-content/uploads/2019/12/Findexable_Global-Fintech-Rankings-2020exSFA.pdf [Accessed: 15 June 2021].

FinTech in Baltic (2020). Estonia FinTech startups map 2020 — First ever draft of the FinTech scene in Estonia. https://fintechbaltic.com/1583/fintechestonia/estonia-fintech-startups-map-2020-first/ [Accessed: 16 August 2021].

Fintech Law (2019). Estonia building regulatory sandbox. https://www.fintechlawmagazine.com/2019/02/19/estonia-building-regulatory-sandbox/ [Accessed: 5 September 2021].

Furber, S. (2018). Baltic Fintechs juggle growth ambitions with tougher checks for financial crime. https://www.spglobal.com/market intelligence/en/news-insights/trending/t6zsrr0orvi8rk_qqpb08a2 [Accessed: 16 August 2021].

Fybish, A. (2021). Top Estonian startups to watch in 2021. https://www.startupstash.com/estonian-startups/ [Accessed: 15 August 2021].

Heston, T. (2017). A case study in blockchain healthcare innovation. *International Journal of Current Research*, *9*(11), 60587–60588. https://www.researchgate.net/publication/321478417_A_case_study_in_blockchain_health_care_innovation [Accessed: 20 June 2021].

International Monetary Fund (2018). E-stonia takes off. https://www.imf.org/external/pubs/ft/fandd/2018/03/pdf/trenches.pdf [Accessed: 9 August 2021].

Invest in Estonia (n.d.). FinTech. https://investinestonia.com/business-opportunities/fintech/ [Accessed: 16 August 2021].

Kazmi, R. (2021). *8 uses of AI in FinTech: Using Machine Learning.* https://www.koombea.com/blog/8-uses-of-ai-and-machine-lear ning-in-fintech/ [Accessed: 20 August 2021].

Kemp, S. (2021). Digital 2021: The latest insights into the 'state of digital'. *We Are Social.* Weblog. https://wearesocial.com/us/blog/2021/01/digital-2021-the-latest-insights-into-the-state-of-digital/ [Accessed: 25 May 2021].

Klein, C., Havrylchyk, O., & Casullo, L. (2017). *Reviving Productive Investment in Estonia.* OECD Economics Department Working Papers.

Laidroo, L., Tamre, A., Kukk, M. Tasa, E., & Avarmaa, M. (2021). FinTech report Estonia 2021. https://www.researchgate.net/publication/352381420_FinTech_Report_Estonia_2021 [Accessed: 28 June 2021].

Lee, I., & Shin, Y. J. (2016). FinTech: Ecosystem, business models, investment decisions, and challenges. *Business Horizons*, *61*, 35–46.

Lumiste, R., Robert, P., & Purju, A. (2008). *Estonia's Economic Development: Trends, Practices, and Sources. A Case Study.* The World Bank. https://openknowledge.worldbank.org/bitstream/handle/10986/28035/577240NWP0Box353766B01PUBLIC10gcwp025web.pdf?sequence=1&isAllowed=y [Accessed: 30 August 2021].

Mastercard Lighthouse (2020). Mastercard Lighthouse — Join the 2020 edition. https://mclighthouse.com/mastercard-lighthouse-join-the-2020-edition/ [Accessed: 1 September 2021].

Mastercard Lighthouse (2021). Spring 2021 starts with a new name and 15 promising Nordic and Baltic tech start-ups joining Mastercard Lighthouse. https://mclighthouse.com/spring-2021-starts-with-a-new-name-and-15-promising-nordic-and-baltic-tech-start-ups-joining-mastercard-lighthouse/ [Accessed: 6 October 2021].

Mention, A. (2019). The future of Fintech. *Research-Technology Management*, *62*, 59–63.

Mittal, V. (2019). *Estonia FinTech Landscape.* doi:10.13140/RG.2.2.25217.10080 [Accessed: 5 September 2021].

Peyton, A. (2019). EBRD and Estonia unveil regulatory sandbox. https://www.fintechfutures.com/2019/02/ebrd-and-estonia-unveil-regulatory-sandbox/ [Accessed: 5 September 2021].

Raiffeisen Bank International in Austria (2021). How Finance Estonia contributes to developing their country's FinTech ecosystem. https://www.cee-fintechatlas.com/2021/07/12/how-financeestonia-contributes-to-developing-their-countrys-ecosystem/ [Accessed: 10 September 2021].

Schueffel, P. (2016). Taming the beast: A scientific definition of Fintech. *Journal of Innovation Management*, *4*, 32–54.

SEB (2020). The success story continues: only Estonian companies represent the Baltics in Mastercard's financial technology accelerator. https://www.seb.ee/en/news/2020-02-27/the-success-story-continues-only-estonian-companies-represent-the-baltics-in-mas [Accessed: 7 September 2021].

Startup Estonia (2021). Estonian startup database. https://startupestonia.ee/startup-database [Accessed: 10 September 2021].

Startup Wise Guys (2021). Why FinTech accelerator? https://startupwiseguys.com/fintech/ [Accessed: 1 October 2021].

Still, K., Lähteenmäki, I., & Seppänen, M. (2019). Relationships in the emergence of FinTech ecosystems. In *Proceedings of the 52nd Hawaii International Conference on System Sciences.*

Sumedrea, S. (2020). Regional development of financial innovation in eastern European countries. *Series V — Economic Sciences*, *12*(61–62), 133–142.

The Iyer Report: Understanding FinTech (2017). FinTech: Where did it start? http://www.theiyerreport.com/2017/fintech-where-did-it-start/ [Accessed: 17 August 2021].

The New Economy (2019). How Estonia became Europe's tech hotspot. https://www.theneweconomy.com/technology/how-estonia-became-europes-tech-hotspot [Accessed: 10 September 2021].

The World Bank Group (2020). FinTech in Europe and Central Asia: Maximizing benefits and managing risks. https://openknowledge.worldbank.org/handle/10986/33591 [Accessed: 7 September 2021].

Tichy, N., & Charan, R. (1990). Citicorp faces the world: An interview with John Reed. https://hbr.org/1990/11/citicorp-faces-the-world-an-interview-with-john-reed [Accessed: 2 September 2021].

Tirmaste, K. (2019). *FinTech Ecosystem Development in Estonia.* Tallinn University of Technology.

Tirmaste, K., Voolma, L., Laidroo, L., Kukk, M., & Avarmaa, M. (2019). FinTech Report Estonia 2019. Tal Tech Department of Economics and Finance. http://www.financeestonia.ee/priority_niche/financial-technology/attachment/fintech-report-estonia-2019/ [Accessed: 15 June 2021].

Tracxn (2021). FinTech startups in Estonia. tracxn.com/explore/FinTech-Startups-in-Estonia [Accessed: 1 September 2021].

Van de Wiele, W. (2018). European FinTech: New rules on the way. *Banking & Financial Services Policy Report*, *37*(5), 16–31.

Wojcik, D. (2021). Financial geography I: Exploring FinTech — Maps and concepts. *Progress in Human Geograph*, *45*(3), 566–576.

https://doi.org/10.1142/9781800612723_0011

Chapter 11

Digital Remittances: The Role of Alternative Money Transfer Channels

Martina Metzger*,‡, Tim Riedler†,§ and Jennifer Pédussel Wu*,¶

**Institute for International Political Economy Berlin, Berlin School of Economics and Law, Berlin, Germany*

†Department of Economic and Social Geography, University of Cologne, Cologne, Germany

‡martina.metzger@hwr-berlin.de

§riedler@wiso.uni-koeln.de

¶jennifer.pedussel-wu@hwr-berlin.de

Abstract

This chapter explores the role of digital financial services, e.g., mobile money systems and cryptocurrency-based systems, for migrants to send remittances. We discuss whether digital remittance channels increase access to financial services for remittance-sending and remittance-receiving households. Africa, and in particular Kenya, are pioneers in digital money transfer systems; thus, our chapter focuses on Kenya, however taking into account other experiences of the Global South. We find that digital remittance channels are often superior in terms of service-related features. However, the choice to use a specific transfer channel might be restricted by the lack of physical and technological availability of providers, means, and technological illiteracy. In addition, sending and receiving households might be cautious to use mobile cash systems due to a lack of trust in the system, the providers, or regulatory authorities. Accordingly, financial inclusion beyond e-payments and outreach to the poor is not automatic. In contrast, the use of Bitcoin-based transfer systems is more ambivalent; these systems are technically more challenging in terms of both infrastructure and literacy and more vulnerable to fraud. Some findings also indicate that Bitcoin is an incomplete and inferior substitute to other digital remittance channels.

Keywords: Digital financial services, digital remittances, financial inclusion, mobile money, cryptocurrency-based systems.

1. Introduction

There is already a vast literature exploring the benefits of a continued stream of economic remittances to migrants' home countries. Two aspects have not yet received sufficient attention. The first is the role digital financial services might play in facilitating remittance transfers by overcoming the deficiencies of traditional formal and informal transfer channels, of which one is the high cost of transfers systematically limiting the development potential of remittances. In 2015, reducing the transfer costs of remittances was included into the sustainable development goals (SDGs) of the UN reflecting the outstanding role remittances could play for development. The subsequent 2016 UN SDG Report shows the worldwide average rate of remittance fees at that time at 7.5% declining from around 10% a few years earlier (United Nations, 2016, p. 31). Since then remittance costs continued declining even through the pandemic; in the final quarter of 2020, average costs for sending US$200 descended to 6.5%, with some Pacific islands still at 9.1%, followed by Sub-Saharan Africa with 8.5% (United Nations, 2021, p. 47). Accordingly, there is still a long way to go to achieve the SDG goal to downsize the costs for remittance transactions to less than 3% and to eliminate those remittance corridors that charge more than 5% by 2030 (World Bank Group, 2016a, p. 1).

An increase in the use of digital financial services and crypto currencies has enabled customers to send money around the world quickly at lower fees than with traditional remittance methods. A trend to which the IMF Managing Director only recently referred when stating that '(W)e are witnessing a *revolution* in digital money that could make remittances easier, faster, and cheaper' (Georgieva, 2021). Hence, this chapter explores the potential of these digital money transfer channels to contribute to the premature achievement of SDGs; so we also intend to create and contribute knowledge to the broader discussion of the G20 Global Partnership for Financial Inclusion (GPFI, 2017) and the G20 financial inclusion action plan (FIAP).

A second aspect not broadly absorbed in literature is whether digital remittance services increase access to financial services for remittance-sending and remittance-receiving households. Although FinTech markets are still small, they might offer potential for financial inclusion by reducing transaction costs through the digitalization of their activities and providing alternative funding to borrowers with limited access to bank credit. This chapter will carefully examine these technologies and critically assess their developmental potential, including their value in times of economic or health crises. In doing so, this chapter also provides an overview of the competition between existing traditional remittance channels and the newly emerged digital channels.

Remittances are relevant for many low-income and even for middle-income countries all over the world, but they are of particular interest in Africa for four reasons. First, many low-income countries in Africa receive a relatively high share of remittances in terms of GDP and per capita incomes in comparison to other financial inflows. Second, while still a relevant population share is cut-off from traditional financial services, the access to digital services and the coverage with mobile phones is comprehensive in the overwhelming majority of African countries. Third, in some African countries, we find several pioneers of digital financial services. The best-known country pioneering digital financial services is Kenya, in which the traditional rift between telecommunication and financial services is largely resolved. Several other countries are also displaying innovative entrepreneurial initiatives making it worthwhile to explore the initiation and obstruction factors in diverse macroeconomic and regulative environments. Finally, transfer costs of non-digital remittances both to and within Africa are globally the highest. These factors make Africa, and in particularly *the* worldwide pioneer Kenya, an interesting case study for all developing countries who intend to promote FinTechs in general and facilitate digital remittances in particular.

This chapter is structured as follows. Section 2 briefly reviews the relevance of remittances, in terms of senders' motives, which provides an indication concerning sending preferences, and compared to other financial flows, illustrating their exceptional economic importance for many developing countries. In Section 3, we evaluate the existing, traditional, formal and informal remittance channels frequently used by migrants while identifying several obstacles to send and receive non-digital remittances, focusing on those service-related features, which drive the choice of remittances channels. Section 4 explains the functioning of mobile cash systems and Bitcoin-based systems which are the most important digital remittances sending channels. In this section, the Kenyan market with its well-explored and booming FinTech industry will serve as a reference country for the case studies; we will particularly focus on M-Pesa and its Bitcoin equivalent, BitPesa. We will compare these two digital financial services to traditional formal and informal channels on the basis of those features which are most relevant for remittance sending and receiving households — e.g., cost, speed, dissemination and access, reliability, and low risk of loss — and thus explain why certain digital channels are used. Moreover, we will address the obstacles identified in section three and show how digital remittances channels are able to overcome these obstacles or turn them into non-binding deficiencies. In Section 5, we change our perspective and add to the individual household point of view of section three and four the macroeconomic prospect. We critically assess the development potential of digital remittance channels, including their capability to reach out to the poor and to contribute to financial inclusion of low-income households. Section 6 concludes.

2. Relevance of Remittances

We define economic remittances as the procedure of pecuniary transfers in any manner to a receiver distant from the sender, either intra-nationally or across borders. The World Bank Group (2017a) and the IMF (2009) differentiate between three types of personal remittances: compensation of employees, capital transfers between households, and personal transfers. Capital transfers global data availability is very limited and the compensation of employees is a transfer from an employer to its employee and receive no further consideration here. This chapter will therefore focus on remittances sent by migrants working in a foreign country back home to their relatives and friends;

these are categorized as personal transfers covering '(...) all current transfers in cash or in kind made or received by resident households to or from non-resident households' (World Bank Group, 2017a, p. 17). This section provides a brief introduction of the relevance of remittances both in terms of the senders' motives and in comparison to other financial flows.

2.1. ... *in terms of senders' motives*

This section examines *four possible motives* for remitting income that are often mentioned in the literature. They are not evaluated as to which of them is a more likely and more important driving force to migrate. We rather review these motives in order to explain the use of a particular sending channel and hence to identify what is important for the sending household, who will also select the channel of transfer according to its own motives and the perception of need on the side of the recipient household. The motives of migrants sending remittances to their home country can vary, since each has a unique story. Finding out what drives migrants to remit has been the purpose of many empirical studies. Altruism in the sense of the selfless support of families and friends in the home country is seen as a leading motive for remittances. This theory is based on the supposition that people have an *intrinsic interest to support their families and friends.* This act of remitting is assumed to be completely voluntarily (for this passage Piracha and Saraogi, 2011, p. 7).

Furthermore, remittances can be seen as *a form of insurance* for those who stayed home. This so-called insurance payment is a primary focus of remittance researchers. In the literature, the insurance-payment argument is often referred to as a contractual relationship between the sender and receiver of remittances. A quasi insurance payment is made to the family, which provides a small, regular income and can cover actual health or insurance costs of the receiving households. As many of the families in the home countries are dependent on agriculture, remittances can also compensate for crop failures or subsidize the farming activities of the family. The initiator for this kind of dependency can be migrants themselves when they feel responsible for the family, which raised them or for their own children and spouse. The migration can also be initiated by the family itself who send their children abroad when they are old enough. The contractual basis of this insurance-like remittance relationship is more figurative and implicit in most of the cases (for this paragraph Piracha and Saraogi, 201, p. 10).

The sender of remittances can also *pay for services* with their remittances. A person who intends to migrate to another country and leaves a house, business or farm behind needs someone to take care of it during his or her stay abroad. By remitting to a contact person, housekeeper, security guard or employee, the remittance sender is able to take care of his or her belongings back home (Ansala, 2012, pp. 17–18). Finally, migrant workers remit *in order to invest*, e.g., by participations in SMEs, by purchasing land or other real estate. Literature considers a repayment of loans for their own education also as a use of remittances for investment purposes, similarly to the financing of education of the migrant's own children. The real or nominal assets might be owned by the sender or the sender's family (Ansala, 2012, p. 20). These investments can have long-lasting growth and development effects for the receiving households.

2.2. ... *in terms of comparative financial flows*

The worldwide monetary flow of international remittances has been rapidly increasing over the last decades. In 1990, approximately US$29 billion was sent as remittances to developing countries; 10 years later in 2000, the amount already more than doubled to US$73 billion, followed by another doubling in only 5 years when international remittances had risen to US$194 billion in 2005 (World Bank Group, 2017a). After only 2 years of small decline due to the Global Financial Crisis, the remittances flows quickly recovered and rebounded to record levels. Remittances remained resilient during the COVID-19 crisis, only falling from $507.37 billion in 2019 to 505.95 billion in 2020 (World Bank Indicators, 2021). Excluding FDI to China, remittances flows to low- and middle-income countries are the largest source of external financing (World Bank Group, 2021c). Here we refer only to *recorded* digital and non-digital remittances, which are transferred via formal digital and non-digital channels. Estimations suggest that total remittances to these countries, including those sent via informal channels, amount to a multiple of the official figures.

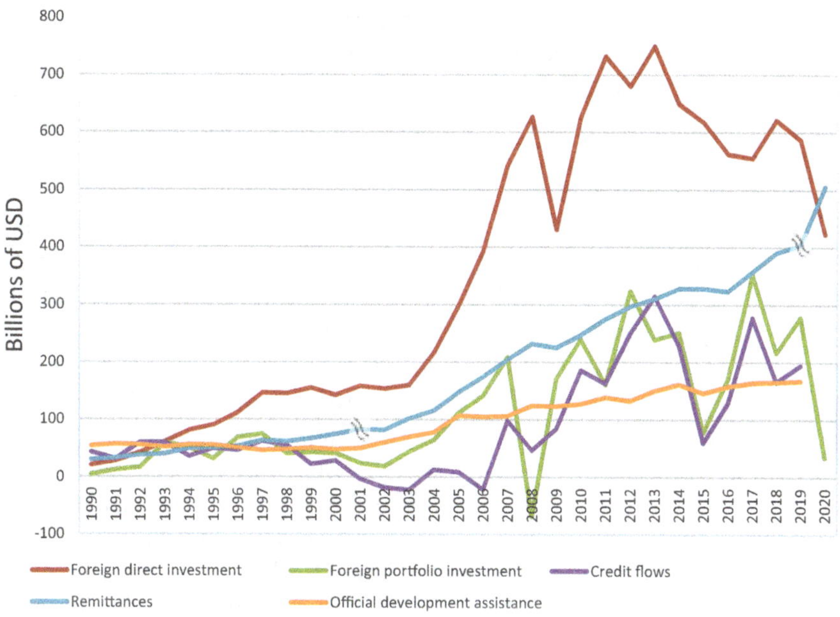

Figure 1. Financial inflows to low- and middle-income countries (1990–2020).

Sources: FDI value in 2020 originates from UNCTAD (2021, Annex Table 1, p. 248) and is calculated using World Development Indicator systematic (own elaboration). All other data is from the World Bank Development Indicators online database; FDI include FDI to China. FPI: PPG bonds, PNG bonds, equity flows. Credit flows: all public, public guaranteed and private credit flows. Remittances: personal transfers, receipts for the period 2002–2019; for the other years there is no data for personal transfers alone; accordingly, for 1991–2001 we used personal remittances received, which include personal transfer *and* compensation of employees. Own elaboration.

Remittances also grew much faster compared to other financial flows. Figure 1 shows that international remittances are the second largest international financial flow to low and middle income countries after FDI and are meanwhile about three times as high as global official development aid. If Chinese FDI were excluded from the total FDI flows as the UN SDG Report suggests (2019, p. 58), then international remittances were even higher than the non-Chinese FDI and thus would constitute the biggest global monetary flow (World Bank Group, 2019, p. 1). In 2020, remittances flows to low and middle-income countries are even higher than FDI including FDI to China;

this is due to the extraordinary situation of the pandemic during which domestic and international investment plummeted. However, we expect investment dynamic to catch up after the pandemic. Even so, the figure shows that the significance of remittances steadily increased.

In absolute terms, high population countries like China, India, and Bangladesh or countries with a large diaspora like the Philippines and Mexico are the main receiving countries. However, in terms of remittances as a percentage of GDP, countries smaller both in population and per capita income belong to the main beneficiaries which show all a remittance-to-GDP ratio of more than 10% To these countries belong Comoros, Lesotho, The Gambia, Liberia and Cabo Verde from Sub-Saharan Africa, Tajikistan, Kyrgyz Republic, Moldova, Georgia, Armenia, Ukraine, Bosnia and Herzegovina, and Montenegro from Europe and Central Asia, Haiti, Honduras, El Salvador, Jamaica, Nicaragua and Guatemala from Latin America and Caribbean, West Bank and Gaza, Yemen, Lebanon, and Jordan from Middle East and North Africa, and Nepal from South Asia. From East Asia and Pacific, only the tax havens Tonga, Samoa, and the Marshall Islands receive more remittances than 10% of GDP; the Philippines receive remittances equivalent of percent of GDP (for this paragraph World Bank Group, 2020).

Countries small in population and per capita income have only marginal access to international capital markets and is restricted in attracting private capital flows in form of FDI or FPI, when they are not resource-rich. With three quarters of global remittances directed to low- and middle income countries (AFI, 2018, p. 3) they have a much broader dissemination across low-income countries and a more equal distribution than traditional capital flows, which are highly concentrated in both sending and receiving countries.

Moreover, remittance flows are the least volatile and most reliable of all financial flows to developing countries. In contrast to traditional capital flows, which are highly pro-cyclical from the point of view of the receiving countries, remittances show a pronounced counter-cyclical character. The amount of remittances will rise, when there is an economic boom in the sending country resulting in better employment opportunities, including for migrants, and second, when there is a downturn or an outright crisis in the receiving country, i.e., when the need for more financial resources is strongest (Frankel,

2010, p. 10). Experience shows that this counter-cyclical behavior from the perspective of the receiving country holds true for any kind of crisis, be it due to natural catastrophes (e.g., in Haiti), financial or economic mismanagement (e.g., Zimbabwe), or social and political upheaval. An example is Egypt during the Arab Spring when all official subsidies and private capital flows decreased and yet the amount of monetary remittances doubled from US$7.15 billion in 2009 to US$14.32 billion in 2011 (Ratha, 2013, p. 6).

The economic and health crisis triggered by COVID-19 strongly affects developing countries, which might experience the deepest slump since post-World War II. Cross-border mobility has been suspended on a broad scale, global value chains have been broken, commodity prices were plummeting in 2020, and financial flows abruptly interrupted. Even in the modest scenario, COVID-19 might cause between 85 and 135 million individuals falling below the poverty line (Sumner *et al.*, 2020); in the medium-contraction scenario, poverty will even increase to such an extent that it will reverse the improvements made since the mid-1990s in countries of the Middle East and North Africa (MENA) as well as those of Sub-Saharan Africa. 'The pandemic is expected to reverse a consistent global trend in poverty reduction for the first time since 1996' (UN Committee for Development Policy, 2021, p. 30).

Until the third quarter of 2020 international organizations expected that COVID-19 would have strong effects on the amounts of remittances sent due to the shutdown in particularly the service sector in advanced countries; however, remittance transfers bounced back surprisingly quick and proved again to be crisis-resilient in the sending countries and counter-cyclical in receiving countries (Garcia-Mora and Rutkowski, 2020; Sayeh and Chami, 2020, p. 17; World Bank Group, 2021b, p. 5).

Gender also plays an important role in remittances flows. Although the majority of migrants are male and despite the gender pay gap, '(a)t the global level, female migrants send approximately the same amount of remittances as male migrants' (International Organization for Migration, 2010, p. 1). In the economics and sociology literature, the issues women face when sending remittances are often not taken into account. A 2006 study on gender specific determinants in remittances analysed a data set with 3,566 observations (Orozco *et al.*, 2006). The data is based on questionnaires responded to by random remitters in metropolitan areas exclusively interviewed in formal remittance shops in Germany, the UK, and the USA. Receiving regions were South America, Central America, the Caribbean and Africa. On average, the remitters were 36.7 years old and 38.6% of them were women; the remittance sending migrants had an average education of 12.35 years (Orozco *et al.*, 2006, p. 22). A sample of another study, this time in the Netherlands with 1,680 remittance sending respondents had a share of 53% female remitters; 79% of the 1,680 people received a higher than secondary education (Kosse and Vermeulen, 2014, p. 31). Women tend to send remittances to other women who take care of their children, make their education possible, or oversee the housekeeping, while men tend to send remittances to their female family members (usually spouses) who take care of the children (cf. *Ibid.*). This conforms to classic gender roles. Women remit smaller amounts on average than men remit and more often remit non-monetary assets, e.g., clothes, food and household items (Holst *et al.*, 2010, p. 5).

Since the turn of the century there is a vast literature on exploring the benefits of a continued stream of monetary remittances to migrants' home countries (e.g., Ambrosius and Cuecuecha, 2016; Butkus and Matuzeviciute, 2016; Bakker, 2015; Aga and Martínez-Peria, 2014; Ratha, 2013; Sirkeci *et al.*, 2012; UNCTAD, 2011; Giuliano and Ruiz-Arranz, 2009; Ekanayake and Halkides, 2008; Rocher and Pelletier, 2008). Monetary remittances are a way for migrant workers to provide a livelihood to those who remain in the home country. Hence, at an individual household level, remittances strengthen the financial situation of home country recipients and improve their living conditions, ceteris paribus. Recipient households have the choice to spend remittances to increase their consumption or to increase their savings, thus accumulating nominal and real wealth; in addition, they might channel remittances towards capacity building and self-financed small investments, increasing their own, and their children's educational level, creating minimum employment opportunities for themselves. As many studies show, remittances have a positive impact on the general income level of receiving households and their spending power and are thus instrumental in decreasing the risk of sliding into poverty. Overall, monetary remittances might be critical for the advancement of the economic and social development of recipient countries. Consequently, from a developmental perspective, it is crucial to facilitate and improve methods to remit.

3. Choice of Remittances Channels

There are three major groups of determinants of migrants' choices of payments channels. Firstly, individual features such as legal status in the host country, gender, age, educational level, general payments habits or financial literacy of the sender and/or the receiver. Secondly, country-specific features, in particularly of the receiving household, e.g., macroeconomic instability and a fragile banking system, capital controls or inconvertibility of the domestic currency in home countries. Finally, there are service-related features such as costs of transfers, speed of delivery, availability and access to the remittances by receiving households or security of transaction.

This section[1] focuses on service-related features driving the individual choices for particular payment channels; the payment channel might not be part of the formal economy, implying informal transactions with risks of fraud for individual migrants and establishing non-official, and sometimes even illegal, economic structures in home countries. The following section introduces the transfer channels that are frequently used by migrants for monetary remittances. The single transfer channel's working mechanisms will be briefly explained and evaluated, identifying several obstacles and deficiencies to sending and receiving non-digital remittances.

3.1. *Formal versus informal channels*

Transfer channels need a sender in one country and a receiver, usually in another country. Also, an intermediary in both countries is necessary to transfer the money and make it possible to collect or to access. Between both intermediaries, a transfer communication method or so-called interface is used to enable the transfer of the money from point A to point B (International Monetary Fund, 2009, p. 4).

[1]Partially drawing on Metzger *et al.* (2019).

Migrants have many different options for sending money to their country of origin. Besides the sender and the recipient of remittances, three traditional, non-digital stations are involved; they are the point of remittance transfer on both the sending and receiving side and finally a network linkage or transfer interface in the middle. These intermediaries reach from commercial telecommunication networks, like SWIFT,[2] to the private physical transport of money.

In general, the transfer channels are classified as informal and formal channels. Formal channels include every officially verified and publicly used monetary transfer service, such as financial institutions like banks or registered money transfer operators (MTOs), but also electronic web-based money sending systems. Other ways to send remittances are autonomously managed transfers and informal MTOs with no official transferring registration. These are commonly referred to as informal sending channels (International Monetary Fund, 2009, p. 13).

Considering formal payments channels, the most reputable and secure way to transfer money cross-border is via bank transfer. Banks are perceived to guarantee for the money to arrive at the country cross-border and in many cases, have their own transfer interface, so that transfer failures should be unlikely; in the case that they do occur, the customer is reimbursed. Although commercial banks are the most reliable money transfer provider, they do not dominate the remittance market. Commercial banks are an attractive transfer channel when they have a broad network of branches and/or ATMs in both the sending and the receiving countries. If they cannot offer a widespread access to their services, they risk having other (formal and informal) market participants poaching their customers.

Even if migrants do not use banks as their payment channels, banks are sometimes included in the clearing process of cross-border transacting MTOs, which are financial enterprises that are specialized in remittance transfers and which offer a second formal payment channel. Through this practice, banks are invisibly involved in the MTOs business model and, depending on the fees, they are able to

[2]Behind most international money and security transfers is the Society for Worldwide Interbank Financial Telecommunications (SWIFT) system. This messaging network is used by most banks and formal financial institutions.

enforce for balancing the accounts, and clearing activities, they profit from the remittance process of MTOs. The biggest MTOs with a total market share of 26% of the formal remittances market are Western Union (14%), UAE Exchange (5%), Money Gram (4%), and Ria (3%) sum a total of 26% of the formal remittance market (McCann, 2019). The annual increase in remittances also attracts companies from other fields of activities to join in and function as an MTO, for example postal services.[3]

The general input payment for remittances through MTOs is made in cash. There are large MTO-networks with many agents and branches in countries worldwide. Some agents are linked to local convenience stores, post offices or mobile communication shops. Some have their own internal clearing interface and some, as mentioned above, include a bank's transfer interface. The receiving channel is an agent or branch at a location in the sender's country of origin and the receiving individual is paid out cash again by the agent. One important advantage of MTOs is that their customers need no membership or bank account; together with a higher speed of disbursal and lower fees than those which banks charge, MTOs are highly competitive. Fees tend to be lower because (i) MTOs move a high amount of money transfers and thus dispose of higher negotiation power vis-à-vis banks than individual migrants with the result that costs for unit sent can be reduced; (ii) MTOs have their network on both ends of sending remittances and thus need to charge the money transfer only once in contrast to remittances sent via the banking sector where in most of the cases two different banks, each at one end of the transfer, charge fees; and finally (iii) MTO customers do not have to be audited as customers of banks.

A third formal payments channel, though still in its infancy, but with high growth rates,[4] comprises web-based money sending

[3]For African countries see IFAD (2016); for Asian countries see Boon (2017) in the bloc of the Asian Development. See also the Irish An Post and the German Deutsche Postbank which both entered into a co-operation with Western Union.

[4]'Global P2P Payment Market accounted for $1,845.29 million in 2019 and is expected to reach $4,491.14 million by 2027, growing at a CAGR of 11.8% during the forecast period' (Globe Newswire, 2020).

institutes or FinTechs. The money transaction enabled by mainstream web-based transfer providers happens peer-to-peer,[5] meaning that one device can directly send money to another. These rapid peer-to-peer transfers are undertaken by peer-to-peer intermediaries, which are usually linked to traditional financial institutes as banks and MTOs.

A well-known example for a web-based international money transfer platform is the web application PayPal, which directly recalculates the transferred sum into a foreign currency. In 2015, the PayPal group acquired the FinTech Xoom, which focuses on sending remittances from the United States of America to other countries (PayPal, 2016). Apart from Xoom in the USA, for the time being PayPal is nearly non-existent in worldwide remittance competition,[6] or as Cuevas-Mohr (2015) states, '(...) why PayPal, who offers an international personal payments service, has never made a concerted push on the remittance market, is also an intriguing question' (p. 12). Finally, since 2018 it is possible to send funds from Paypal to M-Pesa wallets and vice versa, but only if wallet and account run on the same name (Paypal, 2019). TransferWise and WorldRemit are the biggest players in the online remittance segment. To date, WorldRemit has generated funding of a total of US$140 million. Another feature of web-based transfer activity is the ability to send credits to mobile wallets that are connected to mobile cash systems like M-Pesa.

Web-based, licensed applications like Xoom and WorldRemit are considered as formal channels because they are licensed (affiliated) FinTechs and each of their transfers can be tracked and located. The target of every transfer is clear and there cannot be veiled transactions.

There is limited transparency in the informal remittance market and informal transfers are very difficult to track. Thus, informal remittance statistics are based on questionnaires and surveys as a basis for projections, which vary widely depending on the source of estimations and the underlying assumptions. The World Bank

[5]Peer-to-peer connection is the direct communication between two devices. A mobile phone or PC connects to another device within a network. Both connected devices are equivalent and data can be sent directly.

[6]In 2013, PayPal acquired Venmo, a money transaction platform, which is used for domestic transfers and purchasing goods rather than for remittances.

Group's suggestions are somewhat in the middle of other assessments and indicate that the informal sector is about half the size of the formal remittance sector in 2006 (World Bank Group, 2006, p. 92). In a more recent paper showing a shift from informal to formal remittances due to travel restrictions during the pandemic, Kpodar *et al.* (2021, p. 8) indicate that estimates about the informal remittances market vary from 50% to 250% of official remittances flows.

Complex transfer systems such as Hawala in Pakistan, Fei Ch'ein in China, Hundi in India and Padala in the Philippines (El Qorchi *et al.*, 2003, p. 3) also belong to the informal remittance sector; most of these build on traditional banking networks that have existed for thousands of years. These channels play an important role in the remittance industry and are widely accepted and approved of by migrants. Informal networks of numerous agents in several countries generally have their own self-organized clearing system; the only monetary transaction occurs when a cross-border clearing system is used and the balances of both involved agents are compensated. Passwords, codes or official IDs are used for authentication and the entire process is quick and free of regulation. These networks provide anonymity, fast pay-outs, and an absence of third-party intervention.

3.2. *Deficiencies of channels*

3.2.1. *Costs*

The cost of remitting money and the level of financial services that are available in participating countries significantly affect remittance levels (Dermine, 2016). Although the *average costs* of remittances have decreased by 30% between 2008 and 2020, displayed in Figures 2 and 3, costs are still a drag on remittances and are significantly above the UN Sustainable Develop Goal of 3%. The average remitting cost for \$200 is meanwhile below 7% of the remittances sent (World Bank Group, 2021a, p. 12). However, the average remitting cost for the \$200 is still above 7% of the remittances sent for the receiving households as Figure 3 shows.

The costs are decreasing mainly due to technical innovation in particularly by FinTechs, which has led more start-ups and companies entering the international transfer market with business models involving transfer platforms. While the average MTO and Bank remittance costs from 2014 until 2017 were static and post office

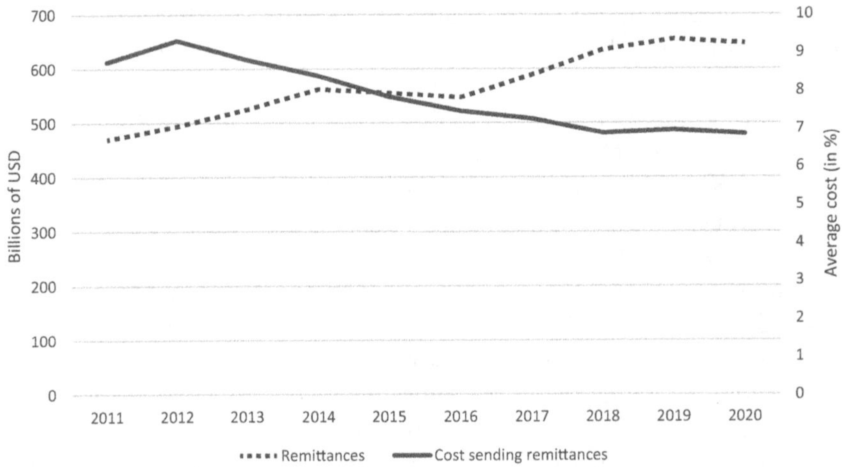

Figure 2. Remittances volume and cost for selected sending countries (2011–2020).

Notes: Remittances are personal transfers, receipts; only the values of countries were considered for which data on costs are continuously available; in total, these were 29 advanced and developing countries. Costs: Average transaction cost of sending remittances from a specific country (%); values are for the first quarter.

Sources: World Bank Development Indicators online database (remittances), Remittances Prices Worldwide (Sending Countries) online database. Own elaboration.

costs even increased, overall average costs decreased due to newcomers entering the market. The latter usually follow a strategy of low costs to enter the market and offer customers an affordable alternative to bank channels.

The costs may vary strongly across the *channels* used and the *regions* to which remittances are sent. Among the three most used formal traditional remittance channels, the MTO transfer charges a budget price, followed by post offices and finally traditional banks with the most expensive rates (World Bank Group, 2021a, p. 14). Globally, South Asia is one of the most cost-effective regions of the world both in terms of receiving and sending remittances, with average transfer costs of around 4.7% (World Bank Group, 2021a, p. 14). This is due to the high share of total remittances channeled to this region. In contrast, the most expensive region to send money is Sub-Saharan Africa, with an average cost of more than 8% (World Bank Group, 2021a, p. 14). Two trends are notable: firstly, the poorest

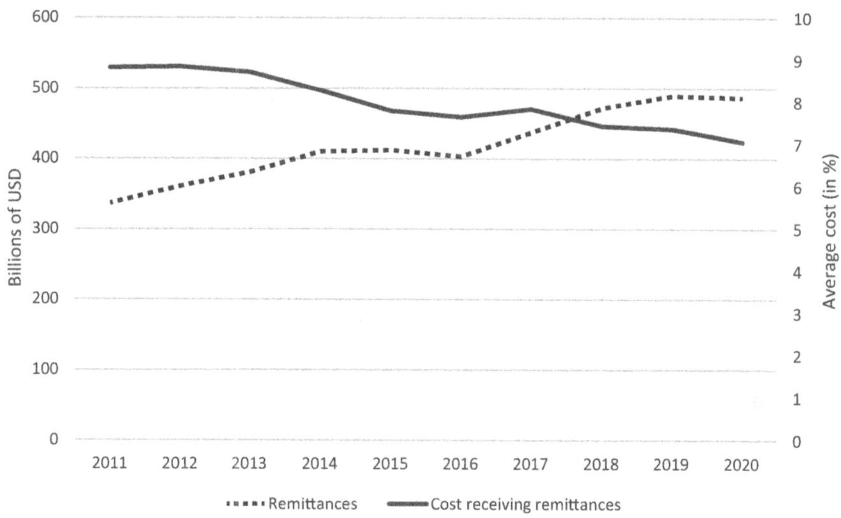

Figure 3. Remittances volume and cost for selected receiving countries (2011–2020).

Notes: Remittances are personal transfers, receipts; only the values of developing countries were considered for which data on costs are continuously available; in total, these were 82 countries. Costs: Average transaction cost of sending remittances to a specific country (%); values are for the first quarter.

Sources: World Bank Development Indicators online database (remittances), Remittances Prices Worldwide (Receiving Countries) online database. Own elaboration.

countries in Africa tend to display the highest cost of remittance; and secondly, the transfer costs of intra-regional or intra continental remittances within Africa and some domestic remittance transfers are even higher than those of remittances, which are sent from outside the continent to Sub-Saharan Africa (IFAD, 2009, p. 3).

One reason for the high cost is the low absolute market size; the Sub Saharan African market is growing, but still small in terms of the global market with $43 billion of a total $667 billion transfers in the 2019 forecast (World Bank Group, 2018, p. 4). A second hurdle is the relatively high share of rural and remote areas, which are not comprehensively covered by official remittances channels; hence, outreaching remittances to clients in remote areas comes at some cost. Finally, widespread capital account regulations and existence of administered exchange rate regimes contribute to remittances costs involving a change in currencies.

Even if there is a sizeable amount of remittances sent and a moderate banking infrastructure existing in the receiving countries, costs might still be high. For Lesotho, remittances are relatively important in terms of GDP, just below 16% in 2020 (World Bank Group, 2020). If not sent informally, including personal cross-border migration, migrants from Lesotho overwhelmingly use South African banks to transfer their remittances, as do many other migrants from the region who migrate to South Africa. Accordingly, the South African-SADC remittances channel is quite active (Metzger, 2008, p. 3, 7ff). However, the costs to remit are considerable; one of the reasons is that the South African banking sector is highly concentrated and thus can afford to charge higher fees as the domestic, meaning South African competition is limited. On the other side, South African banks are present in Lesotho as well as in most of the other SADC countries. In addition, they comply with national and international banking regulation — which some of the other (Southern) African banks do not — and hence have a relatively good reputation. Accordingly, South African banks do not currently have to fear competition from foreign peers or digital financial services, either.

A survey based on data for migrants living in the Netherlands shows that the larger remittance sums are usually transferred via bank accounts, while migrants rely on other channels, including informal ways, for smaller sums. There seems to be evidence that '(...) the use of informal channels is strongly driven by cost considerations' (Kosse and Vermeulen, 2014, p. 3). The latter is also supported by a World Bank cross-country regression in 2006 showing that in corridors with higher prices and a higher black-market exchange rate, the informal flows are higher and the formal flows are lower (World Bank Group, 2006, p. 92).

Since informal transactions are generally opaque, one can only make suggestions about their users, their motives to choose a specific channel and the costs associated with these kinds of transactions. It can be suggested that those households which are financially excluded — either involuntary or by choice — will often resort to informal channels due to lack of alternatives. To the best of our knowledge, in term of costs, no actual studies have found evidence as to what factors exactly determine the pricing rates for informal remittance systems. However, we can reliably infer that informal transactions are much cheaper than formal ones, because informal remittance providers do not actually transfer the amount of money cross-border in every transaction but use an individual clearing system. Thus, there are no fees for a banking interface and there is no need of a currency exchange before arrival at the receiver. Moreover, informal systems do not adhere to government financial market regulations, capital controls, or other foreign exchange rules. Then the avoidance of capital and wealth taxes, which senders and receivers might understand as government enforced costs using the formal way, may also be an impetus for using informal channels.

Apart from high costs for remittance products, another problem migrants face is the *uncertainty of* not knowing the *total costs* of a product at all (Holmes *et al.*, 2007, p. 12). Sometimes, they might only been given a range in which the price settles. Besides, in low-priced transfer products hidden costs can arise (*ibid.*). Fees can be subtracted from the remitted sum or marked up upon the remitted sum. Moreover, the fees are in some cases paid as a trade excluded from the actual transfer. Senders have to keep that in mind when they want their counterpart to receive a precise sum.

3.2.2. *Other obstacles*

One major factor restricting migrants from using a direct remittance payment via a bank or credit institute as an intermediary is the requirement that the sender has to have a bank account in the same bank *and* the receiver has to have a bank account in any bank, which would be the addressee of the payment. This locks out migrants without residency papers as customers as they are severely limited in opening bank accounts. Moreover, given the level of *financial exclusion* in developing countries, many receiving households might not have access to the formal banking system. Almost 52.2% of all adults have an account at a formal financial institution in East Asia and Pacific, which is the most financially inclusive developing region; on the other hand, only up to 30.1% of adults in Sub-Saharan Africa have accounts, which marks it as the most financially excluded region in the world.[7]

The *lack of accurate delivery times* often forces migrants to use other remittance channels with adverse attributes when the sender wants the money to arrive at a certain closing date. This is not

[7]The data is of 2017 and refers to adults from age of 15 years on (World Bank Group, 2020, Table A.1.2).

valid for the majority of MTOs who are able to tell their clients precisely when the money transfer is going to be completed (Holmes *et al.*, 2007, pp. 16–17). On the other hand, banks seem to have the most difficulties to reliably disclose the exact duration for the money transfer; for instance, the transfers to Ghana, Morocco, Serbia, and Vietnam in 2007 took longer than the transfer providers had signaled upfront (Holmes *et al.*, 2007, pp. 16–17).

The *security* of international money transfers in the case of remittances defines the concerns of senders that the transferred money could get lost in the intermediary or retained by non-serious providers. Since the major reputation of transfer providers is via word-of-mouth recommendation, the issue of picking an insecure remittance channel is above all faced by new senders and people whose focal point is a low price that trades in reliability and safety (Profile Business Intelligence Ltd., 2005, p. 21).

A further obstacle for senders in picking an adequate transfer channel can be the limited *availability of physical remittance providers* in their area. When conducting an offline transaction, the sender is forced to remain with banks and MTOs, which have branches within a certain radius. 'Often these remittances are picked up far from home and families must add substantial travel costs and time to the already high transfer fees' (IFAD, 2009, p. 2). In addition, traveling with amounts of cash exposes receiving households to physical assaults and robbery on their way home.

When providers offer their products online, senders can also have problems reaching them in rural areas with poor internet access. The internet penetration in Africa is, with 40%, very low and corresponds to only two thirds of the penetration rate compared to the rest of the world; in addition, while 17% of the global population are located in Africa, it is the home of only 12% of the worldwide internet users and thus shows that Africa is still underrepresented in terms of internet access (Internet World Stats, 2019a).[8]

[8]IWS uses the following definition for its statistics: Someone is defined as an internet user if he or she has the capacity to use the internet; there are two requirements: (1) The person must have available access to an Internet connection point; and (2) The person must have the basic knowledge required to use web technology. All ways to enter the internet are covered by these figures (Internet World Stats, 2019b).

Thus, the lack of technological availability excludes receiving households and therefore also sending households from using online remittance services and exposes them to either the traditional formal channels with high costs, or falling back on informal transfer means. Even if there is internet access, some, especially low-skilled households, lack sufficient technical comprehension to understand how online money transfers work and accordingly use a computer or a smart phone for online remittances (TechnoServe, 2016, p. 8). Consequently, it is the combination of costs, speed, and safety, which are the driving factors for migrants in choosing their remittances channel, while it is the lack of physical and technological availability of providers and means, financial exclusion, and technological illiteracy, which all restrict the choices of migrants from the very beginning.

4. Digital Remittance Channels

Since the 2010s, there has been an intensified search for digital payment channels in order to reduce costs, facilitate access, and lower thresholds for new users. This development has shaped an alternative remittance market with its own digital channels. Two types of these remittance channels will be analysed in this section.[9] Section 4.1 deals with mobile cash systems enabling the cashless money transfer via mobile telephones. It focuses on the most reputable player and pioneer in this business field, M-Pesa in Kenya. Subsequently, the Bitcoin-based business models of FinTechs are examined. The focus will be on the start-up Bitpesa, a Bitcoin equivalent to M-Pesa, also located in Kenya. The present use of both channel types in remittances will be evaluated after describing the functional mechanisms. Both types will be compared to the traditional remittance channels concerning transfer fees and practical examples of FinTech start-ups will be considered.

4.1. *Mobile cash systems*

Any type of payment system that allows the user to send money from one mobile device to another is classified as a mobile cash

[9]This section draws on Metzger *et al.* (2019).

system. There is no internet connection nor a computer required for the mobile cash system; money is sent using the communications system and net technologies of telecom companies. Besides sending and receiving money, households can use these systems to purchase goods and services, receive government payments or pay taxes.

These mobile cash-only systems entered the African market in the last few years with great success. There were more than six billion people using a mobile device, which corresponds to a penetration rate of 78.05% (Statista, 2021a). In Africa, the mobile phone penetration increased rapidly with a continental penetration of 67% (Adepetun, 2015). Kenya has one of the fastest growing mobile device penetration rates worldwide with a total of over 90% already in 2016 (Kemibaro, 2016), bringing it into the top position of African countries and far above the global average.[10] In the Kenyan market, the mobile communication provider Safaricom is the market leader with a market share of approximately 70% (Kenyan Wall Street, 2017).

In 2007, Safaricom introduced the mobile money transfer and payment system M-Pesa to the Kenyan market. The system exploits the USSD technology for sending financial payments between the cell phones users. The individual current account is available as a deposit on the respective user's mobile devices (Jack and Suri, 2014, p. 187), allowing access to the account with a simple SIM-card application. Users can withdraw cash via an M-Pesa agent, an extra M-Pesa ATM or a co-operating bank ATM; the fee for the withdrawal depends on the amount paid-out, e.g., the cost for a cash-outflow of US$200 at an M-Pesa agent equals a pricing rate of about 0.9% (Safaricom, 2017a). The customer, however, will be paid out in Kenyan Shilling.

On the other side, each M-Pesa user can approach agents in different stores and buy electronically credited money with their cash. Airtime, as M-Pesa's virtual money is referred to, is freely transferable to both users and non-users. Accordingly, even vendors, who do not use the M-Pesa payment system themselves, accept it for purchasing

[10]This figure seems to contradict the figures given for internet penetration in Section 3.2. With mobile phones access to internet is not always possible. Not every mobile phone is a smart phone and not every smart phone contract covers using the internet. However, there is a positive link between mobile phone penetration and internet penetration, i.e., Keyna has an internet penetration rate of 90% (Internet World Stats, 2019b).

goods and services in their shops and stores. Another feature, which makes the M-Pesa system very attractive for the vendors, is that it provides its customers with a kind of overdraft to pay their bills. With that, airtime fulfils two of the four functions of money, i.e., the medium of exchange and a limited medium of deferred payments function. As Hughes and Lonie (2007, p. 68) emphasized, the developers wanted to '[...] allow the customer to make payments as conveniently and simply as they do when they buy an airtime top-up [...]'. To raise the acceptance of the M-Pesa payments system, particularly by vendors, the settlement of merchant deposits is automatized as a service by Safaricom, which enables the merchants to settle accounts themselves and receive money almost immediately (Communications Africa, 2015).

M-Pesa was launched in Kenya, but quickly spread to Tanzania, Mozambique, the Democratic Republic of Congo, Lesotho, Ghana, and Egypt. It also entered the Asian market with India already in 2013 and the European market with Romania (2014) and Albania (2015) (EservGlobal, 2016, p. 2). Nevertheless, the major market of M-Pesa is still Kenya; the overall active number of users grew from about one million in 2007 to 33.4 million in 2018 (Medici, 2019). Users residing outside of Kenya increased to 13.4 million in 2019 (Alushula, 2019).

The fee system of M-Pesa for domestic airtime transactions differentiates between registered user transfers and those to unregistered users.[11] Moreover, the fee charged per transaction amount declines per unit by increasing amounts; transfers of 1–100 Kenyan Shilling (KSH) are free of charge. To send 101 KSH, (approximately US$1) incurs a cost of 11% of the total sum; fees fall to 0.15% for 70,000 KSH, the highest possible amount for one transfer and currently worth around US$640 (Safaricom, 2019b). The transfer to unregistered M-Pesa network users follows slightly stricter rules and incurs higher fees. The possible transfer range starts at 101 KSH and is limited to 35,000 KSH for a fee of 0.87%, due to guidelines of the Kenyan Central Bank. Cross border M-Pesa transactions include fees from 100 to 500 KSH with a maximum amount of 70,000 KSH (Safaricom,

[11] For a discussion of domestic remittances transfers in selected African countries see European Investment Bank (2014).

2019a). Should the receiver of a transferred sum of US$200 from the USA to Kenya want to spend the money in cash, the fees for the transfer and the withdrawal have to be calculated although the total amount of 2.65% in fees is still below the SDG range of 3%. M-Pesa Global can also be used to transfer funds directly to bank accounts and over 500,000 Western Union branches (Safaricom, 2019a).

M-Pesa has thus already realized the SDG objective of transferring remittances under 3% and is far superior to any other formal channel.[12] The relatively low transfer fees together with the simple technical handling result in M-Pesa being increasingly used for national and international remittances.

In 2015, Safaricom enabled the international money transfer feature for M-Pesa clients all over the world; a transfer from a bank account to an M-Pesa wallet is possible via USSD code[13] (Safaricom, 2017b). In addition, remittance providers have begun to include M-Pesa and other mobile payment systems as a receiving channel in their operating platforms; the best practice example is WorldRemit, which allows its clients to send mobile credits to people operating an M-Pesa wallet. WorldRemit is thus now the market leader of transfer applications that enables transactions to mobile wallets, '(...) with 30 services in 20+ countries across Europe, Africa, Asia and the Pacific' (WorldRemit, 2016). Fees for a WorldRemit-M-Pesa transfer satisfy the SDG threshold for a US$200 transaction. Moreover, outsiders can charge airtime on Kenyan wallets directly using WorldRemit. A partnership with Western Union enables Kenyan households to receive money via M-Pesa from 45 countries all over the world, including Canada, the UK and the USA (Ntara, 2015, p. 1). Similarly, Azimo, an online remittance provider from Great Britain announced an 80% growth of transfers to M-Pesa wallets from their platform in 2018 (Mavadiya, 2018).

[12]The average pricing rate for the same transfer would be at 8.05%, the cheapest alternatives being WorldRemit with a total cost rate of 3.14%, Ria with 5.35% and Union with 6.04% (World Bank Group, 2017b).

[13]Unstructured Supplementary Service Data — Code consistent of numbers, # and * on the mobile keyboard. A certain sequence functions as control command to arrange a bank-to-wallet transfer.

These co-operations link a traditional, formal remittance channel on the sender's side with a digital formal remittance channel on the receiver's side. The partnership allows the client to remit directly to a mobile M-Pesa wallet. The greatest advantage of M-Pesa in a remittance context is the fact that the whole transfer and clearing system is organized similarly to the networks of informal transfer channels. Clients can send the airtime freely to friends or family and do not require an agent for the transferring process. The agent is solely functioning as a currency exchange from real currency into airtime and vice versa.

M-Pesa also displays advantages in comparison to informal channels. Every transfer is tracked and verified by secure SMS with single transfers capped at US$500, thereby limiting the risk of loss and fraud for the overwhelming majority of remittances transfers. The funds of the M-Pesa users are deposited by a trust with commercial banks in Kenya; however, M-Pesa users continue to own their funds at all times. Even in case of bankruptcy, neither Safaricom nor Safaricom's credit would have access to these funds while the Central Bank of Kenya oversees both commercial banks and M-Pesa.

Since actual currency is not involved in the transfer process, the airtime is free floating and there are marginal costs involved in this kind of transfer. In addition, the transfer agent, here Safaricom, is not involved in the transaction process; payments are made by individual users so the only effort made by Safaricom is the clearing process and the customer service.[14] Accordingly, transactions are completed in a short, predictable, and reliable amount of time; furthermore, the user is not geographically bound to any (physical or technological) local institution except for cellular network access (Herzog and Bolli, 2014, p. 4).

There is no doubt that the adaption of M-Pesa as a payment method is a success story in Kenya as is indicated in Figure 4. Ntara (2015) surveyed the use of M-Pesa for international transfers.

[14]Safaricom pays fixed costs for maintaining the cellular network and the variable costs for the secure SMS transfer are negligible indicating that the extra services provided by Safaricom do not have associated additional costs apart from staffing as transfers happen nearly in real-time.

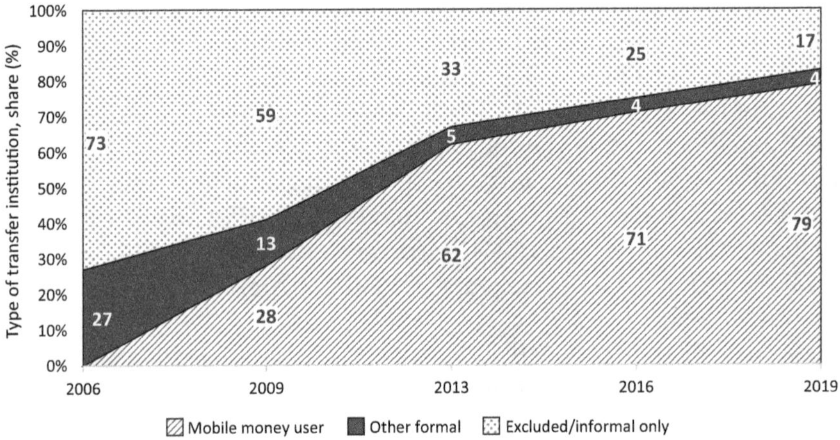

Figure 4. Financial access in Kenya (2006–2019).
Source: FinAccess data, cited in Metzger *et al.* (forthcoming).

Her study covers transfer data of M-Pesa, nine banks, and Western Union for a period of 8 months; it was observed that M-Pesa, with the smallest sum within the observed institutions, has a share of 5% in this market segment of the 11 biggest players in international transfers in Kenya, however it is still higher than 34 other Kenyan banks (Ntara 2015, p. 77).

M-Pesa spreads across the borders to many African countries, but also to Europe and Asia. The business implications of M-Pesa in these other countries have not reached the Kenyan level, yet, but it seems that they also have an impact on the local financial markets. However, it is not as engaging as it is in Kenya. For example, 14 months after the introduction of M-Pesa in Kenya there were 2.7 million registered users and 3,000 registered agents; in Tanzania after 14 months there were only 280,000 registered users and 930 registered agents, although Tanzania has more inhabitants than Kenya (International Finance Corporation, 2010b, p. 2). In contrast, the case of M-Paisa, which is the name of the client in Afghanistan, commercially launched in 2008, shows that in countries with a highly competitive telecommunication market and low technology adaption there can be many hurdles in setting up a mobile cash system (International Finance Corporation, 2010a, pp. 1–3).

4.2. *Bitcoin-based transfer systems*

Bitcoin is referred to as cryptocurrency, or virtual currency, scientifically and in the media.[15] Bitcoin received great attention by the mainstream media. Its price increased to 5-digit numbers with a value of almost $50,000 at the peak per Bitcoin and the price has shown considerable volatility. Bitcoin is not an actual currency in the classical sense because the four main monetary functions — unit of account, medium of exchange, store of value, and medium of deferred payments — are not present.[16] Using Bitcoin as a unit of account is very difficult due to its eight decimal places and odd pricing numbers.

Further, a currency should function as a medium of exchange and should thus be a commonly accepted means and payment method for current transactions; although the number of merchants accepting Bitcoin is increasing, it is still far from crossing a minimum threshold to be of relevance. In addition, its practical infeasibility in terms of usage for small amounts limits its dissemination for payments for ordinary goods and services. Lastly, the price volatility and the insecurity about the future performances rules out Bitcoin taking over the function of the store of value and the medium of deferred payments which both require (expected) long-term stability. The volatility and instability of Bitcoin discourages creditors from accepting Bitcoins as a medium to fulfil medium- and long-term contracts, e.g., debt contracts.

There are four ways, in which Bitcoin remittances are organized. First, Bitcoin users can privately send Bitcoin from their own wallet to the receiving wallet. All this happens without a remittance service provider involved and thus without the safety risks linked to such a provider. Another way is to use a service provider that manages the customer's transfer process in Bitcoin. A third alternative is that the service provider collects the customer's real currency, uses Bitcoin as a transfer currency, and pays the receiver in another, or the same real

[15]A technical explanation of the Bitcoin functional mechanisms can be found in the Bitcoin introduction paper by Satoshi Nakamoto (2008).

[16]See also Lo and Wang (2014) in particular pp. 3–12 on Bitcoin's unsustainability. As a reason why it is unfavourable to adapt see https://www.economist.com/the-economist-explains/2018/07/09/why-bitcoin-uses-so-much-energy.

currency. The fourth method is for the provider to use Bitcoin as a settlement currency and abstain from processing every transaction.

The African remittance FinTech start-up Bitpesa uses Bitcoin for international money transfers, advantageously connecting both technologies Bitcoin and the already widely accepted and trusted M-Pesa payments system, in the transaction process. To get started with using Bitpesa as a remittance provider, users have to trade their local fiat currency into Bitcoin. They can do so through purchase at one of the numerous Bitcoin exchange online platforms or directly from Bitpesa. Bitbond, a Bitcoin lending platform, has a partnership with Bitpesa, which allows them to quickly access Bitcoin. The Bitcoins can then be sent from over 85 countries in the world to Kenya, Tanzania, Uganda, and Nigeria. After receiving the Bitcoin in an African country, Bitpesa converts Bitcoin into the local currency. The receiver can then decide whether the Bitcoins should be paid out in cash or sent to a mobile M-Pesa wallet. For receiving the money as M-Pesa airtime, a second conversion is mandatory and for this Bitpesa charges a consistent fee of 3% per transfer (Maxim, 2015) which is on average higher than using M-Pesa without Bitcoin.

One advantage of digital payments, which use standard money or virtual currency is that the receiver has the opportunity to make their payments fully digital. There is subsequently no need to collect money from an agent. More people in rural Africa then have the chance to receive their remittances via mobile phone and can also process their transactions directly without contacting an agent (only for in-payments). Therefore, travel from distant rural areas to the agent destination need not be undertaken and the risk of being robbed while carrying a lot of paper cash is reduced to zero. When no paying-out agent is involved, the cash also cannot be collected by third parties. Unbanked people have more opportunities to send and receive money besides MTOs and informal channels. Bitcoin wallets can be created easily online and be accessed directly via mobile phones. The Bitcoin wallet complies with a banking account without accounting fees and small transaction fees (Krause, 2016, p. 22). This also applies to M-Pesa, while their service is locally limited and Bitcoin is tradable worldwide (*ibid.*). In this way, undocumented migrants have access to the financial system. However, WiFi and internet penetration still limit sending Bitcoin remittances, since every transaction has to be made online.

Bitcoin presents the possibility of creating a linkage between the pay-out and the spending purpose. If a remittance sender wants to ensure that the money s/he sends is exclusively used in a certain disposition, for example their children's education, then this can be achieved via blockchain based smart contracts.[17] For instance, education fees in Kenya can also directly be paid via M-Pesa (Vodacom, 2017). The intermediary role played by the family in Kenya paying the educational fees is thus avoided, which could be an advantage for the sender.

One strength of Bitcoin in the remittance context is its potential and already established use as an intermediary currency and as a settlement currency. The advantages of a Bitcoin transaction being complete in about 10 minutes and the very small transfer fee qualify Bitcoin to work as an intermediary between fiat currencies. Bitcoin can serve as the settlement currency, because even if the settlement sum is high, there is no effect on the cost since the transfer fees are calculated by file size and not by the value transferred (Caffyn, 2015). Furthermore, a fee can be added voluntarily if the sender wants to incentivize completing their transfer faster. However, a liquid market must exist, and Bitcoin should be attainable and resalable in a short period for a relatively stable price (Scott, 2016, p. 5).

Altogether the higher fees and the volatility of the Bitcoin value together with the technological requirements, which in many rural areas are only marginally existent, and the technological knowledge necessary to manage secure Bitcoin transfers, are obstacles to wider use in low income countries. In addition, Bitcoin exchanges are prone to several forms of fraud and cyberattacks in which course the exchanges either were shut down or even disappeared completely like Kipotchi (see below) with the result that the deposits were gone (Carlisle, 2017, p. 19). Hence, it is not surprising that the market share of Bitcoin-based services to transfer digital remittances is relatively limited.

Today, Bitpesa is still preferred for international business transactions even by SMEs due to its convertibility and reduced foreign

[17]Smart contracts can be set up between two partners and are monitored and accomplished by themselves. That means that if a certain condition is fulfilled the digital money gets paid out.

exchange costs in comparison to the provision of a full-scale web-based credit card system.

Scott (2016) reports in his paper on social finance through cryptocurrencies, that:

> (...) Bitcoin also has potential to facilitate small-scale international commerce. Local merchants in poorer countries may struggle to access international payments systems to sell their goods abroad. For example, a rural crafts cooperative from Zimbabwe might struggle to set up a website with an integrated credit card payments system, but getting a Bitcoin address might enable them to sell products in exchange for Bitcoin tokens, thereby avoiding traditional e-commerce systems (which often involve having to set up a merchant account with a formal bank). Provided that a market exists to exchange such Bitcoins received in trade back into a usable local currency, this could prove useful. For example, imagine a scenario where a small-scale independent producer of sustainable cocoa butter products sold them to US clients in exchange for Bitcoin tokens that were then redeemed for local — or foreign — currency on a Bitcoin exchange. Likewise, a small-scale non-governmental organization can easily set up to receive Bitcoin tokens as donations (p. 5).

Another FinTech start-up in Kenya was Kipochi, founded, like Bitpesa, in 2013. It was a platform also directly connected to M-Pesa and adapted their wallet service to make it possible for customers to buy and sell Bitcoin via SMS. A conversion in local currency was unnecessary. In 2016, Pelle Braendgaard, the founder of Kipochi, wrote about the disappearance in his financial blog, StakeVentures claiming that Kopo Kopo, responsible for the operation, shut down the M-Pesa-Kipochi connection. This attracted the interest of the Central Bank of Kenya, which allowed Kipochi to continue its business only if it would be co-operating with a telecom provider or a financial institution, which are both supervised and monitored (Buenaventura, 2017, p. 29). This example shows that it is essential to place money transfer systems — with or without resorting to Bitcoins — under strict and thorough scrutiny and involve both regulatory and supervisory institutions.

To respond to the competitive disadvantage of higher fees for Bitcoin transfers, the company OKLink, which is a subsidiary of OKCoin from Hong Kong and a settlement network for Bitcoin remittance platforms, announced in 2016 that they will take over the transfer costs for international Bitcoin transfers by their customers of accumulated amounts up to US$100,000.[18] The costs will be balanced for every transaction of under US$500, so that particularly senders of small sums will be assisted. Bitpesa is involved in the settlement network and the subsidizing deal, however not as the only player in the Bitcoin remittance market. For instance, Coins.ph, Rebit or Coinplug also take a share in the settlement. With that the costs for Bitcoin remittances will be reduced to a range between 0.6% and 1.6%, meaning Bitcoin-based remittance transfers will not only be well below the costs of traditional remittance channels, but are able to compete with mobile cash systems.

5. The Role of Digital Remittances Channels

While there are numerous studies, surveys and research papers on the evolution of remittances, very few contributions evaluate, (i) to what extent and why households use digital remittance channels like mobile cash systems and Bitcoin-based transfer systems; (ii) what exactly is the developmental potential of digital remittance channels in terms of overcoming obstacles of traditional sending channels, outreach to low-income households, and financial inclusion; and finally (iii) what characterizes their relationship to the traditional financial sector. Given the limited studies available addressing the intersection of digital financial services, remittances, and development, we will offer only a preliminary assessment of the developmental impacts of the use of digital money transfer channels for sending and receiving remittances in terms of overcoming obstacles identified in traditional remittance channels, improving financial inclusion and reaching out to the poor. However, we begin with offering an overview of the current remittance transfer market in order to assess the share of digital remittances channels and its prospects.

[18]The complete para rests on Bergmann (2016).

5.1. *Dynamics of the market*

While all digital financial services in developing countries and emerging markets, as for instance the value of digital payments and of digital lending have grown in recent years, none of them has surged as strong as digital remittances, alone between 2017 and 2019 by 55% (Agur *et al.*, 2020, p. 3). The amount of annual cross-border remittances transactions via mobile money quadrupled from US$3.1 billion in 2015 to US$12.7 billion in 2020 (GSMA 2021, p. 37). Statista's (2021b) forecasts that the transaction value of total digital remittances will hit €107 billions in 2021 with an extraordinary transaction value growth in this year of more than 20% due to the pandemic; still, forecasts suggests that the transaction value will nonetheless continue to rise by 10.55% at least until 2025. Mobile money has meanwhile 1.2 billion registered customer accounts across more than 96 countries (GSMA, 2021, p. 6), serving 184 remittances corridors, including seven fragile countries in Sub-Saharan Africa (GSMA, 2018, p. 3). In total, the digital remittances market is highly vibrant. Domestic and international migrant will increasingly process remittances online in the next years — unless there are no cases of fraud or other, the digital services disrupting incidents.

Mobile cash systems and cryptocurrency-based models with digital money that can be used for direct payments are able to compete with other remittance-transferring entities, e.g., banks, MTOs or informal channels, including the physical transport of money. Many of the Bitcoin remittance start-ups are targeting numerous corridors at once and are also providing an alternative receiving channel besides banks. Digital remittance sending channels challenge other remittances transfer systems from different angles such as the *cost of processing the transfer* and the *cost of maintenance of the transfer network* as well as *speed of transaction* and *clearing*.

This new global competition initiated by start-ups tackles the average *transfer price for remittance* in all remittance channels as they cover all sending and receiving destinations and keep expanding them on an ongoing basis. Mobile operators offer a pricing rate of 3.12% on average making them almost half as expensive as their nearest competitors Money Transfer Operators (World Bank Group, 2021a, p. 15).

Especially in the upscale Kenyan market, where some remitters have to pay fees of 17%, the fixed price rate of 3% of BitPesa and low-priced transfers via M-Pesa makes a real difference (Heuler, 2015). Overall, there is a huge opportunity for FinTechs inventing new and expanding existing digital financial services with the financial service market locally and globally being in a transition with new players entering.

Nearly all remittance Bitcoin start-ups and M-Pesa use a *clearing and settlement system* with local pay-out channels. This makes them superior to banks and competitive against MTOs and informal remittance providers that use similar systems. Furthermore, the MTO system is generally much more complicated, inefficient, and dependent on banks. M-Pesa transactions are processed in almost real time, which means that when the SMS is sent and received, the receiver owns the funds, is able to access the money immediately and pay at shops that accept M-Pesa via mobile payment. A direct Bitcoin transfer peer-to-peer takes no longer than 10 minutes until the transfer is verified. Bitcoin remittance services take a little longer depending on the pay-in method and how many times the money must be converted into other currencies. This relatively *fast speed of digital channels* is helpful for migrants with a short time preference. If they send money spontaneously, digital channels and informal channels should be their method of choice. Also, if there was an incident back home and the money is needed immediately, migrants can depend on these types of payment. Bitcoin is open source and can easily be adapted by start-ups and emerging small businesses. Bitcoin and M-Pesa constitute a serious threat for both informal and formal remittance channels in pricing and transaction speed; accordingly, these digital channels have the chance to attract also customers who normally rely on informality.

Because Bitcoin-based systems and M-Pesa are superior in *cost and speed of remittances transfer* as well as *low costs of maintenance due to their leveraging of existing networks* they influence market prices for sending remittances resulting in decreasing average costs of remittance transfers. Competition is the main factor for the 2.5% decrease of remittance costs between 2008 and 2016 (World Bank Group, 2019, p. 5). As the study 'What explains the cost of remittances?' found out the more competition among providers in remittance corridors persists, the lower the transaction costs tend to be (Beck and Pería, 2009, p. 120). Moreover, '(...) the average prices of remittances are significantly lower in corridors with a higher number of migrants, smaller share of rural population, and a common language' (Beck and Pería, 2009, p. 120). Conversely, there are certain sending corridors with only few migrants and without real competition to rural areas in Africa where only MTOs will offer their service of transferring and accordingly charge high fees. The strong competition by FinTechs enabling digital remittances puts pressure in particular on traditional financial intermediaries, which dispose over a *banking network with branches*, which need to be maintained and determine a floor and lower bound under which their transfer costs cannot sink without *compromising the network and their financial resilience.*

One way to cope with this competition for traditional banks is to improve bank-to-mobile interoperability (GSMA, 2017a) or to enter this market with an own digital financial service vehicle in order to internalize the technological benefits; traditional companies like Western Union and Money Gram have done so and launched their online money transfer clients by now.

Though M-Pesa and Bitcoin are regulated, conditions vary depending on the country. M-Pesa has a maximum limit of airtime that can be transferred with one transaction. In contrast, the amount of Bitcoin that can be transferred within one transaction is not capped. Many countries and organizations recognize Bitcoin but show many diverse ways to approach it. Certain laws could exacerbate activities by Bitcoin remittances companies if there is no international level playing field as for instance in anti-money laundering rules and laws, but rather specific Bitcoin regulations, which differ from country to country.

5.2. *Overcoming obstacles*

Mobile cash systems do suspend critical restrictions under which other formal channels suffer, for instance from the lack of physical and technological methods and providers, financial exclusion, and a limited technological understanding. These restrictions might still exist; however, they no longer have an effect on the choice of the chosen sending and receiving channel. The only restrictions for remittances transfers via mobile cash systems are the use of a SIM card and the operation of a cellular system. Thus, mobile cash systems empower migrants to choose the remittance channel according to their own preferences and needs and, in so doing, involve developmental potential far beyond its economic advantages.

According to many surveys and case studies, to these preferences and needs belong a short, predictable, and reliable amount of time for the transfer and protection against loss and fraud. However, the major impact of mobile cash systems consists of the enduring and sustainable cost-cutting of the remittances transfer. The SDG objective of fees of fewer than 3% per transaction is envisaged globally for 2030, but cash mobile systems enable it already today for many of the existing country corridors (GSMA, 2017b, p. 9).

In addition, remittances have generally proved to be crisis-resilient. In circumstances like COVID-19 and other epidemics though, when lockdowns and social distancing are required, and cash payments and physical queuing is to be limited as they entail the risk of contagion, digital remittances have made a difference for private households and small businesses striving to stay in the market (Frost *et al.*, 2021; Agur *et al.*, 2020; Were, 2020) and offered the state the opportunity for government-to-person transfers.

Most of these benefits also apply to Bitcoin-based transfer systems; however, these systems are challenging for households and impossible to handle for those who are technically illiterate. In addition, other cryptocurrencies than Bitcoin are often not viable; it is very difficult to project which of the numerous crypto currencies invented each year will have a lasting effect and which ones will level out and cease to exist during the next years. Finally, all cryptocurrencies suffer of a high volatility of their values. Accordingly, a Bitcoin-based stand-alone system might be difficult to establish as a major remittances channel due to the above mentioned limitations as well as its vulnerability to fraud. Therefore, Bitcoin-based transfer systems have strived to advance co-operations with mobile cash systems in order to respond to these concerns and to offer their customers the advantages of both systems.

There is one basic motivation when customers prefer to use Bitcoin-based transfer systems, even if they do not operate a co-operation with mobile cash systems; customers apprehend Bitcoins as an insurance either against a perceived predatory state threatening to limit the disposal over and the amount of transferred money by capital controls and tax claims, or against macroeconomic instability in the receiving country. A recent study (Krause, 2016) about the determinants of Bitcoin usage for remittances in a sample with 21 countries showed that the demand for Bitcoin is positively correlated to inflation and financial regulation while negatively correlated with financial openness. The study uses explanatory variables such as '(...) multiple exchange rates, restrictions on current account transactions, and the requirement of surrender of export proceeds' (Krause, 2016, p. 25). The response and behavior displayed in the study is similar to that observed in circumstances of currency substitution or dollarization in highly unstable economic or political environments.

Another insight of Krause (2016) is that while, unsurprisingly, the usage of Bitcoin is positively correlated with internet penetration rates, it is negatively correlated with financial inclusion in terms of access to a bank account. On first sight, this contradicts the evaluations of many observers that the use of digital financial services increases financial inclusion. If the results of this study were to be generalized, then this would again indicate that the usage of Bitcoin is an incomplete *and* inferior substitute to which customers refer *only* if their first option suffers from deficiencies or is unavailable.

Finally, to the best our knowledge M-Pesa and Bitcoin are not (yet) subject to capital controls, although sending and receiving money constitutes a nominal asset with which the receiver might settle or create liabilities. While the airtime movement of M-Pesa can still be tracked, Bitcoin sending and receiving locations are not visible, only the remitted amount, providing users with more possibilities to anonymously send remittances.

5.3. *Financial inclusion*

Our analysis about the functioning of the most important digital remittances sending channels, mobile cash systems and Bitcoin-based systems, focused on the global pioneer market Kenya. However, in many high-remittances receiving countries, in particular in Sub-Saharan Africa, there are already alternative banking structures evolving in the form of FinTech start-ups and young companies that offer non-traditional, digital banking services such as virtual payments and low-cost money transfers. While still a relevant share of population is cut-off from traditional financial services, the access to digital services and the coverage with mobile phones (and to a lesser extent internet availability) is in the overwhelming majority of for instance African countries comprehensive. Hence, digital financial services, including blockchain technology and the use of cryptocurrencies, seems to offer cost-cutting and broadly disseminated services to remittances receiving households so far excluded from traditional financial markets. In that context, mobile money in particular, and digital financial services, in general, might provide a 'gateway to financial inclusion for both remittance senders and recipients, allowing them to join the digital financial ecosystem and to access a broad range of digital financial services beyond remittances, such as storing money in a secured account or performing digital payments' (GSMA, 2016, p. 5).

This argument derives increased financial inclusion from the technical availability of mobile cash systems or digital financial services to underbanked households. While the deducted positive impact on financial inclusion relies on the acceptance of these services by potential clients, consumer acceptance is not automatic. Many studies, which give evidence for a positive impact of digital financial services, through facilitating remittances and hence financial inclusion, indicate that consumer protection and a regulatory environment perceived as supportive are decisive for consumer adoption (Biggs, 2016). For targeting vulnerable and disadvantaged households like women, a UN Capital Development Fund study (2017) shows the creation of specific tailor-made products and services might additionally be required to fit better to the needs of these groups.

In most of the available studies analysing effects of mobile cash systems or the usage of cryptocurrencies on financial inclusion, digital financial inclusion is understood as sending or receiving money and performing purchases or sales. In that respect, financial inclusion increases with the dissemination of the technology and the rise in market shares by mobile-cash or cryptocurrency-based systems. However, it is unclear how far digital financial services actually induce financial inclusion *beyond e-payments*. Empirical evidence is at best mixed, and some experience is even less encouraging in that respect. A study classifying three groups in Kenya (having no access to a SIM card, having access to a SIM, but do not have an M-PESA account, having an M-Pesa account, but not saving on it) shows that digital financial services do not necessarily result in a rise in financial inclusion beyond the use of payment services. Those households who would be technically, and in terms of income, able to save (phone owner and higher educated), are less likely to do so in comparison to other groups (rather poor, less educated, and female households) (van Hove and Dubus, 2019). Alternatively, in Ghana, savings by users of mobile cash systems are facilitated; the mandatory regulation requires mobile money providers to deposit the float money on interest-bearing accounts with formal banking institutes and pass on 90% of the interest earned (Bank of Ghana, 2019; Wolf, 2019). It remains to be seen whether the steps taken by regulatory authorities in Ghana result in an increased amount of savings or a change in saving behavior.

5.4. *Reaching out to the poor*

Without these digital channels, poorer and financially excluded households, in particular those in rural areas, are at the mercy of informal providers of remittances services with all the downsides of this form of business, e.g., high costs, uncertain delivery time, and limited rights to prosecute the agent or the individual in case of loss or fraud. For these households at the lower end of the income spectrum, which are overwhelmingly women, no alternative exists in contrast to those financially included households, who still have the possibility of transferring remittances via banks. In addition, poorer households on average remit and receive smaller amounts and with a higher frequency; thus, these households benefit from the cost reduction offered by digital channels relatively more than households who can afford to remit and receive higher sums now and then. Data on amounts remitted across borders via mobile cash systems supports this assessment; households using mobile money remit on average only US$124, while the average amount transferred across all channels adds up to US$500 (GSMA, 2021, p. 37).

The positive distributional effects of cost-cutting and broadly disseminated digital channels on poorer households might be even more evident for domestic money transfers and especially domestic remittances. At the beginning, more than 90% of the remittances received via M-Pesa in Kenya were domestic transfers from urban to rural areas (Ntara, 2015, p. 73). In that way, rural households may also participate in the economic advancement, which is often concentrated in industrial and service clusters mainly in urban agglomerations.

Using panel data, similar results could be shown for households in rural Uganda; mobile money access had a positive and significant effect on household welfare measured by real per capita consumption due to a decline in transaction costs and the time taken for money transfers to reach remote areas (Munyegera and Matsumoto, 2016, p. 127). Similarly, Reeves (2017) shows for 18 countries in Sub-Saharan Africa that given a certain level of technological infrastructure and the use of cryptocurrencies, there is a positive correlation between remittance transfers and poverty reduction. Should these effects be generally noticeable and significant, then digital remittances channels would enable trickle-down effects and thereby might set disincentives for a further rural exodus.

However, not all case studies result in such positive evaluation. For sending and receiving households the technical requirements might prove to be too challenging and their commitment to traditional functional transfer methods too persistent. Individuals, especially those with a lower education level, tend to stick with processes they know and trust. Although not related to remittances, a study of rural Benin could not show that one mobile cash system in partnership with a single public high school would facilitate school fee payments and thus the hoped-for improved enrollment failed to appear. School fees were and still are an impediment to enrollment and '(...) students often depend on extended family and kinship networks to pay fees' (Adida *et al.*, 2018, p. 1). Parents would not adapt to the new money transfer system even though other payment options were costly and risky in terms of loss and of passing payment deadlines (Adida *et al.*, 2018).

The lack of technological knowledge of senders of remittances, especially among older and female receivers, is a problem that importantly affects the spread of digital channels. Consequently, it is difficult to assess the extent that digital remittances channels actually pull sending and receiving households out of informality. While appreciating all the positive effects digital transmission channels have on poorer households, they are not a panacea, or as the CEO of a leading US think tank on financial inclusion put it: 'It is important for the development community to pause and reflect on how our work fits into this fast-moving new universe. Poor people remain central to the story but are to lose sight of in the excitement around technology and innovation' (Bull, 2019). Hence, realistic expectations concerning the performance and creation of the expertise required to tap the full potential of both remittances and digital transfer channels are of crucial importance.

6. Conclusions

Mobile cash systems and crypto currency-based models are one segment of digital financial services, only some of which is concerned with remittances transfers; however, both the wider FinTech market and the more restricted segment of digital remittance transfer channels are highly dynamic and in permanent transition. New players with the latest innovative products and services enter the market, cooperating and establishing partnerships across industry branches, thereby challenging both traditional rivals and regulatory authorities. In comparison to traditional remittances sending channels, mobile money transfer channels are often superior in terms of service-related features as costs of transfers for sending and receiving households, speed of delivery, availability, and access to the remittances by receiving households or security of transactions. Furthermore, they are increasingly used for all sorts of payments, including digital remittances. Most important, mobile cash systems are able to fulfil the SDG goal of the 3% fee more than 10 years earlier than envisaged in 2030.

The choice of migrants and their families in the home countries to use a specific transfer channel might be restricted by the lack of physical and technological availability of providers and means, and technological illiteracy. Some studies emphasize that even if physical and technological availability is ensured and enough literacy is given, households might be cautious to use mobile cash systems due to a lack of trust in the system, the providers, or regulatory authorities. Therefore, financial inclusion and outreach to the poor is not an automatism but requires an enabling and resilient environment. Although these findings cannot be generalized, they suggest undertaking more comparative studies in order to gain a deeper understanding about the choice of the remittances transfer channels by sending and receiving households and the influence of regulatory and macroeconomic environment on these decisions.

Further research also needs to differentiate sending and receiving households more effectively according to personal features like gender, educational level, age, and place of residence (urban/rural). Research contributions could then make allowances for those vulnerable groups who would benefit the most from using mobile cash systems. In addition, comparative studies should control whether the remittances are sent within a country, within a region or across continents.

Conversely, the use of Bitcoin-based transfer systems is more ambivalent; these systems are technically more challenging both in terms of infrastructure and literacy and more vulnerable to fraud. Some findings have also indicated that Bitcoin is an incomplete and inferior substitute to which migrants refer to only when their first option is not available or suffers from severe deficiencies.

Though our findings are biased by the case study of Kenya with M-Pesa and Bitpesa and by Sub-Saharan Africa in a broader sense, we are convinced that experience gained in Africa holds keen insights and findings for other regions. This region has pioneered digital money transfer systems and tailor-made regulatory initiatives to address digital financial services, of which neither have yet been thoroughly reflected and reviewed outside Africa.

References

Adida, C., Chabi Bouko, A., Verink, A., Chockalingam, G., & Burney, J. (2018). Pilot of a mobile money school fee payment system in rural Benin, *PLoS ONE, 13*(6), e0198240.

Aga, G. A., & Martinez Peria, S. M. (2014). *International Remittances and Financial Inclusion in Sub-Saharan Africa.* Policy Research Working Paper, No. 6991. World Bank, Washington D.C.

Agur, I., Martinez Peria, S., & Rochon, C. (2020). Digital financial services and the pandemic: Opportunities and risks for emerging and developing economies. *International Monetary Fund Special Series on COVID-19, Transactions, 1*, 2–1.

Alliance for Financial Inclusion (AFI, 2018). *Innovative cross-border remittance services: Experiences from AFI member countries.* Guideline Note, No. 30. AFI, Kuala Lumpur.

Ambrosius, C., & Cuecuecha, A. (2016). Remittances and the use of formal and informal financial services. *World Development, 77*, 80–98.

Ansala, L. (2012). *Motives, channels and migration for remittances: Evidence from Uganda, Senegal and Nigeria.* Master's Thesis. Department of Economics, Aalto University School of Economics.

Bakker, M. (2015). *Migrating into financial markets: How remittances became a development Tool.* University of California Press, Oakland.

Bank of Ghana (2019). Payment System and Services Act, Act No. 897.

Beck, T., & Pería, M. (2009). What explains the cost of remittances? — An examination across 119 country corridors. *The World Bank Economic Review, 25*(1), 105–131. World Bank, Washington D.C.

Biggs, D. (2016). How non-banks are boosting financial inclusion and remittance. In Tasca, P., Aste, T., Pelizzon, L., & Perony, N. (eds.), *Banking Beyond Banks and Money* (pp. 181–196). Springer International Publishing, Switzerland.

Buenaventura, L. (2017). *Reinventing Remittances with Bitcoin* (1st edn.). Bloom Solutions, Manila, Philippines.

Butkus, M., & Matuzeviciute, K. (2016). Remittances, development level, and long-run economic growth. *Economies, 4*(4), 28.

Carlisle, D. (2017). V*irtual currencies and financial crime: Challenges and opportunities.* Royal United Services Institute for Defence and Security Studies, RUSI Occasional Paper (March).

Cuevas-Mohr, H. (2015). *Are Telcos, MTOs and Banks on a Collision Course Over Remittances*? Mohr World Consulting LLC, Miami, FL.

Dermine, J. (2016). Digital banking and market disruption: A sense of déjà vu? *Financial Stability Review, 20*, 17–24. Banque de France.

Ekanayake, E., & Halkides, M. (2008). Do remittances and foreign direct investment promote growth? Evidence from developing countries. *Journal of International Business and Economics, 8*(1), 58–68.

El-Qorchi, M. M., Samuel, M., & Wilson, J. F. (2003). An analysis of the informal hawala system. *World Bank Working Paper.*

EservGlobal (2016). *HomeSend and Vodafone to extend M-Pesa Remittance Agreement to Five New Markets in 2016.* EservGlobal, Barcelona.

European Investment Bank & UN Capital Development Fund (2014). *Digital Financial Services in Africa: Beyond the Kenyan Success Story.* European Investment Bank & UN Capital Development Fund.

Frankel, J. (2010). Are bilateral remittances countercyclical? *Faculty Research Working Paper Series, RWP10-037*, Harvard University, Massachusetts.

Frost, J., Gambacorta, L., & Song Shin, H. (2021). From financial innovation to inclusion. In *Finance and Development* (March) (pp. 14–17).

Giuliano, P., & Ruiz-Arranz, M. (2009). Remittances, financial development, and growth. *Journal of Development Economics, 90*(1), 144–152.

GPFI (2017). *G20 Financial Inclusion Action Plan, July 2017.* Report from GPFI Plenary Held in Berlin.

GSMA (2016). *Driving a Price Revolution — Mobile Money in International Remittances.* GSMA, London.

GSMA (2017a). *State of the Industry Report on Mobile Money 2017.* GSMA, London.

GSMA (2017b). *Guidelines on International Remittances through Mobile Money.* Working Paper September 2017. GSMA, London.

GSMA (2018). *Mobile Money — Competing with Informal Channels to Accelerate the Digitisation of Remittances.* GSMA, London.

GSMA (2021). *State of the Industry Report on Mobile Money 2021.* GSMA, London.

Herzog, C., & Bolli, D. (2014). M-PESAL Ein alternatives Finanztransaktionssystem in Entwicklungsländern. University of Zurich, Institute for Computer Science, Zurich.

Holmes, E., Menzel, C., & Schlink, T. (2007). *Remittances aus Deutschland und ihre Wege in die Herkunftsländer der Migranten — Eine Studie zu fünf ausgewählten Ländern.* GTZ, Eschborn.

Holst, E., Schäfer, A., & Schrooten, M. (2010). Gender, transnational networks and remittances: Evidence from Germany, *SOEP papers on Multidisciplinary Panel Data Research.* DIW, Berlin.

Hughes, N., & Lonie, S. (2007). M-PESA: Mobile money for the 'Unbanked': Turning cellphones into 24-hour tellers in Kenya. *Innovations: Technology, Governance, Globalization, 2*(1–2), 63–81.

IFAD (2009). *Sending Money Home to Africa Remittance Markets, Enabling Environment and Prospects.* International Fund for Agricultural Development, Rome.

IFAD (2016). *Remittances at The Post Office in Africa: Serving the Financial Needs of Migrants and their Families in Rural Areas.* International Fund for Agricultural Development, Rome.

International Finance Corporation (2010a). *M-Money Channel Distribution Case — Afghanistan.* World Bank, Washington D.C.

International Finance Corporation (2010b). *M-Money Channel Distribution Case — Tanzania.* World Bank, Washington D.C.

International Monetary Fund (2009). *International Transactions in Remittances: Guide for Compilers and Users.* IM, Washington D.C.

International Organization for Migration (2010). *Gender, Migration and Remittances.* IOM, Geneva.

Jack, W., & Suri, T. (2014). Risk sharing and transaction costs: Evidence from Kenya's mobile money revolution. *American Economic Review, 103*, 183–223.

Kosse, A., & Vermeulen, R. (2014). *Migrant's Choice of Remittance Channels — Do General Payment Habits Play a Role?* European Central Bank, Frankfurt am Main.

Kpodar, K., Mlachila, M. Quayyum, S., & Gammadigbe, V. (2021). *Defying the Odds: Remittances during the COVID-19 Pandemic.* IMF Working Paper, No. WP/21/186.

Krause, M. (2016). *Bitcoin Implications for the Developing World.* Senior Thesis, Paper 1261. Claremont McKenna College, Claremont.

Lo, S., & Wang, J. (2014). Bitcoin as money? *Current policy perspectives No. 14-4.* Federal Reserve of Boston, Boston.

Metzger, M. (2008). *Regional Cooperation and Integration in Sub-Saharan Africa.* UNCTAD Discussion Paper, No. 189 (September).

Metzger, M., Riedler, T., & Wu, J. P. (2019). *Migrant Remittances: Alternative Money Transfer Channels.* IPE Working Paper, No. 127 (October).

Metzger, M., Were, M., & Wu, J. P. (2022). *Mobile money, financial inclusion, and regulatory architecture: The case of Kenya.* IPE Working Paper (forthcoming).

Munyegera, G., & Matsumoto, T. (2016). Mobile money, remittances, and household welfare: Panel evidence from rural Uganda. *World Development, 79*, 127–137.

Ntara, C. (2015). An analysis of M-Pesa use in international transactions. *European Journal of Business and Management, 7*(17), 73–79.

Orozco, M., Lowell, L., & Schneider, J. (2006). Gender-specific determinants of remittances: Differences in structure and motivation. *Report to the World Bank Gender and Development Group, PREM.* World Bank, Washington D.C.

Piracha, M., & Saraogi, A. (2011). Motivations for remittances — Evidence from Moldova. *IZA Discussion Paper No. 5467.* Institute for the Study of Labor (IZA), Bonn.

Profile Business Intelligence Ltd. (2005). *Sending Money Home? — A Survey of Remittance Products and Services in the United Kingdom.* Department for International Development and Banking Code Standards Board, London, UK.

Ratha, D. (2013). The impact of remittances on economic growth and poverty reduction. *Policy Brief, 8*(1), 1–13.

Reeves, M. (2017). *Cryptocurrency-remittance Transfers Futuristic Technologies and Poverty Alleviation.* Student Thesis. Saratoga Springs, Skidmore College.

Rocher, E., & Pelletier, A. (2008). Migrant workers' remittances: What is the impact on the economic and financial development of Sub-Saharan African countries? *Banque de France Bulletin Digest, 174*, 1–18.

https://www.banque-france.fr/sites/default/files/media/2016/11/25/d174migr.pdf.

Scott, B. (2016). How can cryptocurrency and blockchain technology play a role in building social and solidarity finance? *Working Paper 2016-1*. United Nations Research Institute for Social Development (UNRISD), Geneva.

Sayeh, A., & Chami, R. (2020). Lifelines in danger. *Finance and Development*, *57*(2), 16–19.

Sumner, A., Hoy, C., & Ortiz-Juarez, E. (2020). Estimates of the impact of COVID-19 on global poverty. *UNU WIDER Working Paper 2020/43* (April).

Sirkeci, I., Cohen, J. H., & Ratha, D. (eds.). (2012). *Migration and Remittances During the Global Financial Crisis and Beyond*. World Bank, Washington D.C.

TechnoServe (2016). The digital remittance revolution in South Africa: Challenges and next steps for Africa's largest cross-border payment market. TechnoServe.

UN Capital Development Fund (2017). *Remittances as a Driver of Women's Financial Inclusion*. UNCDF & Australian Aid, New York.

UN Committee for Development Policy (2021). Comprehensive Study on the Impact of COVID-19 on the Least Developed Country Category, New York (April).

UNCTAD (2011). *Impact of Remittances on Poverty in Developing Countries*. UNCTAD, Geneva.

UNCTAD (2021). *World Investment Report 2021. Investing in Sustainable Recovery*. UNCTAD, New York.

United Nations (2016). *The Sustainable Development Goals Report 2016*. United Nations Department of Economic and Social Affairs, New York.

United Nations (2019). *The Sustainable Development Goals Report 2019*. United Nations Department of Economic and Social Affairs, New York.

United Nations (2021). *The Sustainable Development Goals Report 2021*. United Nations Department of Economic and Social Affairs, New York.

van Hove, L., & Dubus, A. (2019). M-PESA and financial inclusion in Kenya: Of paying comes saving? *Sustainability*, *11*(3), 568.

Were, M. (2020). *COVID-19 and Socioeconomic Impact in Africa: The Case of Kenya*. UNU WIDER Background Note, No. 3 (April).

Wolf, L. (2019). *Digital solutions to assist inclusive financial systems? Status quo and potential of Ghana*. Master Thesis, Berlin School of Economics and Law, Berlin.

World Bank Group (2006). *Global Economic Prospects: Economic Implications of Remittances and Migration 2006.* World Bank, Washington D.C.

World Bank Group (2016a). *Migration and Remittances Factbook 2016* (3rd ed.). World Bank, Washington D.C.

World Bank Group (2016b). *Remittance Prices Worldwide: An Analysis of Trends in Costs of Remittance Services, Issue 19.* World Bank, Washington D.C.

World Bank Group (2017a). *Migration and Remittances: Recent Development and Outlook, Migration and Development brief No. 27.* World Bank, Washington D.C.

World Bank Group (2018). *Migration and Remittances: Recent Developments and Outlook, Migration and Development Brief No. 29 (Transit Migration).* World Bank, Washington D.C.

World Bank Group (2019). *Migration and Remittances: Recent Developments and Outlook, Migration and Development Brief 31, (Transit Migration).* World Bank, Washington D.C.

World Bank Group (2020). *Global Financial Development Report 2019/2020: Bank Regulation and Supervision a Decade after the Global Financial Crisis.* World Bank, Washington D.C.

World Bank Group (2021a). *Remittance Prices Worldwide Quarterly: An Analysis of Trends in Cost of Remittances Services, Issue 37 (March).* World Bank, Washington D.C.

World Bank Group (2021b). *Remittance Price Worldwide: The Impact of COVID-19 on the Market for International Remittances tn the Short to Medium Term* (April). World Bank, Washington D.C.

Online Sources

Adepetun, A. (2015). Africa's mobile phone penetration now 67%. https://guardian.ng/technology/africas-mobile-phone-penetration-now-67/ [Accessed: 12 September 2020].

Alushula, P. (2019). M-Pesa users outside Kenya hit 13.4 million. https://www.businessdailyafrica.com/corporate/companies/M-Pesa-users-outside-Kenya-hit-13-4-million/4003102-4956208-16s8a9/index.html [Accessed: 12 September 2020].

Bergmann, C. (2016). Gebührenfreie internationale Überweisungen: OKLink subventioniert Bitcoin-Remittance. https://bitcoinblog.de/2016/10/20/gebuehrenfreie-internationale-ueberweisungen-oklinksub ventioniert-bitcoin-remittance/ [Accessed: 18 January 2017].

Boon, H. (2017). Remittances as a trigger for postal financial inclusion. https://www.asiapathways-adbi.org/2017/11/remittances-as-a-trigger-for-postal-financial-inclusion/ [Accessed: 10 September 2019].

Bull, G. (2019). Great expectations: Fintech and the poor. https://www.cgap.org/blog/great-expectations-fintech-and-poor [Accessed: 10 September 2019].

Caffyn, G. (2015). New service finds optimum bitcoin transaction fee. http://www.coindesk.com/new-service-finds-optimum-bitcoin-transaction-fee/ [Accessed: 12 September 2020].

Communications Africa (2015). Faster M-PESA payment settlement for merchants in Kenya. http://www.communicationsafrica.com/commerce/faster-m-pesa-payment-settlement-formerchants-in-kenya [Accessed: 28 February 2017].

Garcia-Mora, A., & M. Rutkowski (2020). Remittances in times of the coronavirus — Keep them flowing. https://blogs.worldbank.org/psd/remittances-times-coronavirus-keep-them-flowing [Accessed: 29 April 2021].

Georgieva, K. (2021). Leveraging digital money to facilitate remittances. Opening remarks at iLab spring meetings virtual workshop on 14 April. https://www.imf.org/en/News/Articles/2021/04/14/sp041421-leveraging-digital-money-to-facilitate-remittances [Accessed: 29 April 2021].

Globe Newswire (2020). Global $4.49 billion Peer to Peer (P2P) payment market outlook to 2027. https://www.globenewswire.com/news-release/2020/10/26/2114054/0/en/Global-4-49-Billion-Peer-to-Peer-P2P-Payment-Market-Outlook-to-2027.html [Accessed: 8 September 2020].

Heuler, H. (2015). Kenyan start-ups tackle expensive remittances through Bitcoin. http://voanews.com/a/kenyan-startups-tackle-expensive-remittances-through-bitcoin/2702724.html [Accessed: 12 September 2020].

Internet World Stats (2019a). World Internet Usage and Population Statistics: 2019 Mid-Year Estimates. https://internetworldstats.com/stats.htm [Accessed: 12 September 2020].

Internet World Stats (2019b). Surfing and site guide. https://www.internetworldstats.com/surfing.htm#1 [Accessed: 12 September 2020].

Kemibaro, M. (2016). Kenya's latest 2016 mobile and internet statistics. http://www.moseskemibaro.com/2016/10/01/kenyas-latest-2016-mobile-internet-statistics/ [Accessed: 12 September 2020].

Kenyan Wall Street (2017). Kenya: Safaricom market share increases to nearly 70%. https://www.african-markets.com/en/stock-markets/

nse/kenya-safaricom-market-shareincreases-to-nearly-70 [Accessed: 8 March 2019].

Mavadiya, M. (2018). Azimo: 80 percent growth in transactions sent to M-PESA wallets in Kenya. https://www.forbes.com/sites/madhvimavadiya/2018/08/29/azimo-80-percent-growth-in-transactions-sent-to-m-pesa-wallets-in-kenya/#59e0b3665158 [Accessed: 12 September 2020].

Maxim, J. (2015). African Bitcoin remittance service BitPesa expands to Tanzania. https://bitcoinmagazine.com/articles/african-bitcoin-remittance-service-bitpesa-expandstanzania-1431993506 [Accessed: 15 December 2017].

McCann, C. (2019). Remittance market-primer and landscape. https://medium.com/proofofcapital/remittance-market-primer-and-landscape-3213c2c81771 [Accessed: 8 September 2021].

Medici (2019). M-Pesa: Mobile phone-based money transfer — Global presence. https://gomedici.com/m-pesa-mobile-phone-based-money-transfer-global-presence/ [Accessed: 12 September 2020].

Nakamoto, S. (2008). *Bitcoin: A Peer-to-Peer electronic cash System.* https://bitcoin.org/bitcoin.pdf. [Accessed: 12 September 2020].

PayPal (2016). Remittances — Public policy. https://www.paypal.com/us/webapps/mpp/public-policy/issues/remittances [Accessed: 12 September 2020].

PayPal (2019). Welcome to Paypal mobile money service with M-PESA, Frequently asked questions. https://www.paypal-mobilemoney.com/m-pesa/faq [Accessed: 12 September 2020].

Safaricom (2017a). M-Pesa rates, M-Pesa tariffs, M-Pesa withdrawal Charges, MPesa transaction fees. https://www.safaricom.co.ke/personal/m-pesa/get-started-with-m-pesa/m-pesa-tariffs [Accessed: 17 February 2017].

Safaricom (2017b). Bank to M-PESA and M-PESA to bank. https://www.safaricom.co.ke/personal/m-pesa/do-more-with-m-pesa/bank-to-m-pesa-andm-pesa-to-bank [Accessed: 28 February 2017].

Safaricom (2019a). M-Pesa global. https://www.safaricom.co.ke/personal/m-pesa/do-more-with-m-pesa/m-pesa-global. [Accessed: 8 April 2019].

Safaricom (2019b). M-Pesa rates. https://www.safaricom.co.ke/personal/m-pesa/getting-started/m-pesa-rates [Accessed: 8 April 2019].

Statista (2021a). Global smartphone penetration rate as share of population from 2016 to 2020. https://www.statista.com/statistics/203734/global-smartphone-penetration-per-capita-sice-2005/ [Accessed: 8 September 2021].

Statista (2021b). Digital remittances. https://www.statista.com/outlook/332/100/digital-remittances/worldwide [Accessed: 9 September 2021].

Vodacom (2017). Pay school fees with M-Pesa. http://www.vodacom.co.ls/ls-personal/services/promotions/pay-school-fees-with-m-pesa [Accessed: 12 September 2020].

World Bank Group (2017b). Remittance prices worldwide, World Bank Database. https://remittanceprices.worldbank.org/en. [Accessed: 1 April 2017].

World Bank Group (2020). Atlas of sustainable development goals 2020, From World Bank Development Indicators. https://datatopics.worldbank.org/sdgatlas/ [Accessed: 13 August 2021].

World Bank Group (2021c). Defying predictions, remittance flows remain strong during COVID-19 crisis. https://www.worldbank.org/en/news/press-release/2021/05/12/defying-predictions-remittance-flows-remain-strong-during-covid-19-crisis [Accessed: 10 September 2021].

World Development Indicators (2021). https://databank.worldbank.org/source/world-development-indicators [Accessed: 10 September 2021].

WorldRemit (2016). WorldRemit launches instant overseas money transfers to M-Pesa in Albania. https://www.worldremit.com/en/news/worldremit-launches-instant-overseas-money-transfersto-m-pesa-in-albania [Accessed: 10 September 2020].

https://doi.org/10.1142/9781800612723_bmatter

Index

CPSIA information can be obtained
at www.ICGtesting.com
Printed in the USA
BVHW050718140323
660052BV00002B/3

9 781800 612716